KB065974

NE능률 영어교과서

대한민국 고등학생 10명 중 4.7 명이 보는 교과서

영어 고등 교과서 점유율 1위

(7차, 2007 개정, 2009 개정, 2015 개정)

능률보카

그동안 판매된 능률VOCA 1,100만 부

대한민국 박스오피스 천만명을 넘은 영화 단 28개

리딩튜터

그동안 판매된 리딩튜터 1,900만 부 차곡차곡 쌓으면 19만 미터

에베레스트 21 배 높이

그래머존

그동안 판매된 450만 부의 그래머존을 바닥에 쭉 ~ 깔면

1000km 서울-부산 왕복가능

LEVEL **2**

지은이	NE능률 영어교육연구소
선임연구원	김지현
연구원	박효빈, 가민아
영문교열	Curtis Thompson, Angela Lan
디자인	민유화
맥편집	허문희

NE능률이
미래를
창조합니다.

건강한 배움의 고객가치를 제공하겠다는 꿈을 실현하기 위해
40년이 넘는 시간 동안 열심히 달려왔습니다.

앞으로도 끊임없는 연구와 노력을 통해
당연한 것을 멈추지 않고

고객, 기업, 직원 모두가 함께 성장하는 NE능률이 되겠습니다.

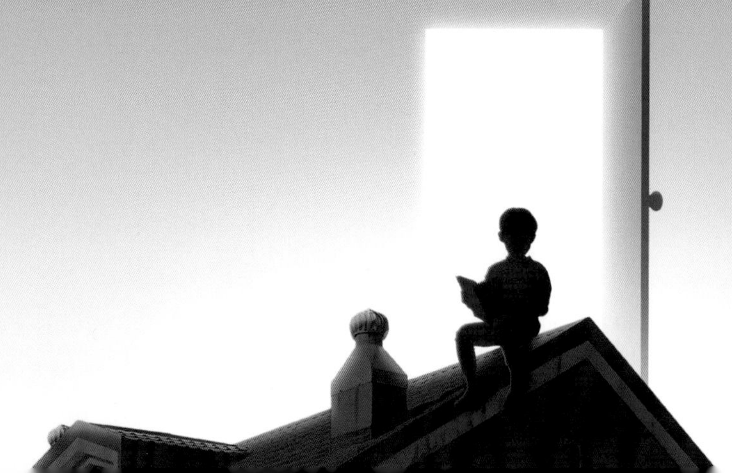

NE 능률

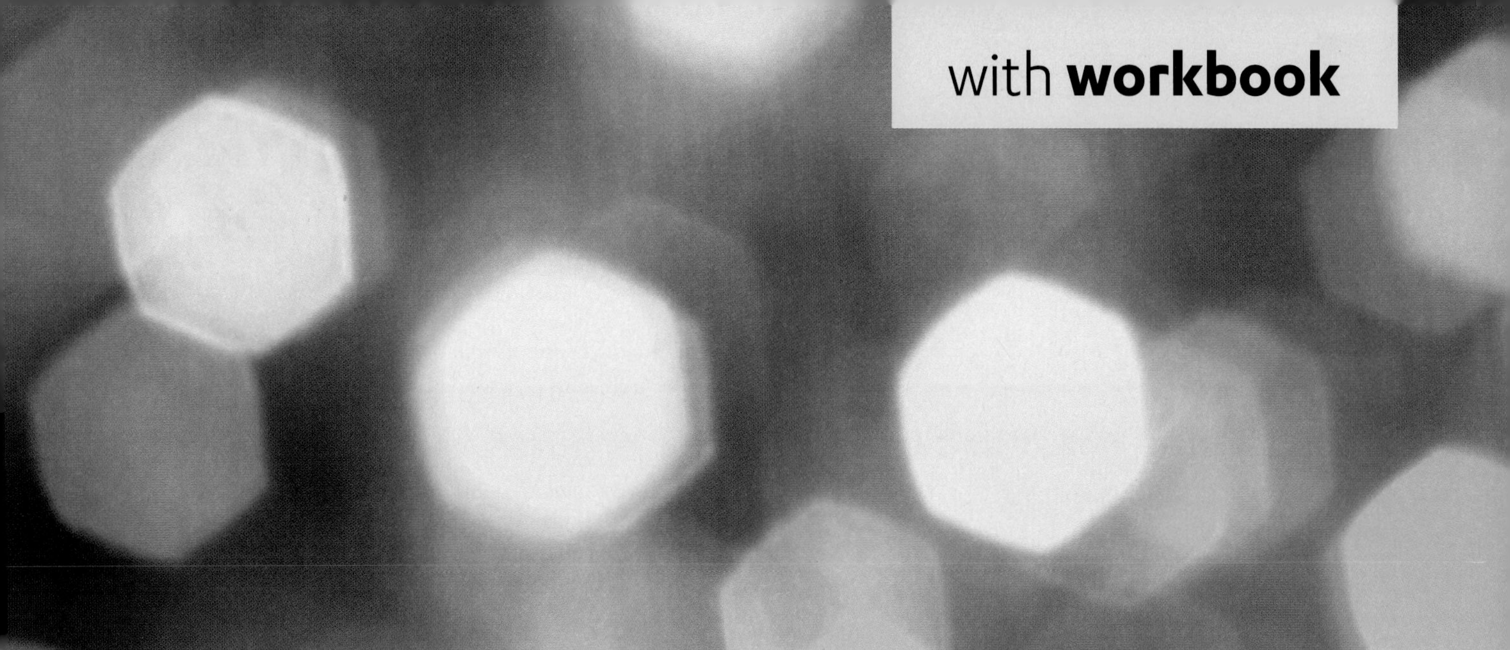

GRAMMAR Inside

LEVEL 2

STRUCTURES

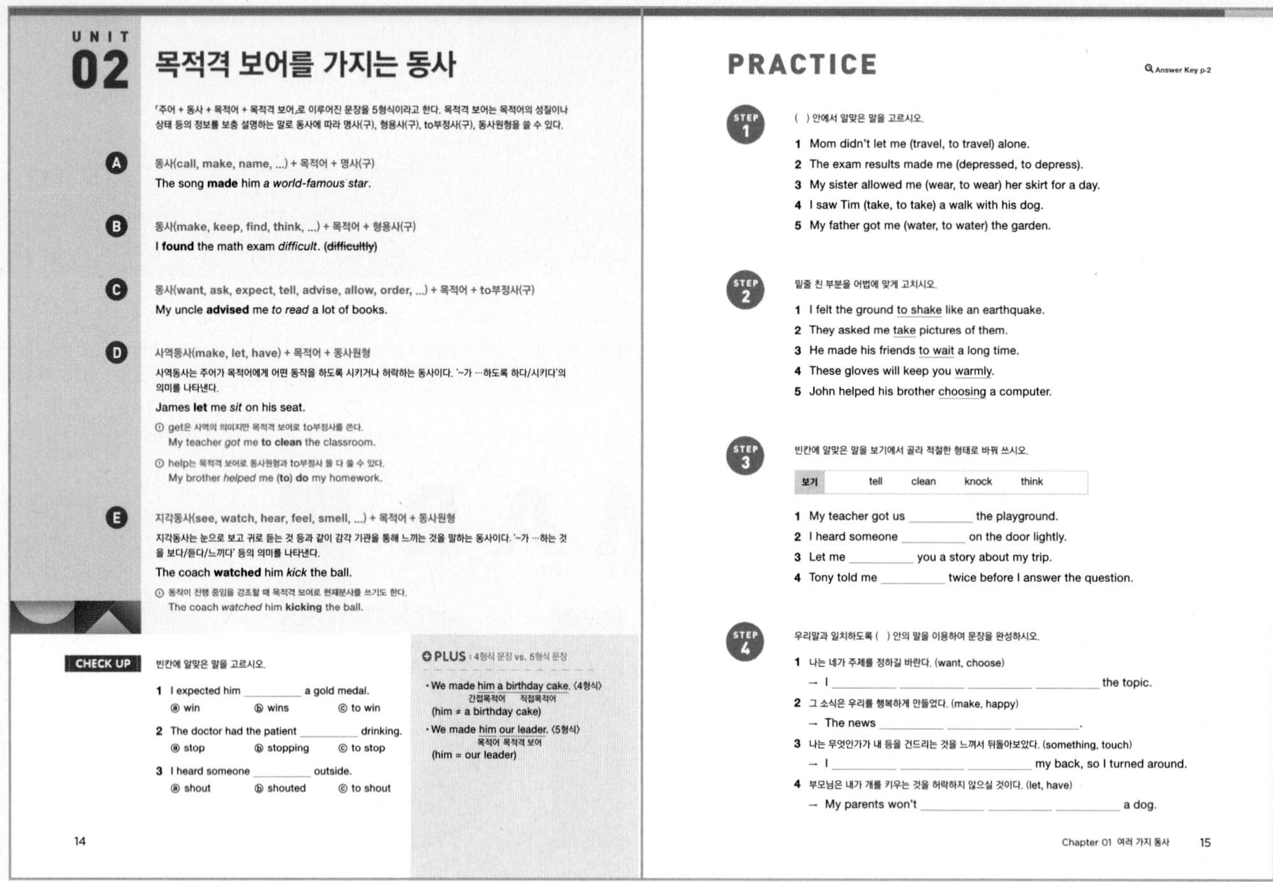

UNIT 02

목적격 보어를 가지는 동사

「주어 + 동사 + 목적어 + 목적격 보어」로 이루어진 문장을 5형식이라고 한다. 목적격 보어는 목적어의 성질이나 상태 등의 정보를 보충 설명하는 말로 동사에 따라 명사(구), 형용사(구), to부정사(구), 동사원형을 쓸 수 있다.

A 동사(call, make, name, ...) + 목적어 + 명사(구)
The song **made** him *a world-famous star*.

B 동사(make, keep, find, think, ...) + 목적어 + 형용사(구)
I **found** the math exam *difficult*. (~~difficultly~~)

C 동사(want, ask, expect, tell, advise, allow, order, ...) + 목적어 + to부정사(구)
My uncle **advised** me *to read* a lot of books.

D 사역동사(make, let, have) + 목적어 + 동사원형
사역동사는 주어가 목적어에게 어떤 동작을 하도록 시키거나 허락하는 동사이다. '~가 …하도록 하다/시키다'의 의미를 나타낸다.
James **let** me *sit* on his seat.
ⓘ get은 사역의 의미지만 목적격 보어로 to부정사를 쓴다.
My teacher *got* me **to clean** the classroom.
ⓘ help는 목적격 보어로 동사원형과 to부정사 둘 다 쓸 수 있다.
My brother *helped* me **(to) do** my homework.

E 지각동사(see, watch, hear, feel, smell, ...) + 목적어 + 동사원형
지각동사는 눈으로 보고 귀로 듣는 것 등과 같이 감각 기관을 통해 느끼는 것을 말하는 동사이다. '~가 …하는 것을 보다/듣다/느끼다' 등의 의미를 나타낸다.
The coach **watched** him *kick* the ball.
ⓘ 동작이 진행 중임을 강조할 때 목적격 보어로 현재분사를 쓰기도 한다.
The coach *watched* him **kicking** the ball.

CHECK UP 빈칸에 알맞은 말을 고르시오.

1 I expected him __________ a gold medal.
ⓐ win ⓑ wins ⓒ to win

2 The doctor had the patient __________ drinking.
ⓐ stop ⓑ stopping ⓒ to stop

3 I heard someone __________ outside.
ⓐ shout ⓑ shouted ⓒ to shout

PLUS : 4형식 문장 vs. 5형식 문장

- We made him a birthday cake. 〈4형식〉
  (him: 간접목적어, a birthday cake: 직접목적어)
  (him ≠ a birthday cake)
- We made him our leader. 〈5형식〉
  (him: 목적어, our leader: 목적격 보어)
  (him = our leader)

14

PRACTICE

Answer Key p-2

STEP 1 ( ) 안에서 알맞은 말을 고르시오.

1 Mom didn't let me (travel, to travel) alone.
2 The exam results made me (depressed, to depress).
3 My sister allowed me (wear, to wear) her skirt for a day.
4 I saw Tim (take, to take) a walk with his dog.
5 My father got me (water, to water) the garden.

STEP 2 밑줄 친 부분을 어법에 맞게 고치시오.

1 I felt the ground to shake like an earthquake.
2 They asked me take pictures of them.
3 He made his friends to wait a long time.
4 These gloves will keep you warmly.
5 John helped his brother choosing a computer.

STEP 3 빈칸에 알맞은 말을 보기에서 골라 적절한 형태로 바꿔 쓰시오.

보기	tell	clean	knock	think

1 My teacher got us __________ the playground.
2 I heard someone __________ on the door lightly.
3 Let me __________ you a story about my trip.
4 Tony told me __________ twice before I answer the question.

STEP 4 우리말과 일치하도록 ( ) 안의 말을 이용하여 문장을 완성하시오.

1 나는 네가 주제를 정하길 바란다. (want, choose)
→ I __________ __________ __________ __________ the topic.
2 그 소식은 우리를 행복하게 만들었다. (make, happy)
→ The news __________ __________ __________.
3 나는 무엇인가가 내 등을 건드리는 것을 느껴서 뒤돌아보았다. (something, touch)
→ I __________ __________ __________ my back, so I turned around.
4 부모님은 내가 개를 키우는 것을 허락하지 않으실 것이다. (let, have)
→ My parents won't __________ __________ __________ a dog.

Chapter 01 여러 가지 동사 15

GRAMMAR POINT

1 GRAMMAR POINT

해당 Unit에서 배워야 할 핵심 문법들을
명확한 설명과 실용적인 예문으로 체계적으로 정리했습니다.

2 CHECK UP

핵심을 묻는 문제를 통해 Grammar Point에서
배운 내용을 이해했는지 확인할 수 있습니다.

3 PLUS

Grammar Point에서 제시한 핵심 문법 외의
추가 정보를 담았습니다.

PRACTICE

1 Grammar Point에서 학습한 내용을 다양한 유형의
문제를 통해 자연스럽게 익힐 수 있습니다.

2 학교 내신 시험에 자주 등장하는 서술형 쓰기 연습문제를
매 Unit마다 경험할 수 있도록 하였습니다.

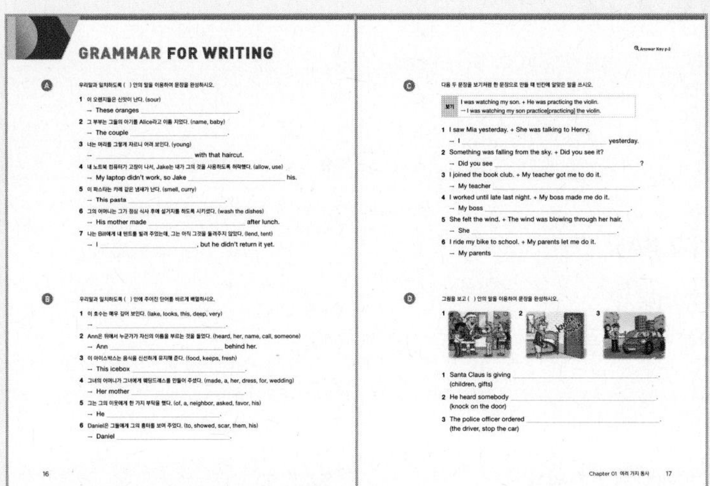

GRAMMAR FOR WRITING

다양한 형태의 쓰기 문제를 풀어봄으로써 Grammar Point를 반복 학습하며 sentence writing의 기초를 마련할 수 있습니다.

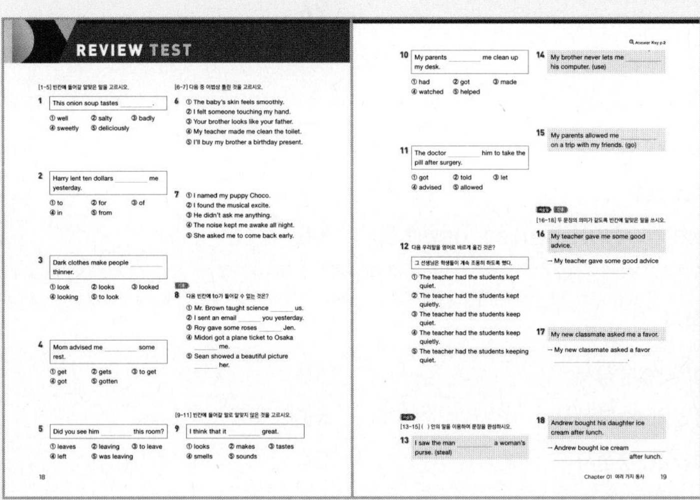

REVIEW TEST

실제 학교 시험과 가장 유사한 유형의 문제들로 구성하여 실전에 대비할 수 있습니다.
고난도 어법 문제와 서술형 문제를 대폭 수록하여 학교 내신 시험의 서술형 주관식 문항에 완벽 대비할 수 있도록 하였습니다.

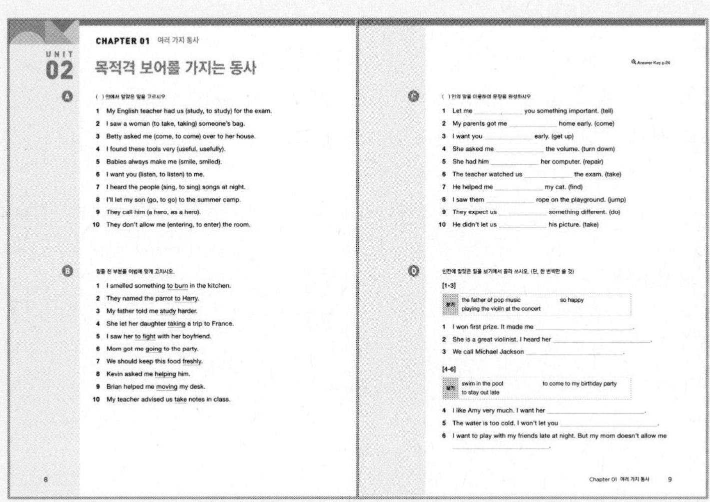

WORKBOOK

각 Unit별 연습문제와 쓰기 문제, Chapter별 Review Test를 수록하였습니다.
더 많은 문제를 풀어봄으로써 문법을 보다 완벽하게 익힐 수 있도록 하였습니다.

CONTENTS

GRAMMAR BASICS

01 문장의 성분

- She is a famous violinist.
  주어 동사 보어
- I learned Spanish in high school.
  주어 동사 목적어 수식어

주어 움직임이나 상태의 주체가 되는 말로, 보통 문장의 맨 앞에 와서 '~은[는, 이, 가]'으로 해석된다. 주어로는 보통 명사나 대명사가 쓰이지만 동명사구나 to부정사구처럼 긴 주어가 쓰이기도 한다.

Emma is a Japanese teacher. **She** speaks Japanese very well.
Meeting new people is exciting.

동사 주어의 상태나 동작을 나타내는 말로, '~이다[하다]'로 해석된다. 대부분 한 단어로 쓰이지만, 두 단어 이상이 모여 하나의 동사 역할을 하기도 하고, 조동사의 도움을 받아 여러 가지 보충의 의미를 갖기도 한다.

Julia **is** a brave girl. She **enjoys** skydiving.
She **looked at** my face.
You **must finish** your homework tonight.

목적어 동사 다음에 오는 말로, 우리말의 '~을[를]'에 해당한다. 보통 목적어로는 명사, 대명사가 쓰이지만, 동명사구나 to부정사구처럼 긴 목적어가 오기도 한다.

You made **a mistake**.
I want **to be a pilot**.

보어 주어나 목적어에 대한 정보를 보충 설명해 주는 말이다. 주격 보어는 동사 뒤에서 주어를 보충 설명하고 목적격 보어는 목적어 뒤에서 목적어를 보충 설명한다.

She became **a doctor**. (she = a doctor) 〈주격 보어〉
We elected Angelina **class president**. (Angelina = class president) 〈목적격 보어〉

수식어 문장의 다른 요소들을 꾸며줘서 문장 내용을 풍부하게 만드는 말이다. 형용사처럼 쓰여 명사를 수식할 수도 있고, 부사처럼 쓰여 동사나 형용사, 다른 부사를 수식하기도 한다.

The **tall** boy is my son.
Alice works **very** hard.
They stayed **in a small hotel**.

02 품사

- Oh, grammar is very difficult but interesting.
  감탄사 명사 동사 부사 형용사 접속사 형용사
  동사 관사
- It is an important part of a language.
  대명사 관사 형용사 명사 전치사 명사

명사 사람, 동물, 사물, 장소 등 세상에 존재하는 모든 것들의 이름을 말한다. 문장에서 주어, 목적어, 보어로 쓰인다.
(man, woman, girl, boy, Jane, Alice, Andy, computer, pen ...)

This **laptop** is his present. 〈주어〉
I bought a **bag**. 〈목적어〉
She is a **cellist**. 〈보어〉

ⓘ 관사: 명사와 결합하여 명사의 의미와 성질을 나타내는 말로, 불특정한 (어떤) 하나를 나타내는 a(n)와 특정한 대상을 가리키는 the가 있다.
a table, **an** elephant, **the** computer ...

대명사 명사를 대신하는 말로, 문장에서 주어, 목적어, 보어로 쓰인다.
(I, you, we, he, she, it, they, this, that, these, those ...)

It is my old school album. 〈주어〉
She loves **him**. 〈목적어〉
The problem is **this**. 〈보어〉

동사 주어의 상태나 동작을 나타내는 말로, 언제를 이야기하는지, 주어가 무엇인지에 따라 형태가 달라진다.
(be, work, look, go, come, buy, expect ...)

I **am** a movie star.
You **are** a movie star.
He **is** a movie star.

We **will go** to the cinema.
We **are going** to the cinema.
We **went** to the cinema.

형용사 명사나 대명사의 성질, 상태 등을 설명하는 말로, 문장에서 명사나 대명사를 꾸며주는 수식어 또는 보어로 쓰인다.
(lovely, nice, brave, bright, pretty, beautiful, smart ...)

Andy has **brown** eyes, **dark** hair, and **good** manners. 〈수식어〉
You look **great** today. 〈보어〉

부사 문장에서 동사나 형용사, 다른 부사, 문장 전체를 꾸며주며, 시간, 장소, 방법, 정도, 빈도 등을 나타낸다.
(then, now, yesterday, here, there, really, always, frequently, much ...)

This black dress fits you **well**. 〈동사를 꾸며줌〉
My new boss is **very** strict. 〈형용사를 꾸며줌〉
He ran **really** fast. 〈다른 부사를 꾸며줌〉
Fortunately, we found a house in the forest. 〈문장 전체를 꾸며줌〉

전치사 명사(구)와 함께 쓰여 시간, 장소, 목적, 방법 등을 나타내는 말이다.
(in, at, on, across, over, under, about, by, for, to, with ...)

I will meet Daniel **in** the lobby **at** noon. 〈장소, 시간〉
We took a walk **across** the bridge. 〈장소〉
I will go to Australia **for** a business meeting. 〈목적〉

접속사 단어와 단어, 구와 구, 절과 절을 이어주는 말이다.
(and, but, or, so, when, before, after, until, because, if, that ...)

I bought a *T-shirt* **and** *sunglasses*. 〈단어와 단어〉
He will stay *in a hotel* **or** *at my home*. 〈구와 구〉
I walked for seven hours, **so** *I feel exhausted*. 〈절과 절〉

감탄사 기쁨, 슬픔, 놀람 등의 감정을 나타내는 말이다.
(oh, wow, oops, bravo ...)

Wow, she is so beautiful!
Bravo, you really did a good job!

03 구와 절

- Pam made a long and boring speech.
  명사구
- We waited until the couple came back.
  부사절

구

1 둘 이상의 단어가 모여 문장 내에서 명사, 형용사, 부사의 역할을 한다.
a beautiful song, very pretty, here and there, in the park ...

2 문장에서의 역할에 따라 명사구, 형용사구, 부사구로 나뉜다.

❶ 명사구: 명사처럼 문장에서 주어, 목적어, 보어로 쓰인다.

The white cap is a present from my father. 〈주어〉
We need **something to eat**. 〈목적어〉
The problem is **his poor health**. 〈보어〉

❷ 형용사구: 형용사처럼 문장에서 명사를 꾸며주는 수식어 또는 보어로 쓰인다.

The building **on the hill** is mine.
His voice was **really attractive**.

❸ 부사구: 부사처럼 문장에서 동사나 형용사, 다른 부사, 문장 전체를 꾸며주는 수식어로 쓰인다.

We saw each other **in the park**.
Her name is easy **to remember**.

절

1 「주어 + 동사」를 포함한 여러 단어가 모여 문장 내에서 명사, 형용사, 부사의 역할을 한다.
that you are honest, whom I love, when I was young ...

2 문장에서의 역할에 따라 명사절, 형용사절, 부사절로 나뉜다.

❶ 명사절: 명사처럼 문장에서 주어, 목적어, 보어로 쓰인다. 절이 주어로 쓰인 경우 가주어 it을 사용하는 경우가 많다.

That I loved her is true. (= *It* is true **that I loved her**.) 〈주어〉
I didn't know **that he was your father**. 〈목적어〉
The fact is **that we should leave right now**. 〈보어〉

❷ 형용사절: 형용사처럼 문장에서 명사를 꾸며주는 수식어로 쓰인다.

It was the story **which my grandmother told me**.

❸ 부사절: 부사처럼 문장에서 동사나 형용사, 다른 부사를 꾸며주는 수식어로 쓰인다.

Please lock the door **before you leave the room**.

CHAPTER

01

여러 가지 동사

영어 문장에서는 동사의 종류에 따라
뒤에 오는 말이 달라진다.

UNIT 01

감각동사와 수여동사

A

감각동사 + 형용사 (2형식)

감각동사는 look, feel, smell, sound, taste와 같이 감각을 표현하는 동사로, 뒤에는 형용사를 쓴다.

- look + 형용사: ~하게 보이다
- feel + 형용사: ~하게 느끼다
- smell + 형용사: ~한 냄새가 나다
- sound + 형용사: ~하게 들리다
- taste + 형용사: ~한 맛이 나다

You **look** *different* without your glasses.

cf. 감각동사 + like + 명사(구)

That cloud **looks like** *a puppy*.

B

수여동사 + 간접목적어 + 직접목적어 (4형식)

수여동사는 give, send, tell, teach, make, buy와 같이 '~에게 …을 (해)주다'의 의미를 가진 동사로, '~에게(간접목적어)'와 '…을(직접목적어)'에 해당하는 두 개의 목적어를 가진다.

I **told** *my best friend* *a secret*.
(my best friend: 간접목적어, a secret: 직접목적어)

「수여동사 + 간접목적어 + 직접목적어」는 「수여동사 + 직접목적어 + to/for/of + 간접목적어」의 형태로 바꿔 쓸 수 있다.

1 간접목적어 앞에 전치사 to를 쓰는 동사: give, send, show, tell, teach, lend, write, pass 등

Ted *sent* me a text message last night.
→ Ted **sent** a text message **to** me last night.

2 간접목적어 앞에 전치사 for를 쓰는 동사: make, buy, get 등

My friend *made* me a cake on my birthday.
→ My friend **made** a cake **for** me on my birthday.

3 간접목적어 앞에 전치사 of를 쓰는 동사: ask

Can I *ask* you a favor?
→ Can I **ask** a favor **of** you?

CHECK UP 빈칸에 알맞은 말을 고르시오.

1 The singer's voice sounds ____________.
ⓐ beauty ⓑ beautiful ⓒ beautifully

2 A Canadian teacher taught English ____________ us at school.
ⓐ to ⓑ for ⓒ of

PRACTICE

Answer Key p.2

STEP 1

( ) 안에서 알맞은 말을 고르시오.

1 Your sneakers look (new, newly).

2 Your plan for summer vacation sounds (interesting, interestingly).

3 I will tell (him my secret, my secret him).

4 Alan made a meal (for, of) his friends.

5 The man asked (me, of me) my phone number.

STEP 2

밑줄 친 부분을 어법에 맞게 고치시오.

1 I would like to ask a favor to you.

2 The apple pie tastes deliciously.

3 Lily showed a note from James for me.

4 I will get some sandwiches of you.

STEP 3

두 문장의 의미가 같도록 빈칸에 알맞은 말을 쓰시오.

1 Lewis sent me some files by email.

→ Lewis sent some files __________ __________ by email.

2 Jay wrote his parents a letter.

→ Jay wrote a letter __________ __________ __________.

3 My parents bought me a winter coat for Christmas.

→ My parents bought a winter coat __________ __________ for Christmas.

STEP 4

우리말과 일치하도록 ( ) 안의 말을 이용하여 문장을 완성하시오.

1 Ron은 빗속에서 춥다고 느꼈다. (cold)

→ Ron __________ __________ in the rain.

2 그 감자튀김은 맛이 짜다. (salty)

→ The french fries __________ __________.

3 Emma는 나에게 그녀의 공책을 빌려주었다. (notebook)

→ Emma lent __________ __________ __________ __________.

4 나는 Chris에게 내 일기를 보여 주었다. (diary)

→ I showed __________ __________ __________ Chris.

5 부모님께서 내게 나의 선생님의 성함을 물어보셨다. (teacher's name)

→ My parents asked __________ __________ __________ __________.

UNIT 02

목적격 보어를 가지는 동사

「주어 + 동사 + 목적어 + 목적격 보어」로 이루어진 문장을 5형식이라고 한다. 목적격 보어는 목적어의 성질이나 상태 등의 정보를 보충 설명하는 말로 동사에 따라 명사(구), 형용사(구), to부정사(구), 동사원형을 쓸 수 있다.

A **동사(call, make, name, ...) + 목적어 + 명사(구)**

The song **made** him *a world-famous star*.

B **동사(make, keep, find, think, ...) + 목적어 + 형용사(구)**

I **found** the math exam *difficult*. (~~difficultly~~)

C **동사(want, ask, expect, tell, advise, allow, order, ...) + 목적어 + to부정사(구)**

My uncle **advised** me *to read* a lot of books.

D **사역동사(make, let, have) + 목적어 + 동사원형**

사역동사는 주어가 목적어에게 어떤 동작을 하도록 시키거나 허락하는 동사이다. '~가 …하도록 하다/시키다'의 의미를 나타낸다.

James **let** me *sit* on his seat.

ⓘ get은 사역의 의미지만 목적격 보어로 to부정사를 쓴다.
My teacher *got* me **to clean** the classroom.

ⓘ help는 목적격 보어로 동사원형과 to부정사 둘 다 쓸 수 있다.
My brother *helped* me (**to**) **do** my homework.

E **지각동사(see, watch, hear, feel, smell, ...) + 목적어 + 동사원형**

지각동사는 눈으로 보고 귀로 듣는 것 등과 같이 감각 기관을 통해 느끼는 것을 말하는 동사이다. '~가 …하는 것을 보다/듣다/느끼다' 등의 의미를 나타낸다.

The coach **watched** him *kick* the ball.

ⓘ 동작이 진행 중임을 강조할 때 목적격 보어로 현재분사를 쓰기도 한다.
The coach *watched* him **kicking** the ball.

CHECK UP 빈칸에 알맞은 말을 고르시오.

1 I expected him __________ a gold medal.
ⓐ win ⓑ wins ⓒ to win

2 The doctor had the patient __________ drinking.
ⓐ stop ⓑ stopping ⓒ to stop

3 I heard someone __________ outside.
ⓐ shout ⓑ shouted ⓒ to shout

PLUS : 4형식 문장 vs. 5형식 문장

- We made him a birthday cake. 〈4형식〉
  (him: 간접목적어, a birthday cake: 직접목적어)
  (him ≠ a birthday cake)
- We made him our leader. 〈5형식〉
  (him: 목적어, our leader: 목적격 보어)
  (him = our leader)

PRACTICE

Answer Key p.2

( ) 안에서 알맞은 말을 고르시오.

1 Mom didn't let me (travel, to travel) alone.

2 The exam results made me (depressed, to depress).

3 My sister allowed me (wear, to wear) her skirt for a day.

4 I saw Tim (take, to take) a walk with his dog.

5 My father got me (water, to water) the garden.

STEP 2

밑줄 친 부분을 어법에 맞게 고치시오.

1 I felt the ground <u>to shake</u> like an earthquake.

2 They asked me <u>take</u> pictures of them.

3 He made his friends <u>to wait</u> a long time.

4 These gloves will keep you <u>warmly</u>.

5 John helped his brother <u>choosing</u> a computer.

STEP 3

빈칸에 알맞은 말을 보기에서 골라 적절한 형태로 바꿔 쓰시오.

보기	tell	clean	knock	think

1 My teacher got us __________ the playground.

2 I heard someone __________ on the door lightly.

3 Let me __________ you a story about my trip.

4 Tony told me __________ twice before I answer the question.

우리말과 일치하도록 ( ) 안의 말을 이용하여 문장을 완성하시오.

1 나는 네가 주제를 정하길 바란다. (want, choose)

→ I __________ __________ __________ __________ the topic.

2 그 소식은 우리를 행복하게 만들었다. (make, happy)

→ The news __________ __________ __________.

3 나는 무엇인가가 내 등을 건드리는 것을 느껴서 뒤돌아보았다. (something, touch)

→ I __________ __________ __________ my back, so I turned around.

4 부모님은 내가 개를 키우는 것을 허락하지 않으실 것이다. (let, have)

→ My parents won't __________ __________ __________ a dog.

GRAMMAR FOR WRITING

A 우리말과 일치하도록 ( ) 안의 말을 이용하여 문장을 완성하시오.

1 이 오렌지들은 신맛이 난다. (sour)
→ These oranges ______________________.

2 그 부부는 그들의 아기를 Alice라고 이름 지었다. (name, baby)
→ The couple ______________________.

3 너는 머리를 그렇게 자르니 어려 보인다. (young)
→ ______________________ with that haircut.

4 내 노트북 컴퓨터가 고장이 나서, Jake는 내가 그의 것을 사용하도록 허락했다. (allow, use)
→ My laptop didn't work, so Jake ______________________ his.

5 이 파스타는 카레 같은 냄새가 난다. (smell, curry)
→ This pasta ______________________.

6 그의 어머니는 그가 점심 식사 후에 설거지를 하도록 시키셨다. (wash the dishes)
→ His mother made ______________________ after lunch.

7 나는 Bill에게 내 텐트를 빌려 주었는데, 그는 아직 그것을 돌려주지 않았다. (lend, tent)
→ I ______________________, but he didn't return it yet.

B 우리말과 일치하도록 ( ) 안에 주어진 단어를 바르게 배열하시오.

1 이 호수는 매우 깊어 보인다. (lake, looks, this, deep, very)
→ ______________________.

2 Ann은 뒤에서 누군가가 자신의 이름을 부르는 것을 들었다. (heard, her, name, call, someone)
→ Ann ______________________ behind her.

3 이 아이스박스는 음식을 신선하게 유지해 준다. (food, keeps, fresh)
→ This icebox ______________________.

4 그녀의 어머니가 그녀에게 웨딩드레스를 만들어 주셨다. (made, a, her, dress, for, wedding)
→ Her mother ______________________.

5 그는 그의 이웃에게 한 가지 부탁을 했다. (of, a, neighbor, asked, favor, his)
→ He ______________________.

6 Daniel은 그들에게 그의 흉터를 보여 주었다. (to, showed, scar, them, his)
→ Daniel ______________________.

Answer Key p.2

C 다음 두 문장을 보기처럼 한 문장으로 만들 때 빈칸에 알맞은 말을 쓰시오.

보기	I was watching my son. + He was practicing the violin. → I was watching my son practice[practicing] the violin.

1 I saw Mia yesterday. + She was talking to Henry.
→ I ______________________________ yesterday.

2 Something was falling from the sky. + Did you see it?
→ Did you see ______________________________?

3 I joined the book club. + My teacher got me to do it.
→ My teacher ______________________________.

4 I worked until late last night. + My boss made me do it.
→ My boss ______________________________.

5 She felt the wind. + The wind was blowing through her hair.
→ She ______________________________.

6 I ride my bike to school. + My parents let me do it.
→ My parents ______________________________.

D 그림을 보고 ( ) 안의 말을 이용하여 문장을 완성하시오.

1

2

3

1 Santa Claus is giving ______________________________.
(children, gifts)

2 He heard somebody ______________________________.
(knock on the door)

3 The police officer ordered ______________________________.
(the driver, stop the car)

REVIEW TEST

[1-5] 빈칸에 들어갈 알맞은 말을 고르시오.

1

This onion soup tastes ________.

① well ② salty ③ badly
④ sweetly ⑤ deliciously

2

Harry lent ten dollars ________ me yesterday.

① to ② for ③ of
④ in ⑤ from

3

Dark clothes make people ________ thinner.

① look ② looks ③ looked
④ looking ⑤ to look

4

Mom advised me ________ some rest.

① get ② gets ③ to get
④ got ⑤ gotten

5

Did you see him ________ this room?

① leaves ② leaving ③ to leave
④ left ⑤ was leaving

[6-7] 다음 중 어법상 틀린 것을 고르시오.

6 ① The baby's skin feels smoothly.
② I felt someone touching my hand.
③ Your brother looks like your father.
④ My teacher made me clean the toilet.
⑤ I'll buy my brother a birthday present.

7 ① I named my puppy Choco.
② I found the musical excite.
③ He didn't ask me anything.
④ The noise kept me awake all night.
⑤ She asked me to come back early.

빈출

8 다음 빈칸에 to가 들어갈 수 없는 것은?

① Mr. Brown taught science ________ us.
② I sent an email ________ you yesterday.
③ Roy gave some roses ________ Jen.
④ Midori got a plane ticket to Osaka ________ me.
⑤ Sean showed a beautiful picture ________ her.

[9-11] 빈칸에 들어갈 말로 알맞지 않은 것을 고르시오.

9

I think that it ________ great.

① looks ② makes ③ tastes
④ smells ⑤ sounds

Answer Key p.2

10

My parents ________ me clean up my desk.

① had ② got ③ made
④ watched ⑤ helped

11

The doctor ________ him to take the pill after surgery.

① got ② told ③ let
④ advised ⑤ allowed

12 다음 우리말을 영어로 바르게 옮긴 것은?

그 선생님은 학생들이 계속 조용히 하도록 했다.

① The teacher had the students kept quiet.
② The teacher had the students kept quietly.
③ The teacher had the students keep quiet.
④ The teacher had the students keep quietly.
⑤ The teacher had the students keeping quiet.

서술형

[13-15] ( ) 안의 말을 이용하여 문장을 완성하시오.

13

I saw the man ________ a woman's purse. (steal)

14

My brother never lets me ________ his computer. (use)

15

My parents allowed me ________ on a trip with my friends. (go)

서술형 빈출

[16-18] 두 문장의 의미가 같도록 빈칸에 알맞은 말을 쓰시오.

16

My teacher gave me some good advice.

→ My teacher gave some good advice ________ ________.

17

My new classmate asked me a favor.

→ My new classmate asked a favor ________ ________.

18

Andrew bought his daughter ice cream after lunch.

→ Andrew bought ice cream ________ ________ ________ after lunch.

19 다음 중 어법상 옳은 것은?

① Lucy found the book usefully.
② I saw him walk down the dark street.
③ I feel sadly when I listen to the song.
④ He expected the package arrive today.
⑤ Dad had me to bring his jacket.

서술형

[20-22] 우리말과 일치하도록 ( ) 안의 말을 이용하여 문장을 완성하시오.

20 좋은 약은 쓴 맛이 난다. (bitter)

→ Good medicine ________________.

21 경비원은 내가 건물로 들어가도록 허락하지 않았다. (not, let, enter)

→ The guard ________________ the building.

22 영어 선생님이 나에게 영어로 일기를 쓰게 하셨다. (get, keep a diary)

→ My English teacher ________________ in English.

23 문장의 형식이 나머지 넷과 다른 것은?

① I want the air to be clean.
② She made the kids wash their hands.
③ The café doesn't let people use straws.
④ Dad made us fresh potato salad.
⑤ They thought the rules unfair.

서술형

[24-25] 우리말과 일치하도록 ( ) 안에 주어진 단어를 바르게 배열하시오.

24 그 이야기는 이상하게 들렸지만 사실이었다. (sounded, story, the, strange)

→ ____________________________, but it was true.

25 나는 여동생이 그녀의 방에서 바이올린을 켜는 소리를 들었다. (play, the, my, heard, sister, I, violin)

→ ____________________________ in her room.

고난도

26 다음 중 어법상 옳은 것을 모두 고르면?

① I told my friends the news.
② This bread tastes good with butter.
③ This soup looks like spicy.
④ Can you get some water of me?
⑤ I'll send an invitation to you tomorrow.

27 다음 중 어법상 옳은 것으로 바르게 짝지어진 것은?

a. I saw the singer dancing on stage.
b. My teacher allowed us play football.
c. My parents let me go to the concert.
d. I got my brother to do his homework.
e. Her book made her very successfully.

① a, b, c ② a, b, d
③ a, c, d ④ b, c, e
⑤ c, d, e

고난도

28 다음 중 어법상 옳은 것의 개수는?

- We found the sofa very comfortable.
- I helped my dad fix his car.
- Mom asked me cleaning the house.
- Jay had the waiter to bring more water.
- I heard Stewart shout at his brother.

① 1개 ② 2개 ③ 3개
④ 4개 ⑤ 5개

서술형

[29-30] 밑줄 친 부분이 어법상 옳은지 판단하고, 틀리면 바르게 고치시오.

29 My boyfriend gave a card for me on my birthday.

(O / X) ______________

30 Parents should keep their kids safe in any situation.

(O / X) ______________

서술형

31 우리말과 일치하도록 주어진 조건에 맞게 문장을 완성하시오.

그는 우리가 길을 찾는 것을 도와주었다.

〈조건〉 1. find, help, the way를 이용할 것
2. 6단어로 쓸 것

→ ______________.

서술형 고난도

[32-33] 어법상 틀린 부분을 찾아 바르게 고치시오.

32 Katie just came back from her business trip. She looks very tiredly. (1개)

33 I'm going to dance at the school festival with Justin. He is a good dancer, so I expect him teach me how to dance. (1개)

LET'S REVIEW

주요 예문을 다시 한번 확인하고, 우리말과 일치하도록 빈칸을 채우시오.

- You [1] ______________ different without your glasses. 너는 안경을 안 쓰니 달라 보인다. Unit 01 - A
- That cloud [2] ______________ a puppy. 저 구름은 강아지처럼 보인다. Unit 01 - A

- I **told** my best friend a secret. 나는 가장 친한 친구에게 비밀을 말했다. Unit 01 - B
- Ted **sent** me a text message last night.
  → Ted **sent** a text message [3] ______________ me last night.
  Ted는 지난밤 내게 문자 메시지를 보냈다. Unit 01 - B
- My friend **made** me a cake on my birthday.
  → My friend **made** a cake [4] ______________ me on my birthday.
  나의 친구가 내 생일에 내게 케이크를 만들어 주었다. Unit 01 - B
- Can I **ask** you a favor?
  → Can I **ask** a favor [5] ______________ you?
  당신에게 부탁 하나를 해도 될까요? Unit 01 - B

- The song [6] ______________ him **a world-famous star**.
  그 노래는 그를 세계적으로 유명한 스타로 만들었다. Unit 02 - A

- I **found** the math exam [7] ______________. 나는 그 수학 시험이 어렵다고 생각했다. Unit 02 - B

- My uncle **advised** me [8] ______________ a lot of books.
  나의 삼촌은 내게 책을 많이 읽으라고 조언했다. Unit 02 - C

- James **let** me [9] ______________ on his seat. James는 내가 그의 자리에 앉도록 했다. Unit 02 - D

- The coach **watched** him [10] ______________ the ball.
  그 코치는 그가 공을 차는 것을 지켜보았다. Unit 02 - E

Answers

[1] look [2] looks like [3] to [4] for [5] of [6] made [7] difficult [8] to read [9] sit [10] kick[kicking]

CHAPTER 02

시제

시제란 동사의 형태 변화를 통해 동작이 일어난 때를 표현하는 것을 말한다.

UNIT 01

현재, 과거, 미래시제 / 진행형

A 현재시제

현재의 사실이나 상태, 변함없는 진리, 반복되는 일 및 습관을 나타낼 때 쓴다.

My family **lives** in a small town.
The sun **rises** in the east.
Kate **checks** her email every day.

B 과거시제

이미 지난 과거의 일이나 상태를 나타낼 때 사용하며 과거를 나타내는 표현(yesterday, last ~, ~ ago)과 자주 함께 쓰인다.

Jake **bought** a new smartphone yesterday.

C 미래시제

1 will + 동사원형: 미래에 대한 예측, 주어의 의지나 즉흥적으로 결심한 일을 나타낼 때 쓴다.

The postman **will arrive** here at about two o'clock.
Mom, I **will help** you clean the living room.

2 be going to + 동사원형: 미래에 대한 예측이나, 이미 정해진 미래의 계획을 나타낼 때 쓴다.

Look at the sky. It **is going to rain** soon. (= It **will rain** soon.)
I'm going to attend the meeting next week.

D 진행형

1 현재진행형: 「be동사 현재형 + v-ing」의 형태로, 현재 진행 중인 일을 나타낼 때 쓴다.

She **is playing** an online game now.

2 과거진행형: 「be동사 과거형 + v-ing」의 형태로, 과거 시점에서 진행 중이었던 일을 나타낼 때 쓴다.

Nick **was talking** on the phone when I saw him.

① 소유, 감각, 감정, 인지 등을 나타내는 동사(have, see, hear, like, know, believe 등)는 진행형으로 쓰지 않는다.

Mr. Lee **has** two sons.
~~Mr. Lee is having two sons.~~

CHECK UP 빈칸에 알맞은 말을 고르시오.

1 The earth ____________ around the sun.
ⓐ goes ⓑ went ⓒ will go

2 James ____________ to Italy last year.
ⓐ travels ⓑ traveled ⓒ will travel

3 Molly ____________ when I called.
ⓐ sleeps ⓑ is sleeping ⓒ was sleeping

⊕ PLUS : 미래를 나타내는 현재시제와 현재진행형

- 미래의 확정된 공식 일정, 계획 등은 현재시제로 나타낼 수도 있다.
  The meeting **begins** at ten o'clock.
- 가까운 미래의 계획은 현재진행형으로 나타낼 수도 있다.
  She **is coming** next Friday.

PRACTICE

Answer Key p.3

( ) 안에서 알맞은 말을 고르시오.

1 He (takes, is taking) a walk after dinner every day.

2 She (enters, entered) the university last year.

3 I (am taking, was taking) a shower when the doorbell rang.

4 I (will send, sent) an email to Hal next week.

STEP 2

( ) 안의 말을 이용하여 문장을 완성하시오.

1 I __________ a pizza an hour ago, but it is not here yet. (order)

2 Water __________ at 100°C. (boil)

3 She was __________ dinner at that time. (eat)

4 My dog always __________ happily when it snows. (run)

STEP 3

밑줄 친 부분을 어법에 맞게 고치시오.

1 Paul is knowing her very well.

2 They will take this picture two years ago.

3 She is singing a pop song when I saw her.

4 I going to visit my grandparents tomorrow.

STEP 4

우리말과 일치하도록 ( ) 안의 말을 이용하여 문장을 완성하시오.

1 Tony는 다음 달에 요가를 배울 예정이다. (learn)
→ Tony __________ __________ __________ __________ yoga next month.

2 그는 부엌에서 설거지를 하고 있다. (wash dishes)
→ He __________ __________ __________ in the kitchen.

3 그녀는 지난주에 내 컴퓨터를 고쳐 주었다. (fix, computer)
→ She __________ __________ __________ last week.

4 나는 매일 아침 한 시간씩 자전거를 탄다. (ride, bicycle)
→ I __________ __________ __________ for an hour every morning.

UNIT
02 현재완료

A 과거 vs. 현재완료

1 과거: 현재와는 상관없이 과거의 사실만을 나타낼 때 쓴다.

He **lost** his watch yesterday. (현재 찾았는지 알 수 없음)

2 현재완료: 과거의 한 시점에서 일어난 일이 현재까지 영향을 줄 때 쓴다.

He **has lost** his watch. (현재까지 잃어버린 상태임)

ⓘ 과거를 나타내는 표현(yesterday, last ~, ~ ago 등)은 현재완료와 함께 쓸 수 없다.

~~He has lost his watch yesterday.~~

B 현재완료: have[has] + v-ed

현재완료는 완료, 경험, 계속, 결과 등의 의미를 나타낸다. 부정문은 「have[has] + not + v-ed」, 의문문은 「Have[Has] + 주어 + v-ed ~?」이다.

1 완료: '막 ~했다'의 의미로, 어떤 동작이 현재에 막 완료되었음을 나타낸다. 주로 already, just, yet 등과 함께 쓰인다.

I **have** just **eaten** a sandwich.

2 경험: '~한 적이 있다'의 의미로, 현재까지의 경험을 나타낸다. 주로 ever, never, before, once 등과 함께 쓰인다.

I've never **eaten** Thai food.

3 계속: '지금까지 계속 ~해 왔다'의 의미로, 과거의 어느 시점부터 현재까지 어떤 동작이나 상태가 계속되고 있음을 나타낸다. 주로 since, for 등과 함께 쓰인다.

He **has had** dogs since he was young.

4 결과: '~해 버렸다'의 의미로, 과거 행동으로 인한 결과가 현재까지 영향을 미치고 있음을 나타낸다.

Julie **has gone** to London. (So she is not here now.)

cf. Julie **has been** to London. 〈경험〉

빈칸에 알맞은 말을 고르시오.

1 I have __________ to his house once.
ⓐ be ⓑ being ⓒ been

2 We __________ each other since we were kids.
ⓐ know ⓑ knew ⓒ have known

3 I __________ the actor here yesterday.
ⓐ see ⓑ saw ⓒ have seen

4 I __________ my purse at home, so I can't buy anything now.
ⓐ leave ⓑ am leaving ⓒ have left

PLUS : for vs. since

• for + 기간: ~ 동안
He has been ill **for** a week.

• since + 시점: ~ 이래로
He has been ill **since** last week.

PRACTICE

Answer Key p.3

( ) 안에서 알맞은 말을 고르시오.

1 I (don't see, haven't seen) the film yet.

2 She (sent, has sent) me an email last month.

3 It (snowed, has snowed) heavily since yesterday.

4 He (has been, has gone) to Paris, so you can't meet him now.

STEP 2

밑줄 친 부분을 어법에 맞게 고치시오.

1 A: Do you ever bake bread?
B: Yes, I have several times.

2 She has been in Seoul for 2015.

3 Bob has learned how to drive three years ago.

4 They lived here since last year.

STEP 3

다음을 현재완료 문장으로 바꿀 때, 빈칸에 알맞은 말을 쓰시오.

1 She lost her glasses, so she doesn't have them now.
→ She ________________ her glasses.

2 Winter came, and it is winter now.
→ Winter ________________.

3 My best friend went to Tokyo. He is not here now.
→ My best friend ________________ to Tokyo.

STEP 4

우리말과 일치하도록 ( ) 안의 말을 이용하여 문장을 완성하시오.

1 나는 그의 전화번호를 잊어버렸다. (forget)
→ I __________ __________ his phone number.

2 그는 여기서 5년째 일해 왔다. (work, here)
→ He __________ __________ __________ __________ five years.

3 나는 벌써 기차표를 샀다. (already, buy)
→ I __________ __________ __________ a train ticket.

4 나는 중국에 한 번 가 본 적이 있다. (be)
→ I __________ __________ __________ China once.

5 너는 로봇 청소기를 사용해 본 적이 있니? (ever, use)
→ __________ __________ __________ __________ a robot vacuum cleaner?

GRAMMAR FOR WRITING

A 우리말과 일치하도록 ( ) 안의 말을 이용하여 문장을 완성하시오.

1 우리는 방금 이 도시로 이사 왔다. (just, move)

→ We ______________________________ to this city.

2 Lia는 일요일에 자원봉사를 할 것이다. (do volunteer work)

→ Lia ______________________________ on Sunday.

3 우리 형은 4년째 저 안경을 껴 왔다. (wear, glasses)

→ My brother ______________________________ four years.

4 그녀는 나의 부모님을 두 번 만난 적이 있다. (meet, parents)

→ She ______________________________ twice.

5 그는 그의 방에서 머리를 말리는 중이다. (dry one's hair)

→ He ______________________________ in his room.

6 나뭇잎들은 가을에 빨갛고 노랗게 변한다. (turn, red and yellow, fall)

→ Leaves ______________________________.

7 나는 2년 전에 초등학교를 졸업했다. (graduate from, elementary school)

→ I ______________________________ two years ago.

B 우리말과 일치하도록 ( ) 안에 주어진 단어를 바르게 배열하시오.

1 너는 이번 주말에 무엇을 할 예정이니? (are, to, you, going, what, do)

→ ______________________________ this weekend?

2 내 여동생이 내 이어폰을 고장 내서, 나는 음악을 들을 수 없다.
(my, has, my, sister, broken, earphones)

→ ______________________________, so I can't listen to music.

3 Sue는 어린아이였을 때부터 노래하는 것을 좋아했다. (has, since, liked, to, Sue, sing)

→ ______________________________ she was a kid.

4 네가 전화했을 때 나는 영화를 보고 있었다. (watching, when, a, was, I, movie)

→ ______________________________ you called.

5 우리 어머니는 내년에 마흔 살이 되신다. (mother, years, will, my, forty, old, be)

→ ______________________________ next year.

6 그 식당은 매일 아침 10시에 문을 연다. (the, at, restaurant, opens, ten o'clock)

→ ______________________________ every morning.

Answer Key p.3

C 빈칸에 알맞은 동사를 보기에서 골라 적절한 시제로 바꿔 쓰시오. (단, 한 번씩만 쓸 것)

[1-4]

보기	be	eat	hear	check

1 An elephant only ______________ plants, not meat.

2 Robert ______________ a strange sound last night.

3 Tim is back from Greece. He ______________ to Greece three times.

4 I ______________ my email every day. Emails are important to my work.

[5-8]

보기	have	walk	help	teach

5 The singer ______________ a lot of fans in Korea now.

6 My father ______________ math at a high school since 1995.

7 I ______________ to school when I met my teacher.

8 A: Jay! Help me move this sofa, please.
B: Sure. I ______________ you.

D Lucy의 이번 주 일정표를 보고 일정에 맞게 문장을 완성하시오.

WED	THU	FRI	SAT	SUN
▪ take a math quiz	▪ go to the dentist	today	▪ have dinner with Ryan	▪ practice the violin

1 She ______________________________ on Wednesday.

2 She ______________________________ yesterday.

3 She ______________________________ tomorrow.

4 She ______________________________ on Sunday.

REVIEW TEST

[1-5] 빈칸에 들어갈 알맞은 말을 고르시오.

1

Water ________ at 0°C.

① freezes ② froze
③ will freeze ④ freezing
⑤ has frozen

2

Emma ________ to Laos last month.

① travels ② traveled
③ is traveling ④ will travel
⑤ has traveled

3

Harry ________ the baseball game now.

① watched ② watching
③ is watching ④ was watching
⑤ have watched

4

Jake ________ a smartphone now.

① have ② has
③ is having ④ will have
⑤ has had

5

I ________ to the concert hall five times.

① am ② have
③ going ④ have been
⑤ will be

[6-7] 다음 중 어법상 틀린 것을 고르시오.

6 ① We have not decided yet.
② She got married five years ago.
③ Light was faster than sound.
④ I was talking with Tom then.
⑤ He teaches English at the school.

7 ① I will help you carry the box.
② He has not cleaned his desk yet.
③ They are waiting for a bus now.
④ He has gone to Sydney last year.
⑤ She is going to meet him tonight.

8 빈칸에 들어갈 말이 순서대로 바르게 짝지어진 것은?

• She has studied physics ________ three years. • He has run the company ________ 2006.

① in – at ② for – at
③ since – for ④ in – since
⑤ for – since

빈출

[9-10] 다음 중 보기의 밑줄 친 부분과 쓰임이 같은 것을 고르시오.

9

보기 He has just been to the market.

① I have heard the song before.
② I have already read the magazine.
③ Have you ever been to South Africa?
④ I have used this pen since last year.
⑤ My dad has had this car for ten years.

Answer Key p.3

10

보기	He has worked on the report for two days.

① He has forgotten her name.
② I have never seen a real rainbow.
③ Have you washed your car yet?
④ They have just finished dinner.
⑤ How long have you been in this city?

서술형

[11-12] ( ) 안의 말을 이용하여 문장을 완성하시오.

11 Next week's festival ______________ fun. (be)

12 Christina ___________ in this house since she was ten. (live)

빈출

13 밑줄 친 부분의 쓰임이 올바른 것은?

① He was riding a bicycle next week.
② She is run a blog now.
③ The game will be exciting yesterday.
④ He has lost his watch a few days ago.
⑤ I have been a designer since last year.

14 빈칸에 들어갈 말이 순서대로 바르게 짝지어진 것은?

• He ___________ ill last Saturday.
• He ___________ ill since last Saturday.

① is – was
② was – is
③ was – was
④ was – has been
⑤ has been – was

서술형

[15-16] 밑줄 친 부분을 어법에 맞게 고치시오.

15 I have stayed at the Sunshine Hotel last summer.

16 Josh looks for a new house now.

서술형

[17-18] 다음 두 문장을 한 문장으로 바꿀 때, 빈칸에 알맞은 말을 쓰시오.

17 Mom went to Paris. She is not here now.

→ Mom ______________ to Paris.

18 When Robin first saw Mindy, he liked her. He still likes her.

→ Robin ______________ he first saw her.

서술형

[19-21] 우리말과 일치하도록 ( ) 안의 말을 이용하여 문장을 완성하시오.

19 너 독도에 가 본 적 있니? (ever, be)

→ ____________________ to Dokdo?

20 누군가가 내 지갑을 훔쳐가서 나는 지금 아무것도 살 수 없다. (steal, purse)

→ Because someone ________________ ___________, I can't buy anything now.

21 Amy는 작년에 그녀의 남자 친구를 만났다. (meet, boyfriend)

→ Amy ____________________ last year.

22 다음 대화의 빈칸에 들어갈 알맞은 말은?

A: It's hot in this room!
B: Really? Then I _______ the window.

① open ② opens
③ will open ④ opened
⑤ have opened

서술형

[23-25] 우리말과 일치하도록 ( ) 안에 주어진 단어를 바르게 배열하시오.

23 그 당시에 나는 친구에게 이메일을 쓰고 있었다. (email, my, to, was, an, I, friend, writing)

→ ________________________________ at that time.

24 나는 그 영화 동호회에 가입할 예정이다. (I, to, the, am, movie club, join, going)

→ ________________________________.

25 우리는 십 년째 친구이다. (have, friends, we, for, been)

→ ________________________________ ten years.

고난도

26 다음 중 어법상 옳은 것을 모두 고르면?

① I am knowing those girls.
② She will play the piano since 2018.
③ Did you go shopping yesterday?
④ The new movie is coming soon.
⑤ He is wearing a hat when I saw him.

27 다음 문장이 어법상 옳으면 O, 틀리면 X의 철자를 선택할 때, 순서대로 만들어지는 단어는?

	O	X
I am liking the boy band BTS.	f	p
I went fishing last weekend.	a	o
Do you ever been to Jeonju?	s	r
It has rained since last Sunday.	k	t

① past ② park
③ pork ④ fast
⑤ fork

고난도

28 다음 중 어법상 옳은 것의 개수는?

- I will turn off the light.
- Fruit is having a lot of vitamins.
- People needed water when they are thirsty.
- I have lived in Korea five years ago.
- Andy has studied in America for two years.

① 1개 ② 2개 ③ 3개
④ 4개 ⑤ 5개

서술형

[29-31] 밑줄 친 부분이 어법상 옳은지 판단하고, 틀리면 바르게 고치시오.

29 I'm going to watch a basketball game this weekend.

(O / X) ______________________

30 I was hearing someone crying.

(O / X) ______________________

31 This movie has won lots of awards last year.

(O / X) ______________________

서술형 고난도

[32-33] 어법상 틀린 부분을 찾아 바르게 고치시오.

32 I am believing that Anna is innocent. (1개)

33 John and I have known each other for elementary school. At that time, he was shorter than me, but now he was taller. (2개)

LET'S REVIEW

주요 예문을 다시 한번 확인하고, 우리말과 일치하도록 빈칸을 채우시오.

- My family **lives** in a small town. 내 가족은 소도시에 산다. Unit 01 - A
- The sun [1] ________________ in the east. 태양은 동쪽에서 뜬다. Unit 01 - A
- Kate **checks** her email every day. Kate는 그녀의 이메일을 매일 확인한다. Unit 01 - A

- Jake [2] ________________ a new smartphone yesterday. Jake는 어제 새 스마트폰을 샀다. Unit 01 - B

- The postman **will arrive** here at about two o'clock. 우체부가 2시경에 여기 도착할 것이다. Unit 01 - C
- Mom, I [3] ________________ you clean the living room.
  엄마, 거실 청소하는 것을 제가 도와 드릴게요. Unit 01 - C
- Look at the sky. It **is** [4] ________________ soon. 하늘을 봐. 곧 비가 올 거야. Unit 01 - C
- **I'm going to attend** the meeting next week. 나는 다음 주에 회의에 참석할 것이다. Unit 01 - C

- She [5] ________________ an online game now. 그녀는 지금 온라인 게임을 하고 있다. Unit 01 - D
- Nick [6] ________________ on the phone when I saw him.
  내가 Nick을 보았을 때 그는 통화 중이었다. Unit 01 - D

- He [7] ________________ his watch yesterday. 그는 어제 자신의 시계를 잃어버렸다. Unit 02 - A
- He **has lost** his watch. 그는 자신의 시계를 잃어버렸다. Unit 02 - A

- I [8] ________________ just **eaten** a sandwich. 나는 방금 샌드위치를 먹었다. Unit 02 - B
- I**'ve** never **eaten** Thai food. 나는 태국 음식을 먹어 본 적이 없다. Unit 02 - B
- He **has had** dogs since he was young. 그는 어렸을 때부터 개를 키워 왔다. Unit 02 - B
- Julie [9] ________________ to London. (So she is not here now.)
  Julie는 런던에 갔다. (그래서 그녀는 지금 여기 없다.) Unit 02 - B

Answers

[1] rises [2] bought [3] will[am going to] help [4] going to rain [5] is playing [6] was talking
[7] lost [8] have [9] has gone

CHAPTER 03

조동사

조동사는 본동사의 기본 의미에
능력, 허가, 요청, 미래, 의무, 충고 등의
의미를 더해 준다.

UNIT 01

can, may, will

A can + 동사원형

1 능력: ~할 수 있다(= be able to + 동사원형)

I **can** speak English, but I **can't** speak French.
= I **am able to** speak English, but **I'm not able to** speak French.

ⓘ can이 능력을 의미할 때, 과거는 could 또는 was[were] able to, 미래는 will be able to를 쓴다.
He **could**[**was able to**] read when he was three years old.
I **will be able to** go to your house tonight.

2 허가: ~해도 된다

You **can** eat my chocolate. I don't want to eat it.

3 요청: ~해 주시겠습니까?

Can[**Could**] you help me move this chair?

B may + 동사원형

1 불확실한 추측, 가능성: ~일지도[할지도] 모른다

Kate **may** like me. She always smiles at me.

2 허가: ~해도 된다

You **may** use my computer.

C will + 동사원형

1 예정, 의지: ~할 것이다

I **will** attend the meeting, but he **won't**[**will not**].

2 요청: ~해 주시겠습니까?

Will[**Would**] you do me a favor?

CHECK UP 빈칸에 알맞은 말을 고르시오.

1 Tim can't ___________ shopping. He doesn't have any money now.
ⓐ go ⓑ goes ⓒ to go

2 ___________ you give me a wake-up call?
ⓐ Be able to ⓑ May ⓒ Will

PRACTICE

Answer Key p.4

STEP 1

( ) 안에서 알맞은 말을 고르시오.

1 It is too dark. I (can't, won't) see well.

2 You may (play, playing) soccer after lunch.

3 I didn't hear you well. (May, Would) you say that again?

4 Next week, Mark has a test, so he (will, wills) study this weekend.

STEP 2

주어진 문장과 의미가 통하도록 빈칸에 알맞은 조동사를 쓰시오.

1 Brian is able to play the flute very well.
→ Brian __________ play the flute very well.

2 Is it okay if I leave early today?
→ __________ I leave early today?

3 I was able to speak Japanese well when I was ten.
→ I __________ speak Japanese well when I was ten.

STEP 3

밑줄 친 부분을 어법에 맞게 고치시오.

1 Look at the clouds. It may to rain this afternoon.

2 Mary will can come to the party tonight.

3 Henry is able drive the big bus.

4 I will saving money for the trip.

STEP 4

우리말과 일치하도록 조동사와 ( ) 안의 말을 이용하여 문장을 완성하시오.

1 네가 원한다면, 이 가방을 가져도 된다. (have)
→ If you want, you __________ __________ this bag.

2 다시는 늦지 않겠습니다. (late)
→ I __________ __________ __________ again.

3 Jenny는 그녀의 방에 있을지도 모른다. (be)
→ Jenny __________ __________ in her room.

4 나는 7시까지 보고서를 다 마칠 것이다. (finish)
→ I __________ __________ the report by seven o'clock.

5 그는 100m를 11초 안에 달릴 수 있다. (run)
→ He __________ __________ __________ __________ 100 m in eleven seconds.

UNIT
02 must, should

must + 동사원형

1 의무: ~해야 한다(= have[has] to + 동사원형)

You **must** be back before dinner.

= You **have to** be back before dinner.

ⓘ must와 have to는 의미가 같지만, 부정형은 전혀 다른 의미를 가진다.

- must not: ~해서는 안 된다 〈금지〉
  I **must not** eat peaches. I am allergic to them.
- don't have to: ~할 필요가 없다(= need not, don't need to)
  You **don't have to** answer all the questions.

ⓘ have to의 과거는 had to, 미래는 will have to를 쓴다.
I **had to** study all night because I have a math test tomorrow. 〈과거〉
You **will have to** learn to spend your money wisely. 〈미래〉

2 강한 추측: ~임에 틀림없다

You **must** be Mr. Kim's daughter. You look just like him.

ⓘ 강한 추측을 의미할 때의 must의 부정은 can't[cannot](~일 리가 없다)이다.
She **can't** be at home now. I just saw her here a few minutes ago.

B

should + 동사원형: ~해야 한다, ~하는 것이 좋다 (must보다는 가벼운 의미)

We **should** keep our promise.

You **shouldn't** run in the hall.

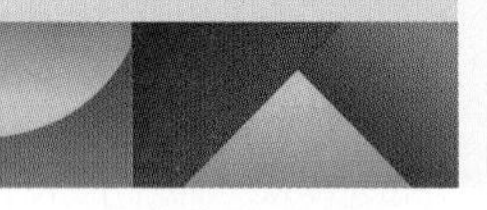

CHECK UP 빈칸에 알맞은 말을 고르시오.

1 He must ___________ late tonight. He has a lot of work.
ⓐ work ⓑ works ⓒ to work

2 She ___________ wait for him in the park yesterday.
ⓐ will have to ⓑ has to ⓒ had to

3 He sings very well. He ___________ be a singer.
ⓐ must ⓑ shouldn't ⓒ can't

4 You should ___________ quiet in the library.
ⓐ are ⓑ be ⓒ to be

PRACTICE

Answer Key p.4

( ) 안에서 알맞은 말을 고르시오.

1 You should (turn, to turn) off your cell phone in the theater.

2 Jessica looks sad. She (must, should) have a problem.

3 You have a lot of time. You (must not, don't have to) hurry.

4 James (cannot, must not) be here. He went to Berlin yesterday.

5 Look at that No Parking sign. You (must not, don't have to) park here.

STEP 2

밑줄 친 부분을 어법에 맞게 고치시오.

1 We must to follow the rules.

2 He should change not the plan.

3 He has to come to the meeting yesterday.

4 You have not to worry about the problem.

STEP 3

주어진 문장과 의미가 통하도록 빈칸에 알맞은 조동사를 보기에서 골라 쓰시오.

보기	can't	must	should

1 It will be good for you to call her right now.
→ You ________ call her right now.

2 It is impossible that he is the robber.
→ He ________ be the robber.

3 Andy has to finish his work before he leaves.
→ Andy ________ finish his work before he leaves.

우리말과 일치하도록 ( ) 안의 말을 이용하여 문장을 완성하시오.

1 수업 시간에 자서는 안 된다. (should, sleep)
→ You ________ ________ ________ during class.

2 문이 열려 있다. 누군가 방 안에 있는 것이 틀림없다. (be)
→ The door is open. Someone ________ ________ in the room.

3 병원 안에서는 절대 담배를 피우면 안 된다. (must, smoke)
→ You ________ ________ ________ in the hospital.

4 우리는 부산에서 지하철을 타야할 것이다. (take)
→ We ________ ________ ________ ________ the subway in Busan.

UNIT
03 would like to, had better, used to

A

would like to + 동사원형: ~하고 싶다

I **would like to** go to the amusement park.

= **I'd like to** go to the amusement park.

Would you **like to** try this tea?

B

had better + 동사원형: ~하는 것이 낫다(충고, 경고)

You **had better** think about it again.

= You**'d better** think about it again.

ⓘ had better의 부정은 「had better not」의 형태로 쓴다.
You **had better not** smoke. It is not good for your health.

C

used to + 동사원형

1 과거의 습관: ~하곤 했다(= would)

Junho **used to** play football on Sunday mornings.
= Junho **would** play football on Sunday mornings.

2 과거의 상태: ~이었다

There **used to** be a big tree here.

ⓘ 과거의 상태를 나타낼 때는 would를 쓸 수 없다.
~~There would be a big tree here.~~

ⓘ used to의 부정은 「didn't use to[used not to]」, 의문문은 「Did + 주어 + use to ~?」로 쓴다.
She **didn't use to** like babies, but now she does.
Did you **use to** work in a bank?

CHECK UP 빈칸에 알맞은 말을 고르시오.

1 Julie ___________ learn Latin dance.
ⓐ would like ⓑ would likes to ⓒ would like to

2 You are late. You ___________ take a taxi.
ⓐ have better ⓑ had better ⓒ had better to

3 You ___________ go to the park alone after midnight.
ⓐ not had better ⓑ had not better ⓒ had better not

4 I used to ___________ to classical music.
ⓐ listen ⓑ listening ⓒ listened

PRACTICE

Answer Key p.5

STEP 1

( ) 안에서 알맞은 말을 고르시오.

1 Mom, I would like (have, to have) a parrot.
2 You (have better, had better) leave now.
3 There (would, used to) be a café at the end of this street.
4 You (had not better, had better not) set up your tent here.

STEP 2

빈칸에 가장 알맞은 말을 보기에서 골라 쓰시오. (단, 한 번씩만 쓸 것)

보기	would like to	had better	would

1 You look very tired. You ______________ take a break.
2 I ______________ change my order. I'll have a hamburger.
3 When I was young, my grandmother ______________ tell me old stories.

STEP 3

주어진 문장과 의미가 통하도록 빈칸에 알맞은 조동사를 쓰시오.

1 I think you should not eat junk food.
→ You __________ __________ __________ eat junk food.
2 I want to go to the concert with you.
→ I __________ __________ __________ go to the concert with you.
3 I went hiking every weekend, but I don't anymore.
→ I __________ __________ go hiking every weekend.

STEP 4

우리말과 일치하도록 조동사와 ( ) 안의 말을 이용하여 문장을 완성하시오.

1 우리는 새해 첫날에 파티를 하곤 했다. (have)
→ We __________ __________ __________ a party on New Year's Day.
2 나는 다시 그녀를 만나고 싶다. (see)
→ I __________ __________ __________ __________ her again.
3 너는 다른 일자리를 찾아보는 것이 좋겠다. (look for)
→ You __________ __________ __________ __________ another job.
4 예전에는 여기에 병원이 있었다. (be, hospital)
→ There __________ __________ __________ __________ __________ here.
5 나와 함께 산책 갈래? (go)
→ __________ __________ __________ __________ __________ for a walk with me?

GRAMMAR FOR WRITING

A 우리말과 일치하도록 조동사와 ( ) 안의 말을 이용하여 문장을 완성하시오.

1 그녀는 러시아어를 말할 수 없다. (speak)
→ She ______________________ Russian.

2 크리스마스에 눈이 올지도 모른다. (snow)
→ It ______________________ on Christmas Day.

3 당신을 저녁 식사에 초대하고 싶습니다. (would, invite)
→ I ______________________ you for dinner.

4 우리 가족은 휴가에 제주도를 가곤 했다. (visit)
→ My family ______________________ Jeju Island on vacation.

5 Robert는 나에게 화가 난 게 틀림없다. (angry)
→ Robert ______________________ with me.

6 너는 너무 밤늦게까지 공부하지 않는 것이 낫다. (study)
→ You ______________________ too late into the night.

7 나는 지난 일요일에 일하러 가야만 했다. (have to, go)
→ I ______________________ to work last Sunday.

B 우리말과 일치하도록 ( ) 안에 주어진 단어를 바르게 배열하시오.

1 Sara는 뉴욕에서 그를 만날 수 있을 것이다. (meet, will, to, be, him, able)
→ Sara ______________________ in New York.

2 아빠는 디저트를 드시지 않았지만, 지금은 드신다. (dessert, to, eat, use, didn't)
→ Dad ______________________, but now he does.

3 히터 좀 켜줄래? (the, can, you, heater, turn on)
→ ______________________?

4 너는 그의 충고를 받아들일 필요가 없다. (have, you, don't, take, advice, his, to)
→ ______________________.

5 너는 나에게 거짓말해서는 안 된다. (lie, you, to, me, not, should)
→ ______________________.

6 그는 내일 너를 만나지 않을지도 몰라. 감기에 걸렸거든. (meet, he, may, not, you)
→ ______________________ tomorrow. He has a cold.

Answer Key p.5

C 보기의 조동사와 ( ) 안에 주어진 말을 이용하여 대화를 완성하시오. (단, 한 번씩만 쓸 것)

보기	had better	will	would like to	can't	used to

1 A: What time will the concert start?
B: The concert ______________ at 6:00 p.m. (start)

2 A: I couldn't sleep last night.
B: You ______________ coffee after dinner. (not, drink)

3 A: Do you play online games?
B: No. I ______________ them, but I don't anymore. (play)

4 A: May I take your order?
B: Yes. I ______________ a sandwich. (have)

5 A: Are Fred and Kevin twins?
B: Well, they ______________ twins. They are not the same age. (be)

D 그림을 보고 보기의 조동사와 ( ) 안의 말을 이용하여 기차 이용 예절에 관한 문장을 완성하시오. (단, 한 번씩 만 쓸 것)

보기	have to	must	may

If you are on the train ...

1 You ______________. (not, smoke)

2 You ______________. (speak quietly)

3 You ______________ at your seat. (eat or drink)

REVIEW TEST

[1-3] 빈칸에 들어갈 알맞은 말을 고르시오.

1

You ________ study now. You have an important exam tomorrow.

① can't ② may not
③ must not ④ have to
⑤ used to

2

I ________ swim in the morning. I don't anymore.

① can ② will
③ should ④ used to
⑤ had better

3

A: I have a headache. B: You ________ take some medicine.

① may not ② should
③ need not ④ used to
⑤ would like to

4 다음 중 보기의 밑줄 친 부분과 의미가 같은 것은?

보기 Anyone may use my laptop.

① Jen may be late for the train.
② The rumor may be true.
③ You may go to the concert.
④ She may not like my present.
⑤ He may be at the school library now.

[5-6] 다음 중 어법상 틀린 것을 고르시오.

5 ① Sam may win first prize.
② He will can attend the party.
③ I won't visit him tomorrow.
④ You must not take pictures here.
⑤ She has to fix her computer today.

6 ① He has better tell the truth.
② I would like to go on a trip.
③ The girl must be her cousin.
④ I used to sleep until noon on Sundays.
⑤ John has to wait for his mother.

빈출

[7-8] 다음 밑줄 친 부분과 바꿔 쓸 수 있는 것을 고르시오.

7

You don't have to worry about it.

① cannot ② may not
③ must not ④ need not
⑤ should not

8

You must come to class on time.

① may ② will
③ have to ④ used to
⑤ would like to

9 다음 중 우리말을 영어로 잘못 옮긴 것은?

① 벤치에 앉아도 될까요?
→ May I sit on the bench?
② 그는 세계 여행을 하고 싶어 한다.
→ He would like to travel the world.
③ 너는 규칙적으로 운동을 해야 한다.
→ You should exercise regularly.
④ 그 가방은 Jenny의 것임에 틀림없다.
→ The bag has to be Jenny's.
⑤ 그는 한때 영어 선생님이었다.
→ He used to be an English teacher.

10 다음 중 밑줄 친 부분을 잘못 고친 것은?

① You had not better go out today.
→ had better not
② I would like have a salad.
→ having
③ You will must call him first.
→ will have to
④ He is able to not swim well.
→ is not able to
⑤ I used going to school on foot.
→ to go

11 빈칸에 들어갈 말로 알맞지 않은 것은?

_________ you recommend a book for me?

① May ② Can ③ Could
④ Will ⑤ Would

서술형

12 대화가 성립되도록 ( ) 안에서 알맞은 말을 골라 쓰시오.

A: Excuse me, ⓐ (may, will) I ask you a question?
B: Sorry. I am very busy. I ⓑ (can, must) go now.

ⓐ _________ ⓑ _________

13 다음 중 두 문장의 의미가 같지 않은 것은?

① May I ask you a question?
→ Can I ask you a question?
② I can pick you up tonight.
→ I am able to pick you up tonight.
③ You must go home before dark.
→ You have to go home before dark.
④ He must be a liar.
→ He may be a liar.
⑤ You don't need to wait for me.
→ You don't have to wait for me.

서술형

[14-15] 빈칸에 공통으로 들어갈 말을 쓰시오.

14
- You _________ better call him now.
- I _________ to get up early yesterday.

15
- Would you like _________ join our bowling club?
- He used _________ live in Mexico.

빈출

[16-17] 밑줄 친 부분의 의미가 나머지 넷과 다른 것을 고르시오.

16 ① He can't drive a truck.
② Ron can't read Chinese.
③ John can't play the guitar.
④ She can't be Tom's sister.
⑤ I can't remember the password.

17 ① You must finish the work today.
② I must find another job.
③ She must get up early tomorrow.
④ She must be angry at me.
⑤ You must be careful with the knife.

서술형

[18-19] 우리말과 일치하도록 빈칸에 알맞은 말을 쓰시오.

18 예전에는 우리 학교 근처에 공원이 있었다.

→ There ________ ________ ________ a park near my school.

19 Mike는 거기에 가길 원하지 않을지도 모른다.

→ Mike ________ ________ ________ to go there.

20 다음 중 not이 들어갈 위치로 적절한 것은?

You ⓐ had ⓑ better ⓒ go ⓓ hiking ⓔ today.

① ⓐ ② ⓑ ③ ⓒ ④ ⓓ ⑤ ⓔ

서술형

[21-22] 주어진 문장과 의미가 통하도록 빈칸에 알맞은 말을 쓰시오.

21 You can use my car if you need to.

→ You ____________ my car if you need to.

22 Cindy is not able to play the drums.

→ Cindy ____________ the drums.

서술형

[23-25] 우리말과 일치하도록 ( ) 안에 주어진 단어를 바르게 배열하시오.

23 그는 오늘 일하러 갈 필요가 없다.
(to, work, doesn't, he, to, go, have)

→ ______________________________ today.

24 나는 새 스마트폰을 사고 싶다.
(buy, a, new, I, like, smartphone, to, would)

→ ______________________________.

25 저에게 이 책을 빌려주시겠어요?
(me, you, this, lend, would, book)

→ ______________________________?

고난도

26 다음 중 어법상 옳은 것을 모두 고르면?

① You had better go to the hospital first.
② Peter will can pick you up tomorrow.
③ Mom used to read me a bedtime story.
④ Adam may to meet his friend tonight.
⑤ There would be old houses in the countryside.

27 다음 중 어법상 옳은 것으로 바르게 짝지어진 것은?

a. You had better wearing a coat.
b. I would like to talk to Mr. Green.
c. The city used to be very crowded.
d. He may being right about the matter.
e. I was able to arrive at work on time.

① a, b, c ② a, c, d
③ a, d, e ④ b, c, e
⑤ b, d, e

고난도

28 다음 중 어법상 옳은 것의 개수는?

- You don't have to prepare dinner for us.
- He is able to not play tennis well.
- I must save a lot of money for a new computer.
- Did you use go skiing?
- I have to study hard for the exam.

① 1개 ② 2개 ③ 3개
④ 4개 ⑤ 5개

서술형

[29-31] 밑줄 친 부분이 어법상 옳은지 판단하고, 틀리면 바르게 고치시오.

29 We should talk not on the phone during the show.

(O / X) ____________________

30 There used to being a big stadium near my school.

(O / X) ____________________

31 You had better change your plan.

(O / X) ____________________

서술형 고난도

[32-33] 어법상 틀린 부분을 찾아 바르게 고치시오.

32 Mia uses to live with me, but she moved to another city. If she moves back, I would like live with her again. (2개)

33 My parents want me to do a few things before I play computer games. First, I should helped my brother with his homework. Also, I had to feed my dog. After that, I can play them. (2개)

LET'S REVIEW

주요 예문을 다시 한번 확인하고, 우리말과 일치하도록 빈칸을 채우시오.

- I **can** speak English, but I **can't** speak French. 나는 영어는 할 수 있지만 프랑스어는 못한다. Unit 01 - A
- You [1] __________ eat my chocolate. 너는 내 초콜릿을 먹어도 된다. Unit 01 - A
- **Can[Could]** you help me move this chair? 제가 이 의자를 옮기는 것을 도와주시겠습니까? Unit 01 - A

- Kate [2] __________ like me. She always smiles at me.
  Kate는 나를 좋아할지도 모른다. 그녀는 언제나 나에게 웃어준다. Unit 01 - B
- You **may** use my computer. 너는 내 컴퓨터를 써도 된다. Unit 01 - B

- I **will** attend the meeting, but he **won't**.
  나는 회의에 참석할 것이지만, 그는 그러지 않을 것이다. Unit 01 - C
- **Will[Would]** you do me a favor? 부탁 하나 들어주시겠습니까? Unit 01 - C

- You **must** be back before dinner. 너는 저녁 식사 전에 돌아와야 한다. Unit 02 - A
- You [3] __________ be Mr. Kim's daughter. You look just like him.
  너는 Kim 씨의 딸임에 틀림없다. 너는 그와 똑 닮았다. Unit 02 - A

- We **should** keep our promise. 우리는 약속을 지켜야 한다. Unit 02 - B
- You [4] __________ run in the hall. 너는 복도에서 뛰면 안 된다. Unit 02 - B

- I **would like to** go to the amusement park. 나는 놀이공원에 가고 싶다. Unit 03 - A
- [5] __________ you **like to** try this tea? 이 차를 마셔 보시겠습니까? Unit 03 - A

- You [6] __________ think about it again. 너는 그것에 대해 다시 생각해 보는 게 좋겠다. Unit 03 - B

- Junho [7] __________ play football on Sunday mornings.
  준호는 일요일 아침마다 축구를 하곤 했다. Unit 03 - C
- There [8] __________ be a big tree here. 여기에 큰 나무가 있었다. Unit 03 - C

Answers

[1] can[may] [2] may [3] must [4] shouldn't[should not] / must not [5] Would [6] had better
[7] used to / would [8] used to

CHAPTER

04

to부정사

to부정사는 「to + 동사원형」 형태로 문장에서 명사, 형용사 혹은 부사의 역할을 한다.

UNIT 01

명사적 용법의 to부정사

to부정사(구)는 명사처럼 문장에서 주어, 보어, 목적어의 역할을 할 수 있다.

A 주어 역할을 하는 to부정사

주어로 쓰인 to부정사가 길어질 경우 보통 「it(가주어) ~ to-v(진주어)」 형태로 쓴다.

To keep a pet in an apartment is not easy.

→ **It** is not easy **to keep** a pet in an apartment.

B 보어 역할을 하는 to부정사

My plan was **to prepare** dinner by six o'clock.

C 목적어 역할을 하는 to부정사

Jake likes **to bake** bread and cookies. He wants **to be** a baker.

ⓘ to부정사의 부정형: 「not[never] to-v」
James decided **not to give up**. He will try again.

D 의문사 + to-v

문장에서 주어, 보어, 목적어의 역할을 하며, 의문사에 따라 그 의미가 달라진다. 「의문사 + to-v」는 「의문사 + 주어 + should + 동사원형」으로 바꿔 쓸 수 있다.

- what to-v: 무엇을 ~할지
- who(m) to-v: 누구를[누구에게] ~할지
- where to-v: 어디서[어디로] ~할지
- how to-v: 어떻게 ~할지
- when to-v: 언제 ~할지

I've finished the work. Please tell me **what to do** next.
= what I should do

CHECK UP 빈칸에 알맞은 말을 고르시오.

1 ____________ is important to follow the school rules.
ⓐ It ⓑ That ⓒ This

2 He wants ____________ new sneakers.
ⓐ buy ⓑ buying ⓒ to buy

3 Tell me when ____________ the room.
ⓐ leave ⓑ leaving ⓒ to leave

PRACTICE

Answer Key p.6

다음 문장을 가주어로 시작하는 문장으로 바꿔 쓰시오.

1 To watch American dramas is interesting.
→ __________ is interesting ______________________________.

2 To travel around the world takes a long time.
→ __________ takes a long time ______________________________.

3 To run 100 m in seven seconds is not possible.
→ __________ is not possible ______________________________.

STEP 2

두 문장의 의미가 같도록 빈칸에 알맞은 말을 쓰시오.

1 I'm not sure what I should say to you.
→ I'm not sure __________ __________ __________ to you.

2 I haven't decided where I should stay in Paris yet.
→ I haven't decided __________ __________ __________ in Paris yet.

3 There are lots of doctors. I don't know whom I should see.
→ There are lots of doctors. I don't know __________ __________ __________.

STEP 3

빈칸에 가장 알맞은 말을 보기에서 골라 to-v 형태로 바꿔 쓰시오.

보기		
	teach students	buy a watch
	draw pictures	memorize thirty English words a day

1 Natalie is a teacher. Her job is ________________________.

2 Tim draws pictures every day. His hobby is ________________________.

3 I want to improve my English. My plan is ________________________.

4 I need ________________________. I lost my old one yesterday.

STEP 4

우리말과 일치하도록 ( ) 안의 말을 이용하여 문장을 완성하시오.

1 나는 어렸을 때 강아지를 갖고 싶어 했다. (want, have)
→ I __________ __________ __________ a puppy when I was a child.

2 어떻게 젓가락질을 하는지 제게 보여주세요. (use)
→ Please show me __________ __________ __________ chopsticks.

3 정크 푸드를 먹는 것은 건강에 좋지 않다. (eat)
→ __________ isn't good for your health __________ __________ junk food.

UNIT 02

형용사적 용법의 to부정사

to부정사(구)는 명사를 수식하거나 「be to-v」 형태로 주어를 설명하는 형용사 역할을 할 수 있다.

A 명사를 수식하는 to부정사

I have a project **to finish** by next week.

ⓘ -thing, -one, -body 등으로 끝나는 대명사 뒤에 수식하는 형용사가 있을 때, to부정사는 형용사 뒤에 온다.
Do you have anything *important* **to say**?

ⓘ 수식 받는 명사가 to부정사 속의 동사에 이어지는 전치사의 목적어일 때, 전치사는 반드시 써야 된다.
He needs a toy **to play with**. (← play with a toy)
~~He needs a toy to play.~~
→ 위 문장에서 play는 자동사이므로 목적어를 취하려면 반드시 전치사가 필요하다.

B 주어를 설명하는 「be to-v」 용법

1 예정: ~할 예정이다
She **is to quit** her job next year.

2 가능: ~할 수 있다
No one **was to be seen** in the shop.

3 의무: ~해야 한다
You **are to keep** your promise.

4 운명: ~할 운명이다
He **was** never **to visit** his hometown again.

5 의도: ~하려고 하다
If you **are to speak** English well, you must practice hard.

CHECK UP 빈칸에 알맞은 말을 고르시오.

1 I need someone ___________ me.
ⓐ help ⓑ helping ⓒ to help

2 He brought up an important topic ___________.
ⓐ talk ⓑ to talk ⓒ to talk about

3 Mom ___________ at the airport at five.
ⓐ is arrive ⓑ is to arrive ⓒ is to arriving

⊕ PLUS : 「be to-v」 용법 vs. 명사적 용법의 보어 역할을 하는 to부정사

- She **is to go** to New York next week. 〈「be to-v 용법」 (예정)〉
- Her plan is **to go** to New York next month. 〈명사적 용법 (보어)〉

PRACTICE

Answer Key p.6

STEP 1 빈칸에 알맞은 말을 보기에서 골라 to-v 형태로 바꿔 쓰시오. (단, 한 번씩만 쓸 것)

보기	finish love eat

1 I couldn't find anything ______________.
2 I don't have enough time ______________ the work.
3 I feel lonely. I need someone ______________ me.

STEP 2 빈칸에 알맞은 전치사를 보기에서 골라 쓰시오. (단, 한 번씩만 쓸 것)

보기	in with to

1 I gave him a pen to write __________.
2 He didn't have anyone to talk __________.
3 Now he is looking for a house to live __________.

STEP 3 두 문장의 의미가 같도록 be동사를 이용하여 빈칸에 알맞은 말을 쓰시오.

1 Andy is going to visit Europe next week.
→ Andy __________ __________ __________ Europe next week.
2 You have to return the books by tomorrow.
→ You __________ __________ __________ the books by tomorrow.
3 The old man was destined to see his family again.
→ The old man __________ __________ __________ his family again.
4 If you intend to stay, you will need a visa.
→ If you __________ __________ __________, you will need a visa.

STEP 4 우리말과 일치하도록 ( ) 안의 말을 이용하여 문장을 완성하시오.

1 나는 10시까지 집에 있어야만 한다. (be, home)
→ I __________ __________ __________ __________ by ten o'clock.
2 냉장고에 차가운 마실 것이 아무 것도 없다. (nothing, drink)
→ There is __________ __________ __________ __________ in the refrigerator.
3 운전할 때 따라야 할 많은 교통 법규가 있다. (traffic rules, follow)
→ There are __________ __________ __________ __________ __________ when you drive.

UNIT 03

부사적 용법의 to부정사

to부정사(구)는 동사, 형용사, 부사를 수식하는 부사의 역할을 할 수 있다.

A **목적을 나타내는 to부정사:** ~하기 위해서

I bought this toy **to make** my daughter happy.
= in order to make
= so as to make

B **결과를 나타내는 to부정사:** (…해서) ~하다

The boy grew up **to become** a fashion designer.

ⓘ 「only to-v」는 '(…했지만) 결국 ~하다'라는 부정적인 결과를 나타낸다.
They played hard, **only to lose** the game.

C **감정의 원인을 나타내는 to부정사:** ~해서, ~하여

I am so happy **to be** back home safely.

D **조건을 나타내는 to부정사:** ~라면, ~한다면

To see him paint, you wouldn't believe he was just three.

E **형용사를 수식하는 to부정사:** ~하기에

The lesson is difficult **to understand**.

F **판단의 근거를 나타내는 to부정사:** ~하다니

She must be smart **to solve** the problem.

CHECK UP 빈칸에 알맞은 말을 고르시오.

1 I was not happy, but I smiled ___________ happy.
ⓐ look ⓑ looked ⓒ to look

2 ___________ her dance, you would think she was a professional.
ⓐ See ⓑ To see ⓒ To seeing

3 They must be close friends ___________ together every day.
ⓐ play ⓑ playing ⓒ to play

PRACTICE

Answer Key p.6

( ) 안에서 알맞은 말을 고르시오.

1 The novel is difficult (understands, to understand).
2 I am happy (know, to know) a nice person like you.
3 I read many books (learn, to learn) a lot of facts.
4 He must be very busy (work, to work) so late every day.

STEP 2

빈칸에 가장 알맞은 말을 보기에서 골라 to-v 형태로 바꿔 쓰시오.

보기		
	see you in New York	take a walk
	be a famous poet	not be late for class

1 I got up early ______________________.
2 She grew up ______________________.
3 I was surprised ______________________.
4 Kate and Tom went to the park ______________________.

밑줄 친 부분에 유의하여 문장을 우리말로 해석하시오.

1 I'll go on a diet to be healthy.
2 The old man lived to be one hundred years old.
3 I went to the store to buy a new winter jacket.
4 She must be foolish to make the same mistake.
5 To hear him sing, you would think him a singer.

STEP 4

우리말과 일치하도록 ( ) 안의 말을 이용하여 문장을 완성하시오.

1 나는 그녀의 죽음에 대해 듣고 충격을 받았다. (hear about, death)
→ I was shocked ______ ______ ______ ______ ______.

2 일본어는 배우기 쉽다. (easy, learn)
→ Japanese ______ ______ ______ ______.

3 그는 자라서 위대한 작가가 되었다. (be, great writer)
→ He grew up ______ ______ ______ ______ ______.

4 나는 나의 고양이를 찾으러 밖으로 나갔다. (look for, cat)
→ I went out ______ ______ ______ ______ ______.

UNIT 04

to부정사의 의미상의 주어, too ~ to-v, enough to-v

A to부정사의 의미상의 주어

to부정사의 행위의 주체가 문장의 주어와 일치하지 않을 때, to부정사 앞에 의미상의 주어를 쓴다.

1 for + 목적격: to부정사의 의미상의 주어는 보통 「for + 목적격」 형태로 나타낸다.

The question was difficult **for me** to answer.

2 of + 목적격: 앞의 형용사가 사람의 성격이나 성질을 나타낼 때(kind, nice, polite, wise, foolish, silly, generous, careless 등) to부정사의 의미상의 주어는 「of + 목적격」 형태로 나타낸다.

It is very *nice* **of you** to remember my birthday.

B to부정사를 이용한 구문

1 too + 형용사/부사 + to-v: 너무 ~하여 …할 수 없다
(= so + 형용사/부사 + that + 주어 + can't + 동사원형)

Ron was **too full to eat** the dessert.
→ Ron was **so full that he couldn't eat** the dessert.

These sneakers are **too expensive for me to buy**.
→ These sneakers are **so expensive that I can't buy** them.

2 형용사/부사 + enough + to-v: ~할 만큼 충분히 …하다
(= so + 형용사/부사 + that + 주어 + can + 동사원형)

The hall is **large enough to fit** a hundred people.
→ The hall is **so large that it can fit** a hundred people.

The game is **easy enough for children to enjoy**.
→ The game is **so easy that children can enjoy** it.

CHECK UP 빈칸에 알맞은 말을 고르시오.

1 It took a long time ___________ to read the essay.
ⓐ me ⓑ for me ⓒ of me

2 It was kind ___________ to give up his seat.
ⓐ him ⓑ for him ⓒ of him

3 Adrian is ___________ shy to speak in public.
ⓐ so ⓑ too ⓒ enough

4 This painting is cheap ___________ for me to buy.
ⓐ so ⓑ too ⓒ enough

PRACTICE

Answer Key p.6

밑줄 친 부분을 어법에 맞게 고치시오.

1 It was careless for you to lose my book.

2 Her feet are enough small to wear these shoes.

3 The juice is so sour for the baby to drink.

4 It is impossible of her to climb Mt. Everest.

빈칸에 for와 of 중 알맞은 전치사를 넣어 문장을 완성하시오.

1 It is hard __________ him to work overtime every day.

2 It was very polite __________ Mr. Lee to say sorry.

3 It seems surprising __________ her to marry him.

4 It is generous __________ you to forgive her.

STEP 3

두 문장의 의미가 같도록 빈칸에 알맞은 말을 쓰시오.

1 Mia is so rich that she can buy the island.
→ Mia is ____________________________________.

2 This bag is so small that I can't put all my books in it.
→ This bag is ____________________________________ in.

3 The English book is easy enough for her to read.
→ The English book is ____________________________________ it.

4 The boy is too big to pass through this hole.
→ The boy is ____________________________________.

우리말과 일치하도록 ( ) 안의 말을 이용하여 문장을 완성하시오.

1 그는 너무나 게을러서 그 일을 제시간에 마칠 수 없다. (lazy, finish)
→ He is ________ ________ ________ ________ the work on time.

2 네가 거짓말을 했다니 어리석었구나! (silly, tell)
→ It was ________ ________ ________ ________ ________ a lie!

3 요리를 하는 것은 내게 있어 흥미진진하다. (exciting, cook)
→ It is ________ ________ ________ ________ ________.

4 그는 부모님을 이해할 수 있을 정도로 충분히 나이가 들었다. (old, understand)
→ He is ________ ________ ________ ________ his parents.

GRAMMAR FOR WRITING

A 우리말과 일치하도록 ( ) 안의 말을 이용하여 문장을 완성하시오.

1 Justin은 장래에 가수가 되고 싶어 한다. (want, be, singer)
→ Justin ______________________ in the future.

2 우리는 눈을 보호하기 위해 선글라스를 꼈다. (wear, sunglasses, protect)
→ We ______________________ our eyes.

3 새로운 사람들을 만나는 것은 재미있다. (meet, new, people)
→ ________ is fun ______________________.

4 그 새로운 시스템은 사용하기 쉽다. (easy, use)
→ The new system ______________________.

5 그 키 큰 소녀는 자라서 슈퍼 모델이 되었다. (grow up, be, supermodel)
→ The tall girl ______________________.

6 Jake의 말을 믿다니 너는 어리석다. 그는 거짓말쟁이다. (believe, Jake's words)
→ You are foolish ______________________. He is a liar.

7 Vanessa는 너무 바빠서 나와 점심을 먹을 수가 없었다. (busy, have lunch)
→ Vanessa was ______________________ with me.

B 우리말과 일치하도록 ( ) 안에 주어진 단어를 바르게 배열하시오.

1 Lucy는 혼자서 결정을 내릴 수 있을 만큼 나이가 들었다. (to, make, a, enough, old, decision)
→ Lucy is ______________________ by herself.

2 저는 추워요. 제게 따뜻한 마실 것을 주세요. (something, hot, me, drink, to, give)
→ I'm cold. ______________________, please.

3 Brian은 항상 바쁘다. 나는 언제 그에게 전화를 해야 할지 모르겠다. (call, I, when, don't, to, know, him)
→ Brian is always busy. ______________________.

4 우리는 앉을 벤치를 찾고 있다. (sit, are, bench, for, a, looking, on, to)
→ We ______________________.

5 Hannah는 음식을 좋아한다. 덜 먹는 것은 그녀에게 매우 힘든 일이다.
(for, it, very, hard, eat less, is, her, to)
→ Hannah likes food. ______________________.

6 나는 9시까지 역에 도착해야 한다. (arrive, I, at, to, the station, am)
→ ______________________ by nine o'clock.

Answer Key p.7

C 주어진 문장과 의미가 통하도록 to부정사를 이용하여 빈칸에 알맞은 말을 쓰시오.

1 I will go to Australia. I will learn English there.
→ I will go to Australia ________ ________ ________.

2 Fred needs to buy a new car. He doesn't have enough money.
→ Fred is not rich ________ ________ ________ a new car.

3 She collects pictures of famous buildings. It is her hobby.
→ Her hobby is ________ ________ ________ of famous buildings.

4 He studied very hard, but he failed the exam.
→ He studied very hard only ________ ________ ________ ________.

5 He didn't remember her name, so he was sorry.
→ He was sorry ________ ________ ________ her name.

6 I feel hot and thirsty. I want to drink something cold.
→ I want something ________ ________ ________.

D 그림을 보고 to부정사와 ( ) 안의 말을 이용하여 문장을 완성하시오.

1 

2 

3 

1 Anthony was ____________________ his teacher at the theater. (surprised, meet)

2 Could you tell me ____________________ Palace Hotel? (get to)

3 The boy is ____________________ the roller coaster. (too, short, ride)

REVIEW TEST

[1-5] 빈칸에 들어갈 알맞은 말을 고르시오.

1 It is interesting __________ a new language.

① learn ② learned
③ be learning ④ to learn
⑤ to learning

2 I need someone __________.

① talk ② talk to
③ talking to ④ to talk
⑤ to talk to

3 She was __________ to go to school.

① to sick ② so sick
③ too sick ④ enough sick
⑤ sick enough

4 She awoke __________ herself famous.

① find ② found
③ to find ④ finding
⑤ to finding

5 It is rude __________ not to apologize.

① he ② him
③ his ④ to him
⑤ of him

빈출

6 밑줄 친 부분의 쓰임이 나머지 넷과 다른 것은?

① I bought a pen to write with.
② We want something to eat.
③ He always has a lot of work to do.
④ She went there to find her brother.
⑤ I don't have time to read the book.

[7-8] 다음 중 어법상 틀린 것을 고르시오.

7 ① His dream is to be a lawyer.
② He found a nice house to live.
③ It is very wise of him to tell the truth.
④ I don't have enough money to buy the shoes.
⑤ You are to be quiet in the library.

8 ① He must be angry to say so.
② The program is not easy to use.
③ I bought something to wear nice.
④ I don't know how to read Russian.
⑤ I plan to stay in Seoul for a week.

9 빈칸에 들어갈 말로 알맞은 것은? (2개)

It is __________ of her to forgive him.

① kind ② easy ③ polite
④ difficult ⑤ hard

Answer Key p.7

10 우리말과 일치하도록 할 때, 빈칸에 들어갈 말로 알맞은 것은?

> 내 목표는 수학 시험에서 100점을 맞는 것이다.
> → My goal is ________ on the math test.

① get one hundred points
② got one hundred points
③ to get one hundred points
④ to getting one hundred points
⑤ not to get one hundred points

11 다음 중 밑줄 친 부분을 바르게 고친 것은?

① Arabic is so difficult to write.
→ enough difficult
② I'm so sad hear about his death.
→ hearing
③ It is careless to you to break the glass.
→ for you
④ He has two sons to take care.
→ to take care of
⑤ I had something tell him.
→ to told

서술형

[12-13] ( ) 안의 말을 이용하여 문장을 완성하시오.

12 We were very upset ________ the news. (hear)

13 Tell me when ________ the national museum. (visit)

서술형

[14-16] 두 문장의 의미가 같도록 빈칸에 알맞은 말을 쓰시오.

14 The work was so complicated that he couldn't do it.

→ The work was ________ ________ ________ ________ ________ ________.

15 The hotel is so large that it can hold 3,000 people at once.

→ The hotel is ________ ________ ________ ________ 3,000 people at once.

16 My boss didn't tell me what I should do.

→ My boss didn't tell me ________ ________ ________.

17 다음 중 어법상 옳은 것은?

① He has a lot of books reading.
② I went to the library to found the book.
③ I like to visiting my friends' blogs.
④ It is not easy to save money regularly.
⑤ My dream is live in a beautiful island.

18 다음 중 보기의 밑줄 친 부분과 쓰임이 같은 것은?

보기	I visited France to see the Eiffel Tower.

① She decided not to go there.
② He quit his job to study more.
③ They bought something to eat.
④ My plan is to pass the exam.
⑤ I don't want to see her again.

19 빈칸에 들어갈 말이 나머지 넷과 다른 것은?

① It was easy ________ us to find your house.
② It was dangerous ________ her to follow him.
③ It is fun ________ me to learn English.
④ It was hard ________ me to solve the problem.
⑤ It is very nice ________ you to call me first.

서술형

[20-21] 우리말과 일치하도록 to부정사와 ( ) 안의 말을 이용하여 문장을 완성하시오.

20 그녀는 빠르게 뛰었지만 결국 그 기차를 놓치고 말았다. (miss, train)

→ She ran quickly ________________________.

21 그가 피아노 연주하는 것을 듣는다면, 너는 그가 피아니스트라고 생각할 것이다. (hear, play)

→ ________________________, you would think he was a pianist.

빈출

22 다음 중 두 문장의 의미가 같지 않은 것은?

① To be a teacher is not easy.
→ It is not easy to be a teacher.
② She told me what to buy.
→ She told me what I should buy.
③ The work is too hard for us to do.
→ The work is so hard that we can do it.
④ I came here to visit him.
→ I came here in order to visit him.
⑤ She is to go to church tomorrow.
→ She will go to church tomorrow.

서술형

[23-24] 우리말과 일치하도록 ( ) 안에 주어진 단어를 바르게 배열하시오.

23 그 상자는 이 모든 옷을 넣을 만큼 충분히 크다. (clothes, enough, all, these, to, big, fit, of)

→ The box is ________________________.

24 나는 적을 만한 종이가 없었다. (write, on, any, paper, to)

→ I didn't have ________________________.

25 주어진 단어를 바르게 배열할 때 네 번째에 오는 단어는?

to, is, for, make, friends, important, teenagers, it

① to ② for
③ make ④ important
⑤ teenagers

고난도

26 다음 중 어법상 옳은 것을 모두 고르면?

① I cleaned the house to help my mom.
② I was disappointed losing the game.
③ Do you have a book to read?
④ It is good of children to do outdoor activities.
⑤ These days, I don't have a close friend to talk to.

27 다음 중 어법상 옳은 것으로 바르게 짝지어진 것은?

a. Jane grew up to be a movie director.
b. He is so weak to carry the desk.
c. It was foolish of you to believe the rumor.
d. It was not nice for you to say that.
e. You must be very sensitive to hear the sound.

① a, b, c ② a, c, e
③ b, c, d ④ b, c, e
⑤ b, d, e

고난도

28 다음 중 어법상 옳은 것의 개수는?

- She is to be a mother next month.
- I didn't study enough hard to pass the exam.
- My sister went to America to meet her friend.
- I'm looking for someone to take care of my dog.
- It is very generous for you to share your knowledge with us.

① 1개 ② 2개 ③ 3개
④ 4개 ⑤ 5개

서술형

[29-30] 밑줄 친 부분이 어법상 옳은지 판단하고, 틀리면 바르게 고치시오.

29 My dream is to help people in need.

(O / X) ______________

30 It is very kind for you to invite me.

(O / X) ______________

서술형

31 우리말과 일치하도록 주어진 조건에 맞게 문장을 완성하시오.

그 노래는 부르기 어렵다.

〈조건〉 1. difficult, sing을 이용할 것
2. The song을 주어로 할 것

→ ______________.

서술형 고난도

[32-33] 어법상 틀린 부분을 찾아 바르게 고치시오.

32 I can't go out with you tonight. I am to finishing the report by tomorrow. (1개)

33 On my mother's birthday, I wanted to do something for her. But I didn't have enough money buying a present. So, I decided write a letter. (2개)

LET'S REVIEW

주요 예문을 다시 한번 확인하고, 우리말과 일치하도록 빈칸을 채우시오.

- [1] ______________ is not easy **to keep** a pet in an apartment.
  아파트에서 반려동물을 기르는 것은 쉽지 않다. Unit 01 - A
- My plan was [2] ______________ dinner by six o'clock.
  내 계획은 6시까지 저녁을 준비하는 것이었다. Unit 01 - B
- Jake likes **to bake** bread and cookies. Jake는 빵과 쿠키를 굽는 것을 좋아한다. Unit 01 - C
- I've finished the work. Please tell me [3] ______________ next.
  저는 일을 끝마쳤습니다. 다음에 제가 무엇을 해야 할지 말씀해 주세요. Unit 01 - D
- I have a project [4] ______________ by next week. 나는 다음 주까지 마쳐야 할 프로젝트가 있다. Unit 02 - A
- You **are** [5] ______________ your promise. 너는 너의 약속을 지켜야 한다. Unit 02 - B
- I bought this toy **to make** my daughter happy. 나는 내 딸을 행복하게 하기 위해 이 장난감을 샀다. Unit 03 - A
- The boy grew up [6] ______________ a fashion designer.
  그 소년은 자라서 패션 디자이너가 되었다. Unit 03 - B
- I am so happy **to be** back home safely. 나는 집에 무사히 돌아와서 매우 기쁘다. Unit 03 - C
- The lesson is difficult [7] ______________. 그 수업은 이해하기에 어렵다. Unit 03 - E
- She must be smart [8] ______________ the problem.
  그 문제를 풀다니 그녀는 똑똑한 것이 틀림없다. Unit 03 - F
- The question was difficult [9] ______________ to answer.
  그 질문은 내가 대답하기에 어려웠다. Unit 04 - A
- Ron was **too full to eat** the dessert. Ron은 너무 배가 불러서 디저트를 먹을 수 없었다. Unit 04 - B
- The hall is **large** [10] ______________ **to fit** a hundred people.
  그 홀은 100명의 사람들을 수용할 만큼 충분히 크다. Unit 04 - B

Answers

[1] It [2] to prepare [3] what to do / what I should do [4] to finish [5] to keep [6] to become[be]
[7] to understand [8] to solve [9] for me [10] enough

CHAPTER

05

동명사

동명사는 문장에서 명사처럼
주어, 보어, 목적어 역할을 한다.

UNIT 01

동명사의 쓰임

동명사는 「v-ing」의 형태로 명사처럼 문장 속에서 주어, 보어, 목적어 역할을 한다.

A 주어 역할

Riding a roller coaster is exciting but scary.
Cooking spaghetti was not difficult.

B 보어 역할

My favorite outdoor activity is **skiing**.
His hobby is **playing** online games.

C 목적어 역할

He *enjoyed* **playing** the drums. 〈동사의 목적어〉
We talked *about* **changing** the plan. 〈전치사의 목적어〉

ⓘ 동명사의 부정형은 동명사 앞에 not을 붙인다.
I thought of **not going** to Spain.

D 자주 쓰이는 동명사 구문

- be busy v-ing: ~하느라 바쁘다
- feel like v-ing: ~하고 싶다
- on v-ing: ~하자마자
- be worth v-ing: ~할 가치가 있다
- cannot help v-ing: ~하지 않을 수 없다
- go v-ing: ~하러 가다

This book **is worth reading** three times.
I **feel like staying** at home all day.

빈칸에 알맞은 말을 고르시오.

1 ____________ up early is very hard for me.
ⓐ Get ⓑ Getting ⓒ To getting

2 I don't like ____________ fun of others.
ⓐ make ⓑ making ⓒ to making

3 She went ____________ with her friends.
ⓐ shop ⓑ shopped ⓒ shopping

PRACTICE

Answer Key p.8

( ) 안에서 알맞은 말을 고르시오.

1 My hobby is (draw, drawing) pictures.
2 I gave up (trying, to try) to make her laugh.
3 (Meet, Meeting) my girlfriend makes me happy.
4 This movie is really long, but it is worth (watching, to watch).

STEP 2

밑줄 친 부분을 어법에 맞게 고치시오.

1 She doesn't mind eats alone.
2 I'm scared of ride a skateboard.
3 Her job is design wedding dresses.
4 Take nice pictures is not difficult for me.

STEP 3

보기를 참고하여 위의 두 문장과 의미가 통하도록 동명사를 이용하여 문장을 완성하시오.

보기	I cook Italian food. It is my job. → My job is cooking Italian food.

1 He likes to go camping with his family. It is his favorite thing.
→ His favorite thing is ______________________.
2 You eat too much fast food. It is not good for your health.
→ ______________________ is not good for your health.
3 Tina didn't keep her promise. She was sorry for it.
→ Tina was sorry for ______________________.

STEP 4

우리말과 일치하도록 ( ) 안의 말을 이용하여 문장을 완성하시오.

1 그는 스테이크를 요리하느라 바쁘다. (cook)
→ He ________ ________ ________ the steak.
2 나는 프랑스어를 말하는 것에 서투르다. (good at, speak)
→ I'm not ________ ________ ________ French.
3 Avery는 나를 향해 계속 미소 지었다. (smile, at)
→ Avery kept ________ ________ ________.
4 나는 재미있는 영화를 보고 싶다. (feel, watch)
→ I ________ ________ ________ a funny movie.

UNIT 02

동명사와 to부정사

A

동명사만 목적어로 취하는 동사: enjoy, avoid, mind, finish, keep, give up, quit, practice 등

Tiffany *avoided* **drinking** too much soda.

B

to부정사만 목적어로 취하는 동사: want, expect, hope, wish, plan, promise, agree, decide 등

I didn't *expect* **to see** the movie star in Paris.

C

동명사와 to부정사를 모두 목적어로 취하는 동사

1 의미 차이가 없는 경우: begin, start, like, love, hate 등

She *began* **playing** the violin when she was four.
She *began* **to play** the violin when she was four.

2 의미 차이가 있는 경우: remember, forget, try 등

- **remember v-ing**: (과거에) ~했던 것을 기억하다 / **remember to-v**: (앞으로) ~할 것을 기억하다

  I *remember* **going** to New York when I was ten.
  Remember **to buy** the book after school.

- **forget v-ing**: (과거에) ~했던 것을 잊다 / **forget to-v**: (앞으로) ~할 것을 잊다

  I can't *forget* **meeting** you last year.
  Don't *forget* **to bring** your passport tomorrow.

- **try v-ing**: 시험 삼아 ~하다[해 보다] / **try to-v**: ~하려고 노력하다[애쓰다]

  I *tried* **using** the new machine, but it didn't work.
  He *tried* **to lose** three kilograms, but it was difficult.

① stop v-ing: ~하는 것을 멈추다 / stop to-v: ~하기 위해 멈추다(부사적 용법의 to부정사)
He *stopped* **looking** at his smartphone.
He *stopped* **to look** at his smartphone.

CHECK UP 빈칸에 알맞은 말을 고르시오.

1 I enjoyed ___________ baseball games.
ⓐ watch ⓑ watching ⓒ to watch

2 Kevin decided ___________ his eating habits.
ⓐ change ⓑ changing ⓒ to change

3 Remember ___________ off the TV before you go out.
ⓐ turn ⓑ turning ⓒ to turn

PRACTICE

Answer Key p.8

( ) 안에서 알맞은 말을 고르시오.

1 We are planning (getting, to get) a cute cat.

2 I don't mind (waiting, to wait) outside.

3 They agreed (buying, to buy) a new sofa.

4 Don't forget (sending, to send) the emails tomorrow.

STEP 2

( ) 안의 말을 이용하여 문장을 완성하시오.

1 My sister and I promised __________ on Saturdays. (exercise)

2 You should finish __________ this book by tomorrow. (read)

3 Do you remember __________ football with me when we were young? (play)

4 You're not telling me the truth. Stop __________ to me. (lie)

두 문장의 의미가 같도록 빈칸에 알맞은 말을 쓰시오.

1 We began studying Spanish last month.
→ We began ______________ Spanish last month.

2 I hate to dance in front of others.
→ I hate ______________ in front of others.

3 She loves having a good time at the beach.
→ She loves ______________ a good time at the beach.

STEP 4

우리말과 일치하도록 ( ) 안의 말을 이용하여 문장을 완성하시오.

1 한꺼번에 너무 많은 음식을 먹는 것을 피해라. (avoid, eat)
→ __________ __________ too much food at once.

2 엄마는 로맨틱한 영화를 보는 것을 좋아하신다. (like, watch)
→ My mom __________ __________ romantic films.

3 나는 수영을 하는 법을 배우기로 결심했다. (decide, learn)
→ I __________ __________ __________ how to swim.

4 그는 그 문을 열기 위해 다른 열쇠를 사용해 보았다. (try, use)
→ He __________ __________ another key to open the door.

5 나는 작년에 그에게서 돈을 빌렸던 것을 잊어버렸다. (forget, borrow, money)
→ I __________ __________ __________ from him last year.

GRAMMAR FOR WRITING

A 우리말과 일치하도록 ( ) 안의 말을 이용하여 문장을 완성하시오.

1 그들은 조만간 그들의 집을 팔기로 결심했다. (decide, sell, house)
→ They ______________________ in the near future.

2 그는 약을 먹을 것을 잊어버렸다. (forget, take)
→ He ______________________ the medicine.

3 그녀는 아침 일찍 일어나는 것을 싫어한다. (hate, get up)
→ She ______________________ early in the morning.

4 그녀는 작년에 그와 만났던 것을 기억하지 못했다. (remember, meet)
→ She didn't ______________________ last year.

5 나는 그 소년을 쳐다보지 않을 수 없었다. (help, look at)
→ I ______________________ the boy.

6 그녀는 실수하는 것을 두려워한다. (make a mistake)
→ She is afraid of ______________________.

7 많이 웃는 것은 당신의 건강에 좋다. (laugh, a lot, good)
→ ______________________ for your health.

B 우리말과 일치하도록 ( ) 안에 주어진 단어를 바르게 배열하시오.

1 수리공은 차 수리를 끝마쳤다. (car, fixing, the, finished, has)
→ The repairman ______________________.

2 다른 비밀번호를 사용해 보는 게 어때? (try, a, using, password, different)
→ Why don't you ______________________?

3 그녀는 많은 돈을 기부하는 것을 꺼리지 않는다. (lots of, donating, doesn't, money, mind)
→ She ______________________.

4 매일 밤을 새는 것은 불가능하다. (night, every, is, staying up)
→ ______________________ impossible.

5 나는 잠자리에 들기 전에 이를 닦는다. (bed, my teeth, to, brush, going, before)
→ I ______________________.

6 그의 새 앨범은 살 만한 가치가 있다. (worth, new album, buying, his, is)
→ ______________________.

Answer Key p.8

C

보기와 같이 주어진 문장과 의미가 통하도록 빈칸에 알맞은 말을 쓰시오.

보기	I like to take pictures. → My hobby is taking pictures.

1 I teach students Japanese.
→ My job is ___________ ___________.

2 It is necessary to be honest.
→ ___________ ___________ is necessary.

3 Remember that you have to send her an email about the project.
→ Remember ___________ ___________ her an email about the project.

4 I forgot that I bought the milk.
→ I forgot ___________ ___________ ___________.

5 She decided not to eat fast food in order to be healthy.
→ She stopped ___________ ___________ ___________ in order to be healthy.

6 Patrick is busy. He is solving a crossword puzzle.
→ Patrick ___________ ___________ ___________ a crossword puzzle.

D

그림을 보고 ( ) 안에 주어진 말을 이용하여 문장을 완성하시오.

1 Emily never gave up ______________________. (complete the marathon)

2 My dad is ______________________ in the kitchen. (busy, prepare dinner)

3 Stefani hopes ______________________ of her favorite band. (go, the concert)

REVIEW TEST

[1-4] 빈칸에 들어갈 알맞은 말을 고르시오.

1

He quit ________ for his health.

① smoke ② smokes
③ smoked ④ smoking
⑤ to smoke

2

They decided ________ yoga.

① learn ② learns
③ learned ④ learning
⑤ to learn

3

I remember ________ my mother's earrings when I was young.

① lose ② loses
③ lost ④ losing
⑤ to lose

4

We cannot help ________ in love with this cute and lovely cat.

① fall ② falls
③ fallen ④ falling
⑤ to fall

[5-6] 다음 중 어법상 틀린 것을 고르시오.

5 ① Writing a poem is not easy.
② I don't like shopping online.
③ His hobby is collecting comic books.
④ She is good at cook Italian food.
⑤ On seeing me, he ran away.

6 ① He started playing the drums last year.
② Don't forget calling him tomorrow.
③ She stopped playing the online game.
④ She tried to persuade him, but failed.
⑤ Remember to clean your room today.

빈출

[7-8] 빈칸에 들어갈 말로 알맞지 않은 것을 고르시오.

7

We ________ to go on a trip.

① wanted ② decided
③ agreed ④ planned
⑤ minded

8

She ________ walking and jogging.

① enjoys ② promises
③ hates ④ loves
⑤ keeps

빈출

9 다음 우리말을 영어로 바르게 옮긴 것은?

그녀는 소음을 내지 않으려고 애쓰고 있다.

① She is trying making not any noise.
② She is trying not making any noise.
③ She is trying to make not any noise.
④ She isn't trying to make any noise.
⑤ She is trying not to make any noise.

Answer Key p.8

서술형

[10-11] 어법상 틀린 부분을 찾아 바르게 고치시오.

10 He was worried about to fail the exam.

__________ → __________

11 Please remember bringing your ticket with you to the event.

__________ → __________

[12-13] 다음 중 어법상 옳은 것을 고르시오.

12 ① I hate to missing class.
② I started to go on a diet.
③ He isn't good at play baseball.
④ His job is sell used computers.
⑤ Read a newspaper is a good habit.

13 ① I hope seeing his concert someday.
② She avoided talking about the issue.
③ He promised giving me the book.
④ Violet kept to practice ballet.
⑤ We enjoyed to watch the soccer game.

서술형

[14-17] ( ) 안의 말을 이용하여 문장을 완성하시오.

14 You can try __________ our product for free. Don't miss this chance! (use)

15 He forgot __________ his alarm last night, so he woke up late. (set)

16 She didn't agree __________ the schedule. (change)

17 I need some clothes for a field trip. Let's go __________. (shop)

18 다음 중 밑줄 친 부분을 바르게 고친 것은?

① I hope buy a new smartphone.
→ buying
② I can't help think about him.
→ to think
③ He promised join our club.
→ joining
④ She gave up attend the meetings.
→ to attend
⑤ He forgot visit my house last week.
→ visiting

서술형

[19-21] 우리말과 일치하도록 ( ) 안에 주어진 단어를 바르게 배열하시오.

19 좋은 직업을 구하는 것은 쉽지 않다.
(is, not, finding, good, a, easy, job)

→ ______________________.

20 그녀는 캠핑을 가지 않을까 생각 중이다.
(not, going, about, camping)

→ She is thinking ______________.

21 그는 자신의 개들과 산책하는 것을 아주 좋아한다.
(he, taking, dogs, his, with, a walk, loves)

→ ______________________.

서술형

[22-24] 우리말과 일치하도록 ( ) 안의 말을 이용하여 문장을 완성하시오.

22 Paul은 지금 그의 수학 숙제를 하느라 바쁘다.
(busy, math, homework)

→ Paul ______________________
now.

23 그는 친구들과 함께 영어 말하기를 연습한다.
(practice, speak)

→ ______________________
English with his friends.

24 내 여동생은 종종 그녀의 휴대 전화를 가져가는 것을 잊어버린다. (take, cell phone)

→ My sister often ______________
______________________.

25 대화를 읽고 빈칸에 들어갈 알맞은 말을 쓰시오.

Adrian: Hi, Mr. Hill!
Mr. Hill: Excuse me, but do I know you?
Adrian: Yes, we met at a museum in Paris last month.
Mr. Hill: Oh, did we? Sorry, I don't remember.

→ Mr. Hill doesn't remember ________
Adrian before.

고난도

26 다음 중 어법상 틀린 것을 모두 고르면?

① My hobby is singing and dancing.
② Adapting to a new place is not easy.
③ Tell lies is morally wrong.
④ I enjoy playing a game on my phone.
⑤ She really hoped meeting the singer.

27 다음 중 어법상 옳은 것으로 바르게 짝지어진 것은?

a. I'm interested in go on a trip.
b. How about seeing a doctor?
c. My hobby is playing the guitar.
d. He was busy to prepare for his wedding.
e. Going outside late at night is not safe.

① a, b, c ② a, c, d
③ a, d, e ④ b, c, d
⑤ b, c, e

고난도

28 다음 중 어법상 옳은 것의 개수는?

- They began dancing on the stage.
- I finally finished to read this book.
- Would you mind turning off the light?
- My mother loves to drink tea with me.
- Monkeys are good at climbing tall trees.

① 1개 ② 2개 ③ 3개
④ 4개 ⑤ 5개

서술형

[29-31] 밑줄 친 부분이 어법상 옳은지 판단하고, 틀리면 바르게 고치시오.

29 I wish traveling abroad this year.

(O / X) ______________

30 On getting up in the morning, he drinks a glass of water.

(O / X) ______________

31 I don't feel like to go to bed now.

(O / X) ______________

서술형 고난도

[32-33] 어법상 틀린 부분을 찾아 바르게 고치시오.

32 Learning a new language is not easy. You have to be patient and enjoy to learn it. (1개)

33 I went to see a musical. The ticket for the show was very expensive, but it was worth to buy. (1개)

LET'S REVIEW

주요 예문을 다시 한번 확인하고, 우리말과 일치하도록 빈칸을 채우시오.

- [1] ______________ a roller coaster is exciting but scary.
  롤러코스터를 타는 것은 신이 나지만 무섭다. Unit 01 - A

- My favorite outdoor activity is **skiing**. 내가 가장 좋아하는 야외 활동은 스키 타는 것이다. Unit 01 - B

- He enjoyed **playing** the drums. 그는 드럼 치는 것을 즐겼다. Unit 01 - C
- We talked about [2] ______________ the plan. 우리는 그 계획을 바꾸는 것에 대해 이야기했다. Unit 01 - C

- This book **is** [3] ______________ three times. 이 책은 세 번 읽을 가치가 있다. Unit 01 - D
- I **feel like staying** at home all day. 나는 온종일 집에 머물고 싶다. Unit 01 - D

- Tiffany avoided [4] ______________ too much soda.
  Tiffany는 너무 많은 탄산음료를 마시는 것을 피했다. Unit 02 - A

- I didn't expect [5] ______________ the movie star in Paris.
  나는 파리에서 그 영화배우를 볼 것을 기대하지 않았다. Unit 02 - B

- She began [6] ______________ the violin when she was four.
  그녀는 네 살이었을 때 바이올린을 연주하기 시작했다. Unit 02 - C
- I remember [7] ______________ to New York when I was ten.
  나는 열 살이었을 때 뉴욕에 갔던 것을 기억한다. Unit 02 - C
- Remember **to buy** the book after school. 방과 후에 그 책을 살 것을 기억해라. Unit 02 - C
- I can't forget **meeting** you last year. 나는 작년에 너를 만났던 것을 잊을 수 없다. Unit 02 - C
- Don't forget [8] ______________ your passport tomorrow.
  내일 네 여권을 가져오는 것을 잊지 마라. Unit 02 - C
- I tried **using** the new machine, but it didn't work.
  나는 그 새 기계를 시험 삼아 이용해 보았지만 그것은 작동하지 않았다. Unit 02 - C
- He tried [9] ______________ three kilograms, but it was difficult.
  그는 3킬로그램을 감량하려고 노력했지만 그것은 어려웠다. Unit 02 - C

Answers

[1] Riding[To ride] [2] changing [3] worth reading [4] drinking [5] to see [6] playing[to play]
[7] going [8] to bring [9] to lose

CHAPTER

06

분사

분사에는 현재분사(v-ing)와 과거분사(v-ed)가 있으며, 이들은 형용사처럼 명사를 수식하거나 보어 역할을 한다.

UNIT 01

현재분사와 과거분사

분사는 형용사처럼 쓰여 명사를 수식하거나 주어나 목적어를 보충 설명하는 보어 역할을 한다.
진행형(be + v-ing), 완료형(have + v-ed), 수동태(be + v-ed)의 동사구 일부로 쓰이기도 한다.

A 현재분사 vs. 과거분사

1 현재분사(v-ing): 능동(~하는)이나 진행(~하고 있는)의 의미를 가진다.

shocking news 〈능동의 의미〉 / a **barking** dog 〈진행의 의미〉

2 과거분사(v-ed): 수동(~된)이나 완료(~한)의 의미를 가진다.

shocked people 〈수동의 의미〉 / **fallen** leaves 〈완료의 의미〉

B 분사의 역할

1 명사 수식: 보통 명사 앞에서 수식하지만 수식어구가 함께 와서 길어질 때는 명사 뒤에서 수식한다.

The **sleeping** puppy is cute.　　Harry has a book **written** in German.

2 보어 역할

Mike came **running** down the stairs.
Katie had her hair **done**. She looks younger.

- exciting (흥분되게 하는) – excited (흥분한)
- surprising (놀라게 하는) – surprised (놀란)
- amazing (놀라운) – amazed (놀란)
- shocking (충격적인) – shocked (충격받은)
- boring (지루한) – bored (지루해하는)
- tiring (피곤하게 하는) – tired (피곤한)

The comic book was **boring**.　　I am **bored** with my work.

CHECK UP 빈칸에 알맞은 말을 고르시오.

1 I heard an ____________ story.
ⓐ interest　ⓑ interesting　ⓒ interested

2 They seemed ____________ at the news.
ⓐ surprise　ⓑ surprising　ⓒ surprised

3 Who is that man ____________ hands with Mr. Lee?
ⓐ shake　ⓑ shaking　ⓒ shaken

⊕ PLUS

현재분사 vs. 동명사

- 현재분사: She is **teaching** English.
(she ≠ teaching English)
- 동명사: My job is **teaching** English.
(my job = teaching English)

현재분사 + 명사 vs. 동명사 + 명사

- 현재분사 + 명사: a **swimming** girl
(→ a girl who is swimming)
- 동명사 + 명사: a **swimming** pool
(→ a pool for swimming)

PRACTICE

Answer Key p.9

( ) 안에서 알맞은 말을 고르시오.

1 He was (shocking, shocked) at the news.
2 The girl (sitting, sat) on the bench is Isabel.
3 There are no seats (leaving, left) on the bus.
4 The friends sat (talking, talked) for hours.
5 I had my eyesight (checking, checked) today.

STEP 2

밑줄 친 부분을 어법에 맞게 고치시오.

1 Do you know that cry girl?
2 I stood watched the snow fall.
3 She looked surprising by my gift.
4 This is the picture painting by my mother.

STEP 3

( ) 안의 말을 이용하여 문장을 완성하시오.

1 Benjamin was looking for his __________ bag. (lose)
2 Don't wake the __________ baby. (sleep)
3 He bought a watch __________ in Switzerland. (make)
4 Who is the boy __________ with my teacher? (talk)
5 The woman __________ the big sunglasses is Tom's mother. (wear)

STEP 4

우리말과 일치하도록 ( ) 안의 말을 이용하여 문장을 완성하시오.

1 그 지루한 영화에 대해 아무 말도 하지 마라. (bore, movie)
→ Don't say anything about __________ __________ __________.
2 나는 영어로 쓰인 이메일 한 통을 받았다. (email, write)
→ I got __________ __________ __________ in English.
3 그 경기장에 있는 사람들은 흥분한 것처럼 보였다. (look, excite)
→ The people in the stadium __________ __________.
4 나는 내 개가 그 소파 밑에서 자고 있는 걸 발견했다. (find, dog, sleep)
→ I __________ __________ __________ __________ under the sofa.

UNIT 02

분사구문

부사절(접속사 + 주어 + 동사)을 분사를 이용해 줄여 쓴 구문이 분사구문이다.

A 분사구문 만들기

부사절의 주어가 주절의 주어와 같을 때, 부사절의 접속사와 주어를 생략하고 동사를 「v-ing」 형태로 바꾼다.

Watching TV, I heard a strange sound.

(← **When *I* was watching** TV, *I* heard a strange sound.)

cf. 부사절의 동사가 진행형인 경우 v-ing만 남긴다.

B 분사구문의 의미

1 시간, 때: ~할 때(when), ~하는 동안(while)

Walking down the street, I saw the singer.

(← **When I was walking** down the street, I saw the singer.)

2 동시동작: ~하면서(as)

Listening to music, I studied math.

(← **As I listened** to music, I studied math.)

3 이유, 원인: ~ 때문에(because, as, since)

Feeling ill, I didn't go shopping.

(← **Because I felt** ill, I didn't go shopping.)

4 조건: ~한다면(if)

Taking this train, you can go to Tokyo.

(← **If you take** this train, you can go to Tokyo.)

5 양보: ~에도 불구하고(though, although)

Though living near the park, I have never been there.

(← **Though I live** near the park, I have never been there.)

cf. 분사구문이 나타내는 뜻을 분명히 하기 위해 접속사를 밝히는 경우도 있다.
특히 양보의 분사구문은 접속사를 주로 남겨 둔다.

CHECK UP 빈칸에 알맞은 말을 고르시오.

1 __________ the news, she was shocked.
ⓐ Hearing ⓑ Hear ⓒ Heard

2 __________ cold, he wore a thick coat.
ⓐ Be ⓑ To be ⓒ Being

3 __________ a taxi, you'll get there soon.
ⓐ Take ⓑ Taking ⓒ Taken

PRACTICE

Answer Key p.9

( ) 안에서 알맞은 말을 고르시오.

1 (Read, Reading) the magazine, I heard a bell ringing.
2 She talked to me, (smiling, smiled) brightly.
3 (Being, Been) poor, he couldn't buy a new car.
4 (To listen, Listening) to the radio, she fell asleep.

다음 문장을 분사구문으로 바꿔 쓰시오.

1 When I cleaned my room, I found some money.
→ ______________________________

2 If you come after 8:00 p.m., you can get a discount.
→ ______________________________

3 Because she is ill, she won't go to work today.
→ ______________________________

밑줄 친 분사구문을 「접속사 + 주어 + 동사」의 형태로 바꾸시오.

1 Standing so long in the rain, he was angry.
→ ______________________________, he was angry.

2 Going straight, you will find the restaurant.
→ ______________________________, you will find the restaurant.

3 Although having an exam the next day, he didn't study at all.
→ ______________________________, he didn't study at all.

우리말과 일치하도록 ( ) 안의 말을 이용하여 문장을 완성하시오.

1 우리의 숙제를 끝내고 난 후, 우리는 밖으로 나갔다. (finish, homework)
→ __________ __________ __________, we went out.

2 음악을 들으면서 그녀는 그림을 그렸다. (listen to, music)
→ __________ __________ __________, she drew a picture.

3 오른쪽으로 돌면 중식당이 보일 것이다. (turn right)
→ __________ __________, you will see a Chinese restaurant.

GRAMMAR FOR WRITING

A 우리말과 일치하도록 ( ) 안의 말을 이용하여 문장을 완성하시오.

1 그 연극은 정말 지루했다. (really, bore)

→ The play ______________________________.

2 깨진 유리를 밟지 마라. (break, glass)

→ Don't step on the ______________________________.

3 아버지는 항상 나에게 재미있는 이야기들을 해주신다. (interest, story)

→ My father always tells me ______________________________.

4 그는 그의 건강을 걱정하는 것처럼 보였다. (look, worry)

→ ______________________________ about his health.

5 우리는 목록에 쓰여 있는 모든 것을 사야 한다. (everything, write)

→ We should buy ______________________________ on the list.

6 그 문 앞에 서 있는 소년은 내 사촌이다. (stand, in front of, door)

→ The boy ______________________________ is my cousin.

7 그녀는 그녀의 차를 거리에 주차된 채로 두었다. (keep, car, park)

→ She ______________________________ on the street.

B 우리말과 일치하도록 ( ) 안에 주어진 단어를 바르게 배열하시오.

1 나를 보자 아기는 울기 시작했다. (began, me, seeing, the, baby)

→ ___________________________________ to cry.

2 경찰은 그 도둑이 나무 뒤로 숨는 것을 보았다. (thief, saw, the, hiding, the, police)

→ ___________________________________ behind a tree.

3 고기를 싫어하기 때문에 그는 스테이크를 주문하지 않았다. (order, he, hating, didn't, meat)

→ ___________________________________ the steak.

4 지금 출발하면 너는 버스를 탈 수 있을 것이다. (will, leaving, you, catch, now)

→ ___________________________________ the bus.

5 너는 Greg Smith라는 이름의 남자를 아니? (a, named, you, know, Greg Smith, do, man)

→ ___________________________________?

6 길을 따라 걸어가는 동안 나는 Jina를 만났다. (walking, I, street, down, the, met)

→ ___________________________________ Jina.

Answer Key p.9

C 주어진 문장과 의미가 통하도록 ( ) 안의 말을 이용하여 빈칸에 알맞은 말을 쓰시오.

1 I had to work a lot yesterday. I felt like having a rest. (tire)

a. Yesterday was a ______________ day.

b. I felt ______________.

2 Sam has a job doing the same thing repeatedly, so he doesn't enjoy it. (bore)

a. Sam's job is ______________.

b. Sam is ______________ with his repetitive work.

3 Brian was very healthy. We didn't expect him to die. (shock)

a. Brian's death was ______________.

b. We were ______________ by Brian's death.

4 Jen is going on a school trip next week. She can't wait to go. (excite)

a. Jen is ______________ about going on the school trip.

b. Jen thinks that the school trip will be ______________.

D 그림을 보고 분사와 ( ) 안의 말을 이용하여 문장을 완성하시오.

1 This is ______________________ by my mom during our summer vacation. (a picture, take)

2 ______________________, I posed for the picture. (talk, on the phone)

3 The girl ______________________ is my sister, Ella. (build, the sandcastle)

4 The man ______________________ next to Ella is my father. (wear, sunglasses)

REVIEW TEST

[1-4] 빈칸에 들어갈 알맞은 말을 고르시오.

1

I am going to see the __________ sun on New Year's Day.

① rise ② rose
③ risen ④ rising
⑤ to rise

2

Some of the people __________ to my birthday party didn't come.

① invite ② invites
③ inviting ④ invited
⑤ to inviting

3

She sat __________ with a teacher.

① talk ② talked
③ talking ④ to talking
⑤ being talked

4

__________ in the rain, I felt cold.

① Walk ② Walking
③ To walk ④ Walked
⑤ Being walked

5 다음 중 어법상 옳은 것은?

① He lay on the sofa, reading a book.
② Hear the news, she began to cry.
③ My father is interesting in playing golf.
④ She had a letter writing by Jim.
⑤ Everybody hates that bored class.

6 빈칸에 들어갈 말이 순서대로 바르게 짝지어진 것은?

• I'm __________ in making robots. • Making robots is very __________.

① interest – interest
② interesting – interested
③ interested – interesting
④ interesting – interesting
⑤ interested – interested

[7-8] 밑줄 친 부분의 의미로 가장 적절한 것을 고르시오.

7

<u>Being tired</u>, she went to bed early.

① If she was tired
② As she was tired
③ After she was tired
④ While she was tired
⑤ Though she was tired

8

<u>Walking down this road</u>, you will see his office.

① Unless you walk down this road
② Because you walk down this road
③ If you walk down this road
④ Though you walk down this road
⑤ Since you walk down this road

Answer Key p.10

[9-10] 다음 중 밑줄 친 부분이 잘못된 것을 고르시오.

9 ① The soccer game was very exciting.
② The online game was not interesting.
③ He is always tired after work.
④ He was boring with reading the same book.
⑤ I was shocked by the news of her accident.

10 ① He has a cat calling Lucky.
② The barking dog looks scary.
③ We enjoyed the exciting musical.
④ The boy sitting on the bench is my son.
⑤ Having a headache, I went to a doctor.

서술형 빈출

[11-12] 밑줄 친 부분을 분사구문으로 바꿔 쓰시오.

11 Because he was sick, he didn't attend the meeting.

→ ________________, he didn't attend the meeting.

12 If you exercise regularly, you will lose weight.

→ ________________, you will lose weight.

빈출

[13-15] 밑줄 친 부분의 쓰임이 나머지 넷과 다른 것을 고르시오.

13 ① Look at the lady wearing a red dress.
② He stood looking at the poster.
③ She saw him walking in the park.
④ His hobby is volunteering for charities.
⑤ Who is that boy swimming in the pool?

14 ① The sleeping baby is so cute.
② He bought a new sleeping bag.
③ A sleeping cat dreams of mice.
④ The sleeping boy next to me is my cousin.
⑤ Don't touch a sleeping dog.

15 ① Although being full, we ordered dessert.
② Being in a bad mood, I went home.
③ Being angry, he didn't say anything.
④ Being rich is good, but it is not everything.
⑤ Being poor, he couldn't go to college.

서술형

[16-18] ( ) 안의 말을 적절한 형태로 써서 문장을 완성하시오.

16 __________ at the back, I couldn't hear well. (sit)

17 The news about the car accident was __________. (shock)

18 They tried hard to open the __________ door. (lock)

19 다음 중 밑줄 친 부분을 잘못 고친 것은?

① Spill coffee, I got my shirt dirty.
→ Spilling

② I picked up the fall leaf.
→ fallen

③ I have a break watch.
→ broken

④ She plans to buy a use car.
→ using

⑤ The man buy flowers is my father.
→ buying

서술형

[20-22] 우리말과 일치하도록 ( ) 안의 말을 이용하여 문장을 완성하시오.

20 나는 사고로 손상된 그 차를 고쳐야만 한다.
(car, damage)

→ I should fix __________________ in the crash.

21 우리는 최선을 다했지만 결과는 실망스러웠다.
(disappoint)

→ We did our best, but the result __________________.

22 눈사람을 만들고 있는 저 소녀들은 행복해 보인다.
(girl, build)

→ __________________ a snowman look happy.

서술형

23 우리말과 일치하도록 주어진 조건에 맞게 문장을 완성하시오.

한국에서 공부하는 동안, 그는 좋은 친구들을 많이 사귀었다.

〈조건〉 1. study, Korea를 이용할 것
2. 접속사를 쓰지 말 것

→ __________________, he made many good friends.

서술형

[24-25] 우리말과 일치하도록 ( ) 안에 주어진 단어를 바르게 배열하시오.

24 나는 그가 기타를 연주하는 것을 들었다.
(heard, him, guitar, I, the, playing)

→ __________________________.

25 밝게 웃으면서 그는 손을 흔들었다.
(smiling, waved, he, brightly)

→ __________________________.

고난도

26 다음 중 어법상 옳은 것을 모두 고르면?

① This is the book writing by Mr. Potter.
② I heard her name shouted loudly.
③ Dan was very excited to win the game.
④ Be careful with the breaking pieces of glass.
⑤ Have you seen any interesting movies recently?

27 다음 중 어법상 옳은 것으로 바르게 짝지어진 것은?

a. She is interesting in construction. b. I felt sad when I saw the bird's broken wings. c. Taken this bus, you can be there on time. d. Being cold, I wore a mask. e. Crying loudly, the baby looked for her mother.

① a, b, c ② a, c, d
③ a, d, e ④ b, d, e
⑤ c, d, e

고난도

28 다음 중 어법상 옳은 것의 개수는?

• Sitting on the sofa, I read a magazine. • Look at the baby holding a doll. • I finally found my lost wallet last week. • Living near the park, I've been there many times. • Do you know the girl stood beside the door?

① 1개 ② 2개 ③ 3개
④ 4개 ⑤ 5개

서술형

[29-31] 밑줄 친 부분이 어법상 옳은지 판단하고, 틀리면 바르게 고치시오.

29 There are many people surprised at the news.

(O / X) ____________

30 The tall woman spoken in front of the audience is my mother.

(O / X) ____________

31 I saw a picture drawing by Leonardo da Vinci.

(O / X) ____________

서술형 고난도

[32-33] 어법상 틀린 부분을 찾아 바르게 고치시오.

32 When I went to Spain, I saw a castle building a long time ago. It looked beautiful. (1개)

33 A car hit a boy ridden a bicycle. People passing by called 119. The boy injuring in the accident is in the hospital now. (2개)

LET'S REVIEW

주요 예문을 다시 한번 확인하고, 우리말과 일치하도록 빈칸을 채우시오.

- The [1] __________ puppy is cute. 그 잠자는 강아지는 귀엽다. Unit 01 - B
- Harry has a book [2] __________ in German. Harry는 독일어로 쓰인 책을 가지고 있다. Unit 01 - B
- Mike came [3] __________ down the stairs. Mike는 계단을 달려서 내려왔다. Unit 01 - B
- Katie had her hair [4] __________. She looks younger.
  Katie는 머리를 했다. 그녀는 더 어려 보인다. Unit 01 - B
- The comic book was [5] __________. 그 만화책은 지루했다. Unit 01 - B
- I am [6] __________ with my work. 나는 내 일이 지루하다. Unit 01 - B

- **Watching** TV, I heard a strange sound. TV를 보다가 나는 이상한 소리를 들었다. Unit 02 - A

- **Walking** down the street, I saw the singer. 길을 걸어가다가 나는 그 가수를 보았다. Unit 02 - B
- [7] __________ to music, I studied math. 나는 음악을 들으면서 수학을 공부했다. Unit 02 - B
- **Feeling** ill, I didn't go shopping. 나는 아파서 쇼핑하러 가지 않았다. Unit 02 - B
- [8] __________ this train, you can go to Tokyo. 이 기차를 탄다면 너는 도쿄에 갈 수 있다. Unit 02 - B
- **Though** [9] __________ near the park, I have never been there.
  나는 공원 근처에 살지만 그곳에 가 본 적이 한 번도 없다. Unit 02 - B

Answers

[1] sleeping [2] written [3] running [4] done [5] boring [6] bored [7] Listening[As I listened] [8] Taking[If you take] [9] living[I live]

CHAPTER 07

수동태

수동태는 주어가 동사의 영향을 받거나
동작을 당할 때 쓴다.

UNIT 01

능동태와 수동태

A 능동태 vs. 수동태

• 능동태: 주어가 어떤 동작을 하는 것을 말할 때 쓴다.
• 수동태: 「be + v-ed」 형태로, 주어가 동사의 영향을 받거나 동작을 당하는 것을 말할 때 쓴다.

Many fans **love** the singer. 〈능동태〉
The singer **is loved** by many fans. 〈수동태〉

B 「by + 행위자」의 생략

행위자가 막연한 일반인일 때나, 분명하지 않거나 중요하지 않을 때 「by + 행위자」는 생략할 수 있다.

English **is spoken** in many countries.
My purse **was stolen** last week.
This wine **was made** in Chile.

C 수동태의 시제

1 과거시제: be동사의 과거형 + v-ed

Anna repaired my computer.
→ My computer **was repaired** by Anna.

2 미래시제: will be + v-ed

Ted will do the new project.
→ The new project **will be done** by Ted.

3 진행형: be동사 + being + v-ed

My dad is cooking dinner.
→ Dinner **is being cooked** by my dad.

빈칸에 알맞은 말을 고르시오.

1 This room ___________ by the staff every day.
ⓐ clean ⓑ is cleaning ⓒ is cleaned

2 This art gallery ___________ in 1982.
ⓐ built ⓑ was built ⓒ is being built

3 The broken window ___________ tomorrow.
ⓐ will fixed ⓑ will be fixed ⓒ will being fixed

PRACTICE

Answer Key p.10

( ) 안에서 알맞은 말을 고르시오.

1 I (made, was made) some sandwiches for the picnic.
2 This app (uses, is used) by many people around the world.
3 The coffee (is be made, is being made) by my sister now.
4 The new movie (will released, will be released) next week.

STEP 2

다음을 수동태 문장으로 바꿔 쓰시오.

1 Many people visit this website.
→ ______________________________

2 The scientists watched the bird.
→ ______________________________

3 They will choose Kate as the best actress.
→ ______________________________

4 John is baking the chocolate cookies now.
→ ______________________________

STEP 3

밑줄 친 부분을 어법에 맞게 고치시오.

1 The math problem was solving by Jack.
2 The Arts Festival is be held in Busan now.
3 The roof will painted green next month.
4 A lot of information is share on the internet.

STEP 4

우리말과 일치하도록 ( ) 안의 말을 이용하여 문장을 완성하시오.

1 이 그림은 피카소에 의해 그려졌다. (draw)
→ This picture ________ ________ ________ Picasso.

2 새로운 쇼핑몰이 우리 동네에 지어질 것이다. (build)
→ A new shopping mall ________ ________ ________ in our town.

3 전화 통화는 지금 녹음되는 중이다. (record)
→ The call ________ ________ ________ now.

4 학급 반장은 학생들에 의해 선출된다. (elect)
→ The class president ________ ________ ________ the students.

UNIT 02

수동태의 여러 가지 형태

A 수동태의 부정문 · 의문문 / 조동사의 수동태

1 수동태의 부정문: be동사 + not + v-ed

This email **wasn't written** by Frank.

2 수동태의 의문문: be동사 + 주어 + v-ed?

Were you **bitten** by a dog?

3 조동사의 수동태: 조동사 + be + v-ed

My homework **should be done** by tomorrow.

B 4형식 · 5형식 문장의 수동태

1 4형식 문장의 수동태: 4형식 문장은 목적어가 두 개(간접목적어, 직접목적어)이므로 보통 두 개의 수동태 문장이 가능하다. 직접목적어를 주어로 수동태를 만들 때는 간접목적어 앞에 전치사를 쓴다. 대개는 to를 쓰지만 동사가 buy, make, get인 경우 for를, ask인 경우 of를 쓴다.

My husband gave me this ring.
→ I **was given** this ring by my husband. 〈간접목적어를 주어로 할 때〉
→ This ring **was given to** me by my husband. 〈직접목적어를 주어로 할 때〉

2 5형식 문장의 수동태: 목적어가 수동태의 주어가 된다.

My brother named our cat Kitty.
→ Our cat **was named** Kitty by my brother.

3 사역동사나 지각동사의 수동태: 사역동사 make 다음에 목적격 보어로 쓰인 동사원형은 수동태 문장에서 to부정사로 바뀌고, 지각동사 다음에 목적격 보어로 쓰인 동사원형은 수동태 문장에서 현재분사나 to부정사로 바뀐다.

Karen made us do the dishes.
→ We **were made to do** the dishes by Karen.

I saw Sam go out with Karen.
→ Sam **was seen going**[**to go**] out with Karen.

CHECK UP 빈칸에 알맞은 말을 고르시오.

1 This ice cream __________ by me.
ⓐ be not made ⓑ was not made ⓒ did not make

2 The computer was bought __________ Tom by his father.
ⓐ to ⓑ for ⓒ of

3 I was made __________ the messy kitchen.
ⓐ clean ⓑ cleaning ⓒ to clean

⊕ PLUS

4형식 동사 중 buy, make, sell과 같은 동사는 사람이 주어인 수동태로 쓰지 않는다.

I bought my brother a watch.
→ A watch was bought for my brother by me.
→ ~~My brother was bought a watch by me.~~

PRACTICE

Answer Key p.10

( ) 안에서 알맞은 말을 고르시오.

1 (Was, Did) the new product announced yesterday?

2 This card was sent (to, for) me by Jane for my birthday.

3 Joy was heard (play, playing) the flute in her room last night.

4 The school rules (must be followed, be must followed) by all the students.

STEP 2

밑줄 친 부분을 어법에 맞게 고치시오.

1 I was didn't invited to Brad's birthday party.

2 Milk must being kept in the refrigerator.

3 My little brother was made wash his hands before dinner.

4 The sneakers were bought to me by my parents.

STEP 3

다음을 수동태 문장으로 바꿔 쓰시오.

1 My mom made me wake up early.

→ I ________________________________.

2 Mr. Smith teaches us English.

→ We ________________________________.

3 My doctor advised me to eat more vegetables.

→ I ________________________________.

4 You can remove this sticker easily.

→ This sticker ________________________________.

STEP 4

우리말과 일치하도록 ( ) 안의 말을 이용하여 문장을 완성하시오.

1 이 사진들은 네가 찍었던 거니? (picture, take)

→ ________ ________ ________ ________ by you?

2 이 주스는 엄마가 나를 위해 만들어 주셨다. (make)

→ This juice ________ ________ ________ ________ by my mom.

3 Brian이 통화하는 것이 나에게 들렸다. (hear, talk)

→ Brian ________ ________ ________ on the phone by me.

4 Julia는 그녀의 부모님에 의해 공주라고 불렸다. (call, Princess)

→ Julia ________ ________ ________ ________ her parents.

UNIT 03

주의해야 할 수동태

A 동사구의 수동태: 동사구는 수동태로 바꿀 때 하나의 동사로 취급한다.

The truck *ran over* the garbage can.
→ The garbage can **was run over** by the truck.

※ 여러 가지 동사구

- take care of: ~을 돌보다
- run over: (차가) ~을 치다
- look up to: ~을 존경하다
- bring up: ~을 키우다
- look after: ~을 돌보다
- laugh at: ~을 비웃다
- look down on: ~을 경멸하다
- put off: ~을 연기하다

B 수동태로 쓰이지 않는 동사

1 목적어가 없는 자동사: appear, disappear, happen 등

My favorite singer **appeared** on TV.
~~My favorite singer was appeared on TV.~~

2 소유나 상태를 나타내는 타동사: have(~을 가지고 있다), resemble(~을 닮다), fit(~에 어울리다) 등

I **have** a blog.
~~A blog is had by me.~~

C by 이외의 전치사를 사용하는 경우

보통 행위자는 by를 사용하여 나타내지만, 다른 전치사를 사용하는 경우도 있다.

- be covered with: ~로 덮여 있다
- be pleased with: ~로 기뻐하다
- be satisfied with: ~에 만족하다
- be disappointed with[at]: ~에 실망하다
- be surprised at: ~에 놀라다
- be interested in: ~에 흥미가 있다
- be filled with: ~로 가득 차다 (= be full of)
- be known to: ~에게 알려지다
- be made of[from]: ~로 만들어지다

This box **is filled with** candy.

We **were surprised at** his sudden visit.

CHECK UP 빈칸에 알맞은 말을 고르시오.

1 My puppy ____________ by my friend Dylan yesterday.
ⓐ looked after ⓑ was looked ⓒ was looked after

2 We were disappointed ____________ the band's new song.
ⓐ from ⓑ with ⓒ to

PRACTICE

Answer Key p.11

밑줄 친 부분을 어법에 맞게 고치시오.

1 The baby was taken care by the nurse.
2 The man suddenly was disappeared.
3 The cake is covered on chocolate.
4 His nose is resembled by his father's.

STEP 2

다음을 수동태 문장으로 바꿔 쓰시오.

1 My boss put off the meeting.
→ The meeting ______________________________.
2 Sophia looks up to Mr. Smith.
→ Mr. Smith ______________________________.
3 Life on Jeju Island satisfies them.
→ They ______________________________ on Jeju Island.

STEP 3

빈칸에 알맞은 말을 보기에서 골라 쓰시오. (단, 한 번씩만 쓸 것)

보기	of	with	to	in

1 Are you interested __________ painting?
2 That bed frame was made __________ wood.
3 They were pleased __________ their son's progress.
4 The news was known __________ all the students in the school.

우리말과 일치하도록 ( ) 안의 말을 이용하여 문장을 완성하시오.

1 그의 시는 다른 사람들에게 비웃음을 샀다. (laugh at)
→ His poem __________ __________ __________ __________ others.
2 나는 그의 사고 소식에 놀랐다. (surprise)
→ I __________ __________ __________ the news of his accident.
3 그 신발 가게는 손님들로 가득 차 있었다. (fill)
→ The shoe store __________ __________ __________ customers.
4 많은 야생 동물이 차에 치였다. (run over)
→ Lots of wild animals __________ __________ __________ __________ cars.

GRAMMAR FOR WRITING

A 우리말과 일치하도록 ( ) 안의 말을 이용하여 문장을 완성하시오.

1 "로미오와 줄리엣"은 셰익스피어에 의해 쓰였다. (write)

→ *Romeo and Juliet* ______________________ Shakespeare.

2 새 중학교가 우리 집 근처에 지어지고 있다. (build)

→ A new middle school ______________________ near my house.

3 그녀의 연설은 다음 주까지 연기될 것이다. (put off)

→ Her speech ______________________ until next week.

4 Chris는 사장에 의해 손님들을 안내하게 되었다. (make, guide)

→ Chris ______________________ the clients by his boss.

5 그 스케이트보드는 삼촌이 나에게 사 주신 것이다. (buy)

→ The skateboard ______________________ by my uncle.

6 이 이메일은 그 회사에서 나에게 보낸 것이다. (send)

→ This email ______________________ by the company.

7 나는 내 우산을 바구니에 놓았는데 그것이 사라졌다. (disappear)

→ I put my umbrella in the basket, but it ______________________.

B 우리말과 일치하도록 ( ) 안에 주어진 단어를 바르게 배열하시오.

1 우리의 계획은 비밀로 지켜져야 한다. (should, secret, be, kept)

→ Our plan ______________________________.

2 그 컴퓨터를 네가 망가뜨렸니? (computer, broken, the, you, by, was)

→ ______________________________________?

3 Sam이 버스 정류장에 서 있는 것을 Jenny가 봤다. (seen, standing, the, was, bus stop, at)

→ Sam ______________________________ by Jenny.

4 그 애플파이는 내가 굽지 않았다. (not, by, was, me, baked)

→ The apple pie ______________________________.

5 그는 그의 친구들에 의해 천사라고 불린다. (friends, is, an angel, he, by, his, called)

→ ______________________________________.

6 "정글북"에서 Mowgli는 늑대에 의해 키워졌다. (brought, was, wolves, up, by, Mowgli)

→ In *The Jungle Book*, ______________________________.

Answer Key p.11

C 수동태와 ( ) 안의 말을 이용하여 대화를 완성하시오.

1 A: How do you like your new job as a firefighter?
B: It is really good. I ______________________ it. (satisfy)

2 A: Let's take the elevator.
B: No, we can't. The elevator ______________________ now. (repair)

3 A: Sorry, Sarah. I wrote your name the wrong way.
B: That's okay. That kind of mistake ______________________.
(can, make, anyone)

4 A: Why did you go to the supermarket?
B: Because I ______________________ some milk. (tell, get)

5 A: Can we use chocolate powder instead of sugar powder?
B: No, the cake ______________________ sugar powder. Our customer asked for that. (should, cover)

D 그림을 보고 ( ) 안의 말을 이용하여 문장을 완성하시오. (단, 현재시제로 쓸 것)

1 
2 
3 
4 

1 The soccer players ______________________ their win. (please)

2 The girl ______________________ the food. (disappoint)

3 The boy ______________________ the singer's beautiful voice. (surprise)

4 My little brother ______________________ my grandfather. (take care of)

REVIEW TEST

[1-5] 빈칸에 들어갈 알맞은 말을 고르시오.

1 This red dress ________ by a famous designer.

① design ② designing
③ to design ④ designed
⑤ was designed

2 The present was sent ________ me by my best friend.

① to ② at ③ of
④ by ⑤ with

3 The potato pizza will ________ in thirty minutes.

① deliver ② delivers
③ delivering ④ delivered
⑤ be delivered

4 The two boys were made ________ fighting by their teacher.

① stop ② stopped
③ stopping ④ to stop
⑤ being stopped

5 My parents were surprised ________ my grades.

① in ② to ③ as
④ at ⑤ of

6 다음 중 어법상 옳은 것은?

① He suddenly was disappeared.
② The sports car is had by the actor.
③ This house built by my grandfather.
④ My sister is resembled by my mother.
⑤ The man was injured in the accident.

[7-8] 다음 중 어법상 <u>틀린</u> 것을 고르시오.

7 ① My watch was stolen.
② Were you hit by the snowball?
③ The file was sent to me by Nora.
④ The show will being finished in twenty minutes.
⑤ Kevin was expected to come to the party.

8 ① Korean history is taught to us by Mr. Kim.
② Ava was seen read a book in the café.
③ Tofu should be kept in the refrigerator.
④ This teddy bear was made for me by my friend.
⑤ The picnic was put off because of the bad weather.

Answer Key p.11

[9-10] 다음 우리말을 영어로 바르게 옮긴 것을 고르시오.

9 이 치즈 케이크는 엄마를 위해 만들어졌다.

① This cheesecake made Mom.
② This cheesecake was made Mom.
③ This cheesecake was made by Mom.
④ This cheesecake was made for Mom.
⑤ This cheesecake was made of Mom.

10 그 나무는 어제 버스에 치였다.

① The tree ran over a bus yesterday.
② The tree ran over by a bus yesterday.
③ The tree was run by a bus yesterday.
④ The tree was run over a bus yesterday.
⑤ The tree was run over by a bus yesterday.

서술형 빈출

[11-13] ( ) 안의 말을 이용하여 문장을 완성하시오.

11 The magazine ______________ by many teenagers in the past. (read)

12 We were made ______________ a diary in English by our English teacher. (keep)

13 The festival will ______________ this weekend. (hold)

빈출

[14-15] 빈칸에 공통으로 들어갈 말을 고르시오.

14
- I am satisfied __________ the result.
- The bottle was filled __________ juice.

① in ② to ③ as
④ by ⑤ with

15
- This mouse pad is given __________ everyone as a free gift.
- The singer's name is known __________ people around the world.

① in ② to ③ as
④ by ⑤ with

서술형

[16-18] 다음을 수동태 문장으로 바꿔 쓰시오.

16 My favorite director filmed this movie.

→ This movie ______________________
______________________.

17 That sitcom made the actress a superstar.

→ The actress ______________________
______________________.

18 Many workers look up to my boss.

→ My boss ______________________
______________________.

19 다음 중 밑줄 친 부분이 잘못된 것은?

① I am pleased with Eric's decision.
② The pretty doll was made of paper.
③ I was disappointed to his answer.
④ The bed was covered with a sheet.
⑤ Jay is interested in hip hop dance.

서술형

[20-22] 우리말과 일치하도록 ( ) 안의 말을 이용하여 문장을 완성하시오.

20 Alice는 반의 모두가 좋아한다. (like)

→ Alice ______________ everyone in the class.

21 재미있는 이야기를 선생님께서 수업 시간에 우리에게 해 주셨다. (tell)

→ An interesting story ______________ by my teacher in class.

22 그의 발명품은 그의 친구들에게 비웃음을 당했다. (laugh at)

→ His invention ______________ his friends.

서술형

[23-25] 우리말과 일치하도록 ( ) 안에 주어진 단어를 바르게 배열하시오.

23 그 도둑은 경찰에 잡힐 것이다. (will, by, police, be, the, caught)

→ The thief ______________.

24 지금 회의에서 중요한 문제들이 이야기되고 있다. (talked, are, issues, about, being, important)

→ ______________ in the meeting now.

25 밖에서 내 어린 남동생이 우는 소리가 들렸다. (little, crying, my, was, heard, brother)

→ ______________ outside.

고난도

26 다음 중 어법상 옳은 것을 모두 고르면?

① Was this report wrote by you?
② Some cars are being sold on the internet.
③ The house will be cleaned by my husband.
④ The players were made practice harder by their coach.
⑤ The advice was given for me by my parents.

27 다음 중 어법상 옳은 것으로 바르게 짝지어진 것은?

a. My mom is satisfied with her new car.
b. The floor was covered with dust.
c. This ice cream was made by fresh milk.
d. The decision cannot be put off any longer.
e. We are very pleased for your service.

① a, b, c ② a, b, d
③ a, d, e ④ b, c, e
⑤ b, d, e

고난도

28 다음 중 어법상 옳은 것의 개수는?

• I was surprised at her response.
• I'm not interested in other opinions.
• The project will be completed in a few days.
• The flowers were not given to me by my boyfriend.
• The accident was happened in the late afternoon.

① 1개 ② 2개 ③ 3개
④ 4개 ⑤ 5개

서술형

29 우리말과 일치하도록 주어진 조건에 맞게 문장을 완성하시오.

그 아이는 영웅에 의해 구조되었니?

〈조건〉 1. the child, rescue, the hero를 이용할 것
2. 7단어로 쓸 것

→ ____________________?

서술형

[30-31] 밑줄 친 부분이 어법상 옳은지 판단하고, 틀리면 바르게 고치시오.

30 Some gold was found in the ship.

(O / X) ____________________

31 Sophia was brought by up her uncle.

(O / X) ____________________

서술형 고난도

[32-33] 어법상 틀린 부분을 찾아 바르게 고치시오.

32 The conference was held in a famous hotel. We arrived there on time. It was filled by many people. (1개)

33 This is a great film. It is been seen all over the world now. Its director is looked up to many film students. (2개)

LET'S REVIEW

주요 예문을 다시 한번 확인하고, 우리말과 일치하도록 빈칸을 채우시오.

- The singer **is loved** by many fans. 그 가수는 많은 팬에 의해 사랑받는다. Unit 01 - A

- English [1] ____________ in many countries. 영어는 많은 나라에서 말해진다. Unit 01 - B

- My computer **was repaired** by Anna. 내 컴퓨터는 Anna에 의해 수리되었다. Unit 01 - C
- The new project [2] ____________ **done** by Ted.
  새 프로젝트는 Ted에 의해 수행될 것이다. Unit 01 - C
- Dinner [3] ____________ **cooked** by my dad. 저녁 식사는 우리 아빠에 의해 요리되고 있다. Unit 01 - C

- This email **wasn't written** by Frank. 이 이메일은 Frank에 의해 쓰이지 않았다. Unit 02 - A
- [4] ____________ by a dog? 너는 개에게 물렸니? Unit 02 - A
- My homework **should be done** by tomorrow. 내 숙제는 내일까지 끝나야 한다. Unit 02 - A

- This ring [5] ____________ me by my husband. 이 반지는 내 남편에 의해 나에게 주어졌다. Unit 02 - B
- Our cat **was named** Kitty by my brother.
  우리 고양이는 내 남동생에 의해 Kitty라고 이름 지어졌다. Unit 02 - B
- We [6] ____________ **do** the dishes by Karen. 우리는 Karen에 의해 설거지를 하게 되었다. Unit 02 - B
- Sam **was seen going[to go]** out with Karen. Sam이 Karen과 함께 나가는 것이 보였다. Unit 02 - B

- The garbage can [7] ____________ the truck. 그 쓰레기통은 그 트럭에 치였다. Unit 03 - A

- My favorite singer **appeared** on TV. 내가 가장 좋아하는 가수가 TV에 나왔다. Unit 03 - B

- This box **is filled** [8] ____________ candy. 이 상자는 사탕으로 가득 차 있다. Unit 03 - C
- We **were surprised** [9] ____________ his sudden visit.
  우리는 그의 갑작스런 방문에 놀랐다. Unit 03 - C

Answers

[1] is spoken [2] will be [3] is being [4] Were you bitten [5] was given to [6] were made to
[7] was run over by [8] with [9] at

CHAPTER

08

대명사

대명사는 명사를 대신하는 말이다.

UNIT 01

부정대명사 I

부정대명사란 불특정한 사람이나 사물을 가리키는 대명사이다.

cf. 일부 부정대명사(some, any, all, both, each)는 대명사로뿐만 아니라 동일한 의미의 형용사로도 쓰인다.

A **one:** 앞에서 언급된 것과 같은 종류의 불특정한 사람이나 사물을 가리킬 때 쓴다. 복수형은 ones이다.

I don't have a smartphone. I need to buy **one**.
= a smartphone

Will you buy the red apples or the green **ones**?
= apples

ⓘ 앞에서 언급된 것과 동일한 것을 가리킬 때는 it을 쓴다.

I've lost my watch. I can't find **it**.
= my watch

B **some / any:** '조금(의)', '약간(의)'의 의미로, some은 주로 긍정문이나 권유문, any는 주로 부정문이나 의문문에 쓴다.

I posted **some** pictures on my blog.

A: Would you like to have **some** snacks? B: Yes, I'd like to have **some**.

Nick has lost his wallet. He doesn't have **any** money.

A: Do you have **any** plans for this weekend? B: No, I don't have **any**.

C **all:** '모든', '모든 것'의 의미로, all이 대명사로 사람을 나타낼 때는 복수, 사물이나 상황을 나타낼 때는 단수 취급한다. 단, 「all (of) + 명사」인 경우 뒤에 나오는 명사의 수에 동사를 일치시킨다.

All *were* satisfied with the results. / **All** *was* calm this morning.

All the students *have* gone home. / **All** the work *is* finished.

D **both:** '둘 다', '양쪽(의)'의 의미로, 복수 취급한다.

Ray and Mike go snowboarding a lot in winter. **Both** *like* snowboarding.

E **each / every:** each는 '각각(의)', every는 '모든'의 의미로, 둘 다 단수 취급한다.

Each of the children *was* given a book.

Every product in this market *is* on sale.

CHECK UP 빈칸에 알맞은 말을 고르시오.

1 I only have small bags. I need a bigger ____________.
ⓐ one ⓑ it ⓒ each

2 Daisy was hungry, so she ate ____________ doughnuts.
ⓐ any ⓑ some ⓒ one

PRACTICE

Answer Key p.12

STEP 1

( ) 안에서 알맞은 말을 고르시오.

1 A: Do you have a computer? B: Yes, I have (one, it).

2 The man didn't catch (some, any) fish yesterday.

3 We have to move (all, every) these boxes.

4 (Each, All) student gave a different answer.

5 Do you prefer white sneakers or black (one, ones)?

STEP 2

빈칸에 some과 any 중 알맞은 것을 쓰시오.

1 Would you like __________ chocolate cookies?

2 Can you play __________ musical instruments?

3 I went to the bakery to buy __________ sandwiches.

4 Don't buy __________ more skirts. You already have a lot of them.

STEP 3

빈칸에 알맞은 말을 보기에서 골라 쓰시오. (단, 한 번씩만 쓸 것)

보기	one	it	both	every	all

1 I sold my old car and bought a new __________.

2 I have two brothers. __________ of them are taller than me.

3 I want to visit __________ country in South America.

4 __________ the members have their membership cards.

5 His new novel is great. I enjoyed __________.

STEP 4

우리말과 일치하도록 ( ) 안의 말을 이용하여 문장을 완성하시오.

1 나는 수영복이 없다. 하나 사고 싶다. (get)
→ I don't have a swimsuit. I want to __________ __________.

2 나는 신선한 딸기들을 약간 샀다. (fresh, strawberry)
→ I bought __________ __________ __________.

3 우리는 둘 다 인도 음식을 좋아한다. (us, like)
→ __________ __________ __________ __________ Indian food.

4 나는 세 명의 외국인을 만났다. 각각은 다른 나라 출신이었다. (be)
→ I met three foreigners. __________ __________ from a different country.

UNIT 02

부정대명사 II

A

another: 또 하나 다른 것(의), 또 하나(의)

I don't like this T-shirt. Can you show me **another**?

cf. another는 대명사로뿐만 아니라 동일한 의미의 형용사로도 쓰인다.

Do you have these shoes in **another** color?

B

one ~ the other ...: (둘 중의) 하나는 ~, 다른 하나는 …

I have two pets. **One** is a hamster, and **the other** is a rabbit.

ⓘ one ~, another ..., the other ...: (셋 중의) 하나는 ~, 다른 하나는 …, 나머지 하나는 …

Today, I have exams in three classes.
One is in math; **another** is in science; **the other** is in history.

C

some ~ others ...: 어떤 것[사람]들은 ~, 다른 어떤 것[사람]들은 …

Some like hip hop, and **others** like ballads.

ⓘ some ~, the others ...: 어떤 것[사람]들은 ~, 나머지 모든 것[사람]들은 …

There are one hundred balls in the box.
Some are black, and **the others** are white.

D

each other / one another: '서로'라는 의미로 보통 each other는 둘 사이에, one another는 셋 이상일 때 쓰지만, 종종 구별 없이 쓰이기도 한다.

Your blouse and pants match well with **each other**.
We all should help **one another**.

CHECK UP 빈칸에 알맞은 말을 고르시오.

1 I don't like the pattern on this plate. Can you show me ____________?
ⓐ another ⓑ other ⓒ each other

2 Julie has two sons. One is three, and ____________ is five.
ⓐ another ⓑ the other ⓒ others

3 Some students walk to school, and ____________ take the school bus.
ⓐ another ⓑ the other ⓒ others

4 This town is very small. All the people in this town know ____________.
ⓐ another ⓑ other ⓒ one another

PRACTICE

Answer Key p.12

( ) 안에서 알맞은 말을 고르시오.

1 I ate a piece of cake, but I'm still hungry. Can I have (another, other)?

2 Julie and Brian looked at (another, each other) and smiled.

3 I bought two cups of ice cream. (One, Some) is for me, and (the other, others) is for you.

4 There are a lot of people in the park. (One, Some) are playing badminton, and (the other, others) are sitting on the grass.

STEP 2

밑줄 친 부분을 어법에 맞게 고치시오.

1 Roses are various colors. Some are red, and the others are pink.

2 My sister and Jason know the other. They have met before.

3 This muffin tastes delicious. Can I have other?

4 Gavin has two nicknames. One is "Prince," and others is "Elephant."

STEP 3

빈칸에 알맞은 말을 보기에서 골라 쓰시오. (단, 한 번씩만 쓸 것)

보기	another	the other	the others	others	one another

1 I have five sons. One has blond hair, and ____________ have brown hair.

2 Five basketball players were passing a ball to ____________.

3 Some people like meat, and ____________ like fish.

4 I have three cats. One is white, ____________ is gray, and ____________ is black.

우리말과 일치하도록 빈칸에 알맞은 말을 쓰시오.

1 James와 Lucy는 서로 좋아한다.

→ James and Lucy like ____________.

2 커피 한 잔 더 마시겠어요?

→ Will you drink __________ cup of coffee?

3 어떤 사람들은 코미디 영화를 좋아하고, 다른 어떤 사람들은 공포 영화를 좋아한다.

→ __________ like comedies, and __________ like horror movies.

4 나는 두 명의 외국인 친구가 있다. 한 명은 일본인이고, 다른 한 명은 프랑스인이다.

→ I have two foreign friends. __________ is Japanese, and ____________ is French.

UNIT 03

재귀대명사

재귀대명사란 인칭대명사의 소유격이나 목적격에 -self[-selves]를 붙인 형태로 '~ 자신'이라는 의미를 가진다.

A

재귀용법: 주어가 하는 동작의 대상이 주어 자신일 때, 즉 목적어가 주어와 같을 때 목적어 자리에 재귀대명사를 쓴다.

1 동사의 목적어

Seth hurt **himself** while he was playing soccer.

2 전치사의 목적어

Amy was proud of **herself** for doing her best.

※ 재귀대명사와 자주 쓰이는 동사

- dress oneself: 옷을 입다
- seat oneself: 앉다
- talk to oneself: 혼잣말하다
- enjoy oneself: 즐거운 시간을 보내다
- hurt oneself: 다치다
- excuse oneself: 변명하다, 자리를 뜨다
- burn oneself: 데다, 화상을 입다
- cut oneself: 베이다

B

강조용법: 주어나 목적어를 강조하며, 이때의 재귀대명사는 생략할 수 있다.

He **himself** fixed the computer. / He fixed the computer **himself**. 〈주어 강조〉
I like the singer **herself**, not her songs. 〈목적어 강조〉

C

재귀대명사를 포함한 관용표현

- by oneself: 홀로, 혼자서(= alone), 혼자 힘으로
- in itself: 원래, 그 자체가
- between ourselves: 우리끼리 이야기인데
- make oneself at home: 편히 쉬다[지내다]
- for oneself: (자기를 위해) 혼자 힘으로
- beside oneself: 제정신이 아닌
- help oneself to: ~을 마음껏 먹다

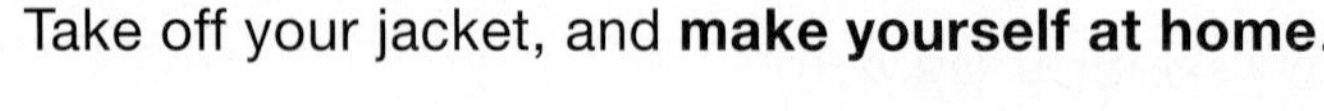

Take off your jacket, and **make yourself at home**.

CHECK UP 빈칸에 알맞은 말을 고르시오.

1 I taught ____________ Italian.
ⓐ me ⓑ my ⓒ myself

2 My sister made the seafood pasta ____________.
ⓐ she ⓑ her ⓒ herself

3 I built my dog's house ____________ myself.
ⓐ by ⓑ beside ⓒ between

PRACTICE

Answer Key p.12

( ) 안에서 알맞은 말을 고르시오.

1 Never mind. I was just talking to (me, myself).
2 Jason wrote the report (him, himself).
3 The children enjoyed (them, themselves) at the playground.
4 I was working in the office (by myself, beside myself) last night.

밑줄 친 부분을 생략할 수 있으면 O표, 생략할 수 없으면 X표 하시오.

1 My sister burned herself on the stove.
2 The five-year-old boy painted this picture himself.
3 I didn't like the musical itself, but I liked the songs in it.
4 We seated ourselves at a table by the window.

빈칸에 알맞은 말을 보기에서 골라 쓰시오.

보기	by	between	beside

1 She was almost __________ herself with excitement when she heard the shocking news.
2 I finished the project __________ myself. I didn't ask for any help.
3 Let's keep this secret __________ ourselves. Don't tell anyone else.

우리말과 일치하도록 ( ) 안의 말을 이용하여 문장을 완성하시오.

1 그 파스타에 들어간 토마토소스 자체가 맵다. (in)
→ The tomato sauce in the pasta is spicy __________ __________.
2 네 숙제는 네가 직접 해야 한다. (do one's homework)
→ You should __________ __________ __________ __________.
3 이 빵을 마음껏 드세요. 제가 방금 구웠어요. (help)
→ Please __________ __________ __________ this bread. I just baked it.
4 Joshua는 중요한 전화를 받기 위해 회의에서 자리를 떴다. (excuse)
→ Joshua __________ __________ from the meeting to take an important phone call.

GRAMMAR FOR WRITING

A 우리말과 일치하도록 ( ) 안의 말을 이용하여 문장을 완성하시오.

1 우리 둘 다 Brown 선생님의 수업을 듣는다. (attend)

→ ____________________ Mr. Brown's class.

2 각각의 사람은 다른 재능을 가지고 있다. (person, have)

→ ____________________ a different talent.

3 이 자판기는 지폐를 받지 않는다. 나는 동전들이 좀 필요하다. (need, coin)

→ This vending machine doesn't take bills. I ____________________.

4 James는 어제 계단에서 떨어져서 다쳤다. (hurt)

→ James fell down the stairs and ____________________ yesterday.

5 Hal은 이미 세 가지 언어를 말할 수 있는데도, 또 다른 언어를 배우고 있다. (one)

→ Hal already speaks three languages, and he is learning ____________.

6 우리 집에 컴퓨터가 두 대 있다. 하나는 데스크톱이고, 다른 하나는 노트북 컴퓨터이다. (desktop)

→ There are two computers in my house. ____________________, and ____________________ is a laptop.

B 우리말과 일치하도록 ( ) 안에 주어진 단어를 바르게 배열하시오.

1 나는 영어 자체는 좋아하지만, 영어 시험은 싫어한다. (English, I, itself, like)

→ ____________________________, but I hate English tests.

2 모든 사람은 행복한 삶을 살고 싶어 한다. (live, person, every, to, wants)

→ ____________________________ a happy life.

3 그 아이들은 그들 힘으로 간식을 만들었다. (snack, themselves, a, for, made)

→ The children ____________________________.

4 여행하는 동안 그녀의 모든 돈이 도난당했다. (her, was, all, stolen, money)

→ ____________________________ during the trip.

5 Mary와 Nancy는 10년 동안 서로 알고 지냈다. (known, years, other, have, each, ten, for)

→ Mary and Nancy ____________________________.

6 어떤 외국인들은 김치를 좋아하지만, 다른 어떤 이들은 좋아하지 않는다.
(foreigners, some, don't, kimchi, but, others, like)

→ ____.

Answer Key p.12

C

다음 대화의 빈칸에 알맞은 말을 보기에서 골라 쓰시오. (단, 한 번씩만 쓸 것)

보기	any	one	both	ourselves	the other	it

1 A: Is there a convenience store near here?
B: Yes, there is ______________ on the corner.

2 A: Do you have Tom's phone number?
B: Yes. I wrote ______________ down.

3 A: Did you hear that? There's something outside!
B: I didn't hear ______________ sounds from outside. Maybe it was the TV.

4 A: Let us keep this between ______________.
B: Don't worry. I won't tell anyone.

5 A: I can't choose between this yellow shirt and this blue one.
B: How about buying ______________ of them? They are on sale now.

6 A: What's the signature dish of this restaurant?
B: There are two. One is a potato pizza, and ______________ is pumpkin soup.

D

그림을 보고 빈칸에 알맞은 말을 써서 문장을 완성하시오.

1 Olivia __________ __________ while she was cooking.

2 As the couple argued, they pointed at __________ __________.

3 The child has three balloons. One is red, __________ __________ yellow, and __________ __________ __________ purple.

REVIEW TEST

[1-5] 빈칸에 들어갈 알맞은 말을 고르시오.

1 My brother gave me his bicycle, but I don't like ________.

① it ② one
③ other ④ another
⑤ the other

2 My computer is too old and slow. I'd like to buy a new ________.

① it ② one
③ other ④ another
⑤ the other

3 ________ airport has its own unique code.

① Both ② All
③ Some ④ Other
⑤ Each

4 There are five people in my family. We love ________.

① the other ② one
③ another ④ each another
⑤ one another

5 A: Is there ________ ice cream in the freezer?
B: No, there is not.

① any ② some
③ all ④ every
⑤ each

[6-8] 다음 중 어법상 틀린 것을 고르시오.

6 ① Some of my friends live in Seoul.
② Do you have any questions?
③ Both of us have smartphones.
④ Each question has five choices.
⑤ Every students in the school like the teacher.

7 ① I can introduce me in English.
② The two dogs barked at each other.
③ Some like movies, and others like plays.
④ I bought a magazine, but I left it on the bus.
⑤ Will you have another glass of milk?

8 ① Jay hurt himself while he was moving.
② Tom and Henry know each other well.
③ This cake tastes good! Can I have another piece?
④ Some students passed the math test, but others didn't.
⑤ I read two books last week: one was interesting, but other was boring.

Answer Key p.13

9 다음 밑줄 친 부분과 바꾸어 쓸 수 있는 것은?

I'm still thirsty. I'd like to have <u>one more</u> glass of water.

① it ② all
③ other ④ another
⑤ each other

서술형

10 두 문장의 의미가 같도록 빈칸에 알맞은 말을 쓰시오.

Chloe traveled to England alone last summer.

→ Chloe traveled to England __________ __________ last summer.

서술형

11 밑줄 친 단어를 올바른 형태로 고쳐 쓰시오.

The pot is very hot. Be careful not to burn <u>you</u>.

서술형

[12-13] 빈칸에 들어갈 알맞은 대명사를 쓰시오.

12 There are two kinds of flowers in the vase. __________ are roses, and __________ are tulips.

13 A: I'm looking for jeans. Can you recommend any good __________ to me?
B: Sure. How about these?

빈출

[14-15] 빈칸에 들어갈 말이 순서대로 바르게 짝지어진 것을 고르시오.

14 I bought __________ cookies. Would you like __________?

① any – any ② any – some
③ any – another ④ another – any
⑤ some – some

15 Every figure skater __________ very hard. All of them __________ many hours at the rink.

① practice – spend
② practices – spend
③ practice – spends
④ practices – spends
⑤ practicing – spending

서술형 빈출

[16-17] 빈칸에 공통으로 들어갈 알맞은 말을 쓰시오.

16
- This spoon is dirty. Could you bring me __________?
- I received three presents on my birthday. One was a bag; __________ was a novel; the other was a doll.

17
- Would you like __________ apples?
- Everyone likes different seasons: __________ like summer, and others like winter.

18 다음 우리말을 영어로 바르게 옮긴 것은?

어떤 사람들은 도시에 살고 싶어 하고, 다른 어떤 사람들은 시골에 살고 싶어 한다.

① One person wants to live in the city; the other wants to live in the country.
② One person wants to live in the city; another wants to live in the country.
③ Some people want to live in the city; the other wants to live in the country.
④ Some people want to live in the city; others want to live in the country.
⑤ Some people want to live in the city; the others want to live in the country.

서술형

[19-21] 우리말과 일치하도록 ( ) 안의 말을 이용하여 문장을 완성하시오.

19 너는 저 칼에 베이지 않도록 조심해야 한다. (cut)

→ You should be careful not to ________ ________ with that knife.

20 이 학교의 모든 학생들은 예술적 재능이 있다. (student)

→ ________ ________ in this school has artistic talent.

21 Lucy와 Joe는 첼로 연주를 잘한다. 왜냐하면 둘 다 연습을 많이 하기 때문이다. (practice)

→ Lucy and Joe are good at playing the cello because ________ ________ it a lot.

22 다음 중 밑줄 친 부분을 생략할 수 있는 것은?

① My hobby is taking pictures of myself.
② Mike wrote this poem himself.
③ I saw Amanda talking to herself.
④ Have you ever traveled by yourself?
⑤ Sue found herself in a strange place.

서술형

[23-25] 우리말과 일치하도록 ( ) 안에 주어진 단어를 바르게 배열하시오.

23 긴 여행 후 우리 모두는 매우 피곤했다. (tired, us, all, very, of, were)

→ ________________ after the long trip.

24 수학여행은 재미있었고, 우리는 아주 즐거운 시간을 보냈다. (enjoyed, very, we, much, ourselves)

→ Our field trip was interesting, and ________________.

25 디저트를 마음껏 드세요. (the, to, dessert, yourself, help)

→ Please ________________.

고난도

26 다음 중 어법상 옳은 것을 모두 고르면?

① Have you seen my jacket? I can't find it.
② I don't have some plans for the trip.
③ Both women were wearing glasses.
④ Every room has a laptop and an internet connection.
⑤ Would you like to have any tea?

27 다음 중 어법상 옳은 것으로 바르게 짝지어진 것은?

a. All the food was delicious.
b. Both players were great today.
c. Romeo and Juliet loved each another.
d. Every cloud have a silver lining.
e. They enjoyed themselves after the victory.

① a, b, c ② a, b, e
③ a, c, e ④ b, c, e
⑤ b, d, e

고난도

28 다음 중 어법상 옳은 것의 개수는?

• She called herself an angel.
• Each of us have our responsibility.
• Tony hurt himself while he was climbing the mountain.
• Both of my parents was very pleased with my graduation.
• Every student in my class takes part in the project.

① 1개 ② 2개 ③ 3개
④ 4개 ⑤ 5개

서술형

[29-31] 밑줄 친 부분이 어법상 옳은지 판단하고, 틀리면 바르게 고치시오.

29 I would like to buy a smartphone. Could you show me a good one?

(O / X) ____________________

30 Some people enjoy cooking, but other don't.

(O / X) ____________________

31 I'm going to travel to Italy by myself next month.

(O / X) ____________________

서술형 고난도

[32-33] 어법상 틀린 부분을 찾아 바르게 고치시오.

32 I met two friends while I was traveling. One is from Italy, and another is from Argentina. (1개)

33 Welcome to our hotel. Every member of our staff are ready to make you feel comfortable. Please make you at home, and enjoy your stay. (2개)

LET'S REVIEW

주요 예문을 다시 한번 확인하고, 우리말과 일치하도록 빈칸을 채우시오.

- Will you buy the red apples or the green [1] ______________?
  너는 빨간 사과를 살 거니 초록 사과를 살 거니? Unit 01 - A
- Would you like to have **some** snacks? 너는 간식을 좀 먹겠니? Unit 01 - B
- Nick has lost his wallet. He doesn't have [2] ______________ money.
  Nick은 지갑을 잃어버렸다. 그는 돈이 조금도 없다. Unit 01 - B
- **All** the students have gone home. 모든 학생들이 집에 갔다. Unit 01 - C
- Ray and Mike go snowboarding a lot in winter. **Both** like snowboarding.
  Ray와 Mike는 겨울에 스노보드를 많이 타러 간다. 둘 다 스노보드를 좋아한다. Unit 01 - D
- [3] ______________ of the children was given a book. 각각의 아이들은 책을 한 권 받았다. Unit 01 - E
- [4] ______________ product in this market is on sale. 이 시장의 모든 상품은 할인 중이다. Unit 01 - E
- I don't like this T-shirt. Can you show me [5] ______________?
  저는 이 티셔츠가 맘에 들지 않아요. 또 다른 것을 보여 줄 수 있나요? Unit 02 - A
- I have two pets. **One** is a hamster, and **the other** is a rabbit.
  나는 애완동물이 두 마리 있다. 하나는 햄스터이고, 다른 하나는 토끼이다. Unit 02 - B
- **Some** like hip hop, and [6] ______________ like ballads.
  어떤 사람들은 힙합을 좋아하고, 다른 어떤 사람들은 발라드를 좋아한다. Unit 02 - C
- Your blouse and pants match well with [7] ______________ **other**.
  너의 블라우스와 바지가 서로 잘 어울린다. Unit 02 - D
- We all should help **one another**. 우리는 모두 서로 도와야 한다. Unit 02 - D
- Amy was proud of [8] ______________ for doing her best.
  Amy는 최선을 다한 것에 대해 그녀 자신이 자랑스러웠다. Unit 03 - A
- He [9] ______________ fixed the computer. 그가 직접 컴퓨터를 고쳤다. Unit 03 - B
- Take off your jacket, and **make yourself at home**. 재킷을 벗고 편히 쉬어라. Unit 03 - C

Answers

[1] ones [2] any [3] Each [4] Every [5] another [6] others [7] each [8] herself [9] himself

CHAPTER 09

형용사나 부사에 '-er', '-est' 또는 'more', 'most'를 붙여 대상의 성질, 상태, 수량의 정도를 비교할 수 있다.

UNIT 01

원급, 비교급, 최상급

A

as + 원급(형용사/부사) + as: ~만큼 …한[하게]

Bill is **as tall as** his father.

She can swim **as fast as** I can.

B

비교급 + than: ~보다 더 …한[하게]

Today is **hotter than** yesterday.

This pencil case is **more expensive than** that one.

ⓘ 비교급을 강조할 때는 비교급 앞에 '훨씬'의 의미를 가지는 much, a lot, even, far 등을 쓴다.

Your room is **much** *bigger* than mine.

C

the + 최상급: 가장 ~한[하게]

1 the + 최상급 + in + 장소나 범위를 나타내는 단수명사: ~안에서 가장 …한[하게]

Cream pasta is **the most popular** dish *in* this restaurant.

2 the + 최상급 + of + 비교의 대상이 되는 명사: ~중에서 가장 …한[하게]

James is **the fastest** runner *of* the three.

ⓘ 비교급과 최상급 만들기(규칙 변화)

일반적인 경우	-(e)r / -(e)st	fast – faster – fastest large – larger – largest
-y로 끝나는 경우	y를 i로 바꾸고 -er / -est	easy – easier – easiest
단모음 + 단자음으로 끝나는 경우	자음을 한 번 더 쓰고 -er / -est	big – bigger – biggest
-ous, -ful, -ing, -ive 등으로 끝나는 대부분의 2음절 단어와 3음절 이상의 단어인 경우	단어 앞에 more / most	famous – more famous – most famous

빈칸에 알맞은 말을 고르시오.

1 Kirk is as ____________ as me.

ⓐ strong ⓑ stronger ⓒ strongest

2 This cell phone is ____________ than that one.

ⓐ small ⓑ smaller ⓒ smallest

3 He is the ____________ boy in his class.

ⓐ smart ⓑ smarter ⓒ smartest

PRACTICE

Answer Key p.13

STEP 1 ( ) 안에서 알맞은 말을 고르시오.

1 The Nile River is the (longer, longest) river in the world.
2 My brother is (very, far) busier than me.
3 She can jump as (high, highest) as her older brother.
4 I think skiing is (exciting, more exciting) than skating.

STEP 2 ( ) 안의 말을 이용하여 문장을 완성하시오.

1 I like seafood ______________ than meat. (much)
2 Jeju Island is the ______________ island in Korea. (large)
3 Tomorrow will be as ______________ as today. (cold)
4 She got up ______________ than me. (early)

STEP 3 주어진 문장과 의미가 통하도록 ( ) 안의 말을 이용하여 문장을 완성하시오.

1 The yellow bag is $10. The red bag is $15.
→ The yellow bag is ______________ the red one. (cheap)
2 I am 160 cm tall. Kevin is 165 cm tall. Ron is 168 cm tall.
→ Ron is ______________ boy of the three of us. (tall)
3 Sue runs 100 m in fifteen seconds. Emily also runs 100 m in fifteen seconds.
→ Emily runs 100 m ______________ Sue. (fast)

STEP 4 우리말과 일치하도록 ( ) 안의 말을 이용하여 문장을 완성하시오.

1 Hailey는 나보다 훨씬 더 힘이 세다. (much, strong)
→ Hailey is __________ __________ __________ me.
2 아빠는 엄마만큼 요리를 잘하신다. (well)
→ Dad cooks __________ __________ __________ Mom.
3 나에게는 수학이 영어보다 더 어렵다. (difficult)
→ For me, math is __________ __________ __________ English.
4 그녀는 그 나라에서 가장 유명한 여배우이다. (famous, actress)
→ She is __________ __________ __________ __________ in the country.

UNIT **02**

비교 구문을 이용한 표현

A **배수사 + as + 원급 + as ~:** ~의 몇 배로 …한[하게](= 배수사 + 비교급 + than)

My burger is **three times as thick as** yours.
= My burger is **three times thicker than** yours.

B **the + 비교급 ~, the + 비교급 ...:** ~하면 할수록 더 …하다

The harder you study, **the better** your grade will be.

C **비교급 + and + 비교급:** 점점 더 ~한[하게]

Laptops are getting **smaller and smaller**.
It is getting **more and more difficult** to see the stars.

D **Which/Who ~ 비교급, A or B?:** A와 B 중에서 어느 것이/누가 더 ~한가?

Which do you like **better**, hip hop **or** rock music?
Who is **taller**, Tom **or** Jimmy?

E **one of the + 최상급 + 복수명사:** 가장 ~한 것들 중 하나

Cristiano Ronaldo is **one of the most popular soccer players** in the world.

CHECK UP 빈칸에 알맞은 말을 고르시오.

1 His hand is ___________ as big as mine.
ⓐ two ⓑ second ⓒ twice

2 The more you practice, ___________ you will be.
ⓐ good ⓑ the good ⓒ the better

3 It is getting colder and ___________.
ⓐ cold ⓑ colder ⓒ coldest

4 Who came to school ___________, Jane or Joe?
ⓐ later ⓑ the later ⓒ latest

5 She is one of the ___________ painters in the world.
ⓐ famous ⓑ more famous ⓒ most famous

PRACTICE

Answer Key p.14

( ) 안에서 알맞은 말을 고르시오.

1 Beijing is (ten, ten times) as big as London.

2 The internet is one of the greatest (invention, inventions) in history.

3 The longer he waited, (the angry, the angrier) he became.

4 Which do you enjoy (more, most), dramas or comedies?

밑줄 친 부분을 어법에 맞게 고치시오.

1 The hole is getting big and big.

2 Which is most difficult, math or science?

3 Your pizza is four as large as his.

4 New York is one of the more busiest cities in the world.

STEP 3

우리말과 일치하도록 ( ) 안의 말을 이용하여 문장을 완성하시오.

1 낮이 점점 더 길어지고 있다. (long)

→ The days are getting ________________.

2 그녀가 더 천천히 말할수록 나는 그녀를 더 많이 이해할 수 있었다. (slowly, much)

→ ________________ she talked, ________________ I could understand her.

3 경복궁은 한국에서 가장 아름다운 건축물 중 하나이다. (beautiful)

→ Gyeongbokgung Palace is one of ________________ buildings in Korea.

우리말과 일치하도록 ( ) 안의 말을 이용하여 문장을 완성하시오.

1 소리가 점점 더 조용해지고 있다. (quiet)

→ The sound is getting ________ ________ ________.

2 네가 더 일찍 도착할수록 너는 더 빨리 들어갈 것이다. (early, soon)

→ ________ ________ you arrive, ________ ________ you will get in.

3 Bill과 Warren 중 누가 더 부자인가요? (rich)

→ ________ ________ ________, Bill or Warren?

4 이 방은 내 방보다 세 배 더 크다. (three, big)

→ This room is ________ ________ ________ ________ mine.

GRAMMAR FOR WRITING

A 우리말과 일치하도록 ( ) 안의 말을 이용하여 문장을 완성하시오.

1 그 빨간 가방은 파란 것만큼 값이 싸다. (cheap)
→ The red bag is ________________________ the blue one.

2 날이 점점 더 따뜻해지고 있다. (get, warm)
→ It is ________________________.

3 이것이 이 도시에서 가장 높은 건물이다. (tall, building)
→ This is ________________________ this city.

4 나의 형은 나보다 돈을 훨씬 더 많이 번다. (much, money)
→ My brother earns ________________________ me.

5 오늘이 내 인생에서 가장 행복한 날 중 하나였다. (happy, day)
→ Today was ________________________ of my life.

6 괌과 하와이 중 어느 것이 한국에 더 가까운가요? (close)
→ ________________________ to Korea, Guam or Hawaii?

7 네가 더 오래 잘수록 너는 더 피곤해질 것이다. (long, tired)
→ ______________ you sleep, ______________ you will be.

B 우리말과 일치하도록 ( ) 안에 주어진 단어를 바르게 배열하시오.

1 셰익스피어는 역사상 가장 위대한 작가 중 한 명이다. (one, is, writers, the, of, greatest)
→ Shakespeare ________________________ in history.

2 Paul과 Alice 중 누가 더 어립니까? (younger, Paul, is, or, who, Alice)
→ ________________________?

3 파리는 나의 고향보다 세 배 더 크다. (three, hometown, than, my, times, bigger)
→ Paris is ________________________.

4 그 소설은 점점 더 유명해졌다. (and, more, more, famous, became)
→ The novel ________________________.

5 Jennifer는 나보다 옷에 돈을 두 배 더 많이 쓴다. (much money, as, me, as, twice)
→ Jennifer spends ________________________ on clothes.

6 내가 더 높이 올라갈수록 더 추워졌다. (the, I, climbed, it, became, higher, colder, the)
→ ________________________.

Answer Key p.14

C 표를 보고 ( ) 안의 말을 이용하여 문장을 완성하시오.

[1-3]

City	Seoul	Tokyo	Beijing
Temperature	22°C	28°C	22°C

1 Tokyo is ________________ Beijing. (hot)

2 Beijing is ________________ Seoul. (cool)

3 Tokyo is ________________ city of the three. (hot)

[4-6]

Dog's Name	Buddy	Coco	Nemo
Age	11	14	2
Weight	8 kg	5 kg	2 kg

4 Buddy and Coco have lived ________________ Nemo. (far, long)

5 Coco is ________________ pet of the three. (old)

6 Buddy is ________________ Nemo. (four, heavy)

D 그림을 보고 ( ) 안의 말을 이용하여 문장을 완성하시오.

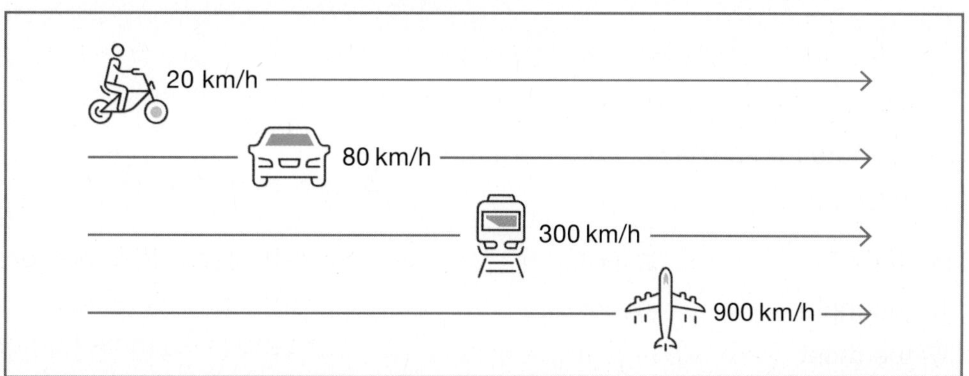

1 The bicycle is ________ ________. (slow)

2 The car is ________ ________ ________ ________ ________ the bicycle. (four, fast)

3 The train is ________ ________ the car. (fast)

4 The plane is ________ ________ ________ ________ the train. (three, fast)

REVIEW TEST

1 다음 중 원급, 비교급, 최상급이 잘못 연결된 것은?

① easy – easier – easiest
② thin – thinner – thinnest
③ weak – weaker – weakest
④ strong – more strong – most strong
⑤ early – earlier – earliest

[2-5] 빈칸에 들어갈 알맞은 말을 고르시오.

2

Jim plays soccer ________ than me.

① well ② good
③ better ④ best
⑤ most

3

His novels are as ________ as his poems.

① difficult ② difficulter
③ difficultest ④ more difficult
⑤ most difficult

4

The more people have, ________ they want.

① much ② more
③ the more ④ most
⑤ the most

5

Who works ________, Max or Ted?

① the hard ② harder
③ the harder ④ hardest
⑤ the hardest

[6-7] 다음 중 어법상 틀린 것을 고르시오.

6 ① She is slimmer than me.
② He is the fastest runner in his class.
③ His smile is as bright as sunshine.
④ It grew bright and bright outside.
⑤ Which is cheaper, going by bus or by train?

7 ① In summer, the days are longer than the nights.
② This car is four as expensive as that one.
③ The faster he spoke, the more confused I got.
④ His illness is getting more and more serious.
⑤ This is one of the most popular books in the store.

8 밑줄 친 단어를 바르게 고친 것으로 짝지어진 것은?

• The pyramid is one of the (A) amazing buildings in Egypt. • Who is (B) most humorous, Bella or Oliver?

	(A)		(B)
①	amazing	…	humorouser
②	more amazing	…	humorouser
③	more amazing	…	more humorous
④	most amazing	…	more humorous
⑤	most amazing	…	humorousest

Answer Key p.14

9 다음 중 밑줄 친 부분을 바르게 고친 것은?

① This is the lightest box in the four.
→ than

② This camera is heavy than that one.
→ heaviest

③ She is as richest as my uncle.
→ richer

④ Which is smaller, your dog and his dog? → or

⑤ Picasso is one of the more famous painters in history. → famous

서술형 빈출

[10-12] 주어진 문장과 의미가 통하도록 ( ) 안의 말을 이용하여 문장을 완성하시오.

10
- Bill spends $30 a week.
- Sam spends $10 a week.

→ Bill spends ______________ Sam. (three, much)

11
- It is 32°C in Paris.
- It is 32°C in Rome too.

→ It is ______________ in Rome as it is in Paris. (hot)

12
- Mike got a 90 on the math test.
- Harry got a 70 on the math test.
- Dean got an 85 on the math test.

→ Mike got ______________ score of the three. (high)

서술형

13 대화를 읽고 비교급을 이용하여 빈칸에 들어갈 알맞은 말을 쓰시오.

A: How old are you?
B: I'm fifteen years old. How about you?
A: I am ________ ________ you. I'm thirteen years old.

14 빈칸에 들어갈 말로 알맞지 않은 것은?

She is ________ taller than her brother.

① even ② far ③ much
④ a lot ⑤ very

15 다음 중 어법상 옳은 것은?

① My brother is twice as old as me.
② The rain grew heavy and heavier.
③ Tom's cat is very bigger than my cat.
④ The more you smile, more people like you.
⑤ He is one of the smartest boy in the school.

서술형

16 표를 보고 ( ) 안의 말을 이용하여 비교급 문장을 완성하시오.

Fruit	Price
an orange	$1.50
an apple	$2.00

→ An orange is ______________ an apple. (cheap)

서술형

17 대화를 읽고 ( ) 안의 말을 이용하여 문장을 완성하시오.

A: The weather is so nice today.
B: Yeah. As the weather is nicer, I feel better than yesterday.
A: Me too.

→ ______________ the weather is, ______________ they feel. (nice, good)

빈출

18 표의 내용과 일치하지 않는 것은?

Name	Height	Weight
Jina	158 cm	48 kg
Hani	155 cm	50 kg
Mina	162 cm	52 kg

① Jina is taller than Hani.
② Mina is lighter than Hani.
③ Hani is heavier than Jina.
④ Mina is the tallest of the three.
⑤ Hani is the shortest of the three.

서술형

[19-21] 우리말과 일치하도록 ( ) 안의 말을 이용하여 문장을 완성하시오.

19 위로 올라갈수록 점점 더 추워진다. (high, cold)

→ ______________ you go, ______________ it gets.

20 이 집은 저 집보다 다섯 배나 더 비싸다. (expensive)

→ This house is ______________________ that house.

21 너는 영화나 뮤지컬 중 어느 것을 더 좋아하니? (much)

→ ______________________, movies or musicals?

22 다음 중 밑줄 친 부분이 잘못된 것은?

① He became more and more confident.
② It snowed much more than last year.
③ His feet are bigger than mine.
④ The more you eat, the more weight you'll gain.
⑤ I play the flute as better as her.

서술형

23 우리말과 일치하도록 주어진 조건에 맞게 문장을 완성하시오.

그 교과서는 공책보다 두 배 더 두껍다.

〈조건〉 1. thick, the notebook, twice를 이용할 것
2. 원급을 이용할 것

→ The textbook ______________________
______________________.

서술형

[24-25] 우리말과 일치하도록 ( ) 안에 주어진 단어를 바르게 배열하시오.

24 그의 영어는 점점 더 나아지고 있다.
(is, better, his, and, better, English, getting)

→ ______________________.

25 Carter는 세계에서 가장 유명한 마술사 중 한 명이다.
(the, is, famous, in, Carter, most, of, world, magicians, the, one)

→ ______________________
______________________.

고난도

26 다음 중 어법상 옳은 것을 모두 고르면?

① She doesn't study as harder as I do.
② Where is nearest bus stop?
③ He can speak English better than me.
④ I feel much best than last week.
⑤ My sister is one of the most popular girls in her school.

27 다음 중 어법상 옳은 것으로 바르게 짝지어진 것은?

a. My eyesight is getting worse and worse.
b. This tower is twice as taller as the building.
c. This desert is one of the driest places on Earth.
d. I don't exercise as often as my brothers do.
e. The farthest you go, the hardest it is to return.

① a, b, c ② a, c, d
③ a, d, e ④ b, c, e
⑤ b, d, e

고난도

28 다음 중 어법상 옳은 것의 개수는?

- Today is as hottest as yesterday.
- China is three times larger than India.
- The more my daughter laughs, the happier I am.
- Pecan pie is the more popular dessert in this restaurant.
- She is one of the greatest artist in the 20th century.

① 1개 ② 2개 ③ 3개
④ 4개 ⑤ 5개

서술형

[29-31] 밑줄 친 부분이 어법상 옳은지 판단하고, 틀리면 바르게 고치시오.

29 The fire is growing large and large.

(O / X) ____________

30 Which season do you like more, summer or winter?

(O / X) ____________

31 Seoul is one of the most crowded city in the world.

(O / X) ____________

서술형 고난도

[32-33] 어법상 틀린 부분을 찾아 바르게 고치시오.

32 My younger brother asks me a lot of questions. Today's question was much more difficult as others. (1개)

33 There are many ways to go to Jeju Island. Taking a ship is cheapest way, but taking an airplane is fast than taking a ship. (2개)

LET'S REVIEW

주요 예문을 다시 한번 확인하고, 우리말과 일치하도록 빈칸을 채우시오.

- Bill is **as tall as** his father. Bill은 그의 아버지만큼 키가 크다. Unit 01 - A
- She can swim [1] ______________ I can. 그녀는 나만큼 빠르게 수영할 수 있다. Unit 01 - A

- Today is [2] ______________ yesterday. 오늘은 어제보다 더 덥다. Unit 01 - B
- This pencil case is [3] ______________ **than** that one. 이 필통이 저것보다 더 비싸다. Unit 01 - B

- Cream pasta is [4] ______________ dish in this restaurant.
  크림 파스타는 이 레스토랑에서 가장 인기 있는 음식이다. Unit 01 - C
- James is [5] ______________ runner of the three.
  James는 그 셋 중에서 가장 빠른 주자이다. Unit 01 - C

- My burger is [6] ______________ **as** yours. 내 버거는 네 것보다 세 배 더 두껍다. Unit 02 - A

- [7] ______________ you study, ______________ your grade will be.
  네가 더 열심히 공부하면 할수록 네 성적은 더 좋아질 것이다. Unit 02 - B

- Laptops are getting **smaller and smaller**. 노트북이 점점 더 작아지고 있다. Unit 02 - C
- It is getting [8] ______________ **difficult** to see the stars.
  별을 보는 것이 점점 더 어려워지고 있다. Unit 02 - C

- [9] ______________ do you like **better**, hip hop ______________ rock music?
  너는 힙합과 록 음악 중에서 어느 것이 더 좋니? Unit 02 - D
- **Who** is **taller**, Tom **or** Jimmy? Tom과 Jimmy 중에서 누가 더 키가 크니? Unit 02 - D

- Cristiano Ronaldo is **one of the** [10] ______________ **soccer** ______________ in the world.
  Cristiano Ronaldo는 세계에서 가장 인기 있는 축구 선수 중 한 명이다. Unit 02 - E

Answers

[1] as fast as [2] hotter than [3] more expensive [4] the most popular [5] the fastest [6] three times as thick [7] The harder, the better [8] more and more [9] Which, or [10] most popular, players

CHAPTER

10

접속사

접속사는 단어와 단어, 구와 구, 절과 절을 연결한다.

UNIT 01

시간, 이유, 결과의 접속사

A 시간을 나타내는 접속사

1 when / as: ~할 때

I was shy **when** I was young.

As I looked at her, she smiled brightly.

2 while: ~하는 동안

I drank a cup of tea **while** I was reading a novel.

ⓘ while은 '~인 반면에'의 의미로 사용되기도 한다.
While I like watching sports, he likes playing them.

3 after / before: ~한 후에 / ~하기 전에

You'll feel better **after** you get some rest.

Let's buy some popcorn **before** we watch the movie.

4 until[till]: ~(할 때)까지

I will wait here **until** he comes back.

ⓘ 시간의 부사절에서는 현재시제가 미래시제를 대신한다.
I'll call you when I **arrive** at the airport. (~~will arrive~~)

B 이유, 결과를 나타내는 접속사

1 because: ~이기 때문에

I wore a coat **because** the weather was cold.

2 as / since: ~이기 때문에(이유가 이미 알려졌을 때 주로 사용)

As[**Since**] he waited for too long, he was angry.

3 so: 그래서

I was late, **so** I took a taxi.

4 so ~ that ...: 매우[너무] ~해서 …하다

This soup is **so** hot **that** I can't eat it now.

CHECK UP 빈칸에 알맞은 말을 고르시오.

1 It was snowing ____________ I got up in the morning.
ⓐ because ⓑ when ⓒ so

2 ____________ he told a lie to me, I don't trust him anymore.
ⓐ As ⓑ When ⓒ While

3 This car is ____________ expensive that I can't buy it.
ⓐ and ⓑ but ⓒ so

PRACTICE

Answer Key p.15

STEP 1

( ) 안에서 알맞은 말을 고르시오.

1 (As, Until) I was really tired, I went to bed early.

2 (While, Since) you were sleeping, he came to see you.

3 The small town was really beautiful, (since, so) I wanted to stay there.

4 She ran so fast (as, that) I couldn't keep up.

5 I will finish my homework before the TV show (will start, starts).

STEP 2

빈칸에 알맞은 말을 보기에서 골라 쓰시오. (단, 한 번씩만 쓸 것)

보기	while	so	that	since	before

1 Wash your face __________ you have breakfast.

2 I was ill, __________ I couldn't attend the meeting.

3 __________ you're busy, I'll call you later.

4 I was cooking __________ she was reading a newspaper.

5 The film was so interesting __________ I watched it several times.

STEP 3

밑줄 친 부분을 어법에 맞게 고치시오.

1 The subway was so crowded as I couldn't take it.

2 Don't go out until I will tell you to.

3 While she was doing the dishes, I clean the living room.

STEP 4

우리말과 일치하도록 ( ) 안의 말을 이용하여 문장을 완성하시오.

1 저녁을 먹고 나서 나는 산책하러 나갔다. (have dinner)

→ I went out for a walk __________ __________ __________ __________.

2 네가 준비가 될 때까지 밖에서 기다리겠다. (be ready)

→ I will wait outside __________ __________ __________ __________.

3 그는 하루 종일 일해서 매우 피곤했다. (work)

→ __________ __________ __________ all day, he was very tired.

4 나갈 때, 문 잠그는 것을 잊지 마라. (leave)

→ __________ __________ __________, don't forget to lock the door.

5 너무 추워서 그들은 밖에 나가지 않았다. (cold)

→ It was __________ __________ __________ they didn't go outside.

UNIT 02

조건, 양보의 접속사 / 명령문 + and, or ~

A 조건을 나타내는 접속사

1 if: ~한다면, ~라면

If you want a good grade, you have to study hard.

2 unless: 만약 ~하지 않으면(= if ~ not)

Unless you call your mom now, she will be very angry.
= **If** you do**n't** call your mom now, ...

ⓘ 조건을 나타내는 부사절에서는 현재시제가 미래시제를 대신한다.
We will have a big party if we **win** the game. (~~will win~~)

B 양보를 나타내는 접속사

though[although]: ~에도 불구하고, 비록 ~지만

Though it rained, the soccer game was not canceled.

C 명령문 + and, or ~

1 명령문, and ~: ~해라, 그러면 …할 것이다

Take the earliest train**, and** you will get there on time.
= **If** you take the earliest train, you ...

2 명령문, or ~: ~해라, 그러지 않으면 …할 것이다

Finish your homework**, or** you can't play the game.
= **Unless** you finish your homework, you ...
= **If** you do**n't** finish your homework, you ...

CHECK UP 빈칸에 알맞은 말을 고르시오.

1 ____________ you get up early, you can see the sunrise.
ⓐ If ⓑ Unless ⓒ Though

2 ____________ she was poor, she tried to help others.
ⓐ If ⓑ And ⓒ Although

3 Push this red button, ____________ the box will open.
ⓐ and ⓑ but ⓒ if

PRACTICE

Answer Key p.15

STEP 1

( ) 안에서 알맞은 말을 고르시오.

1 (Though, If) he is a hundred years old, he is very healthy.
2 (If, Unless) you have any questions, ask me anytime.
3 (If, Unless) you love your work, you won't succeed.
4 Take this bus, (and, or) you'll get to the library.

STEP 2

밑줄 친 부분을 어법에 맞게 고치시오.

1 If I <u>will miss</u> the last train, I will take a taxi.
2 Unless we <u>don't leave</u> now, we'll miss the movie.
3 <u>Followed</u> the rules, or you'll be in trouble.
4 Unless you <u>will study</u> hard, you'll regret it someday.

STEP 3

주어진 문장과 의미가 통하도록 빈칸에 알맞은 접속사를 쓰시오.

1 If you don't make a reservation, you won't get a table.
→ __________ you make a reservation, you won't get a table.
2 I tried my best, but I couldn't win the prize.
→ __________ I tried my best, I couldn't win the prize.
3 If you read a lot of books, you will be wiser.
→ Read a lot of books, __________ you will be wiser.
4 Unless you are careful with that knife, you will get hurt.
→ Be careful with that knife, __________ you will get hurt.

STEP 4

우리말과 일치하도록 ( ) 안의 말을 이용하여 문장을 완성하시오.

1 Jenny를 보면, 나에게 전화하라고 말해라. (see)
→ __________ __________ __________ __________, tell her to call me.
2 네가 조용히 하지 않으면, 아기가 깰 것이다. (unless, be quiet)
→ __________ __________ __________ __________, the baby will wake up.
3 비록 나는 피곤했지만, 그 일을 제시간에 마쳤다. (tired)
→ __________ __________ __________ __________, I finished the work on time.
4 서둘러라, 그러지 않으면 너는 학교에 늦을 것이다. (be)
→ Hurry up, __________ __________ __________ __________ late for school.

GRAMMAR FOR WRITING

A 우리말과 일치하도록 ( ) 안의 말을 이용하여 문장을 완성하시오.

1 네가 전화하기 전에 우리는 점심을 먹었다. (call)
→ We had lunch ________________________.

2 만일 네가 네 계획을 바꾸면, 나에게 알려라. (change, plans)
→ ________________________, let me know.

3 어제는 그의 생일이어서 나는 그에게 선물을 주었다. (give, a present)
→ It was his birthday yesterday, ________________________ to him.

4 그 꿈은 너무 생생해서 나는 그것을 매우 잘 기억할 수 있었다. (vivid, remember)
→ The dream was ________________________ it very well.

5 너의 수업이 끝날 때까지 기다리겠다. (class, be over)
→ I will wait ________________________.

6 나는 베트남을 여행하는 동안 즐거운 시간을 보냈다. (travel)
→ ________________________ in Vietnam, I had a great time.

7 나에게 사실을 말해라, 그러면 내가 너를 용서해 줄 것이다. (forgive)
→ Tell me the truth, ________________________.

B 우리말과 일치하도록 ( ) 안에 주어진 단어를 바르게 배열하시오.

1 나는 그 약을 먹었지만, 여전히 몸이 좋지 않다. (the, took, I, although, medicine)
→ ________________________, I'm still not feeling well.

2 내가 그 방에 들어가자, 모든 사람이 일어났다. (I, entered, as, room, everyone, the)
→ ________________________ stood up.

3 일요일이었기 때문에 그 가게는 문을 닫았다. (shop, was, Sunday, it, was, since, the)
→ ________________________ closed.

4 점심을 다 먹은 후 그는 설거지를 할 것이다. (finishes, wash, lunch, he, will, he, after)
→ ________________________ the dishes.

5 영수증을 가져오지 않으면, 너는 환불을 받을 수 없다. (you, receipt, unless, bring, can't, the, you)
→ ________________________ get a refund.

6 네 코트를 입어라, 그러지 않으면 감기에 걸릴 것이다. (will, or, coat, put on, you, your)
→ ________________________ catch a cold.

Answer Key p.15

C 자연스러운 문장이 되도록 빈칸에 알맞은 말을 보기에서 골라 쓰시오. (단, 한 번씩만 쓸 것)

보기		
	say sorry to him	moved to Paris
	see this photo	taste better
	stayed at home all day	was cooking in the kitchen

1 I was sick, so I ______________________.

2 Ron lived in Seoul before he ______________________.

3 They'll be surprised if they ______________________.

4 Add more salt into the soup, and it'll ______________________.

5 Unless you ______________________, he won't talk to you again.

6 While my aunt ______________________, I took care of her baby.

D 그림을 보고 보기1에 주어진 접속사와 보기2에 주어진 표현을 이용하여 문장을 완성하시오.

1 

2 

3 

4 

보기 1	before	that	until	when

보기 2		
	cry a lot	stop raining
	watch the movie	get out of the movie theater

1 Mia and I bought some popcorn and drinks ______________________.

2 The movie was so touching ______________________.

3 ______________________, it suddenly started to rain.

4 As we didn't have an umbrella, we waited ______________________.

REVIEW TEST

[1-5] 빈칸에 들어갈 알맞은 말을 고르시오.

1

I listened to the radio ________ I was driving to work.

① so　② that
③ though　④ while
⑤ if

2

________ she didn't understand the book well, she kept reading it.

① That　② Though
③ Unless　④ When
⑤ If

3

It was too late, ________ I couldn't call you.

① while　② so
③ as　④ since
⑤ because

4

This cat is so cute ________ I can't stop looking at him.

① as　② if
③ that　④ while
⑤ although

5

Visit our website, ________ you'll get useful information.

① and　② or　③ but
④ if　⑤ unless

6 다음 중 밑줄 친 부분이 자연스럽지 않은 것은?

① Though I didn't have money, I went shopping.
② As there was a lot of traffic, she was late.
③ He completed his painting after he died.
④ When you go abroad, you need a passport.
⑤ The weather is so hot that I can't go outside.

7 다음 중 어법상 틀린 것은?

① Though he is thin, he is very strong.
② Ask her, and you'll get the answer.
③ If he will tell a lie, he will be punished.
④ Please help me when you finish your work.
⑤ As I didn't know what to say, I said nothing.

8 세 문장의 의미가 비슷하도록 할 때, 빈칸에 들어갈 말이 순서대로 바르게 짝지어진 것은?

Study hard, or you will fail the exam. → ________ you don't study hard, you will fail the exam. → ________ you study hard, you will fail the exam.

① If – Though
② When – Unless
③ Unless – When
④ If – Unless
⑤ When – Although

빈출

9 밑줄 친 접속사의 의미가 나머지 넷과 다른 것은?

① As it rained, the picnic was canceled.
② As I entered the house, it was dark.
③ As he lives near me, I often meet him.
④ As Nick had a headache, he stayed in bed.
⑤ As the box was heavy, I couldn't move it.

10 빈칸에 들어갈 접속사가 나머지 넷과 다른 것은?

① ________ you take a nap, you'll feel better.
② ________ you need my help, tell me anytime.
③ ________ you don't get up, you can't see him.
④ ________ it snows tomorrow, I won't drive my car.
⑤ ________ you set the alarm, you won't be able to wake up at seven.

서술형 빈출

[11-13] 주어진 문장과 의미가 통하도록 빈칸에 알맞은 말을 쓰시오.

11 I opened the door after I knocked.

→ I knocked ________ I opened the door.

12 If you turn left, you'll see the art gallery.

→ Turn left, ________ you'll see the art gallery.

13 Hannah enjoys iced tea, but I like hot tea.

→ ________ Hannah enjoys iced tea, I like hot tea.

14 다음 우리말을 영어로 잘못 옮긴 것은?

그 케이크는 맛있어서 많은 사람들이 좋아한다.

① The cake is delicious, so many people love it.
② As the cake is delicious, many people love it.
③ Since the cake is delicious, many people love it.
④ Because the cake is delicious, many people love it.
⑤ Though the cake is delicious, many people love it.

서술형

[15-16] 밑줄 친 부분을 어법에 맞게 고치시오.

15
A: It is raining.
B: It looks like a shower. It'll stop soon. Let's wait here until it will stop.
A: Okay.

16
A: My computer is broken. What should I do?
B: Ask Timmy. He knows computers well. Unless he is not busy, he will be able to help you.
A: Thanks.

고난도

17 다음 중 어느 빈칸에도 들어갈 수 없는 것은?

> Michael left the office late ___ⓐ___ he had a lot of work. It was nearly midnight ___ⓑ___ he arrived home. He watched a movie ___ⓒ___ it was late. The next morning, he was so tired ___ⓓ___ he missed his alarm!

① that ② unless
③ because ④ though
⑤ when

18 다음 중 밑줄 친 부분을 바르게 고친 것은?

① You can come to my new house after I will move. → will be moving
② Daisy was so thirsty than she drank juice. → because
③ Go travel, or you will experience many things. → that
④ If she will see your gift, she'll be amazed. → sees
⑤ As I looked everywhere, I couldn't find my key. → Since

서술형

[19-20] 빈칸에 공통으로 들어갈 접속사를 쓰시오.

19
- ________ I didn't have breakfast, I'm very hungry.
- ________ I looked out the window, the sun started to rise.

20
- Brian read a magazine ________ he was waiting.
- ________ I like listening to music, he likes singing.

서술형

[21-22] 우리말과 일치하도록 ( ) 안의 말을 이용하여 문장을 완성하시오.

21 나는 내 꿈이 이루어질 때까지 포기하지 않을 것이다. (dream, come true)

→ I will never give up ________________
________________.

22 조심해라, 그러지 않으면 너는 실수를 저지를 것이다. (make a mistake)

→ Be careful, ________________.

서술형

[23-25] 우리말과 일치하도록 ( ) 안에 주어진 단어를 바르게 배열하시오.

23 Jimmy가 돌아온 후에 함께 저녁을 먹자. (comes, Jimmy, dinner, together, have, after, back)

→ Let's ________________
________________.

24 그녀의 아들이 아팠기 때문에 그녀는 그가 걱정되었다. (was, son, worried, her, was, sick, she, since)

→ ________________
about him.

25 그 아이는 너무 무서워서 소리를 질렀다. (scared, that, so, screamed, he)

→ The kid was ________________.

고난도

26 다음 중 어법상 옳은 것을 모두 고르면?

① I stirred the soup until it boiled.
② We will play outside if it won't rain tomorrow.
③ Unless you don't get up early, you'll be late.
④ I was so angry that I hung up the phone.
⑤ Drink enough water, and you'll get healthier.

27 다음 중 어법상 옳은 것으로 바르게 짝지어진 것은?

a. Unless you take this bus, you won't arrive on time.
b. Kate skipped lunch since she was very busy.
c. Review today's lesson, and you can't do well on the quiz tomorrow.
d. The weather was too hot that I wore shorts.
e. While Dad watched a baseball game, I played computer games.

① a, b, c ② a, b, d
③ a, b, e ④ b, c, e
⑤ b, d, e

고난도

28 다음 중 어법상 옳은 것의 개수는?

- Don't open your eyes until I tell you.
- As I missed Emily, I didn't keep in touch with her.
- Unless you eat something now, you will be hungry later.
- Finish your vegetables, and I will give you some dessert.
- Though it rained, the tennis match was canceled.

① 1개 ② 2개 ③ 3개
④ 4개 ⑤ 5개

서술형

[29-31] 밑줄 친 부분이 어법상 옳은지 판단하고, 틀리면 바르게 고치시오.

29 Jacob studied so hard that he got a scholarship.

(O / X) ____________

30 I will work on my homework until my mom will come back.

(O / X) ____________

31 He looked very hungry, but we gave him something to eat.

(O / X) ____________

서술형 고난도

[32-33] 어법상 틀린 부분을 찾아 바르게 고치시오.

32 Although I flipped the switch, the light didn't turn on. The room was very dark that I couldn't see anything. (1개)

33 There was a huge desk in front of the door, so I almost fell over it when I came in. If we move it, someone will get hurt. (1개)

LET'S REVIEW

주요 예문을 다시 한번 확인하고, 우리말과 일치하도록 빈칸을 채우시오.

- I was shy **when** I was young. 나는 어렸을 때 수줍음이 많았다. Unit 01 - A
- [1] ________ I looked at her, she smiled brightly.
  내가 그녀를 보았을 때 그녀는 환하게 웃었다. Unit 01 - A
- I drank a cup of tea **while** I was reading a novel. 나는 소설을 읽는 동안 차 한 잔을 마셨다. Unit 01 - A
- You'll feel better **after** you get some rest. 너는 휴식을 좀 취한 후에 더 나아질 것이다. Unit 01 - A
- Let's buy some popcorn **before** we watch the movie.
  우리 영화를 보기 전에 팝콘을 좀 사자. Unit 01 - A
- I will wait here [2] ________ he comes back.
  나는 그가 돌아올 때까지 여기서 기다릴 것이다. Unit 01 - A

- I wore a coat **because** the weather was cold. 날씨가 추웠기 때문에 나는 코트를 입었다. Unit 01 - B
- [3] ________ he waited for too long, he was angry.
  그는 너무 오래 기다렸기 때문에 화가 났다. Unit 01 - B
- I was late, [4] ________ I took a taxi. 나는 늦어서 택시를 탔다. Unit 01 - B
- This soup is [5] ________ hot ________ I can't eat it now.
  이 수프는 너무 뜨거워서 나는 그것을 지금 먹을 수 없다. Unit 01 - B

- [6] ________ you want a good grade, you have to study hard.
  네가 좋은 성적을 원한다면, 너는 열심히 공부해야 한다. Unit 02 - A
- [7] ________ you call your mom now, she will be very angry.
  네가 지금 너희 엄마에게 전화하지 않으면, 그녀는 매우 화가 날 것이다. Unit 02 - A

- [8] ________ it rained, the soccer game was not canceled.
  비가 왔음에도 불구하고, 그 축구 경기는 취소되지 않았다. Unit 02 - B

- Take the earliest train, [9] ________ you will get there on time.
  가장 이른 기차를 타라, 그러면 너는 그곳에 제시간에 도착할 것이다. Unit 02 - C
- Finish your homework, [10] ________ you can't play the game.
  숙제를 끝내라, 그러지 않으면 너는 게임을 할 수 없다. Unit 02 - C

Answers

[1] As[When] [2] until[till] [3] As[Since, Because] [4] so [5] so, that [6] If [7] Unless
[8] Though[Although] [9] and [10] or

CHAPTER 11

관계사

대명사 또는 부사의 역할을 하면서 절을 이끌어 앞의 명사나 대명사에 연결하는 말로, 관계대명사와 관계부사가 있다.

UNIT 01

관계대명사

「접속사 + 대명사」 역할을 하며, 관계대명사가 이끄는 절은 앞의 명사(선행사)를 수식한다.

I have a friend. + He dances very well.

→ I have a friend [**who** dances very well].

선행사	주격	목적격	소유격
사람	who	who(m)	whose
사물, 동물	which	which	whose

A 주격 관계대명사 who, which

I know *a girl* **who** wants to be a news reporter. 〈선행사가 사람〉

← I know a girl. + She wants to be a news reporter.

Mason often visits *blogs* **which** have movie reviews. 〈선행사가 사물〉

← Mason often visits blogs. + They have movie reviews.

B 목적격 관계대명사 who(m), which

I have *an old friend* **who(m)** I've known for ten years. 〈선행사가 사람〉

← I have an old friend. + I've known her for ten years.

The coupon **which** you have is out of date. 〈선행사가 사물〉

← The coupon is out of date. + You have it.

C 소유격 관계대명사 whose

I like *the boy* **whose** hair is brown. 〈선행사가 사람〉

← I like the boy. + His hair is brown.

In Europe, there are *many houses* **whose** roofs are red. 〈선행사가 사물〉

← In Europe, there are many houses. + Their roofs are red.

CHECK UP 빈칸에 알맞은 말을 고르시오.

1 I have an aunt ________ lives in Paris.
ⓐ who ⓑ whom ⓒ whose

2 This is the piano ________ Dad gave to me.
ⓐ whom ⓑ whose ⓒ which

3 Look at the dog ________ tail is very fluffy.
ⓐ who ⓑ whom ⓒ whose

⊕ PLUS : 관계대명사 who vs. 의문사 who

- 관계대명사 who가 이끄는 절은 선행사를 수식한다.
  I know a boy [**who** is good at cooking].
- 의문사 who는 '누가'의 의미이다.
  I know **who** is good at cooking.

PRACTICE

Answer Key p.16

( ) 안에서 알맞은 말을 고르시오.

1 I read a book (which, whose) author is unknown.
2 Ben is my neighbor (who, which) works in a hospital.
3 Jenny read an article (who, which) was written by her friend.
4 Picasso is the famous painter (whose, whom) I like the most.

STEP 2

빈칸에 알맞은 말을 보기에서 골라 쓰시오. (단, 한 번씩만 쓸 것)

보기	who	whom	which	whose

1 She knows a guy ________ job is selling cars.
2 I'll show you the laptop ________ I bought yesterday.
3 He is a baker ________ makes the best apple pie in the world.
4 I remember the boy ________ we saw at the bookstore yesterday.

STEP 3

다음 두 문장을 관계대명사를 이용하여 한 문장으로 쓰시오.

1 Yesterday, I met a girl. + She is from Mexico.
→ ________________________________
2 I want to buy a smartphone. + Its screen is large.
→ ________________________________
3 Mr. Lee is a teacher. + A lot of students respect him.
→ ________________________________
4 The dress is very beautiful. + The actress is wearing it.
→ ________________________________

STEP 4

우리말과 일치하도록 ( ) 안의 말을 이용하여 문장을 완성하시오.

1 그는 자기 어머니에 관한 소설을 썼다. (be)
→ He wrote a novel ________ ________ about his mother.
2 나는 털이 모두 까만 고양이가 한 마리 있다. (fur)
→ I have a cat ________ ________ ________ all black.
3 나는 인도에 사는 사촌에게 선물을 보냈다. (live)
→ I sent a present to my cousin ________ ________ in India.
4 나는 Lily가 좋아하는 그 소년을 본 적이 없다. (like)
→ I haven't seen the boy ________ ________ ________.

UNIT 02

관계대명사 that, what / 관계대명사의 생략

A 관계대명사 that

1 선행사의 종류에 상관없이 주격 혹은 목적격 관계대명사로 쓸 수 있다.

He is the football player **that**[**who**(**m**)] I like the most.
Jim wants to go to the university **that**[**which**] is in Oxford.

2 선행사가 사람과 사물[동물]이거나, 최상급, 서수, the very, the same, the last 등의 수식을 받는 경우, 또는 -thing으로 끝나는 단어 등을 포함하는 경우에는 주로 관계대명사 that을 쓴다.

The drama is about *an old man and a dog* **that** lived on an island.
Jane is wearing *the same dress* **that** I'm wearing.
Buy *anything* **that** you want.

B 관계대명사 what

what은 선행사를 포함하는 관계대명사로서, the thing(s) that[which]의 의미이다.

I didn't hear **what** you just said. Could you repeat it?
= the thing that[which]

C 관계대명사의 생략

1 목적격 관계대명사(who(m), which, that)는 생략이 가능하다.

My father bought me the sneakers (**that**[**which**]) I wanted to have.
This is the house (**that**[**which**]) the singer lives *in*.

ⓘ 목적격 관계대명사절 끝의 전치사는 관계대명사 앞에 둘 수 있는데, 이때는 관계대명사 that을 쓰거나 생략할 수 없다.

This is the house in which the singer lives.
~~This is the house in that the singer lives.~~
~~This is the house in the singer lives.~~

2 「주격 관계대명사 + be동사」는 뒤에 분사구나 형용사구가 올 때 생략이 가능하다.

I know the girl (**who**[**that**] **is**) playing the drums on the stage.

CHECK UP 빈칸에 알맞은 말을 고르시오.

1 The purse ____________ I lost was black.
ⓐ who ⓑ that ⓒ what

2 Ron is the only student ____________ speaks Spanish in class.
ⓐ whom ⓑ that ⓒ what

3 ____________ I really want to do now is sleep.
ⓐ Which ⓑ That ⓒ What

4 The boy ____________ glasses is my cousin.
ⓐ wears ⓑ wearing ⓒ is wearing

PRACTICE

Answer Key p.16

( ) 안에서 알맞은 말을 고르시오.

1 I like movies (that, what) have happy endings.
2 There were a lot of kids (playing, were playing) soccer.
3 Listening to rock music is (that, what) I like best.
4 It is a difficult question (that, what) no one can answer.
5 This is the restaurant in (which, that) I first saw the girl.

STEP 2

다음 문장에서 생략할 수 있는 부분을 찾아 쓰시오. (생략할 수 있는 부분이 없으면 X표 하시오.)

1 This is a film that was made by my favorite director.
2 I don't like people that tell lies to me.
3 The woman to whom Amy is talking is her teacher.
4 This is the job that no one wants to do.
5 I saw an old lady whose hair was all white.

STEP 3

빈칸에 that과 what 중 알맞은 것을 쓰시오.

1 Jake is the only person __________ can help you.
2 __________ is important in my life is my family.
3 These are the cookies __________ my friend made for me.
4 This is __________ I bought for my grandfather's birthday.

우리말과 일치하도록 ( ) 안에 주어진 단어를 바르게 배열하시오.

1 브라질에서 쓰이는 언어는 무엇입니까? (Brazil, language, spoken, in, the)
→ What is ______________________________?
2 내가 좋아하는 과목은 수학과 과학이다. (subjects, I, the, like)
→ ______________________________ are math and science.
3 그녀가 크리스마스에 원하는 것은 인형이다. (what, Christmas, for, wants, she)
→ ______________________________ is a doll.
4 Ian이 모임 장소에 도착했던 첫 번째 사람이었다. (was, the, person, that, arrived, first)
→ Ian ______________________________ at the meeting place.

UNIT 03

관계부사

「접속사 + 부사」의 역할을 하는 말로, 관계부사가 이끄는 절이 형용사처럼 선행사를 수식한다.

ⓘ 관계부사는 「전치사 + 관계대명사」로 바꿔 쓸 수 있다.

when	at/on/in/during which	why	for which
where	at/on/in/to which	how	the way (in which)

A **when:** 시간 (선행사: the time, the day, the year 등)

I can't wait for *the day* **when** my vacation starts.
= on which

← I can't wait for the day. + My vacation starts on that day.

B **where:** 장소 (선행사: the place, the city, the country 등)

I'm looking for *the place* **where** I will stay in Italy.
= at which

← I'm looking for the place. + I will stay at the place in Italy.

C **why:** 이유 (선행사: the reason)

I can't tell you *the reason* **why** I love her so much.
= for which

← I can't tell you the reason. + I love her so much for that reason.

D **how:** 방법 (선행사: the way)

선행사 the way와 관계부사 how는 함께 쓰지 않고 둘 중 하나만 사용한다.

~~This is the way how the story ends.~~

This is **how** the story ends.
= the way in which

= This is **the way** the story ends.

← This is the way. + The story ends in this way.

CHECK UP 빈칸에 알맞은 말을 고르시오.

1 Do you remember the day ____________ we first met?
ⓐ when ⓑ where ⓒ why

2 Austria is a country ____________ a lot of famous musicians were born.
ⓐ when ⓑ where ⓒ why

3 It's rush hour. That is the reason ____________ I want to leave early.
ⓐ where ⓑ why ⓒ how

4 I don't like ____________ he behaves.
ⓐ when ⓑ why ⓒ how

PRACTICE

Answer Key p.17

( ) 안에서 알맞은 말을 고르시오.

1 Tell me the place (when, where) you saw my dog.
2 This is (how, what) I made the seafood spaghetti.
3 Molly may know the reason (how, why) Harper quit her job.
4 It's two o'clock. This is the time (when, why) I always feel sleepy.

STEP 2

빈칸에 알맞은 관계부사를 쓰시오.

1 Shanghai is the city __________ I traveled last summer.
2 Do you know the reason __________ this movie is so popular?
3 I remember the exact date __________ Jake visited my house.
4 I'm worried about __________ he treats his child.

STEP 3

다음 두 문장을 관계부사를 이용하여 한 문장으로 쓰시오.

1 This is the elementary school. + I used to go to the school.
→ ____

2 That is the way. + Harry solved the problem in that way.
→ ____

3 Liz told me the reason. + She left the party early for that reason.
→ ____

4 April 1 is the day. + People play jokes on that day.
→ ____

STEP 4

우리말과 일치하도록 ( ) 안에 주어진 단어를 바르게 배열하시오.

1 뮤지컬이 시작하는 시간을 아니? (starts, when, time, the, musical, the)
→ Do you know ________________________________?

2 그는 나에게 자신이 프랑스어를 공부하는 이유를 말해주었다. (reason, studied, he, the, French, why)
→ He told me ________________________________.

3 나는 네가 네 치마를 샀던 가게에 갈 거야. (where, your, the, you, skirt, shop, bought)
→ I'll go to ________________________________.

GRAMMAR FOR WRITING

A 우리말과 일치하도록 ( ) 안의 말을 이용하여 문장을 완성하시오.

1 Jessica는 나를 잘 아는 오랜 친구이다. (old, know)
→ Jessica is an ______________________________ me well.

2 나는 아버지가 유명한 작곡가인 한 남자를 만날 것이다. (famous, composer)
→ I'll meet a guy ______________________________.

3 그 집은 큰 정원이 있다. 그곳이 내가 찾고 있는 바로 그 집이다. (the very, look for)
→ The house has a big garden. It is ______________________________.

4 Ted는 그가 어제 봤던 뮤지컬에 대해 나에게 말해 줬다. (see)
→ Ted told me about the musical ______________________________.

5 Eric은 서울에서 일을 구했다. 그것이 그가 그곳으로 이사했던 이유이다. (reason, move)
→ Eric got a job in Seoul. That is ______________________________ there.

6 이것이 내가 그 포테이토 피자를 만들었던 방법이다. (make, potato pizza)
→ This is ______________________________.

7 내가 사랑에 빠졌던 그 소녀는 꽃을 좋아했다. (fall in love with)
→ ______________________________ liked flowers.

B 우리말과 일치하도록 ( ) 안에 주어진 단어를 바르게 배열하시오.

1 냉장고 안에 있는 것은 무엇이든 마셔도 된다. (you, that, can, anything, is, drink)
→ ______________________________ in the refrigerator.

2 나는 내가 더 이상 신지 않는 신발을 버릴 것이다. (I, anymore, the, don't, shoes, wear, throw away)
→ I will ______________________________.

3 내일은 2학기가 시작하는 날이다. (the, begins, day, when, the, semester, second)
→ Tomorrow is ______________________________.

4 이곳이 내가 매일 운동하는 그 체육관이다. (gym, exercise, I, where, the, is, this)
→ ______________________________ every day.

5 저기서 커피를 마시고 있는 사람이 나의 부인이다. (drinking, there, the, coffee, over, person)
→ ______________________________ is my wife.

6 Lena의 미소는 아름답다. 그것이 내가 그녀에 대해 좋아하는 것이다. (like, about, what, I, her)
→ Lena's smile is beautiful. That's ______________________________.

Answer Key p.17

C

자연스러운 문장이 되도록 빈칸에 알맞은 말을 보기에서 골라 쓰시오. (단, 한 번씩만 쓸 것)

[1-4]

보기		
	that I didn't agree with	whose job is to design clothes
	which has a lot of vitamin C	that my friend recommended

1 I often eat fruit ________________________________.

2 Ann gave an opinion ________________________________.

3 I watched the movie ________________________________.

4 I have a friend ________________________________.

[5-8]

보기		
	how I got my job	when the car accident happened
	where we can eat Greek food	why I was depressed yesterday

5 This is the restaurant ________________________________.

6 The sad movie was the reason ________________________________.

7 I uploaded my resume online. That is ________________________________.

8 I still remember the day ________________________________.

D

그림을 보고 보기 1에 주어진 관계사와 보기 2에 주어진 표현을 이용하여 문장을 완성하시오.

1 

2 

3 

보기 1	who	what	whose
보기 2	walking the dog	tire is flat	she said to me

1 There's a car ________________________________.

2 I was touched by ________________________________.

3 The boy ________________________________ is my brother.

REVIEW TEST

[1-5] 빈칸에 들어갈 알맞은 말을 고르시오.

1

Tom is the boy ________ is the most popular student in my school.

① who ② whom
③ whose ④ which
⑤ what

2

A koala is an animal ________ lives in Australia.

① who ② whom
③ whose ④ which
⑤ what

3

Stacey is a girl ________ goal is to learn five languages.

① who ② whom
③ whose ④ which
⑤ what

4

That's exactly ________ I wanted to say.

① who ② whose
③ which ④ that
⑤ what

5

Paris is the city ________ the Louvre Museum is located.

① when ② where
③ why ④ how
⑤ which

[6-7] 다음 중 어법상 틀린 것을 고르시오.

6 ① What she said made me angry.
② Logan has a friend whose hair is red.
③ I know a boy that is a big fan of boxing.
④ He is the only boy that knows the answer.
⑤ I sang a song which title was "My Love."

7 ① Tell me the time when the show ends.
② This is the hotel where I want to work.
③ Do you remember the day when we first met?
④ That is the way how I made the salad.
⑤ I don't know the reason why he sold his house.

8 다음 중 빈칸에 that을 쓸 수 없는 것은?

① My father is a man ________ I admire.
② I have the same shoes ________ you have.
③ This is a doll with ________ my sister plays.
④ I have a friend ________ wants to be an actor.
⑤ He is the tallest boy ________ I've ever seen.

빈출

9 밑줄 친 부분의 쓰임이 나머지 넷과 다른 것은?

① Dan is the man who lives next door.
② I know the boy who works here.
③ I don't know who sent me the file.
④ I have a friend who cooks very well.
⑤ The man who is wearing glasses is my teacher.

10 다음 중 밑줄 친 부분을 생략할 수 있는 것은?

① Don't tell anyone what I said.
② Cindy is the girl who I like the most.
③ Joe was the only man that believed me.
④ She bought a shirt whose color was green.
⑤ The people with whom I traveled were nice.

11 다음 중 어법상 옳은 것은?

① Lisbon is the city which my aunt lives.
② The room in where I stayed was dirty.
③ I have a book written in French.
④ I don't know the reason for that they fought.
⑤ The thing what I want to do now is to take a break.

12 빈칸에 들어갈 말이 순서대로 바르게 짝지어진 것은?

- Do you know a quiet place in ______ we can talk?
- Do you know a quiet place ______ we can talk?

① that – which
② where – that
③ which – where
④ which – which
⑤ where – where

13 다음 우리말을 영어로 바르게 옮긴 것은?

그것이 그가 보낸 마지막 메시지이다.

① It's the last message that he sent.
② It's the last message why he sent.
③ It's the last message what he sent.
④ It's the last message whom he sent.
⑤ It's the last message whose he sent.

서술형 빈출

[14-15] 다음 두 문장을 관계사를 이용하여 한 문장으로 쓰시오.

14
- I want to meet the author.
- He wrote the *Dark Tower* series.

→ ______________________________
____

15
- Today is the day.
- My final exams are over on this day.

→ ______________________________
____

서술형

[16-18] 빈칸에 알맞은 관계사를 쓰시오.

16 I visited lots of blogs about traveling in Europe. That is ________ I collected the information for my trip.

17 Look at the baby and the puppy ________ are sleeping side by side. They're so cute.

18 I like November the most. November is the month ________ I was born.

서술형

[19-20] 우리말과 일치하도록 ( ) 안의 말을 이용하여 문장을 완성하시오.

19 젠가는 그 규칙들이 단순한 보드게임이다.
(rule, simple)

→ Jenga is a board game ________ ________ ________ ________.

20 제주도는 내가 이번 여름에 가고 싶은 곳이다.
(want, go)

→ Jeju Island is the place ________ ________ ________ ________ ________ this summer.

서술형

[21-22] 다음 문장에서 생략할 수 있는 부분을 찾아 쓰시오.

21 We saw an elephant that was walking around the fence.

22 I lost the watch that my father bought for me.

서술형

[23-25] 우리말과 일치하도록 ( ) 안에 주어진 단어를 바르게 배열하시오.

23 Jake가 그 소식을 들은 첫 번째 사람이었다.
(news, the, person, that, heard, the, first)

→ Jake was ____.

24 오빠는 내 생일에 내가 가장 필요로 했던 것을 주었다.
(me, needed, what, I, gave)

→ My brother ________________________ the most on my birthday.

25 이곳이 내가 스마트폰을 샀던 가게이다.
(smartphone, in, that, my, I, bought)

→ This is the shop ____.

고난도

26 다음 중 어법상 옳은 것을 모두 고르면?

① I don't trust people whom tell lies.
② I know a man whose job is to dance.
③ I don't believe which you've just said.
④ Is there anything that I can do for you?
⑤ He gave me the book I really wanted to read.

27 다음 중 어법상 옳은 것으로 바르게 짝지어진 것은?

> a. I have a friend which lives in Spain.
> b. That is the cup what I'm looking for.
> c. I have a dog whose fur is brown.
> d. Tom has no one that he can trust.
> e. Mia is looking forward to the day when she will meet her parents.

① a, b, c ② a, b, d
③ a, c, d ④ b, c, d
⑤ c, d, e

고난도

28 다음 중 어법상 옳은 것의 개수는?

> • I need a bag what has many pockets.
> • My dad doesn't like people who are often late.
> • I don't remember the year when I hurt my leg.
> • We hired a man which speaks Spanish very well.
> • Do you know the reason why he left the country?

① 1개 ② 2개 ③ 3개
④ 4개 ⑤ 5개

서술형

[29-31] 밑줄 친 부분이 어법상 옳은지 판단하고, 틀리면 바르게 고치시오.

29 This is the way how I use the coffee machine.

(O / X) ______________________

30 We can go to the restaurant when we celebrated your birthday.

(O / X) ______________________

31 The doctor explained the reason what people get cancer.

(O / X) ______________________

서술형 고난도

[32-33] 어법상 틀린 부분을 찾아 바르게 고치시오.

32 I have been friends with Tom for five years. He is someone whose I can trust in any situation. (1개)

33 King Sejong was a great leader whom made Hangeul for his people. Hangeul is very scientific and logical. (1개)

LET'S REVIEW

주요 예문을 다시 한번 확인하고, 우리말과 일치하도록 빈칸을 채우시오.

- I know a girl **who** wants to be a news reporter. 나는 뉴스 기자가 되기를 원하는 한 소녀를 안다. Unit 01 - A
- Mason often visits blogs [1] ______________ have movie reviews.
  Mason은 영화 리뷰가 있는 블로그들을 자주 방문한다. Unit 01 - A
- I have an old friend [2] ______________ I've known for ten years.
  나는 10년 동안 알고 지낸 오랜 친구가 있다. Unit 01 - B
- The coupon **which** you have is out of date. 네가 갖고 있는 쿠폰은 기한이 지났다. Unit 01 - B
- I like the boy [3] ______________ hair is brown. 나는 머리가 갈색인 그 소년을 좋아한다. Unit 01 - C
- The drama is about an old man and a dog [4] ______________ lived on an island.
  그 드라마는 어느 섬에 살았던 한 노인과 개에 관한 것이다. Unit 02 - A
- Jane is wearing the same dress **that** I'm wearing.
  Jane은 내가 입고 있는 것과 똑같은 드레스를 입고 있다. Unit 02 - A
- I didn't hear **what** you just said. 나는 네가 방금 말한 것을 듣지 못했다. Unit 02 - B
- My father bought me the sneakers (**that**[**which**]) I wanted to have.
  우리 아버지는 내가 갖고 싶어 했던 스니커즈를 내게 사 주셨다. Unit 02 - C
- I know the girl ([5] ______________) playing the drums on the stage.
  나는 무대에서 드럼을 치고 있는 그 소녀를 안다. Unit 02 - C
- I can't wait for the day [6] ______________ my vacation starts.
  나는 내 방학이 시작하는 날을 몹시 기다린다. Unit 03 - A
- I'm looking for the place [7] ______________ I will stay in Italy.
  나는 내가 이탈리아에서 머물 장소를 찾고 있다. Unit 03 - B
- I can't tell you the reason [8] ______________ I love her so much.
  나는 내가 그녀를 정말 많이 사랑하는 이유를 네게 말해줄 수 없다. Unit 03 - C
- This is **how** the story ends. 이것이 그 이야기가 끝나는 방식이다. Unit 03 - D

Answers

[1] which[that] [2] who(m)[that] [3] whose [4] that [5] who[that] is [6] when[on which]
[7] where[at which] [8] why[for which]

CHAPTER

12

가정법

가정법이란 실제 일어나지 않았거나 일어나지 않을 것 같은 일에 대한 가정이나 소망을 표현하는 어법이다.

UNIT 01

가정법 과거, 가정법 과거완료

A 가정법 과거

• 형태: If + 주어 + 동사의 과거형, 주어 + would[could, might] + 동사원형

• 의미: '만일 ~라면 …할 텐데'의 의미로, 현재 사실에 반대되거나 실현 가능성이 없는 일을 가정할 때 쓴다.

If I **had** time, I **could go** to the party.
(← As I don't have time, I can't go to the party.)

If I **won** the lottery, I **would buy** a nice house.

ⓘ 가정법 과거에서 if절의 be동사는 주어의 인칭에 관계없이 were를 쓴다.
If I **were** an adult, I would not have to go to school.

B 가정법 과거완료

• 형태: If + 주어 + had v-ed, 주어 + would[could, might] + have v-ed

• 의미: '만일 ~였다면 …했을 텐데'의 의미로, 과거 사실과 반대되는 가정을 할 때 쓴다.

If I **had taken** the subway, I **would have arrived** on time.
(← As I didn't take the subway, I didn't arrive on time.)

If Mia **had brought** her umbrella, she **wouldn't have bought** another.
(← As Mia didn't bring her umbrella, she bought another.)

CHECK UP 빈칸에 알맞은 말을 고르시오.

1 If Leo liked playing soccer, he __________ with us now.
ⓐ will play ⓑ would play ⓒ would have played

2 If she __________ in Korea, she could come to my wedding.
ⓐ is ⓑ were ⓒ had been

3 If my brother hadn't told me, I __________ my mom's birthday.
ⓐ will forget ⓑ had forgotten ⓒ would have forgotten

4 If I __________ asleep, I could have watched the final game.
ⓐ haven't been ⓑ hadn't been ⓒ wouldn't have been

⊕ PLUS : 단순 조건문 vs. 가정법 과거

• 단순 조건문: 실제로 발생 가능한 일을 가정할 때 쓰인다.
If Bob **joins** our club, we all **will be** happy.
(Bob이 가입을 할지 안 할지 알 수 없음)

• 가정법 과거: 현재 사실의 반대나 실현 불가능한 일을 가정할 때 쓰인다.
If Bob **joined** our club, we all **would be** happy.
(Bob이 가입할 가능성이 희박함)

PRACTICE

Answer Key p.18

( ) 안에서 알맞은 말을 고르시오.

1 Tomorrow is test day. If I (am, were) you, I would study now.

2 If you had gone to the café, you (could see, could have seen) the actor.

3 If Lily had a boyfriend, she (wouldn't be, won't be) alone on Valentine's Day.

4 If I (had gotten, would have gotten) a better grade, my parents would have bought me a new smartphone.

STEP 2

밑줄 친 부분을 어법에 맞게 고치시오.

1 The jeans are too expensive. If I were you, I will not buy them.

2 If it had been cold yesterday, I could go skating on the frozen river.

3 If I speak English fluently, I could make a lot of foreign friends.

4 If Liz heard your problem, she would have given some advice.

STEP 3

다음 문장을 가정법으로 바꿀 때 빈칸에 알맞은 말을 쓰시오.

1 As I am scared of flying, I can't go skydiving.
→ If I ______________ scared of flying, I ______________ skydiving.

2 As I didn't know her number, I couldn't call her.
→ If I ______________ her number, I ______________ her.

3 As I don't know him, I cannot invite him to the party.
→ If I ______________ him, I ______________ him to the party.

4 As the man stole her purse, he went to jail.
→ If the man ______________ her purse, he ______________ to jail.

우리말과 일치하도록 ( ) 안의 말을 이용하여 문장을 완성하시오.

1 내가 18살이라면, 그 영화를 볼 수 있을 텐데. (watch)
→ If I __________ eighteen years old, I __________ __________ the movie.

2 내게 충분한 돈이 있다면, 세계 여행을 할 텐데. (have, enough, travel)
→ If I __________ __________ __________, I __________ __________ around the world.

3 내가 배부르지 않았다면, 그 피자를 먹었을 텐데. (be full, eat)
→ If I __________ __________ __________ __________, I __________ __________ __________ the pizza.

UNIT 02

I wish + 가정법, as if + 가정법

I wish + 가정법

1 I wish + 가정법 과거

- 형태: I wish + 주어 + 동사의 과거형
- 의미: '~라면 좋을 텐데'의 의미로, 현재의 이룰 수 없는 소망을 표현한다.

I wish Tom **didn't have** a girlfriend. I want to be his girlfriend.
(← I'm sorry that Tom has a girlfriend.)

2 I wish + 가정법 과거완료

- 형태: I wish + 주어 + had v-ed
- 의미: '~했더라면 좋을 텐데'의 의미로, 과거 일에 대한 유감이나 아쉬움을 표현한다.

I wish I **had charged** my cell phone last night. It's out of battery.
(← I'm sorry that I didn't charge my cell phone last night.)

B as if + 가정법

1 as if + 가정법 과거

- 형태: as if + 주어 + 동사의 과거형
- 의미: '마치 ~인 것처럼'의 의미로, 현재 사실과 반대되는 내용을 가정할 때 쓴다.

She talks **as if** she **knew** the actress very well.
(← In fact, she doesn't know the actress very well.)

2 as if + 가정법 과거완료

- 형태: as if + 주어 + had v-ed
- 의미: '마치 ~였던 것처럼'의 의미로, 과거 사실과 반대되는 내용을 가정할 때 쓴다.

Jake looks **as if** he **had not been** sick.
(← In fact, Jake was sick.)

CHECK UP 빈칸에 알맞은 말을 고르시오.

1 It is Thursday. I wish today ___________ Sunday.
ⓐ is ⓑ were ⓒ had been

2 I am tired now. I wish I ___________ up late last night.
ⓐ don't stay ⓑ didn't stay ⓒ hadn't stayed

3 Elena acts as if she ___________ our boss, but she is not.
ⓐ be ⓑ were ⓒ had been

4 Ken talks as if he ___________ Europe, but he hasn't been there.
ⓐ visit ⓑ visited ⓒ had visited

PRACTICE

Answer Key p.18

STEP 1

( ) 안에서 알맞은 말을 고르시오.

1 I like Karen, but she doesn't like me. I wish she (liked, had liked) me.

2 I wish I (didn't spend, hadn't spent) so much money at the mall yesterday.

3 My grandmother treats me as if I (were, had been) a kid, but I'm not.

4 She talks as if she (saw, had seen) a ghost, but she hasn't seen one.

STEP 2

밑줄 친 부분을 어법에 맞게 고치시오.

1 I heard the concert was amazing. I wish I went to the concert.

2 Ted doesn't want to do his homework now. He wishes he doesn't have any homework.

3 Chris and I are friends, but he treats me as if I had been his younger sister.

STEP 3

주어진 문장과 의미가 통하도록 빈칸에 알맞은 말을 쓰시오.

1 I'm sorry that I had a fight with my brother.
→ I wish I ________________________.

2 I'm sorry that Susie and I are not in the same class.
→ I wish Susie and I ________________________.

3 In fact, my sister doesn't clean her room every day.
→ My sister talks as if she ________________________.

4 In fact, Gary heard the news.
→ Gary acts as if he ________________________.

STEP 4

우리말과 일치하도록 ( ) 안에 주어진 단어를 바르게 배열하시오.

1 내가 노래를 잘하면 좋을 텐데. (I, were, at, wish, I, singing, good)
→ ________________________.

2 오늘 아침에 우산을 가져왔더라면 좋을 텐데. (I, had, an, wish, I, umbrella, brought)
→ ________________________ this morning.

3 진호는 한국인이지만, 그는 마치 중국 출신인 것처럼 중국어를 한다.
(Chinese, if, he, he, speaks, were, as)
→ Jinho is Korean, but ________________________ from China.

GRAMMAR FOR WRITING

A 우리말과 일치하도록 ( ) 안의 말을 이용하여 문장을 완성하시오.

1 내가 너라면, 그 일을 포기하지 않을 텐데. (be, give up)

→ If I ________________ you, I ________________ the work.

2 나는 매우 피곤하다. 지금 당장 한 시간 동안 잘 수 있으면 좋을 텐데. (wish, sleep)

→ I am very tired. ______________________________ for an hour right now.

3 내가 더 일찍 도착했더라면, 그를 만날 수 있었을 텐데. (arrive, meet)

→ If I ________________ earlier, I ________________ him.

4 햇빛이 너무 강하다. 내 선글라스를 가져왔더라면 좋을 텐데. (bring, sunglasses)

→ The sun is too strong. I wish __________________________________.

5 이 로봇은 마치 사람인 것처럼 말한다. (a human)

→ This robot talks as if ______________________________.

6 네가 서둘렀다면, 그 열차를 탈 수 있었을 텐데. (hurry up, take)

→ If you ________________, you ________________ the train.

7 그녀가 내 충고를 받아들였다면, 실패하지 않았을 텐데. (take, fail)

→ If she ________________ my advice, she ________________.

B 우리말과 일치하도록 ( ) 안에 주어진 단어를 바르게 배열하시오.

1 내가 지금 어른이면 좋을 텐데. (I, a, grown-up, wish, I, were)

→ ______________________________________ now.

2 비가 오지 않았다면, 나는 소풍을 갔을 텐데. (on, I, gone, a, picnic, would, have)

→ If it had not rained, ______________________________________.

3 Anne이 우리와 함께 있다면, 우리는 더 재미있을 텐데. (more, fun, we, have, would)

→ If Anne were with us, ______________________________________.

4 James에게 내 비밀을 말하지 않았더라면 좋을 텐데. (I, told, not, secret, had, wish, my)

→ I ______________________________________ to James.

5 Sarah는 가끔 다섯 살 아이인 것처럼 행동한다. (if, she, behaves, kid, a five-year-old, as, were)

→ Sarah sometimes ______________________________________.

6 그는 마치 스페인에 가 봤던 것처럼 말했지만 그는 거기에 가 본 적이 없다.
(if, to, been, he, he, had, talked, as, Spain)

→ ______________________________________, but he hasn't been there.

Answer Key p.18

C 다음 문장을 가정법으로 바꿀 때 빈칸에 알맞은 말을 쓰시오.

1 I'm sorry that I can't play the drums.
→ I wish I __________ __________ the drums.

2 I don't have a car, so I can't give him a ride.
→ If I __________ a car, I __________ __________ him a ride.

3 I'm sorry that I didn't buy the coat then.
→ I wish I __________ __________ the coat then.

4 As the weather is fine now, we can go for a walk.
→ If the weather __________ fine now, we __________ __________ for a walk.

5 In fact, the accident didn't happen yesterday.
→ I feel as if the accident __________ __________ yesterday.

6 As I didn't miss the bus, I was not late for the meeting.
→ If I __________ __________ the bus, I __________ __________ __________ late for the meeting.

7 In fact, he can't drive a truck.
→ He talks as if he __________ __________ a truck.

D 그림을 보고 ( ) 안의 말을 이용하여 가정법 문장을 완성하시오.

1 2 3

1 If I had enough money, I ____________________. (buy this dress)

2 I wish ____________________. I can't finish the project by the deadline. (have more time)

3 I wish ____________________. It is so cold now. (lose one's gloves)

REVIEW TEST

[1-5] 빈칸에 들어갈 알맞은 말을 고르시오.

1

I have to go now. If I had more time, I ________ longer.

① stay ② stayed
③ had stayed ④ would stay
⑤ would have stayed

2

If I had missed the bus, I ________ the airplane.

① miss ② missed
③ had missed ④ would miss
⑤ would have missed

3

I only have a younger sister, but I wish I ________ an older brother.

① have ② had
③ have had ④ had had
⑤ haven't had

4

I wish I ________ harder when I was young.

① study ② studied
③ have study ④ had studied
⑤ would have studied

5

My teacher loves us as if we ________ his children.

① are ② were
③ had been ④ would
⑤ would have been

[6-7] 다음 중 밑줄 친 부분이 잘못된 것을 고르시오.

6 ① Alice wishes she has long hair.
② He talks as if he had helped us.
③ If I were free, I could visit you.
④ My uncle treats me as if I were a baby.
⑤ If he hadn't come to this city, he couldn't have met me.

7 ① I wish I had a lot of friends.
② Alex talks as if he were married.
③ I wish I had brought my camera with me this morning.
④ If you had a million dollars, what would you do with it?
⑤ If you saw the movie, you would have liked the ending.

빈출

8 다음 문장을 가정법으로 바르게 고친 것은?

Because I came late, I couldn't see Ted.

① If I came late, I couldn't see Ted.
② If I didn't come late, I saw Ted.
③ If I had not come late, I had seen Ted.
④ If I had come late, I couldn't have seen Ted.
⑤ If I had not come late, I could have seen Ted.

빈출

[9-11] 다음 우리말을 영어로 바르게 옮긴 것을 고르시오.

9 내가 19살이라면, 운전면허증을 딸 수 있을 텐데.

① If I am nineteen years old, I can get a driver's license.
② If I was nineteen years old, I got a driver's license.
③ If I were nineteen years old, I could get a driver's license.
④ If I were nineteen years old, I could have gotten a driver's license.
⑤ If I had been nineteen years old, I could have gotten a driver's license.

10 내가 더 일찍 일어났더라면, 나는 아침을 먹었을 텐데.

① If I wake up earlier, I will have breakfast.
② If I woke up earlier, I would have breakfast.
③ If I woke up earlier, I would have had breakfast.
④ If I had woken up earlier, I would have breakfast.
⑤ If I had woken up earlier, I would have had breakfast.

11 내 휴대 전화를 떨어뜨리지 않았더라면 좋을 텐데.

① I wish I drop my cell phone.
② I wish I dropped my cell phone.
③ I wish I didn't drop my cell phone.
④ I wish I had dropped my cell phone.
⑤ I wish I hadn't dropped my cell phone.

서술형

[12-14] ( ) 안의 말을 이용하여 문장을 완성하시오.

12 I already have three cars. I wish I __________ a nice sports car too. (have)

13 You play online games too much. If I __________ you, I wouldn't play online games so much. (be)

14 Laura talks as if she __________ me yesterday. In fact, she didn't call. (call)

서술형

[15-17] 우리말과 일치하도록 ( ) 안의 말을 이용하여 문장을 완성하시오.

15 Brian이 담배를 끊는다면, 그는 더 건강할 텐데. (stop, be)

→ If Brian __________ smoking, he __________ healthier.

16 내가 그에게 사과했더라면, 그가 나를 용서했을 텐데. (apologize, forgive)

→ If I __________ to him, he __________ me.

17 한국 전쟁이 일어나지 않았더라면 좋을 텐데. (happen)

→ I wish the Korean War ____________.

18 다음 중 어법상 옳은 것은?

① I wish I can speak Chinese.
② He talks as if he had written the book.
③ If she have worked harder, she would not have been fired.
④ I wish my friends have not missed my birthday.
⑤ If he had seen you, he will have told you.

서술형

[19-21] 다음 문장을 가정법으로 바꿀 때 빈칸에 알맞은 말을 쓰시오.

19 As I don't have a car, I can't drive you to the airport.

→ If I ____________ a car, I ____________ you to the airport.

20 As Jason lied to me, I didn't trust him.

→ If Jason ____________ to me, I would have trusted him.

21 I'm sorry that winter vacation isn't longer.

→ I wish ____________.

22 빈칸에 공통으로 들어갈 말은?

- If I ____________ you, I would not go to the party.
- Amy walks as if she ____________ a top model, but she is not.

① be ② am ③ is
④ were ⑤ had been

서술형

[23-25] 우리말과 일치하도록 ( ) 안에 주어진 단어를 바르게 배열하시오.

23 Tony는 마치 그 수학 시험이 쉬웠던 것처럼 말한다. (if, the, had, test, math, been, easy, as)

→ Tony talks ____________.

24 내가 그 비싼 코트를 사지 않았더라면 좋을 텐데. (not, the, I, coat, had, expensive, bought)

→ I wish ____________.

25 그녀가 바쁘지 않다면, 우리와 함께 여행 갈 수 있을 텐데. (she, she, could, busy, go, if, weren't)

→ ____________ on the trip with us.

고난도

26 다음 중 어법상 옳은 것을 모두 고르면?

① He talks as if he didn't know me.
② I wish I haven't been here with you.
③ If I didn't live with my family, I would be very lonely.
④ I wish I had spent more time with my grandmother before she died.
⑤ If we hadn't worn dresses, we could have climbed the mountain.

27 다음 중 어법상 옳은 것으로 바르게 짝지어진 것은?

a. I wish I could speak Italian.
b. She acts as if she were my sister.
c. I would have bought a new laptop now if I had enough money.
d. If you knew her, you can introduce her to me.
e. If I had worn a hat, I wouldn't have gotten sunburned.

① a, b, c ② a, b, d
③ a, b, e ④ b, c, e
⑤ b, d, e

고난도

28 다음 중 어법상 옳은 것의 개수는?

- If I drive, I could have arrived sooner.
- I wish I had long hair.
- I wish my family had stayed together.
- If we practiced harder, we could have won last night.
- If I hadn't given up, I would have become a singer.

① 1개 ② 2개 ③ 3개
④ 4개 ⑤ 5개

서술형

[29-31] 밑줄 친 부분이 어법상 옳은지 판단하고, 틀리면 바르게 고치시오.

29 She speaks as if she had known my secret. In fact, she doesn't.

(O / X) ____________________

30 He will call you if he had your phone number.

(O / X) ____________________

31 If I hadn't met you, I would have lived a meaningless life.

(O / X) ____________________

서술형 고난도

[32-33] 어법상 틀린 부분을 찾아 바르게 고치시오.

32 I heard the show was exciting. I wish I went to it. (1개)

33 Next month, I am going to go abroad for college. I am so excited, but my mother is worried about it. She acts as if I am a baby. If I were her, I wouldn't have worried so much. (2개)

LET'S REVIEW

주요 예문을 다시 한번 확인하고, 우리말과 일치하도록 빈칸을 채우시오.

- **If** I [1]____________ time, I ____________ to the party.
  만일 내가 시간이 있다면, 나는 그 파티에 갈 수 있을 텐데. Unit 01 - A
- **If** I [2]____________ the lottery, I ____________ a nice house.
  만일 내가 복권에 당첨된다면, 나는 좋은 집을 살 텐데. Unit 01 - A
- **If** I **had taken** the subway, I [3]____________ on time.
  만일 내가 지하철을 탔다면, 나는 제시간에 도착했을 텐데. Unit 01 - B
- **If** Mia [4]____________ her umbrella, she **wouldn't** ____________ another.
  만일 Mia가 그녀의 우산을 가져왔더라면, 그녀는 또 하나를 사지 않았을 텐데. Unit 01 - B
- **I** [5]____________ Tom ____________ a girlfriend. I want to be his girlfriend.
  Tom이 여자 친구가 없으면 좋을 텐데. 나는 그의 여자 친구가 되고 싶다. Unit 02 - A
- **I** [6]____________ I ____________ my cell phone last night. It's out of battery.
  내가 어젯밤에 내 휴대 전화를 충전했더라면 좋을 텐데. 휴대 전화에 배터리가 없다. Unit 02 - A
- She talks **as if** she [7]____________ the actress very well.
  그녀는 마치 그녀가 그 여배우를 매우 잘 아는 것처럼 말한다. Unit 02 - B
- Jake looks [8]____________ he ____________ sick.
  Jake는 마치 아프지 않았던 것처럼 보인다. Unit 02 - B

Answers

[1] had, could go [2] won, would buy [3] would have arrived [4] had brought, have bought
[5] wish, didn't[did not] have [6] wish, had charged [7] knew [8] as if, hadn't[had not] been

CHAPTER 13

일치와 화법

주절과 종속절은 시제를 일치시킨다.
화법은 말이나 생각을 전달하는 방법으로
직접화법과 간접화법이 있다.

UNIT 01

시제의 일치

A 시제 일치

주절의 시제	종속절의 시제
현재	모든 시제 가능
과거	현재 → 과거
	현재완료, 과거 → 과거완료
	will → would, can → could, may → might, must → must[had to]

1 주절의 시제가 현재인 경우 종속절에는 모든 시제가 올 수 있다.

I *think* that Julie **has** a boyfriend.
I *think* that Julie **had** a boyfriend.
I *think* that Julie **will have** a boyfriend soon.

2 주절의 시제가 과거인 경우 종속절에는 과거 또는 과거완료가 와야 한다.

I *thought* that Max **was** absent from school.
I *thought* that Max **had been** absent from school.
I *thought* that Max **would be** absent from school.

B 시제 일치의 예외

1 과학적 사실, 일반적 진리, 속담 등은 주절의 시제와 상관없이 종속절에 항상 현재시제를 쓴다.

I learned that oil **is** lighter than water. 〈과학적 사실〉
~~I learned that oil was lighter than water.~~
She said that good medicine **tastes** bitter. 〈속담〉
~~She said that good medicine tasted bitter.~~

2 역사적 사실은 주절의 시제와 상관없이 종속절에 항상 과거시제를 쓴다.

My art teacher said that Vincent van Gogh **killed** himself in 1890.
~~My art teacher said that Vincent van Gogh had killed himself in 1890.~~

3 과거의 상황이 현재에도 지속되는 경우, 주절의 시제가 과거이더라도 종속절에 현재시제를 쓸 수 있다.

Kate *said* that she **updates** her blog every day.

CHECK UP

빈칸에 알맞은 말을 고르시오.

1 Long ago, people didn't know that the earth ____________ round.
ⓐ is ⓑ was ⓒ had been

2 I knew that Shakespeare ____________ born in England in 1564.
ⓐ is ⓑ was ⓒ had been

PRACTICE

Answer Key p.19

STEP 1

( ) 안에서 알맞은 말을 고르시오.

1 They said that the baseball game (is, had been) canceled.
2 I didn't know that potatoes (grow, will grow) underground.
3 My teacher said that slow and steady (wins, won) the race.
4 I read that the remote control (was, had been) invented in 1956.

STEP 2

밑줄 친 부분을 어법에 맞게 고치시오.

1 My science teacher said that light moved faster than sound.
2 My father said that a friend in need was a friend indeed.
3 I heard that George Washington had been the first president of the US.

STEP 3

문장의 주절을 과거시제로 바꿀 때, 빈칸에 알맞은 말을 쓰시오.

1 Insu says that the Korean team will win the final game.
→ Insu said that the Korean team __________ the final game.
2 Kevin doesn't know that he lost his cell phone.
→ Kevin didn't know that he __________ his cell phone.
3 The book says that the Second World War started in late 1939.
→ The book said that the Second World War __________ in late 1939.
4 The boy knows that one and one makes two.
→ The boy knew that one and one __________ two.

STEP 4

우리말과 일치하도록 ( ) 안의 말을 이용하여 문장을 완성하시오.

1 모든 사람들이 네가 최선을 다했다는 것을 알고 있다. (do one's best)
→ Everybody knows that ______ ______ ______ ______.
2 Jake는 루브르 박물관이 1793년에 지어졌다고 읽었다. (be built)
→ Jake read that the Louvre Museum ______ ______ in 1793.
3 우리는 뱀들이 겨울 동안 잠을 잔다고 배웠다. (snake, sleep)
→ We learned that ______ ______ during the winter.

UNIT 02

화법

• 직접화법: 다른 사람이 말한 내용을 인용 부호를 이용하여 그대로 전달할 때 쓰는 화법
• 간접화법: 다른 사람이 말한 내용을 전달하는 사람 입장에서 바꾸어 전달할 때 쓰는 화법

A 평서문의 화법 전환 (직접화법 → 간접화법)

① 전달동사를 바꾼다. (say[said] → say[said] / say to[said to] → tell[told])
② 주절의 콤마와 인용 부호를 없애고 접속사 that을 쓴다. (that은 생략 가능)
③ 인용 부호 안의 인칭대명사는 전달자에 맞춰서 바꾸고, 동사도 시제에 맞춰 바꾼다.

Ryan said to me, "I want to invite you to my birthday party." 〈직접화법〉
→ Ryan **told** me (**that**) **he wanted** to invite **me** to **his** birthday party. 〈간접화법〉

B 의문문의 화법 전환 (직접화법 → 간접화법)

1 의문사가 없는 의문문

① 주절의 동사는 ask로 바꾼다.
② 주절의 콤마와 인용 부호를 없애고 접속사 if[whether]를 쓴다.
③ if[whether] 다음의 어순을 「주어 + 동사」로 바꾼다. 인용 부호 안의 인칭대명사는 전달자에 맞춰서 바꾸고, 동사도 시제에 맞춰 바꾼다.

Jay said to me, "Do you like snowboarding?" 〈직접화법〉
→ Jay **asked** me **if[whether] I liked** snowboarding. 〈간접화법〉

2 의문사가 있는 의문문

① 주절의 동사는 ask로 바꾼다.
② 주절의 콤마와 인용 부호를 없애고 의문사를 그대로 쓴다.
③ 의문사 다음의 어순을 「주어 + 동사」로 바꾼다. 인용 부호 안의 인칭대명사는 전달자에 맞춰서 바꾸고, 동사도 시제에 맞춰 바꾼다.

Mia said to me, "Why do you study Japanese?" 〈직접화법〉
→ Mia **asked** me **why I studied** Japanese. 〈간접화법〉

ⓘ 의문사가 주어인 경우에는 「의문사 + 동사」의 어순을 그대로 쓴다.
Tim said to me, "Who made you angry?"
→ Tim asked me **who had made** me angry.

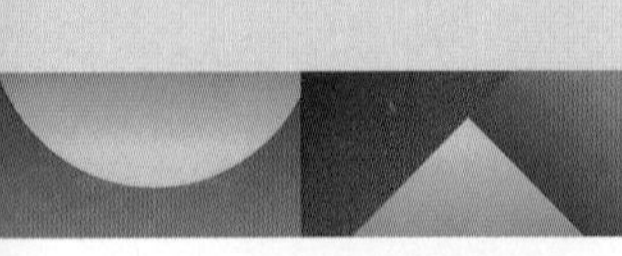

CHECK UP 다음을 간접화법으로 바꿀 때, 빈칸에 알맞은 말을 고르시오.

1 Aaron said to me, "I don't know your phone number."
→ Aaron told me that ____________ phone number.
ⓐ I don't know your ⓑ he doesn't know your ⓒ he didn't know my

PRACTICE

Answer Key p.20

( ) 안에서 알맞은 말을 고르시오.

1 Elijah (said, told) me that he had to work overtime.

2 The boy asked me (if, that) I knew the way to city hall.

3 I asked Jane where (had she bought, she had bought) the mug.

4 The teacher asked us (who had kicked, had who kicked) the trash can.

STEP 2

다음을 간접화법으로 바꿀 때, 빈칸에 알맞은 말을 쓰시오.

1 The weather forecast said, "It will snow on Christmas Day."
→ The weather forecast ______________________________.

2 Sarah said to me, "Do you like musicals?"
→ Sarah ______________________________.

3 I said to Tom, "I have something to tell you."
→ I ______________________________.

4 Harry said to me, "Where are you going?"
→ Harry ______________________________.

5 Tommy said, "I got an F in history."
→ Tommy ______________________________.

6 My boss said to me, "Who sent the fax?"
→ My boss ______________________________.

7 Ted said to me, "Do you want to change the schedule?"
→ Ted ______________________________.

8 I said to Lisa, "How did you make the potato pizza?"
→ I ______________________________.

우리말과 일치하도록 ( ) 안의 말을 이용하여 문장을 완성하시오.

1 Nick은 나에게 좋은 선생님이 되고 싶다고 말했다. (want)
→ Nick ________ me ________ ________ to be a good teacher.

2 Anne은 내게 그녀가 내 공책을 빌릴 수 있는지 물었다. (can, borrow)
→ Anne ________ me ________ ________ ________ ________
________ notebook.

3 그녀가 나에게 왜 그 배우를 좋아하냐고 물었다. (like)
→ She ________ me ________ ________ ________ the actor.

GRAMMAR FOR WRITING

A 우리말과 일치하도록 ( ) 안의 말을 이용하여 문장을 완성하시오.

1 Mike는 나에게 인도 음식을 좋아하는지 물었다. (like)
→ Mike ________________________ Indian food.

2 우리는 물이 100°C에서 끓는다고 배웠다. (boil)
→ We learned ________________________ at 100°C.

3 나는 한국 전쟁이 1950년에 시작됐다고 들었다. (the Korean War, start)
→ I heard ________________________ in 1950.

4 Susie는 언젠가 유럽을 여행하고 싶다고 말한다. (want, travel)
→ Susie says that ________________________ to Europe someday.

5 그 아이는 일본이 섬나라라는 것을 몰랐다. (Japan, be)
→ The child didn't know ________________________ an island country.

6 나는 내 여동생이 어제 내 재킷을 입었다고 생각한다. (my sister, wear)
→ I think ________________________ my jacket yesterday.

7 그들은 나에게 왜 의사가 되고 싶은지 물었다. (want, become)
→ They ________________________ a doctor.

B 우리말과 일치하도록 ( ) 안에 주어진 단어를 바르게 배열하시오.

1 James는 그 영화를 이미 봤다고 내게 말했다. (me, seen, that, had, told, already, he)
→ James ________________________ the movie.

2 그 외국인은 나에게 영어를 할 수 있는지 물었다. (could, me, I, English, speak, asked, if)
→ The foreigner ________________________.

3 할아버지께서는 두 개의 머리가 하나보다 낫다고 말씀하셨다. (that, two, said, are, better, heads)
→ My grandfather ________________________ than one.

4 Ben은 누가 저 큰 집에 사는지 나에게 물었다. (who, in, me, big, that, asked, house, lived)
→ Ben ________________________.

5 나는 피카소가 스페인에서 태어났다고 들었다. (Spain, that, was, heard, born, in, Picasso)
→ I ________________________.

6 엄마가 슈퍼마켓에서 우리 선생님을 만났다고 나에게 말씀하셨다.
(teacher, me, told, she, my, that, had, met)
→ Mom ________________________ at the supermarket.

Answer Key p.20

C 주어진 대화를 간접화법으로 바꿀 때 빈칸에 알맞은 말을 쓰시오.

Mike: **1.** I will go to America to study.
Rosie: **2.** What do you want to study in America?
Mike: **3.** I plan to study marketing.
Rosie: That's great!

1 Mike told Rosie ______________________.
2 Rosie asked Mike ______________________.
3 Mike told Rosie ______________________.

Seth: **4.** Did you hear the noise coming from Maple Street last night?
Lucy: No, I didn't. I went to bed early. **5.** What happened?
Seth: **6.** There was a car accident.

4 Seth asked Lucy ______________________ coming from Maple Street the previous night.
5 Lucy asked Seth ______________________.
6 Seth told Lucy ______________________.

D 그림을 보고 대화를 읽은 뒤 빈칸에 알맞은 말을 써서 문장을 완성하시오.

1
Mia: Can you play the drums?
Liam: No, I can't.

2

Mom: What did you learn today?
Jimin: Humans first landed on the moon in 1969. I didn't know that.

3
Asher: What did you do last weekend?
Luna: I rode a bike along the river.

1 Mia asked Liam ______________________.
2 Jimin learned that ______________________.
3 Luna told Asher ______________________ last weekend.

REVIEW TEST

[1-5] 빈칸에 들어갈 알맞은 말을 고르시오.

1

She thought that Jake ________ in trouble.

① is being ② was
③ were ④ will be
⑤ have been

2

I learned that light ________ faster than sound.

① travel ② travels
③ traveled ④ has traveled
⑤ had traveled

3

The book says the light bulb ________ invented by Thomas Edison.

① be ② is
③ was ④ has been
⑤ had been

4

Tommy asked me ________ I had ever gone scuba diving.

① that ② if
③ unless ④ what
⑤ though

5

Jacob told me that he ________ well soon.

① gets ② will get
③ is getting ④ would get
⑤ has gotten

[6-7] 다음 중 어법상 틀린 것을 고르시오.

6 ① Jessica said that she had a cold.
② I know that she doesn't eat meat.
③ She said that she wakes up at seven.
④ He learned Mars was smaller than Earth.
⑤ I heard that Shakespeare wrote *Hamlet*.

7 ① He asked me if did I like movies.
② She asked me who had broken the glass.
③ Mia asked me where my hometown was.
④ Tom said that he had met Jay on the street.
⑤ He told me that he was looking for his cell phone.

빈출

8 다음을 간접화법으로 바꿀 때, 빈칸에 들어갈 알맞은 말은?

My teacher said to me, "What do you want to be in the future?" → My teacher asked me ________ to be in the future.

① what did I want
② what I wanted
③ what you wanted
④ what did you wanted
⑤ what do I want

Answer Key p.20

빈출

[9-11] 대화를 읽고 빈칸에 들어갈 말이 순서대로 바르게 짝지어진 것을 고르시오.

9

Mira: What is your hobby?
Steve: I like to draw pictures.
→ Steve ________ that ________ to draw pictures.

① said – I liked ② said – he liked
③ told – I liked ④ told – he liked
⑤ asked – I liked

10

Kirk: Do you have a smartphone?
Max: Yes, I do.
→ Kirk ________ Max ________ a smartphone.

① said – if he has
② told – if he had
③ told – if did he have
④ asked – if he had
⑤ asked – if did he have

11

Repairman: When did you buy the computer?
Ann: I bought it two years ago.
→ The repairman ________ Ann ________ the computer.

① said – when she had bought
② told – when did she buy
③ told – when she bought
④ asked – when had she bought
⑤ asked – when she had bought

12 다음 대화의 빈칸에 들어갈 알맞은 말은?

A: When can she start the work?
B: I don't know. She didn't tell me when she ________ it.

① start ② starts
③ can start ④ could start
⑤ has started

서술형

[13-15] 우리말과 일치하도록 ( ) 안의 말을 이용하여 문장을 완성하시오.

13 우리는 지구가 태양 주변을 돈다고 배웠다.
(the earth, move around)

→ We were taught that ________ ________ the sun.

14 그녀는 나에게 내가 나이에 비해 어려 보인다고 말했다.
(look, young)

→ She ________ for my age.

15 그는 나에게 방학 동안 무엇을 할 것인지 물어보았다.
(what, will)

→ He ________ during vacation.

서술형

[16-18] 밑줄 친 부분을 어법에 맞게 고치시오.

16 My friend says that no news <u>was</u> good news.

17 We learned that the First World War <u>had started</u> in July of 1914.

18 I knew that water <u>froze</u> at 0°C.

서술형

[19-20] 다음을 간접화법으로 바꿀 때, 빈칸에 알맞은 말을 쓰시오.

19 He said to me, "I had a fight with my girlfriend."

→ He ______________________________
______________________________.

20 Bill said to me, "What made you think so?"

→ Bill ______________________________
______________________________.

서술형

21 우리말과 일치하도록 주어진 조건에 맞게 문장을 완성하시오.

Amy는 나에게 커피를 원하는지 물어보았다.

〈조건〉 1. want, some coffee를 이용할 것
2. 간접화법으로 쓸 것

→ ______________________________.

서술형

[22-24] 우리말과 일치하도록 ( ) 안에 주어진 단어를 바르게 배열하시오.

22 지훈이는 항상 스쿨버스를 타고 학교에 간다고 말했다. (said, always, he, school, to, goes, that)

→ Jihun ______________________________
by school bus.

23 선생님께서 내게 그 문제를 어떻게 풀었는지 물어보셨다. (solved, asked, the, I, me, problem, had, how)

→ My teacher ______________________________
______________________________.

24 John이 내게 숙제를 끝냈냐고 물었다. (finished, asked, I, had, me, homework, if, my)

→ John ______________________________
______________________________.

25 대화를 읽고 빈칸에 들어갈 알맞은 말을 쓰시오.

Lucas: Amy, do you have any plans for tomorrow?
Amy: Yes. I will go to the baseball stadium.
Lucas: Wow! That sounds exciting.

→ Amy told Lucas ______________________________
______________________________ the next day.

고난도

26 다음 중 어법상 옳은 것을 모두 고르면?

① I thought she wouldn't like me.
② I asked him what had he had for dinner.
③ My dad says that blood was thicker than water.
④ My teacher said that Napoleon had become Emperor of France in 1804.
⑤ I didn't know you go swimming every morning.

27 다음 중 어법상 옳은 것으로 바르게 짝지어진 것은?

a. She said that she had seen me at the department store.
b. David asked me that I played any musical instrument.
c. Emma told me that she wanted to be a ballerina.
d. Phil asked me how long had I known Jane.
e. The police officer asked us who had called the police.

① a, b, c ② a, c, d
③ a, c, e ④ b, c, d
⑤ b, c, e

고난도

28 다음 중 어법상 옳은 것의 개수는?

• My father realized that he had left the door open.
• I thought that my sister would be a great scientist.
• Jane asked me what had I done on my vacation.
• I heard that Yun Dong-ju had died at the age of twenty-seven.
• He told me that he had a headache.

① 1개 ② 2개 ③ 3개
④ 4개 ⑤ 5개

서술형

[29-31] 밑줄 친 부분이 어법상 옳은지 판단하고, 틀리면 바르게 고치시오.

29 I learned that Antarctica was colder than the Arctic.

(O / X) ______________________

30 She asked me what flower did I like best.

(O / X) ______________________

31 Gary asked me which team had won the match.

(O / X) ______________________

서술형 고난도

[32-33] 어법상 틀린 부분을 찾아 바르게 고치시오.

32 Timmy told me that he will go to the movies after school. (1개)

33 When I met the couple two years ago, they said that they have been married for five years. I also told them if they had children. (2개)

LET'S REVIEW

주요 예문을 다시 한번 확인하고, 우리말과 일치하도록 빈칸을 채우시오.

- I think that Julie [1] ______________ a boyfriend. 나는 Julie가 남자 친구가 있었다고 생각한다. Unit 01 - A
- I think that Julie **will have** a boyfriend soon. 나는 Julie가 곧 남자 친구가 생길 거라고 생각한다. Unit 01 - A
- I thought that Max **had been** absent from school. 나는 Max가 학교에 결석했었다고 생각했다. Unit 01 - A
- I thought that Max [2] ______________ absent from school.
  나는 Max가 학교에 결석할 거라고 생각했다. Unit 01 - A

- I learned that oil [3] ______________ lighter than water.
  나는 기름이 물보다 더 가볍다고 배웠다. Unit 01 - B
- She said that good medicine **tastes** bitter. 그녀는 좋은 약은 더 쓰다고 말했다. Unit 01 - B
- My art teacher said that Vincent van Gogh [4] ______________ himself in 1890.
  나의 미술 선생님은 빈센트 반 고흐가 1890년에 자살했다고 말했다. Unit 01 - B
- Kate said that she **updates** her blog every day.
  Kate는 자신의 블로그를 매일 업데이트한다고 말했다. Unit 01 - B

- Ryan said to me, "I want to invite you to my birthday party."
  Ryan은 나에게 "나는 너를 내 생일 파티에 초대하고 싶어."라고 말했다.

  → Ryan [5] ______________ me **that he** ______________ to invite ______________ to ______________ birthday party.

  Ryan은 나에게 그가 나를 그의 생일 파티에 초대하고 싶다고 말했다. Unit 02 - A

- Jay said to me, "Do you like snowboarding?"
  Jay는 나에게 "너는 스노보드 타는 것을 좋아하니?"라고 말했다.

  → Jay [6] ______________ me ______________ snowboarding.

  Jay는 나에게 내가 스노보드 타는 것을 좋아하는지 물었다. Unit 02 - B

- Mia said to me, "Why do you study Japanese?" Mia는 나에게 "너는 왜 일본어를 공부하니?"라고 말했다.

  → Mia [7] ______________ me ______________ Japanese.

  Mia는 나에게 내가 왜 일본어를 공부하는지 물었다. Unit 02 - B

Answers

[1] had [2] would be [3] is [4] killed [5] told, wanted, me, his [6] asked, if[whether] I liked
[7] asked, why I studied

MEMO

MEMO

MEMO

MEMO

MEMO

지은이

NE능률 영어교육연구소

NE능률 영어교육연구소는 혁신적이며 효율적인 영어 교재를 개발하고
영어 학습의 질을 한 단계 높이고자 노력하는 NE능률의 연구조직입니다.

GRAMMAR Inside 〈Level 2〉

펴 낸 이 주민홍
펴 낸 곳 서울특별시 마포구 월드컵북로 396(상암동) 누리꿈스퀘어 비즈니스타워 10층
㈜NE능률 (우편번호 03925)
펴 낸 날 2022년 1월 5일 개정판 제1쇄 발행
2024년 8월 15일 제17쇄
전 화 02 2014 7114
팩 스 02 3142 0356
홈페이지 www.neungyule.com
등록번호 제1-68호
I S B N 979-11-253-3708-9 53740
정 가 15,500원

NE 능률

고객센터

교재 내용 문의: contact.nebooks.co.kr (별도의 가입 절차 없이 작성 가능)
제품 구매, 교환, 불량, 반품 문의: 02-2014-7114
☎ 전화문의는 본사 업무시간 중에만 가능합니다.

NE능률 교재 MAP

문법 구문 서술형

아래 교재 MAP을 참고하여 본인의 현재 혹은 목표 수준에 따라 교재를 선택하세요.
NE능률 교재들과 함께 영어실력을 쑥쑥~ 올려보세요!
MP3 등 교재 부가 학습 서비스 및 자세한 교재 정보는 www.nebooks.co.kr 에서 확인하세요.

초1-2

초3
- 그래머버디 1
- 초등영어 문법이 된다 Starter 1

초3-4
- 그래머버디 2
- 초등영어 문법이 된다 Starter 2
- 초등 Grammar Inside 1
- 초등 Grammar Inside 2

초4-5
- 그래머버디 3
- Grammar Bean 1
- Grammar Bean 2
- 초등영어 문법이 된다 1
- 초등 Grammar Inside 3
- 초등 Grammar Inside 4

초5-6
- Grammar Bean 3
- Grammar Bean 4
- 초등영어 문법이 된다 2
- 초등 Grammar Inside 5
- 초등 Grammar Inside 6

초6-예비중
- 능률중학영어 예비중
- Grammar Inside Starter
- 원리를 더한 영문법 STARTER

중1
- 능률중학영어 중1
- Grammar Zone 입문편
- Grammar Zone 워크북 입문편
- 1316 Grammar 1
- 문제로 마스터하는 중학영문법 1
- Grammar Inside 1
- 열중 16강 문법 1
- 쓰기로 마스터하는 중학서술형 1학년
- 중학 천문장 1

중1-2
- 능률중학영어 중2
- 1316 Grammar 2
- 문제로 마스터하는 중학영문법 2
- Grammar Inside 2
- 열중 16강 문법 2
- 원리를 더한 영문법 1
- 중학영문법 총정리 모의고사 1
- 중학 천문장 2

중2-3
- Grammar Zone 기초편
- Grammar Zone 워크북 기초편
- 1316 Grammar 3
- 원리를 더한 영문법 2
- 중학영문법 총정리 모의고사 2
- 쓰기로 마스터하는 중학서술형 2학년
- 중학 천문장 3

중3
- 능률중학영어 중3
- 문제로 마스터하는 중학영문법 3
- Grammar Inside 3
- 열중 16강 문법 3
- 중학영문법 총정리 모의고사 3
- 쓰기로 마스터하는 중학서술형 3학년

예비고-고1
- 문제로 마스터하는 고등영문법
- 올클 수능 어법 start
- 천문장 입문

고1
- Grammar Zone 기본편 1
- Grammar Zone 워크북 기본편 1
- Grammar Zone 기본편 2
- Grammar Zone 워크북 기본편 2
- 필히 통하는 고등 영문법 기본편
- 필히 통하는 고등 서술형 기본편
- 천문장 기본

고1-2
- 필히 통하는 고등 영문법 실력편
- 필히 통하는 고등 서술형 실전편
- TEPS BY STEP G+R Basic

고2-3
- Grammar Zone 종합편
- Grammar Zone 워크북 종합편
- 올클 수능 어법 완성
- 천문장 완성

고3

수능 이상/ 토플 80-89 · 텝스 600-699점
- TEPS BY STEP G+R 1

수능 이상/ 토플 90-99 · 텝스 700-799점
- TEPS BY STEP G+R 2

수능 이상/ 토플 100 · 텝스 800점 이상
- TEPS BY STEP G+R 3

workbook

GRAMMAR Inside

LEVEL 2

A 4-level grammar course
with abundant writing practice

NE Neungyule

CONTENTS

01 문장의 성분

A

주어에는 O표를 하고, 동사에는 밑줄을 그으시오.

1 Cats eat fish.

2 You should go home now.

3 The picture was painted by Edward Munch.

4 His grandparents took care of him.

5 My love for my family will last forever.

6 Exercising every day keeps me healthy.

7 You and I have to finish this together.

8 My younger sister laughed at the story.

9 That he didn't receive my letter must be a lie.

10 What she borrowed from me was some books.

B

밑줄 친 부분의 문장 성분을 보기에서 골라 쓰시오.

보기	주어	동사	목적어	보어	수식어

1 Daniel studies very hard.

2 We must follow the rules.

3 I go to church on Sundays.

4 This bus goes to the station.

5 Logan asked me to speak nicely.

6 My sister wants to be a lawyer.

7 The girl became a hairdresser.

8 I must finish my homework today.

9 The book is popular among teenagers.

10 I look forward to seeing my favorite singer.

Answer Key p.24

02 품사

A

다음 중 품사가 다른 하나를 고르시오.

1 about, look, take, teach, leave, find

2 special, easy, great, always, warm

3 slowly, really, salt, forever, twice

4 mountain, airplane, hobby, listen, house

5 night, grandmother, pretty, week, picture

6 impossible, pleasant, young, beautiful, language

7 in, under, without, oh, for, during, before

8 I, they, it, me, those, her, this, his, the

9 and, after, if, or, so, when, with

10 oh, oops, bravo, wow, now

B

밑줄 친 부분의 품사를 보기에서 골라 쓰시오.

보기	명사	대명사	동사	형용사	부사	전치사	접속사	감탄사

1 This is my grandfather.

2 What can I do for you?

3 Oh, look at the cute baby!

4 They are going to Spain next week.

5 Which do you prefer, coffee or tea?

6 I enjoy drinking hot cocoa in winter.

7 I like to ride bikes.

8 Luckily, we have found your lost dog.

9 My brother plays the violin well.

10 Charlotte lived in Seattle when she was a child.

03 구와 절

A 밑줄 친 부분이 구인지 또는 절인지 쓰시오.

1 Her son is really cute.
2 The hat on the desk is not yours.
3 They say that Jonathan is honest.
4 The black cat followed my brother.
5 Would you like something to drink?
6 I waited until my parents came home.
7 He was my best friend when I was young.
8 Joyce doesn't wake up early in the morning.
9 The woman who is smiling at me is my mom.
10 She doesn't know that you are older than her.

B 자연스러운 문장이 되도록 두 절을 연결하시오.

1 Are you sure •	• a. but she doesn't like candy.
2 I took a shower •	• b. because he is kind.
3 Amelia has a dog, •	• c. and it is eight years old.
4 This is the house •	• d. if you don't mind.
5 Yuna likes chocolate, •	• e. until she comes back.
6 I will wait for her •	• f. that my grandparents live in.
7 Jacob was hungry, •	• g. that he forgot my birthday.
8 It made me sad •	• h. so he ordered a sandwich.
9 Everyone likes him •	• i. that you can do it by yourself?
10 Please open the window •	• j. after I played soccer.

UNIT 01

감각동사와 수여동사

Answer Key p.24

A

( ) 안에서 알맞은 말을 고르시오.

1 Your mother looks (young, like young).

2 This chocolate cake tastes (sweet, sweetly).

3 I will buy (my son a bike, a bike my son).

4 This bread smells (fresh, freshly).

5 He showed his photo albums (me, to me).

6 Please get the baby (a doll, for a doll).

7 My father made a toy car (to, for) me.

8 That idea sounds (good, well) to me.

9 The police asked (her, of her) some questions.

10 Dean sent an email (to, for) his boss.

B

두 문장의 의미가 같도록 빈칸에 알맞은 말을 쓰시오.

1 My grandfather gave my brother some advice.
→ My grandfather gave some advice ________________.

2 I got my younger sister the concert tickets.
→ I got the concert tickets ________________.

3 He sent his daughter some science books.
→ He sent some science books ________________.

4 He taught us a few good lessons.
→ He taught a few good lessons ________________.

5 May I ask you a favor?
→ May I ask a favor ________________?

6 I showed her the letter from my parents.
→ I showed the letter from my parents ________________.

7 She bought her mother leather boots.
→ She bought leather boots ________________.

C 밑줄 친 부분을 어법에 맞게 고치시오.

1 I will show the book for you.
2 The actor's new hairstyle looks greatly.
3 The milk smells badly. Don't drink it.
4 I will give my brother to some money.
5 That cotton sheet feels softly.
6 My brother lent his laptop of me.
7 This hot dog tastes really terribly.
8 The melody of the song sounds beautifully.
9 He taught table manners for us.
10 The reporter asked to me many questions.

D 빈칸에 알맞은 전치사를 쓰시오.

1 This fish looks __________ a snake.
2 He got some free coupons __________ me.
3 I gave my old toys and books __________ my little brother.
4 He told the truth __________ me last night.
5 The old man asked a favor __________ me a few minutes ago.
6 My mother will buy a new suit __________ me.
7 When we visited her house, she made coffee __________ us.
8 I wrote a letter __________ my brother in the army.
9 Please send a text message __________ your parents.
10 My neighbor lent the hammer __________ me.

WRITING PRACTICE

Answer Key p.24

A 우리말과 일치하도록 ( ) 안의 말을 이용하여 문장을 완성하시오.

1 너의 노트북 컴퓨터는 무거워 보인다. (heavy)

→ Your laptop ______________________.

2 나는 그녀에게 아름다운 목걸이를 빌려주었다. (lend, a beautiful necklace)

→ I ______________________ her.

3 한국의 전통 음식은 환상적인 맛이 난다. (fantastic)

→ Traditional Korean food ______________________.

4 엄마가 나에게 긴 드레스를 사주셨다. (a long dress)

→ Mom ______________________.

5 이 초콜릿 쿠키들은 달콤한 향이 난다. (sweet)

→ These chocolate cookies ______________________.

6 그가 그녀에게 자신의 사물함 열쇠를 주었다. (his locker key)

→ He ______________________.

B 우리말과 일치하도록 ( ) 안에 주어진 단어를 바르게 배열하시오.

1 나는 그녀에게 유행하는 티셔츠 하나를 사주었다. (her, T-shirt, bought, trendy, a)

→ I ______________________.

2 Caroline은 정말 졸려 보였다. (looked, sleepy, really)

→ Caroline ______________________.

3 기자가 그들에게 그 행사에 대해 다양한 질문을 했다. (questions, them, asked, various)

→ A reporter ______________________ about the event.

4 이 포테이토 피자는 맛있는 냄새가 난다. (delicious, this, smells, potato pizza)

→ ______________________.

5 그녀는 그녀의 고객에게 잘못된 제품을 보냈다. (sent, the, customer, wrong, to, her, product)

→ She ______________________.

6 내 남자친구는 나에게 많은 편지를 썼다. (me, lots of, wrote, letters, to)

→ My boyfriend ______________________.

UNIT 02

목적격 보어를 가지는 동사

A

( ) 안에서 알맞은 말을 고르시오.

1 My English teacher had us (study, to study) for the exam.
2 I saw a woman (to take, taking) someone's bag.
3 Betty asked me (come, to come) over to her house.
4 I found these tools very (useful, usefully).
5 Babies always make me (smile, smiled).
6 I want you (listen, to listen) to me.
7 I heard the people (sing, to sing) songs at night.
8 I'll let my son (go, to go) to the summer camp.
9 They call him (a hero, as a hero).
10 They don't allow me (entering, to enter) the room.

B

밑줄 친 부분을 어법에 맞게 고치시오.

1 I smelled something to burn in the kitchen.
2 They named the parrot to Harry.
3 My father told me study harder.
4 She let her daughter taking a trip to France.
5 I saw her to fight with her boyfriend.
6 Mom got me going to the party.
7 We should keep this food freshly.
8 Kevin asked me helping him.
9 Brian helped me moving my desk.
10 My teacher advised us take notes in class.

Answer Key p.24

C

( ) 안의 말을 이용하여 문장을 완성하시오.

1 Let me ______________ you something important. (tell)

2 My parents got me ______________ home early. (come)

3 I want you ______________ early. (get up)

4 She asked me ______________ the volume. (turn down)

5 She had him ______________ her computer. (repair)

6 The teacher watched us ______________ the exam. (take)

7 He helped me ______________ my cat. (find)

8 I saw them ______________ rope on the playground. (jump)

9 They expect us ______________ something different. (do)

10 He didn't let us ______________ his picture. (take)

D

빈칸에 알맞은 말을 보기에서 골라 쓰시오. (단, 한 번씩만 쓸 것)

[1-3]

보기	the father of pop music	so happy
	playing the violin at the concert	

1 I won first prize. It made me ____________________________.

2 She is a great violinist. I heard her ____________________________.

3 We call Michael Jackson ____________________________.

[4-6]

보기	swim in the pool	to come to my birthday party
	to stay out late	

4 I like Amy very much. I want her ____________________________.

5 The water is too cold. I won't let you ____________________________.

6 I want to play with my friends late at night. But my mom doesn't allow me ____________________________.

WRITING PRACTICE

Answer Key p.25

A 우리말과 일치하도록 ( ) 안의 말을 이용하여 문장을 완성하시오.

1 우리 선생님은 내가 사실을 말하길 원하셨다. (want, tell)

→ My teacher ______________________________ the truth.

2 나는 너의 개가 거리에서 달리는 것을 보았다. (see, run)

→ I ______________________________ down the street.

3 그는 나에게 그녀한테 사과하라고 충고했다. (advise, say sorry)

→ He ______________________________ to her.

4 엄마는 나에게 빨래를 하도록 시키셨다. (get, do)

→ My mom ______________________________ the laundry.

5 우리는 그 쇼가 지루하다는 걸 알게 되었다. (find, the show, boring)

→ We ______________________________.

6 나의 아버지는 나를 작은 공주라고 부르신다. (call, a little princess)

→ My father ______________________________.

B 우리말과 일치하도록 ( ) 안에 주어진 단어를 바르게 배열하시오.

1 내 여동생은 항상 그녀의 방을 깨끗하게 유지한다. (her, clean, room, keeps)

→ My sister always ______________________________.

2 그는 나에게 그의 카메라를 가져오게 했다. (bring, me, camera, had, his)

→ He ______________________________.

3 나는 그의 차가 건물 앞에 서는 것을 보았다. (saw, car, stop, his, in front of)

→ I ______________________________ the building.

4 그들은 나에게 조용히 해달라고 요청했다. (me, be, quiet, to, asked)

→ They ______________________________.

5 우리가 그를 우리의 회장으로 만들었다. (him, our, made, president)

→ We ______________________________.

6 엄마는 내게 야채를 더 먹게 하셨다. (eat, made, me, more vegetables)

→ Mom ______________________________.

REVIEW TEST

Answer Key p.25

[1-5] 빈칸에 들어갈 알맞은 말을 고르시오.

1

Mom won't let me ________ her car.

① drive ② to drive
③ driving ④ drove
⑤ driven

2

Your plan sounds ________.

① well ② perfectly
③ boring ④ interestingly
⑤ excitingly

3

She told me ________ the project by tomorrow.

① finish ② finishing
③ finished ④ to finish
⑤ will finish

4

The comedian's funny joke made us ________.

① laughed ② laugh
③ will laugh ④ to laugh
⑤ laughing

5

I made a cheesecake ________ you.

① to ② of ③ for
④ from ⑤ at

[6-7] 다음 중 어법상 틀린 것을 고르시오.

6 ① She got me to hold her bag.
② I asked him open the window.
③ I heard him walking down the stairs.
④ He advised me to do some exercises.
⑤ They didn't allow the baby to climb onto the table.

7 ① Did he tell you to move away?
② She looked fine yesterday.
③ My mom bought me a new bike.
④ I saw him drop his smartphone.
⑤ This tea tastes very bitterly.

빈출

8 빈칸에 들어갈 전치사가 다른 하나는?

① He showed his essay ________ me.
② I'll lend ten dollars ________ you.
③ She didn't write a card ________ me.
④ My friend bought a book ________ me.
⑤ Did you send the letter ________ her?

[9-11] 빈칸에 들어갈 말로 알맞지 않은 것을 고르시오.

9 This toy looks ________.

① cute ② really
③ great ④ fun
⑤ like a real train

10 Kristen ________ me to learn a new language.

① told ② advised
③ wanted ④ made
⑤ helped

11 He ________ me climb the mountain.

① made ② helped
③ got ④ let
⑤ had

12 다음 우리말을 영어로 바르게 옮긴 것은?

그의 부모님은 그가 훌륭한 야구 선수가 되길 원했다.

① His parents wanted him is a good baseball player.
② His parents wanted him be a good baseball player.
③ His parents wanted him to be a good baseball player.
④ His parents wanted him being a good baseball player.
⑤ His parents wanted him was a good baseball player.

서술형

[13-14] ( ) 안의 말을 이용하여 문장을 완성하시오.

13 I heard him ____________ the flute. (play)

14 My teacher had us ____________ a classroom newspaper. (make)

15 다음 중 어법상 옳은 것은?

① Did you tell her your idea?
② She didn't make me to do it.
③ The clothes smell badly.
④ My dad had me to clean my desk.
⑤ I want you call me tonight.

서술형 빈출

[16-18] 두 문장의 의미가 같도록 빈칸에 알맞은 말을 쓰시오.

16 I made her a small hair pin.

→ I made a small hair pin ________.

17 They asked me many favors.

→ They asked many favors ________.

18 Anna will pass him the ball.

→ Anna will pass the ball ____________.

서술형

19 우리말과 일치하도록 주어진 조건에 맞게 문장을 완성하시오.

태양은 식물에게 에너지를 준다.

〈조건〉 1. give, energy, plants를 이용할 것
2. 전치사를 쓸 것

→ The sun ________________________.

서술형

[20-21] 우리말과 일치하도록 ( ) 안의 말을 이용하여 문장을 완성하시오.

20 네 목소리가 전화상으로 다르게 들린다.
(sound, different)

→ Your voice ________________ on the phone.

21 나는 그에게 그의 선생님께 전화를 하라고 시켰다.
(have, make a call)

→ ________________________ to his teacher.

서술형

[22-23] 우리말과 일치하도록 ( ) 안에 주어진 단어를 바르게 배열하시오.

22 그는 나에게 자신의 책을 돌려달라고 요청했다.
(return, he, book, to, me, his, asked)

→ ________________________.

23 나는 네가 나에게 저녁을 만들어 주길 원한다.
(you, to, I, make, want, dinner)

→ ________________________ for me.

서술형 고난도

[24-25] 어법상 틀린 부분을 찾아 바르게 고치시오.

24 The doctor advised me exercise. That will keep me healthily. (2개)

25 In this game, I will show some pictures for you. Then I will ask you picking your favorite picture. (2개)

UNIT 01

현재, 과거, 미래시제 / 진행형

A ( ) 안에서 알맞은 말을 고르시오.

1 She (saw, is going to see) a movie next Friday.
2 My cousins (are visiting, visited) me last week.
3 My father (goes, go) fishing every Saturday.
4 Jake (talking, is talking) on the phone now.
5 I (am watching, was watching) a TV show when you called.
6 Two and five (make, made) seven.
7 Mike (bought, will buy) some bread yesterday.
8 Brad (has, is having) two dogs and a cat.
9 I (am looking, was looking) for my grammar book now.
10 The man on TV (am, was) a mayor last year.

B 밑줄 친 부분을 어법에 맞게 고치시오.

1 I wore a school uniform when I go to school.
2 The composer writes a song last night.
3 He is knowing a lot of funny stories. He sometimes tells them to us.
4 Jessica takes pictures right now.
5 They are fighting when their mother came.
6 He is an English teacher. He taught English.
7 I learned to ride a horse next summer vacation.
8 Hot air was lighter than cold air.
9 I plan to travel to Europe with my family last summer.
10 Look at the monkeys! They were eating bananas now.

Answer Key p.25

C

( ) 안의 말을 이용하여 문장을 완성하시오.

1 The actress ______________ born in 1985. (be)

2 I ______________ to Italy next year. (go)

3 Lily ______________ a business five years ago. (start)

4 The sun ______________ necessary for life on earth. (be)

5 I ______________ to Jeju Island with my friends last year. (travel)

6 Steven ______________ a reality show on TV now. (watch)

7 Dana always ______________ happy when she receives gifts. (feel)

8 I ______________ a movie tomorrow. (not, watch)

9 Ask Bruce. He ______________ a lot of things about cars. (know)

10 I ______________ a computer game when Mom came into my room. (play)

D

우리말과 일치하도록 빈칸에 알맞은 말을 보기에서 골라 적절한 형태로 바꿔 쓰시오.

보기	pass	ride	write	cook	get

1 나는 오늘 저녁 부모님을 위해 저녁 식사를 요리할 것이다.

→ I ______________________ dinner for my parents this evening.

2 Peter는 매일 아침 7시에 일어난다.

→ Peter ______________________ up at seven o'clock every morning.

3 나는 미국에 있는 형에게 이메일을 쓰는 중이다.

→ I ______________________ an email to my brother in the US.

4 그는 매우 열심히 공부했기 때문에 시험에 합격했다.

→ He ______________________ the exam because he studied very hard.

5 나는 그때 한강을 따라 자전거를 타고 있었다.

→ I ______________________ a bicycle along the Han River at that time.

WRITING PRACTICE

Answer Key p.25

A 우리말과 일치하도록 ( ) 안의 말을 이용하여 문장을 완성하시오.

1 나는 어제 그의 사무실을 방문하였다. (visit, his office)

→ I ______________________________ yesterday.

2 그녀는 지금 자신의 지갑을 찾고 있다. (look for, purse)

→ She ______________________________ now.

3 개구리는 매해 겨울 동면을 한다. (frogs, hibernate)

→ ______________________________ every winter.

4 나는 그에게 세 통의 이메일을 보냈다. (send, email)

→ I ______________________________ to him.

5 그는 오늘 오후에 그의 차를 수리할 것이다. (repair, car)

→ He ______________________________ this afternoon.

6 그 도서관은 매일 오전 11시에 문을 연다. (library, open)

→ ______________________________ at 11:00 a.m. every day.

B 우리말과 일치하도록 ( ) 안에 주어진 단어를 바르게 배열하시오.

1 나는 아버지와 함께 매주 목요일에 테니스를 친다. (play, with, I, father, my, tennis)

→ ______________________________ every Thursday.

2 나의 가족은 3년 전에 서울로 이사왔다. (three, ago, years, moved, Seoul, to)

→ My family ______________________________.

3 우리는 내일 그 기차를 탈 예정이다. (going, the, to, train, are, take)

→ We ______________________________ tomorrow.

4 나의 형은 집에서 저녁을 만들고 있다. (at, dinner, making, home, is)

→ My brother ______________________________.

5 그 농구 경기는 3시에 시작할 것이다. (basketball, start, the, will, game)

→ ______________________________ at three o'clock.

6 아빠가 내게 전화하셨을 때 나는 내 친구와 놀고 있었다. (was, my, playing, friend, with)

→ I ______________________________ when Dad called me.

UNIT 02

현재완료

Answer Key p.25

A

( ) 안에서 알맞은 말을 고르시오.

1 I have (use, used) this pencil case for three years.

2 He (studied, has studied) English since he was five.

3 I (has been, have been) to New Zealand four times.

4 Jake (doesn't read, hasn't read) the magazine yet.

5 Mina has lived in Tokyo (for, since) two years.

6 Susan (lost, has lost) her wedding ring last month.

7 She (has been, has gone) to Cuba, so you can't meet her now.

8 He (reads, has read) this letter many times before.

9 I (saw, have seen) this talk show last night.

10 It has been cold (for, since) last month.

B

우리말과 일치하도록 밑줄 친 부분을 고쳐 쓰시오.

1 우리 수학 선생님은 지난주부터 아프시다.
→ My math teacher be sick since last week.

2 Serena는 전에 자신만의 방을 가져본 적이 없다.
→ Serena never has her own room before.

3 나는 지난 여름에 가족과 함께 한라산에 갔었다.
→ I go to Mt. Halla with my family last summer.

4 그는 미국으로 가 버려서 여기에 없다.
→ He go to the US, so he is not here.

5 Sam은 지난 일요일에 화장실 청소를 했다.
→ Sam clean the bathroom last Sunday.

6 그들은 전에 춤 동아리에서 만난 적이 있다.
→ They met in the dancing club before.

C 다음을 현재완료 문장으로 바꿀 때, 빈칸에 알맞은 말을 쓰시오.

1 I first knew her ten years ago. I still know her.
→ I ______________________ her for ten years.

2 She lost her favorite sneakers, so she doesn't have them now.
→ She ______________________ her favorite sneakers.

3 He went to Vietnam. He isn't here now.
→ He ______________________ to Vietnam.

4 I left my smartphone at home. I don't have it now.
→ I ______________________ my smartphone at home.

5 She ate all the cookies. There's nothing left.
→ She ______________________ all the cookies.

6 Mr. Brown was busy last week. He is still busy now.
→ Mr. Brown ______________________ busy since last week.

D 밑줄 친 부분에 유의하여 문장을 우리말로 해석하시오.

1 I haven't finished the math homework yet.
2 Stella has lived in Mexico for five years.
3 Have you ever eaten German food?
4 I have already washed the clothes.
5 Harry has visited my house several times.
6 Earl and I have been close friends since we were five.
7 My boss has gone to Seoul on business.
8 Somebody has left a suitcase at the hotel.
9 Jenny has just bought her mom's birthday present.
10 I have never been to China.

WRITING PRACTICE

Answer Key p.25

A 우리말과 일치하도록 ( ) 안의 말을 이용하여 현재완료 시제로 문장을 완성하시오.

1 나는 태국에 간 적이 한 번 있다. (be)

→ I ______________________________ Thailand once.

2 그는 벌써 그 소설을 읽었다. (already, read)

→ He ______________________________ the novel.

3 나는 유령을 본 적이 없다. (never, see)

→ I ______________________________ a ghost.

4 어제 이후로 눈이 많이 내렸다. (snow)

→ It ______________________________ a lot since yesterday.

5 그들은 여름 캠프에 가고 없다. (go)

→ They ______________________________ the summer camp.

6 그녀는 20살 때부터 여기서 일해 왔다. (work, here)

→ She ______________________________ she was twenty.

B 우리말과 일치하도록 ( ) 안에 주어진 단어를 바르게 배열하시오.

1 그녀는 방금 집에 도착하였다. (she, arrived, just, has)

→ ______________________________ home.

2 나는 그 영화를 여러 번 봤다. (movie, I, watched, the, have)

→ ______________________________ several times.

3 그녀는 그녀의 목걸이를 어제 찾았다. (yesterday, found, necklace, her)

→ She ______________________________.

4 그는 5년 동안 이 컴퓨터를 사용해 왔다. (he, this, for, computer, used, has)

→ ______________________________ five years.

5 그 의사는 아직 공항에 도착하지 않았다. (has, the, not, doctor, arrived)

→ ______________________________ at the airport yet.

6 그녀는 자신의 영어 교과서를 잃어버렸다. (has, her, she, English textbook, lost)

→ ______________________________.

REVIEW TEST

[1-5] 빈칸에 들어갈 알맞은 말을 고르시오.

1 Seawater __________ salty.

① taste ② tastes
③ is tasting ④ tasted
⑤ has tasted

2 I __________ dinner ten minutes ago.

① eat ② ate
③ am eating ④ have eaten
⑤ am going to eat

3 He __________ a singer someday.

① be ② is
③ was ④ will be
⑤ has been

4 I __________ Chinese since I entered middle school.

① study ② will study
③ was studying ④ have studied
⑤ am going to study

5 My brother __________ hiking every Sunday.

① go ② is gone
③ goes ④ was gone
⑤ have gone

[6-8] 다음 중 어법상 틀린 것을 고르시오.

6 ① I visited the new bakery last week.
② James is studying at the library now.
③ I have lost my necklace yesterday.
④ He walks his dog every day.
⑤ We are going to study together tonight.

7 ① I have met him three times.
② Maria called me last night.
③ I study for five hours every day.
④ There was no air in space.
⑤ My sister is sleeping in her bed now.

8 ① We were talking about the actor then.
② I will take the English test tomorrow.
③ He is having a nice sports car.
④ Julie has been to England before.
⑤ I'm checking my email.

[9-10] 빈칸에 들어갈 말이 순서대로 바르게 짝지어진 것을 고르시오.

9
• I __________ Harry last week.
• I __________ Harry tomorrow morning.

① meet – met
② met – am going to meet
③ met – have met
④ will meet – met
⑤ am meeting – will meet

Answer Key p.25

10

• It __________ yesterday.
• It __________ since last night.

① has rained – was raining
② has rained – rains
③ rained – will rain
④ rained – has rained
⑤ rains – is going to rain

빈출

[11-12] 다음 중 보기의 밑줄 친 부분과 쓰임이 같은 것을 고르시오.

11

보기	I have forgotten his phone number.

① He has lived in this town since 2017.
② I have never seen a UFO.
③ She has already eaten her sandwich.
④ I have liked the show for five years.
⑤ He has lost his laptop computer.

12

보기	I have just finished the project.

① I have seen a circus show before.
② He has never driven a truck.
③ Jim has been sick for three days.
④ I have left my hometown.
⑤ He has already decided on his daughter's name.

[13-14] 다음 중 어법상 옳은 것을 고르시오.

13 ① He was jogging along the beach now.
② I have known him since five years.
③ I will have a cheeseburger for lunch.
④ Kate is liking pop music.
⑤ Jane is wearing blue jeans then.

14 ① The next train arrives at 5:30 p.m.
② He is knowing her well.
③ I did my homework tomorrow.
④ Have you read the book yesterday?
⑤ I saw them since yesterday.

서술형

[15-17] ( ) 안의 말을 이용하여 문장을 완성하시오.

15 They ______________ friends since they were young. (be)

16 She ______________ her teeth now. (brush)

17 I ______________ a very handsome man on the street yesterday. (meet)

서술형

[18-19] 다음 두 문장을 한 문장으로 바꿀 때, 빈칸에 알맞은 말을 쓰시오.

18 My computer broke. It doesn't work now.

→ My computer ____________________.

19 Tim started working here five years ago. He still works here.

→ Tim ____________________ here for five years.

서술형

[20-21] 자연스러운 대화가 되도록 빈칸에 알맞은 말을 쓰시오.

20 A: Do you drink milk every morning?
B: Yes. I ____________ a glass of milk every morning.

21 A: Was he talking to you?
B: No. He ____________ on the phone.

서술형

[22-23] 우리말과 일치하도록 ( ) 안에 주어진 단어를 바르게 배열하시오.

22 그가 지난달에 그 기계를 고쳤다.
(machine, he, the, fixed)

→ ____________________ last month.

23 그녀는 내년이면 열여섯 살이 될 것이다.
(going, old, she, to, sixteen, be, is, years)

→ ____________________ next year.

서술형 고난도

[24-25] 어법상 틀린 부분을 찾아 바르게 고치시오.

24 Amy has always wanted to make her own movie. So she was going to make a school movie club next month. (1개)

25 Tom invites me to his new house a few days ago. On that day, he prepared a delicious pizza for me. I was liking it very much. (2개)

CHAPTER 03 조동사

UNIT 01 can, may, will

Answer Key p.26

A ( ) 안에서 알맞은 말을 고르시오.

1 I can (play, playing) the cello.
2 My family will (spend, spent) our holidays on a small island.
3 I (can't, wasn't able to) swim last year.
4 She must (be, being) interested in jazz.
5 You (may, would) turn on the heater if you want.
6 The rumor about Jenny may not (be, is) true.
7 Can I (take, took) John to the movie this evening?
8 She (is, was) not able to eat spicy food when she was young.
9 (Will, May) you pass me the chili sauce?
10 You will (can, be able to) look at my pictures soon.

B 밑줄 친 부분을 어법에 맞게 고치시오.

1 Tommy may to be wrong.
2 Will I see your passport, please?
3 May you dance with me this Friday night?
4 You may left the office after six.
5 Is she able apply for this job?
6 You will leave now if you are busy.
7 I can't living without my family.
8 My mother can't speak English last year.
9 He will can find his way someday.
10 The man is able to jumping very high.

C

주어진 문장과 의미가 통하도록 빈칸에 알맞은 조동사를 쓰시오.

1 Is it okay for me to use your bathroom?

→ __________ I use your bathroom?

2 It's possible that Emily has that old novel.

→ Emily __________ have that old novel.

3 I was not able to pass the exam because I was not ready for it.

→ I __________ pass the exam because I was not ready for it.

4 Can you give me a hand?

→ __________ you give me a hand?

5 It's okay to start cleaning the room in the afternoon.

→ You __________ start cleaning the room in the afternoon.

6 Eric is able to help you move the boxes.

→ Eric __________ help you move the boxes.

D

밑줄 친 부분에 유의하여 문장을 우리말로 해석하시오.

1 You can eat my crackers if you want.
2 I will sing a song for you on your birthday.
3 They are able to fix the machine.
4 You may go to the movies with your friends this evening.
5 We will be able to travel through space.
6 His story may not be true.
7 Your parents may be surprised at the news.
8 He won't say anything to me.
9 Would you tell me your email address?
10 I can read Chinese, but I can't speak it at all.

WRITING PRACTICE

Answer Key p.26

A 우리말과 일치하도록 ( ) 안의 말을 이용하여 문장을 완성하시오.

1 그가 스파게티를 만드는 법을 알지도 모른다. (know)
→ He ______________________ how to make spaghetti.

2 너는 내 만화책을 빌려가도 된다. (borrow)
→ You ______________________ my comic books.

3 그는 휴가 기간에 우리에게 차를 빌려줄 수 있을 것이다. (will, lend)
→ He ______________________ us a car during the holidays.

4 우리 할머니는 어렸을 때 빨리 달릴 수 있었다. (run)
→ My grandmother ______________________ fast when she was young.

5 나는 제시간에 그 일을 마칠 수 없었다. (finish)
→ I ______________________ the work in time.

6 너는 내가 외출할 동안 내 개를 돌봐줄래? (take care of)
→ ______________________ my dog while I'm out?

B 우리말과 일치하도록 ( ) 안에 주어진 단어를 바르게 배열하시오.

1 그들은 결석에 대해 거짓말을 할지도 모른다. (a lie, may, about, tell)
→ They ______________________ their absence.

2 집에 돌아가는 길에 우체국에 들러줄 수 있니? (the post office, can, you, by, stop)
→ ______________________ on your way back home?

3 너는 내 집에 자유롭게 들어와도 된다. (may, come, my house, into)
→ You ______________________ freely.

4 Mark는 5m 다이빙대에서 다이빙할 수 있다. (able, is, to, dive, from)
→ Mark ______________________ a five-meter platform.

5 저를 위해 이 짐을 날라줄 수 있나요? (carry, you, this baggage, for, will, me)
→ ______________________, please?

6 그녀는 내일까지 보고서를 끝낼 수 없을 것이다. (won't, finish, to, be, able, the report)
→ She ______________________ by tomorrow.

UNIT 02

must, should

A

( ) 안에서 알맞은 말을 고르시오.

1 We should (stop, stopping) using paper cups.

2 You (must not, don't must) run around.

3 What (should, have to) I prepare before the interview?

4 She (can, can't) be this late. She left there an hour ago.

5 What do I have to (do, doing) next?

6 We must (save, to save) energy.

7 You need not (take, to take) care of me. I can take care of myself.

8 You (may, should) see that movie. It is really amazing.

9 I (have to, had to) wait in a long line at the bank yesterday.

10 The concert is free. You (must not, don't have to) buy a ticket.

B

밑줄 친 부분을 어법에 맞게 고치시오.

1 Does a young child have to paying an entrance fee?

2 Mike not need take care of his sister tonight.

3 She doesn't has to buy an expensive present.

4 You don't should take pictures in this museum.

5 Does he have to stay in the hospital last night?

6 You don't need run. You are not late.

7 When must I returned to the office, Mr. Scott?

8 He should to speak to the teacher first.

9 Henry has to go to bed early last night.

10 She should not be his sister. They look very different.

Answer Key p.26

C

주어진 문장과 의미가 통하도록 빈칸에 알맞은 말을 보기에서 골라 쓰시오. (단, 한 번씩만 쓸 것)

보기	cannot	must	must not	need not	should

1 I advise you to be kind to your friends.
→ You ______________ be kind to your friends.

2 I'm sure this is not Nick's diary. He doesn't keep one.
→ This diary ______________ be Nick's. He doesn't keep a diary.

3 It is not allowed for you to enter this room before the meeting ends.
→ You ______________ enter this room before the meeting ends.

4 You don't have to bring your car. Tom will bring his car.
→ You ______________ bring your car. Tom will bring his car.

5 I'm sure you are a big fan of the singer.
→ You ______________ be a big fan of the singer.

D

밑줄 친 부분에 유의하여 문장을 우리말로 해석하시오.

1 You must not laugh at your friends.
2 That dog must be very clever.
3 You don't have to copy the file. I already have a copy.
4 There must be another way to open the door.
5 We should pick up our trash after the picnic.
6 I had to wait a day to meet her.
7 You must prepare for the final match.
8 You will have to go to see a dentist.
9 He had to stay up all night.
10 Tony can't be in his room. I didn't see him come into the house.

WRITING PRACTICE

Answer Key p.26

A 우리말과 일치하도록 ( ) 안의 말을 이용하여 문장을 완성하시오.

1 Alex는 피아노를 더 연습해야 한다. (should, practice)

→ Alex ______________________ the piano more.

2 Clark은 지금 당장 그의 숙제를 제출해야 한다. (have to, hand in)

→ Clark ______________________ his homework right now.

3 이 영화는 네가 이해하기에 어려운 게 분명하다. (must, difficult)

→ This movie ______________________ for you to understand.

4 이 카메라는 Ron의 것일 리가 없다. 그의 것은 다르게 생겼다. (camera, be)

→ ______________________ Ron's. His looks different.

5 그녀는 지금 출발할 필요가 없다. 그녀의 기차는 오후 2시까지 오지 않을 것이다. (have to, leave)

→ ______________________ now. Her train won't come until 2:00 p.m.

6 나는 집을 청소하는 데 나의 주말을 써야 했다. (have to, spend)

→ I ______________________ my weekend cleaning my house.

B 우리말과 일치하도록 ( ) 안에 주어진 단어를 바르게 배열하시오.

1 그들은 더 이상 마스크를 쓸 필요가 없다. (need, to, masks, they, don't, wear)

→ ______________________ anymore.

2 너는 50분 이내에 이 문제들을 풀어야 한다. (should, solve, these, you, questions)

→ ______________________ within fifty minutes.

3 너는 이 방에서 조용히 해야 한다. 우리 아기가 지금 자고 있다. (be, this room, in, you, must, quiet)

→ ______________________. Our baby is sleeping now.

4 나는 중학교 때 교복을 입어야 했다. (wear, to, I, had, a, uniform)

→ ______________________ when I was in middle school.

5 우리는 모든 규칙을 지킬 필요는 없다. (we, follow, need, to, don't)

→ ______________________ all the rules.

6 나는 다음 주 월요일 전에 보고서를 끝마쳐야 한다. (finish, the, report, should, I)

→ ______________________ before next Monday.

UNIT 03

would like to, had better, used to

Answer Key p.26

A ( ) 안에서 알맞은 말을 고르시오.

1 The weather is so hot. I'd like to (have, having) some ice cream.

2 I used to (study, studying) after dinner.

3 I (would like to, would like) buy a bottle of water.

4 I (used to, would like to) like math, but now I do not.

5 Mary (uses to, used to) be very friendly.

6 Emma (didn't use to, wasn't used to) be afraid of dogs.

7 Jack (had not better, had better not) miss the class.

8 (Would, Will) you like to go snowboarding this weekend?

9 The bell (would, used to) be in the tower.

10 Kate (has better, had better) drive more carefully.

B 빈칸에 가장 알맞은 말을 보기에서 골라 쓰시오.

보기	would like to	had better	used to

1 I ____________________ travel Europe with my family someday.

2 I ____________________ have many foreign friends but not anymore.

3 You ____________________ not talk about the rumor anymore.

4 Damon ____________________ help us a lot before he moved to France.

5 You ____________________ ask Mike about the homework. He can help you.

6 Mina ____________________ live near my house, but she moved to Busan.

7 I ____________________ watch that movie. It looks interesting.

8 You ____________________ not say anything about her son.

9 A: Can I help you?
B: I ____________________ book a table.

10 My grandmother ____________________ knit sweaters for me when she was alive.

C 주어진 문장과 의미가 통하도록 빈칸에 알맞은 말을 보기에서 골라 쓰시오.

보기	would like to	had better	used to

1 I want to listen to Bach's symphony.

→ I ____________________ listen to Bach's symphony.

2 I think you should study hard for your future.

→ You ____________________ study hard for your future.

3 I dreamed of becoming an astronaut, but I don't anymore.

→ I ____________________ dream of becoming an astronaut.

4 I think she should not talk about the matter.

→ She ____________________ not talk about the matter.

5 This car was mine before I gave it to Olivia.

→ This car ____________________ be mine before I gave it to Olivia.

D 밑줄 친 부분에 유의하여 문장을 우리말로 해석하시오.

1 What would you like to have for dinner?

2 She had better not lend Tom her money.

3 You had better take the subway.

4 Dave used to be a rich man.

5 There used to be an old house here.

6 No one would like to work with him.

7 I would like to play computer games this weekend.

8 My mom used to be a basketball player.

9 Dan would travel alone when he was healthy.

10 You had better do your science homework first.

WRITING PRACTICE

Answer Key p.27

A 우리말과 일치하도록 보기의 조동사와 ( ) 안의 말을 이용하여 문장을 완성하시오.

보기	would like to	had better	used to

1 나는 할아버지를 방문하러 기차로 가곤 했었다. (go)

→ I ______________________ by train to visit my grandfather.

2 Jack은 백화점을 둘러보고 싶어 한다. (look)

→ Jack ______________________ around the department store.

3 Brian은 그녀에게 뮤지컬 표를 사 주고 싶어 한다. (buy)

→ Brian ______________________ her a ticket to a musical.

4 나는 대도시에서 살았었다. (live)

→ I ______________________ in a big city.

5 Brad는 그 노래 대회에 참가하지 않는 게 낫겠다. (take part in)

→ Brad ______________________ the singing contest.

6 너는 그 셔츠를 환불 받는 게 낫겠다. (get)

→ You ______________________ a refund for the shirt.

B 우리말과 일치하도록 ( ) 안에 주어진 단어를 바르게 배열하시오.

1 Peter는 아침마다 산책을 하곤 했다. (would, take, a, Peter, walk)

→ ______________________________ every morning.

2 Greg은 다른 사람들에게 친절하지 않았었다. (be, didn't, kind, Greg, use, to)

→ ______________________________ to others.

3 너는 회의에 제시간에 오는 게 낫겠다. (better, be, time, on, you, had)

→ ______________________________ for the meeting.

4 당신은 의사가 될 생각을 했었나요? (you, did, think, use, to)

→ ______________________________ about becoming a doctor?

5 이 차가운 강에서는 수영하지 않는 게 낫겠다. (not, better, had, swim)

→ You ______________________________ in this cold river.

6 고등학교를 졸업하면 무엇을 하고 싶니? (would, what, like, do, to, you)

→ ______________________________ when you graduate from high school?

REVIEW TEST

[1-3] 빈칸에 들어갈 알맞은 말을 고르시오.

1 Matthew __________ practice hard if he wants to win the speech contest.

① can't
② have to
③ could
④ should
⑤ used to

2 Do I __________ wait longer?

① can
② must
③ have to
④ used to
⑤ would like to

3 I __________ drink some water. I feel very thirsty.

① cannot
② won't
③ may
④ used to
⑤ would like to

4 다음 중 보기의 밑줄 친 부분과 의미가 같은 것은?

보기	The rumor must be wrong.

① He must call me tonight.
② You must not talk during the exam.
③ We must finish the report today.
④ You must tell him the truth.
⑤ She must be a middle school student.

[5-6] 다음 중 어법상 틀린 것을 고르시오.

5
① Jessica, will you marry me?
② Can you open this bottle, please?
③ What should I packing for the trip?
④ You'd better go to bed now.
⑤ Would you like to have some dessert?

6
① You must be joking!
② You should ask your teacher first.
③ I'll have to try this once again.
④ I was not able solve the question.
⑤ Can you bring me a glass of water?

빈출

[7-8] 밑줄 친 부분의 의미가 나머지 넷과 다른 것을 고르시오.

7
① They may be full now.
② You may go to the party.
③ He may not like his teacher.
④ They may be in the hospital.
⑤ My father may not be at home.

8
① Can you speak German?
② You can leave now if you want.
③ David can drive this car.
④ I can memorize thirty words a day.
⑤ She can show you the way to my house.

Answer Key p.27

9 다음 중 우리말을 영어로 잘못 옮긴 것은?

① 그가 Tiffany의 오빠일 리가 없다.
→ He must not be Tiffany's brother.

② 내가 에세이 쓰는 거 도와줄래?
→ Will you help me write the essay?

③ 너는 오늘 이 일을 끝마칠 필요가 없어.
→ You don't have to finish this work today.

④ 오디션을 위해 제가 어디로 가야 하나요?
→ Where should I go for the audition?

⑤ 너는 아침 일찍 일어나는 게 낫겠다.
→ You had better get up early in the morning.

10 다음 중 밑줄 친 부분을 잘못 고친 것은?

① I'll to come back by noon tomorrow.
→ come

② I would like have a steak and salad.
→ to have

③ I won't can get there by six o'clock.
→ be able to

④ I used to reading a lot of comic books.
→ read

⑤ He not had better meet her for a while.
→ had not better

빈출

[11-12] 다음 밑줄 친 부분과 바꿔 쓸 수 있는 것을 고르시오.

11

She must go home early to take care of Ted.

① can ② may
③ used to ④ has to
⑤ would

12

He could attend the meeting on time.

① would like to ② need not
③ used to ④ was able to
⑤ didn't have to

13 빈칸에 들어갈 말로 알맞지 않은 것은?

________ you lend your notebook to me?

① Will ② Can ③ May
④ Could ⑤ Would

서술형

[14-16] 주어진 문장과 의미가 통하도록 빈칸에 알맞은 조동사를 쓰시오.

14

It's okay for you to visit my office today.

→ You ________ visit my office today.

15

David played computer games a lot, but he doesn't now.

→ David ________ ________ play computer games a lot.

16

I think you should go to see a doctor today because tomorrow is a holiday.

→ You ________ ________ go to see a doctor today because tomorrow is a holiday.

빈출

17 다음 중 두 문장의 의미가 같지 않은 것은?

① May I go home now?
→ Is it okay if I go home now?

② He is able to read books in Spanish.
→ He can read books in Spanish.

③ I have to clean my room.
→ I must clean my room.

④ You don't have to read the book.
→ You need not read the book.

⑤ This must be his last chance to see her.
→ This may be his last chance to see her.

서술형

[18-19] 우리말과 일치하도록 ( ) 안에 주어진 단어를 바르게 배열하시오.

18 그녀는 무대로 나가기 전에 긴장을 풀어야 한다.
(she, relax, before, going, should)

→ ______________________________ out on the stage.

19 버스에서 내릴 때에는 조심해야 한다.
(be, have, careful, to, you)

→ ______________________________ when you get off the bus.

서술형

[20-21] 우리말과 일치하도록 빈칸에 알맞은 말을 쓰시오.

20 Sam은 이 수업을 받을 필요가 없다.

→ Sam ________ ________ ________ take this lesson.

21 Curt는 직접 파스타를 요리하고 싶어 한다.

→ Curt ________ ________ ________ cook the pasta himself.

서술형

[22-23] 빈칸에 공통으로 들어갈 말을 쓰시오.

22
• Would you like ________ have something else?
• Arthur had ________ hurry this morning.

23
• Laura ________ get up early. She has an important meeting tomorrow morning.
• Jay ________ like red. He always wears red shirts.

서술형 고난도

[24-25] 어법상 틀린 부분을 찾아 바르게 고치시오.

24 You don't had better tell the truth to Liam. He may be shocked. (1개)

25 I would like go to the department store with you this Saturday. Please let me know if you will able to go with me. (2개)

UNIT 01

명사적 용법의 to부정사

Answer Key p.27

A

( ) 안에서 알맞은 말을 고르시오.

1 (It, that) is easy to make new friends.

2 Anne wanted (stay, to stay) inside because it was cold outside.

3 My dream is (become, to become) a famous musician.

4 His hobby is (take, to take) pictures of wild animals.

5 She decided (going, to go) to the hospital with me.

6 It's not possible (carried, to carry) the suitcase by yourself.

7 I haven't decided what (wearing, to wear) for the party yet.

8 I have promised (not to see, to not see) him again.

9 This website provides information about where (going, to go) in Seoul.

10 I'll let you know when (moving, to move) into the new office.

B

다음 문장을 가주어로 시작하는 문장으로 바꿔 쓰시오.

1 To keep two cats in this small house is not easy.

→ ___________ is not easy ______________________________.

2 To finish the homework before dinner is my plan.

→ ___________ is my plan ______________________________.

3 To go to Europe this summer will be exciting.

→ ___________ will be exciting ______________________________.

4 To make her follow my order was impossible.

→ ___________ was impossible ______________________________.

5 To listen to his advice is not wise.

→ ___________ is not wise ______________________________.

6 To exercise regularly is good for your health.

→ ___________ is good for your health ______________________________.

C 두 문장의 의미가 같도록 빈칸에 알맞은 말을 쓰시오.

1 Tell me how I should solve the problem.

→ Tell me ______________________.

2 I don't know who I should ask about my application.

→ I don't know ______________________.

3 They are talking about where they should go next.

→ They are talking about ______________________.

4 My mother told me what I should prepare for dinner.

→ My mother told me ______________________.

5 Let me know how I should arrange the furniture.

→ Let me know ______________________.

6 I don't know when I should start recording.

→ I don't know ______________________.

D 밑줄 친 부분을 어법에 맞게 고치시오.

1 I need buy a new cell phone.

2 His job is clean the rooms in the hotel.

3 It was difficult to accept not her offer.

4 I don't know where buying such a stylish skirt.

5 We're not sure when tell him the truth.

6 His plan was invite everyone over to his house this Friday.

7 He told the students what to not do at the camp.

8 It is necessary finish your work before you go to bed.

9 Elizabeth didn't want go hiking yesterday.

10 My mom taught me how reading when I was young.

WRITING PRACTICE

Answer Key p.27

A 우리말과 일치하도록 to부정사와 ( ) 안의 말을 이용하여 문장을 완성하시오.

1 새로운 곳을 방문하는 것은 언제나 재미있다. (visit, places)
→ ______________ is always fun ______________________________.

2 나는 그녀의 사고에 대해 무슨 말을 해야 할지 모르겠다. (what, say)
→ I don't know ______________________________ about her accident.

3 그의 일은 잡지를 편집하는 것이다. (edit, the magazine)
→ His job is ______________________________.

4 그 시험에서 100점을 맞는 것은 불가능하다. (score 100)
→ ______________ is impossible ______________________________ on the exam.

5 그는 다음 달에 인도네시아로 떠나기로 결정했다. (decide, leave)
→ He ______________________________ for Indonesia next month.

6 넌 내일 아침까지 그 컴퓨터를 고칠 필요가 있다. (need, fix, the computer)
→ You ______________________________ by tomorrow morning.

B 우리말과 일치하도록 ( ) 안에 주어진 단어를 바르게 배열하시오.

1 이 텐트를 빌리는 데는 200달러가 든다. (to, this, rent, tent, 200 dollars)
→ It costs ______________________________.

2 우리는 여름 휴가 때 어디를 갈지 정해야만 한다. (go, where, to, summer, vacation, for, decide)
→ We have to ______________________________.

3 온라인에서 표를 산 것은 현명했다. (was, it, to, buy, wise, the tickets)
→ ______________________________ online.

4 Jessica는 돌아가서 Terry를 데려오길 원했다. (go back, get, to, wanted, and)
→ Jessica ______________________________ Terry.

5 나는 다음 주 야영을 위해 스테이크 요리하는 법을 배우고 싶다. (to, to, how, learn, steak, cook)
→ I want ______________________________ for our camping trip next week.

6 나는 여행을 위해 뭘 준비해야 할지 모르겠다. (the trip, prepare, what, for, to)
→ I don't know ______________________________.

UNIT 02

형용사적 용법의 to부정사

A

( ) 안에서 알맞은 말을 고르시오.

1 Paul has a lot of homework (do, to do) today.
2 I have a sore throat. Give me something (warm to drink, to drink warm).
3 I don't have any reason (sell, to sell) this house.
4 I have some problems (dealing, to deal) with.
5 Nothing was (to be, to being) seen on the street.
6 She (is study, is to study) abroad next year.
7 I ordered something (sweet to eat, to eat sweet).
8 Jacob wanted someone (to talk to, to talk).
9 You are (finish, to finish) the project by this Saturday.
10 I need a notebook (to write, to write in).

B

빈칸에 알맞은 말을 보기에서 골라 to-v 형태로 바꿔 쓰시오. (단, 한 번씩만 쓸 것)

[1-3]

보기	answer	call	study

1 Emma decided __________ harder.
2 I couldn't find anyone __________ my question.
3 She gave me a phone number __________ in case of an emergency.

[4-6]

보기	explain	lead	ask

4 I have a lot of questions __________ the professor.
5 He is known for his ability __________ his team.
6 Please give me a chance __________ why I was late.

Answer Key p.27

C

빈칸에 알맞은 전치사를 보기에서 골라 쓰시오. (단, 각 전치사를 두 번씩만 쓸 것)

보기	in	to	on	with

1 For this job, I need an office to work __________.

2 I downloaded some music files to listen __________ last night.

3 Dana asked me for a computer to work __________.

4 Can you give me a pen to write __________, please?

5 I have no partner to work __________.

6 He's the only one to talk __________ about that problem.

7 They needed a big sofa to relax __________.

8 We don't have a house to live __________.

D

두 문장의 의미가 같도록 be동사를 이용하여 빈칸에 알맞은 말을 쓰시오.

1 She is going to arrive at the airport at 8:30 p.m.
→ She __________ __________ __________ at the airport at 8:30 p.m.

2 Nothing could be seen in the sky that night.
→ Nothing __________ __________ __________ seen in the sky that night.

3 Selina is going to meet the new manager tomorrow.
→ Selina __________ __________ __________ the new manager tomorrow.

4 The couple are going to be married next week.
→ The couple __________ __________ __________ __________ next week.

5 You have to clean your dirty room.
→ You __________ __________ __________ your dirty room.

6 If you are going to enjoy your life, you need to learn to love yourself.
→ If you __________ __________ __________ your life, you need to learn to love yourself.

WRITING PRACTICE

Answer Key p.27

A 우리말과 일치하도록 to부정사와 ( ) 안의 말을 이용하여 문장을 완성하시오.

1 나는 중요한 할 말이 있다. (important, say)

→ I have something ______________________________.

2 그는 나에게 그릴 붓을 빌려 주었다. (paint)

→ He lent me a brush ______________________________.

3 Ted는 월요일까지 돈을 갚아야 한다. (be, pay)

→ Ted ______________________________ the money back by Monday.

4 Mary는 자기 사업을 시작할 예정이었다. (be, start)

→ Mary ______________________________ her own business.

5 나는 내가 힘들 때 이야기할 친구가 없다. (any friends, talk to)

→ I don't have ______________________________ when I have difficulties.

6 그 소년은 그의 어머니를 다시 보지 못할 운명이었다. (be, never, see)

→ The boy ______________________________ his mother again.

B 우리말과 일치하도록 ( ) 안에 주어진 단어를 바르게 배열하시오.

1 Luke는 함께 살 룸메이트를 구하고 있다. (with, looking, is, live, for, a, to, roommate)

→ Luke ______________________________.

2 나는 걱정할 것이 아무것도 없다. (have, to, about, worry, don't, anything)

→ I ______________________________.

3 Chad는 그의 고향에 다시 돌아오지 못할 운명이었다. (return, hometown, not, was, to, his, to)

→ Chad ______________________________ again.

4 그녀는 오늘 밤에 입을 예쁜 무언가가 필요하다. (pretty, needs, wear, to, something)

→ She ______________________________ tonight.

5 다음 주에 내가 병원에 있을 때, 읽을거리 좀 보내줘. (read, to, something, send, me)

→ When I'm in the hospital next week, ______________________________.

6 겨울은 그 섬을 방문하기 가장 좋은 계절이다. (visit, to, the, best, island, season, the)

→ Winter is ______________________________.

UNIT 03

부사적 용법의 to부정사

Answer Key p.28

A

( ) 안에서 알맞은 말을 고르시오.

1 Jake must be eager (see, to see) his score.

2 (Get, To get) over this difficulty, we must work together.

3 We should stay in the building (be, to be) safe.

4 The last question was very difficult (to solve, solving).

5 The bus stop is not far away (to walk, walking) to.

6 She felt so happy (see, to see) her son again.

7 (To see, Saw) her, you would think she was very rich.

8 Joy saved some money (buy, to buy) a bicycle.

9 The little boy grew up (be, to be) a journalist.

10 I wake up at eight o'clock (go, to go) to church every Sunday.

B

빈칸에 가장 알맞은 말을 보기에서 골라 to-v 형태로 바꿔 쓰시오. (단, 한 번씩만 쓸 것)

[1-3]

보기	be a hundred years old	start his new job
	hear his accent	

1 Jake must be excited ______________________________.

2 ______________________________, you would think he was from England.

3 My grandmother lived ______________________________.

[4-6]

보기	make your vacation fun	have such a wonderful family
	carry in my pocket	

4 This smartphone is quite large ______________________________.

5 I am lucky ______________________________.

6 ______________________________, you should have a good plan.

C 두 문장의 의미가 같도록 빈칸에 알맞은 말을 쓰시오.

1 I cleaned the bathroom in order to help my mother.
→ I cleaned the bathroom __________ __________ my mother.

2 If you want to get good grades, you should study harder.
→ __________ __________ good grades, you should study harder.

3 Olivia decided to leave early in order to arrive on time.
→ Olivia decided to leave early __________ __________ on time.

4 Alice tried to open the heavy door, but she failed.
→ Alice tried to open the heavy door, __________ __________ __________.

5 The baby must be hungry because she keeps crying so much.
→ The baby must be hungry __________ __________ crying so much.

D 밑줄 친 부분에 유의하여 문장을 우리말로 해석하시오.

1 Dean was happy <u>to win</u> the singing contest.
2 She would be disappointed <u>to hear</u> the news.
3 I was sad <u>to hear</u> that story.
4 He grew up <u>to be</u> one of the world's best hairdressers.
5 <u>To study</u> in the US, I should study English harder.
6 The church is quite hard <u>to get</u> to from here.
7 We need to practice more <u>to win</u> the championship.
8 Logan went to work <u>only to find</u> that it was a holiday.
9 Those big containers are not easy <u>to move</u>.
10 Be careful <u>not to wake</u> your dad.

WRITING PRACTICE

Answer Key p.28

A 우리말과 일치하도록 to부정사와 ( ) 안의 말을 이용하여 문장을 완성하시오.

1 그 웹 사이트에 접속하기 위해서는 비밀번호를 알아야 한다. (log in)
→ You have to know the password ____________ to the website.

2 엄마는 내가 거짓말한 것을 알고 화가 나셨다. (angry, find out)
→ Mom was ____________ that I told her a lie.

3 George는 자라서 유명한 배우가 되었다. (grow up, be)
→ George ____________ a famous actor.

4 그 컵을 떨어뜨리다니 그녀는 조심성이 없었다. (careless, drop)
→ She ____________ the cup.

5 한자는 쓰기 어렵다. (difficult, write)
→ Chinese characters are ____________.

6 그가 일본어를 말하는 것을 듣는다면, 너는 그가 일본에서 자랐다고 생각할 것이다. (hear)
→ ____________ speak Japanese, you would think he grew up in Japan.

B 우리말과 일치하도록 ( ) 안에 주어진 단어를 바르게 배열하시오.

1 우리는 그 상점에 갔지만, 결국 문이 닫힌 것을 알게 되었다. (it, only, closed, find, to)
→ We went to the store, ____________.

2 그녀가 춤추는 것을 보면 너는 그녀가 발레리나였다고 생각할 것이다.
(her, you, to, dance, see, would, think)
→ ____________ she was a ballerina.

3 그 입학 시험은 합격하기 아주 어렵다. (hard, pass, very, to, is)
→ The entrance exam ____________.

4 Sam은 그 소식을 듣고 충격을 받았다. (shocked, news, to, the, hear)
→ Sam was ____________.

5 우리는 너를 또 보게 되어 기쁘다. (you, see, are, to, pleased, again)
→ We ____________.

6 Walter는 좋은 대학에 들어가기 위해 열심히 공부했다. (university, to, a, get into, good)
→ Walter studied hard ____________.

UNIT 04

to부정사의 의미상의 주어, too ~ to-v, enough to-v

A 밑줄 친 부분을 어법에 맞게 고치시오.

1 It is impossible of me to read three books in a day.
2 That bag is so large to carry.
3 She is too tired that she can't go hiking with us.
4 The tea was too bitter of me to drink.
5 It was wise for Jane to bring her umbrella.
6 He's tall enough reaching the top shelf.
7 Carey is enough smart to solve this math question.
8 The dog is clever enough understand my words.
9 It was very clever for him to be quiet at the moment.
10 He was too tired do anything.

B 빈칸에 for와 of 중 알맞은 전치사를 넣어 문장을 완성하시오.

1 It's possible __________ you to stay here a few more days.
2 It was so kind __________ Olivia to meet me at the airport.
3 It was silly __________ him to leave his bag on the bus.
4 It would be very dangerous __________ her to go there alone.
5 It was stupid __________ you to trust a stranger.
6 It was difficult __________ him to get a satisfying job.
7 It was polite __________ her to say sorry first.
8 It's not easy __________ me to wake up at six o'clock.
9 It is very wise __________ you to eat healthy food.
10 It is fun __________ me to play online games.

Answer Key p.28

C 두 문장의 의미가 같도록 빈칸에 알맞은 말을 쓰시오.

1 He can jump so high that he can touch the ceiling.
→ He can jump high ______________________ the ceiling.

2 The bus was so big that I couldn't drive it.
→ The bus was ______________________.

3 Mary is so strong that she can lift the table by herself.
→ Mary is ______________________ the table by herself.

4 Peter was so fast that he won the race easily.
→ Peter was ______________________ the race easily.

5 The camera was so cheap that young students could buy it.
→ The camera was ______________________.

6 That bag is so small that it can't contain more than four books.
→ That bag is ______________________ more than four books.

D 밑줄 친 부분에 유의하여 문장을 우리말로 해석하시오.

1 The T-shirt is <u>too small for me to wear</u>.
2 The girl was <u>smart enough to solve</u> the riddle.
3 My son is <u>too young to watch</u> the drama.
4 The coffee was <u>sweet enough for me to drink</u>.
5 The movie was <u>too difficult for me to understand</u>.
6 He was <u>clever enough to find</u> the answer.
7 My sister is <u>too careless to have</u> a dog.
8 Mark is <u>talented enough to be</u> a famous actor.
9 This book is <u>too interesting for me to stop</u> reading.
10 The TV is <u>cheap enough for me to buy</u>.

WRITING PRACTICE

Answer Key p.28

A 우리말과 일치하도록 to부정사와 ( ) 안의 말을 이용하여 문장을 완성하시오.

1 가장 중요한 것은 너의 최선을 다하는 것이다. (do one's best)
→ The most important thing is ______________________.

2 그 아이를 집에 혼자 두고 오다니 너는 어리석었다. (leave)
→ It was stupid ______________________ the child alone in the house.

3 Dana는 너무 어려서 혼자 지하철을 탈 수 없다. (young, take the subway)
→ Dana ______________________ by herself.

4 이 노트북 컴퓨터는 어디든 갖고 다닐 수 있을 만큼 가볍다. (light, carry)
→ This laptop is ______________________ anywhere.

5 Jim은 너무 당황해서 내 질문에 답하지 못했다. (embarrassed, answer)
→ Jim was ______________________ my question.

6 네가 그런 식으로 행동을 한 것은 어리석었다. (foolish, behave)
→ It was ______________________ like that.

B 우리말과 일치하도록 ( ) 안에 주어진 단어를 바르게 배열하시오.

1 그가 어렸을 때, 그는 너무 왜소해서 농구팀에 가입할 수 없었다.
(small, too, he, join, to, was, a, basketball team)
→ When he was young, ______________________________.

2 그 칼은 종이를 자를 수 있을 정도로 날카롭다. (is, cut, enough, the paper, sharp, to)
→ The knife ______________________________.

3 그 여행용 가방은 너무 무거워서 내가 옮길 수 없었다. (carry, heavy, me, too, was, to, for)
→ The suitcase ______________________________.

4 이 방은 너무 더워서 나는 잘 수 없다. (hot, can't, is, so, sleep, that, I)
→ This room ______________________________.

5 그녀가 그 집 안에서 어떤 것도 만지지 않았던 것은 현명했다. (not, touch, wise, of, to, her, it, was)
→ ______________________________ anything in the house.

6 한국인이 일본어를 배우는 것은 쉽다. (learn, is, Koreans, easy, for, Japanese, it, to)
→ ______________________________.

REVIEW TEST

Answer Key p.28

[1-5] 빈칸에 들어갈 알맞은 말을 고르시오.

1

It is my goal __________ the race.

① win ② wins
③ won ④ to win
⑤ to winning

2

I was looking for a couch __________.

① sit ② sat
③ to sit ④ sit on
⑤ to sit on

3

He went to the store __________ some fruits.

① buy ② buying
③ bought ④ to buy
⑤ to buying

4

It is dangerous __________ to climb the cliff without any equipment.

① for us ② of us
③ to us ④ for our
⑤ of our

5

I didn't know what __________ in that situation.

① do ② doing
③ to do ④ to doing
⑤ did

빈출

6 밑줄 친 부분의 쓰임이 나머지 넷과 다른 것은?

① I didn't expect to see her again.
② I just want to know the truth.
③ She decided to go to Europe next week.
④ There's nothing to be afraid of.
⑤ Her job is to fix any broken computers in the office.

[7-9] 다음 중 어법상 틀린 것을 고르시오.

7
① I have nothing more to lose.
② I decided to take not the exam.
③ It's not difficult to keep cats at home.
④ We should do our best to finish the task.
⑤ Ellen had some questions to ask you.

8
① She planned to leave the town.
② I need some friends to talk.
③ It's not easy to sing that song.
④ Owen is to take the exam tomorrow.
⑤ He knows where to get a good deal on a laptop.

9 ① It's necessary to dress formally there.
② It is important to read the manual.
③ Mia came to the restaurant to eat curry.
④ David is to arrive at the airport at nine.
⑤ It is silly to you to believe the gossip.

10 다음 중 밑줄 친 부분을 바르게 고친 것은?

① It's so kind for you to invite me to the party. → to you
② I was happy hearing from Luke. → heard
③ I don't know what telling Jake now. → to tell
④ He decided staying here for two more weeks. → to staying
⑤ The guidebook is enough easy for us to read. → easy too

11 우리말과 일치하도록 할 때, 빈칸에 들어갈 알맞은 말은?

내가 파스타를 만드는 것은 한 시간이 걸렸다. → It took an hour ___________ pasta.

① to me to make
② of me making
③ for me to make
④ of me to make
⑤ for me making

서술형

[12-13] ( ) 안의 말을 이용하여 문장을 완성하시오.

12 I decided ______________ your offer. (accept)

13 A: I'm going to city hall. Can you tell me ______________ the bus? (where, get off)
B: Get off at the next stop.

서술형

[14-16] 두 문장의 의미가 같도록 빈칸에 알맞은 말을 쓰시오.

14 This kimchi is so spicy that I can't eat it.

→ This kimchi is ______________.

15 This shelf is so strong that it can support more than a hundred books.

→ This shelf is ______________ more than a hundred books.

16 Tell me what I should do next.

→ Tell me ______________ next.

17 빈칸에 들어갈 말로 알맞지 않은 것은?

It was ___________ of her to say so.

① kind ② polite
③ rude ④ foolish
⑤ dangerous

18 빈칸에 들어갈 말이 나머지 넷과 다른 것은?

① It was fun ________ me to play chess with her.
② It's impossible ________ him to fix the earphones.
③ It was kind ________ her to help me with the homework.
④ It won't be easy ________ you to persuade him.
⑤ It is hard ________ me to taste the difference.

빈출

19 다음 두 문장의 의미가 같지 않은 것은?

① You need to pay more in order to buy the ticket.
→ To buy the ticket, you need to pay more.
② Ted taught me how to use the tool.
→ Ted taught me how I should use the tool.
③ This wood is so hard that I can't break it.
→ This wood is hard enough to break.
④ It was brave of Zoe to call the police.
→ Zoe was brave to call the police.
⑤ Nobody was to be seen in the park.
→ Nobody could be seen in the park.

서술형

[20-21] 우리말과 일치하도록 ( ) 안의 말을 이용하여 문장을 완성하시오.

20 그는 깨어나 보니 자신이 낯선 장소에 있음을 알게 되었다. (find, himself)

→ He woke up ________________ in a strange place.

21 이 단어의 의미는 알아맞히기 어렵다. (difficult, guess)

→ The meaning of this word ________________________.

서술형

[22-23] 우리말과 일치하도록 ( ) 안에 주어진 단어를 바르게 배열하시오.

22 그녀는 그 시험을 합격할 만큼 영리하지 않다. (pass, the test, enough, smart, to)

→ She's not ________________.

23 나는 내 친구에게 줄 좋은 무언가가 필요하다. (friend, to, nice, to, my, give, something)

→ I need ________________.

서술형 고난도

[24-25] 어법상 틀린 부분을 찾아 바르게 고치시오.

24 Last night, my mom called me. She said my grandmother passed away. I was too shocked saying anything. (1개)

25 My dream is travel around the world, but I don't have enough money. And I don't know what do. Can you give me some advice? (2개)

UNIT 01 동명사의 쓰임

A ( ) 안에서 알맞은 말을 고르시오.

1 (Wait, Waiting) for a long time made him angry.

2 His hobby is (build, building) model cars.

3 (Take, Taking) a taxi will be necessary to arrive on time.

4 Freddie quit (do, doing) yoga last month.

5 His job is (repair, repairing) big trucks.

6 On (to finish, finishing) his homework, he started playing computer games.

7 I feel like (to go, going) out with her this weekend.

8 The movie is worth (watch, watching) more than twice.

9 Would you mind (smoking not, not smoking) in this building?

10 Jennifer couldn't help (cry, crying) at the news.

B 밑줄 친 부분을 어법에 맞게 고치시오.

1 He is interested in take pictures of plants.

2 Julie doesn't like dance in front of people.

3 Would you mind to hold this for a second?

4 Her favorite thing is watch sports on TV.

5 She is never good at tell lies.

6 Carrie was tired of listen to the same music over and over.

7 Kyle was busy studied math for the exam next week.

8 Live without light is impossible.

9 Bret was fond of made model robots.

10 Tomorrow Abby will go ski with Stacie.

Answer Key p.29

C 보기를 참고하여 위의 두 문장과 의미가 통하도록 동명사를 이용하여 문장을 완성하시오.

보기	I often read fantasy novels. It is my hobby. → My hobby is <u>reading fantasy novels</u>.

1 I met a lot of people during the trip. I enjoyed it.
→ I enjoyed ______________________________.

2 I couldn't understand my parents. It was difficult for me.
→ ______________________________ was difficult for me.

3 He collects comic books. It is his hobby.
→ His hobby is ______________________________.

4 Do not point at someone. It is quite rude in Korea.
→ ______________________________ is quite rude in Korea.

5 The singer is busy. She is making her new album.
→ The singer ______________________________.

D 밑줄 친 부분에 유의하여 문장을 우리말로 해석하시오.

1 <u>Keeping</u> a diary every day is not easy.

2 My favorite activity is <u>hiking</u> with my children.

3 Lyle <u>went fishing</u> with his friends.

4 Tony <u>was busy preparing</u> dinner yesterday.

5 Jina doesn't <u>feel like going out</u> tonight.

6 Peter <u>couldn't help laughing</u> at her suggestion.

7 Would you <u>mind helping</u> me open this jar?

8 The shirts are <u>worth buying</u> because they look great.

9 <u>On arriving</u> home from his trip, he immediately wanted to go traveling again.

WRITING PRACTICE

Answer Key p.29

A 우리말과 일치하도록 ( ) 안의 말을 이용하여 문장을 완성하시오.

1 그녀의 취미는 여행 블로그를 작성하는 것이다. (write, a travel blog)
→ Her hobby is ______________________.

2 Ethan은 돈을 버는 데 흥미가 없다. (be interested in, make)
→ Ethan ______________________ money.

3 Dave와 Jean은 모임 시간을 바꾸는 것에 대해 이야기했다. (talk about, change)
→ Dave and Jean ______________________ the meeting time.

4 Wesley는 어렸을 때 농구를 잘했다. (be good at, play basketball)
→ Wesley ______________________ when he was young.

5 그는 너무 긴장해서, 진실을 말하지 않을 수 없었다. (help, tell the truth)
→ He ______________________ because he was so nervous.

6 이 책은 여러 번 읽을 가치가 있다. (be worth)
→ This book ______________________ several times.

B 우리말과 일치하도록 ( ) 안에 주어진 단어를 바르게 배열하시오.

1 그녀는 그 상을 받는 것을 자랑스러워했다. (was, winning, of, proud, she)
→ ______________________ the award.

2 Ron은 그 책에 대한 보고서를 쓰느라 바빴다. (a report, busy, writing, was)
→ Ron ______________________ about the book.

3 그의 습관은 그의 손톱을 깨무는 것이다. (nails, is, his, biting)
→ His habit ______________________.

4 Maggie는 맛이 없어서 저녁 식사를 끝내지 못했다. (finish, dinner, Maggie, eating, didn't)
→ ______________________ because it did not taste good.

5 다른 문화를 존중하는 것은 중요하다. (cultures, different, respecting, important, is)
→ ______________________.

6 그는 많은 관중 앞에서 말하는 것을 두려워했다. (of, speaking, was, he, afraid)
→ ______________________ in front of large audiences.

UNIT 02

동명사와 to부정사

Answer Key p.29

A ( ) 안에서 알맞은 말을 고르시오.

1 We are planning (going, to go) to the beach.
2 He didn't avoid (doing, to do) difficult jobs.
3 Damon forgot (buying, to buy) the pen, so he bought one more.
4 I began (feel, to feel) that something was not right.
5 Ramon wanted (going, to go) swimming this summer.
6 Don't forget (locking, to lock) the door before you go out.
7 Wade hoped (buying, to buy) a brand new car.
8 I decided (cleaning, to clean) my room before my friends came over.
9 Someone kept (knocking, to knock) on the door last night.
10 Clark enjoys (traveling, to travel), so he is always planning to go somewhere.

B 밑줄 친 부분을 어법에 맞게 고치시오.

1 April promised buy her brother an iPad.
2 Do you mind to move this chair outside?
3 Because of the traffic, we needed leaving earlier.
4 Remember turn off the light before you go to bed.
5 She just finished to writing her tenth novel.
6 Greg practiced shoot the ball all night.
7 I gave up to be a vegetarian last year.
8 I stopped to take the medicine because I felt better.
9 Don't forget calling me tomorrow.
10 I never expected seeing his sister here.

C (　) 안에 주어진 말을 이용하여 문장을 완성하시오.

1 I remember ________________ in Jinju when I was young. (live)

2 I forgot ________________ my wallet, so I don't have any money. (bring)

3 Paul practices ________________ 1 km every morning. (run)

4 Noah tried ________________ the drawer, but he couldn't. (open)

5 He avoided ________________ Mia because he didn't like her. (meet)

6 Lisa didn't expect ________________ a medal in the contest. (win)

7 Anna doesn't plan ________________ abroad for this summer vacation. (go)

8 They stopped ________________ when their teacher arrived. (fight)

9 Clair decided ________________ her parents her secret. (tell)

10 Carl finished ________________ for his math test. (study)

D 밑줄 친 부분에 유의하여 문장을 우리말로 해석하시오.

1 The baby started crying as soon as she saw me.

2 Don't forget to bring the car key with you.

3 Diane stopped smoking for her health.

4 He tried to concentrate on his work, but he couldn't.

5 Nick tried putting on the jeans.

6 My mom loves to drink coffee.

7 She forgot adding salt to the soup, so she added some more.

8 William remembered lending his money to Zoe.

9 She stopped to answer her cell phone.

10 Remember to turn off the stove when you go out.

WRITING PRACTICE

Answer Key p.29

A 우리말과 일치하도록 ( ) 안의 말을 이용하여 문장을 완성하시오.

1 Nate는 과식하는 것을 피했다. (avoid, eat)

→ Nate ______________________________ too much.

2 그 노인은 죽기 전에 그의 딸을 보고 싶어 했다. (want, see, daughter)

→ The old man ______________________________ before he died.

3 그녀는 아기들 사진 찍는 걸 즐긴다. (enjoy, take pictures)

→ She ______________________________ of babies.

4 Michelle은 우리에게 작별 선물을 주기로 약속했다. (promise, give)

→ Michelle ______________________________ farewell presents.

5 내 시계는 이틀 전에 작동하는 것을 멈췄다. (stop, work)

→ My watch ______________________________ two days ago.

6 나는 오래전에 그를 만났던 것을 기억한다. (remember, meet)

→ I ______________________________ long ago.

B 우리말과 일치하도록 ( ) 안에 주어진 단어를 바르게 배열하시오.

1 그녀는 어머니에게 전화해야 하는 것을 잊었다. (forgot, her mother, call, to, she)

→ ______________________________.

2 내 슬리퍼 좀 갖다 주지 않을래? (bringing, would, me, you, mind)

→ ______________________________ my slippers?

3 Mandy는 거리의 장미꽃 냄새를 맡으려고 멈춰 섰다. (to, roses, Mandy, stopped, the, smell)

→ ______________________________ on the street.

4 Alex는 그 대회까지 계속 연습해야 한다. (the competition, should, keep, until, practicing)

→ Alex ______________________________.

5 그녀는 Tom과 시간 보내는 것을 좋아한다. (time, with, spending, she, Tom, likes)

→ ______________________________.

6 호텔에 예약해야 하는 것을 기억해라. (make, a, remember, to, reservation)

→ ______________________________ at the hotel.

REVIEW TEST

[1-3] 빈칸에 들어갈 알맞은 말을 고르시오.

1

________ too much soda is not good for your health.

① Drink ② Drinks
③ Drank ④ Drinking
⑤ To drinking

2

Percy was busy ________ an essay about his life.

① write ② wrote
③ written ④ writing
⑤ to write

3

They talked about ________ a TV for their new house.

① buy ② bought
③ buying ④ to buy
⑤ to buying

4 다음 문장에서 not이 들어갈 위치로 적절한 것은?

How ⓐ about ⓑ wearing ⓒ that ⓓ hat ⓔ?

① ⓐ ② ⓑ ③ ⓒ ④ ⓓ ⑤ ⓔ

[5-6] 다음 중 어법상 틀린 것을 고르시오.

5 ① Henry decided to change his major.
② I'm afraid of going out alone at night.
③ Dave avoided to do the hard work.
④ Being silent is sometimes the best solution.
⑤ He gave up teaching his younger brother.

6 ① Andy planned to buy a new cell phone.
② I enjoyed having dinner with Bob.
③ Jenny stopped to talk to the stranger.
④ He likes to walk along the beach.
⑤ My sister is fond of buy clothes.

빈출

7 다음 우리말을 영어로 바르게 옮긴 것은?

Greg은 집세 내는 것을 잊었다.

① Greg forgot pay the rent.
② Greg forgot paying the rent.
③ Greg forgot to paying the rent.
④ Greg forgot to pay the rent.
⑤ Greg forgot paid the rent.

빈출

[8-9] 빈칸에 들어갈 말로 알맞지 않은 것을 고르시오.

8

Christina didn't ________ having a conversation with her mom.

① avoid ② enjoy
③ mind ④ finish
⑤ agree

9 | I ________ to learn how to dribble the ball. |

① wanted ② started
③ hoped ④ quit
⑤ wished

서술형

[10-12] 우리말과 일치하도록 어법상 틀린 부분을 찾아 바르게 고치시오.

10 Carl은 엄마를 위해 그 일을 한 것을 자랑스러워했다.

→ Carl was proud of do the job for his mom.

11 내 시계를 다시 가져오는 거 잊지 말아라.

→ Don't forget bringing my watch back.

12 그녀는 오후 내내 그의 기분을 낫게 해주려고 노력했다.

→ She tried making him feel better all afternoon.

[13-14] 다음 중 어법상 옳은 것을 고르시오.

13 ① I never expected to go there again.
② Kirk wants taking a shower now.
③ He quit to play the electric guitar.
④ She has just finished to take a walk.
⑤ He was afraid of to make mistakes.

14 ① He planned visiting his aunt in July.
② She stopped to buy some fruit.
③ He promised buying me coffee.
④ On arrive here, I felt dizzy.
⑤ This book is not worth to read.

서술형

[15-17] ( ) 안의 말을 이용하여 문장을 완성하시오.

15 Don't forget ____________ your medicine before you go to bed. (take)

16 If you're finished ____________, please do the dishes. (eat)

17 The movie is worth ____________ in the theater. (see)

18 다음 중 밑줄 친 부분을 바르게 고친 것은?

① She was busy look around.
→ to look

② I kept sing a song.
→ sang

③ He wanted learning French.
→ learns

④ He gave up to exercise every day.
→ exercising

⑤ She couldn't help take notes.
→ to take

서술형

[19-21] 우리말과 일치하도록 ( ) 안에 주어진 단어를 바르게 배열하시오.

19 어둠 속에서 핸드폰을 사용하는 것은 너의 눈에 좋지 않다. (in, phone, using, dark, your, the)

→ ______________________ is not good for your eyes.

20 그녀는 수업 시간에 자는 나쁜 버릇을 가지고 있다. (of, she, a, habit, bad, has, sleeping)

→ ______________________ during the class.

21 Ted는 새로운 사람들을 만나는 것을 좋아한다. (new, people, likes, meet, to, Ted)

→ ______________________.

서술형

[22-23] 우리말과 일치하도록 ( ) 안의 말을 이용하여 문장을 완성하시오.

22 그는 그의 발음을 향상시키기 위해서 영어로 말하는 것을 연습했다. (practice, speak)

→ He ______________________ in English to improve his pronunciation.

23 그녀는 그 책에 집중하려고 음악 듣는 것을 멈췄다. (stop, listen to)

→ She ______________________ to focus on the book.

서술형 고난도

[24-25] 어법상 틀린 부분을 찾아 바르게 고치시오.

24 After the breakup, Eric tried to forget about his ex-girlfriend, but he couldn't help to think about her. (1개)

25 When the plane started to shake, I remembered to be in a car accident when I was ten years old. And I felt like to throw up. (2개)

UNIT 01

현재분사와 과거분사

Answer Key p.30

A

( ) 안에서 알맞은 말을 고르시오.

1 The girl (talked, talking) with Connor is my sister.

2 I can read a book (writing, written) in Latin.

3 She felt (boring, bored) with the show.

4 Gary was (satisfying, satisfied) with his grade.

5 Don't wake up the (sleeping, slept) twins.

6 Kelly is a doctor (knowing, known) to everyone in that town.

7 My father sat (reading, read) the newspaper on the sofa.

8 Universal Studios is an (exciting, excited) place for kids.

9 We had an (amazing, amazed) trip to the museum.

10 He has a big dog (naming, named) Bruce.

B

밑줄 친 부분을 어법에 맞게 고치시오.

1 I heard shock news about the actor.

2 She was interesting in sports cars.

3 The people wait in line outside are mostly girls.

4 They were exciting when they saw the singer.

5 Jim seemed surprise by the show.

6 I can hardly walk with my breaking leg.

7 English is the language speak in Australia.

8 The girl play in the garden is Ray's second daughter.

9 They stood looked at the pictures on the wall.

10 That amusement park is famous, but it was bored to me.

C ( ) 안의 말을 이용하여 문장을 완성하시오.

1 The woman ______________ the gray hat is Brad's mother. (wear)

2 People all over the world like cars ______________ in Korea. (make)

3 The service at the hotel was quite ______________. (satisfy)

4 This is the house ______________ by David ten years ago. (build)

5 I am looking for someone ______________ in science. (interest)

6 Ryan looked ______________ after running. (tire)

7 I haven't had my hair ______________ for a few months. (cut)

8 Do you know the girl ______________ on the stage? (dance)

9 Harry told me an ______________ story. (excite)

10 The baby sat ______________ with toys on the floor. (play)

D 보기와 같이 두 문장을 한 문장으로 바꿀 때, 빈칸에 알맞은 말을 쓰시오.

보기	I brought a box. The box was made of wood. → I brought a box made of wood.

1 The picture is valuable. It was painted by Picasso.

→ The picture ______________________________ is valuable.

2 They talked about a girl. She was wearing a long coat.

→ They talked about a girl ______________________________.

3 They shouted at a man. He was carrying a yellow backpack.

→ They shouted at a man ______________________________.

4 I like the black tea. It was imported from India.

→ I like the black tea ______________________________.

5 I saw a boy. He was practicing basketball in the rain.

→ I saw a boy ______________________________.

WRITING PRACTICE

Answer Key p.30

A 우리말과 일치하도록 분사와 ( ) 안의 말을 이용하여 문장을 완성하시오.

1 종이로 덮인 상자는 내 것이다. (cover, with paper)

→ The box ________________ is mine.

2 나는 그 무대 위에서 노래하고 있는 남자의 사진을 찍었다. (sing, the stage)

→ I took a photo of a man ________________.

3 Brian은 그 고장난 문을 고칠 수 있다. (fix, break, door)

→ Brian can ________________.

4 그의 제안은 내게 놀랍게 들렸다. (sound, amaze)

→ His proposal ________________ to me.

5 찬물이 가득 찬 병 세 개를 제게 가져다주세요. (bottle, fill with)

→ Please bring me ________________ cold water.

6 여왕은 나무 한 그루가 그녀의 정원에 심어지게 했다. (have, a tree, plant)

→ The queen ________________ in her garden.

B 우리말과 일치하도록 ( ) 안에 주어진 단어를 바르게 배열하시오.

1 그 남자는 통화를 하면서 앉아 있었다. (the man, phone, sat, the, on, talking)

→ ________________.

2 Susie가 입은 저 치마는 꽤 비싸다. (Susie, skirt, worn, that, by)

→ ________________ is quite expensive.

3 저쪽에서 날 기다리고 있는 소년은 Tim이다. (there, over, the boy, for, waiting, me)

→ ________________ is Tim.

4 Tony는 이야기 나누기에 아주 흥미로운 사람이다. (to, very, to, person, a, talk, interesting)

→ Tony is ________________.

5 이것이 파파라치에게 찍힌 그 사진이다. (by, picture, taken, the paparazzi, the)

→ This is ________________.

6 너와 식당에서 저녁을 먹던 그 남자는 누구였니? (with, man, dinner, was, the, who, having, you)

→ ________________ in the restaurant?

UNIT 02 분사구문

A ( ) 안에서 알맞은 말을 고르시오.

1 (Hand, Handing) in her report, she said sorry to her teacher.

2 He always does his homework (sat, sitting) on that couch.

3 (Hugging, Hugged) me, she thanked me for coming.

4 (See, Seeing) the police officer, the boy ran away.

5 (Wanting, Wanted) to learn Korean, he decided to go to Korea.

6 (Be, Being) late, I missed the beginning of the movie.

7 (Turn, Turning) left, you will find the clothing store.

8 (Lie, Lying) on my bed, I played games online.

9 (Wear, Wearing) only a thin jacket, I felt cold.

10 (Smiled, Smiling) brightly, Dad winked at me.

B 다음 문장을 분사구문으로 바꿔 쓰시오.

1 When I looked out the window, I saw my teacher.
→ ______________________, I saw my teacher.

2 If you take the bus, you can get there in ten minutes.
→ ______________________, you can get there in ten minutes.

3 As I felt tired, I didn't cook dinner last night.
→ ______________________, I didn't cook dinner last night.

4 While he was lifting heavy boxes, he hurt his arm.
→ ______________________, he hurt his arm.

5 Because I wanted to learn how to play tennis, I started taking lessons.
→ ______________________, I started taking lessons.

6 After he put down his book, he walked over to the door.
→ ______________________, he walked over to the door.

Answer Key p.30

C 밑줄 친 분사구문을 「접속사 + 주어 + 동사」의 형태로 바꾸시오.

1 Though being upset with her, he tried to be calm.
→ ______________________, he tried to be calm.

2 Sitting on the beach, I watched the sunset.
→ ______________________, I watched the sunset.

3 Turning right at City Tower, you can see an old gray building.
→ ______________________, you can see an old gray building.

4 Getting off the bus, she fell down.
→ ______________________, she fell down.

5 Having no money, I couldn't buy pizza.
→ ______________________, I couldn't buy pizza.

6 After having dinner, I took a walk.
→ ______________________, I took a walk.

D 밑줄 친 부분에 유의하여 문장을 우리말로 해석하시오.

1 Waiting for my turn, I read a magazine.
2 Being overwhelmed by the results, she couldn't even say a word.
3 Taking him to my home, I showed him around.
4 Being tired after work, I don't want to do anything.
5 Being Korean, he always likes to eat kimchi and rice.
6 Arriving at the airport, I called my mother.
7 Driving through the traffic jam, he became worried about arriving late.
8 Listening to the radio, James did his homework.
9 Before going to bed, I always set my alarm.
10 Turning left, you will see a house.

WRITING PRACTICE

Answer Key p.30

A 우리말과 일치하도록 분사구문과 ( ) 안의 말을 이용하여 문장을 완성하시오.

1 지하철을 타면 우리는 시간을 절약할 수 있다. (take, the subway)

→ ______________________________, we can save time.

2 그 오래된 다리를 건너면서 그녀는 불안함을 느꼈다. (cross, the old bridge)

→ ______________________________, she felt nervous.

3 Tommy는 우울해서 하루종일 집에 있었다. (feel, depressed)

→ ______________________________, Tommy stayed home all day.

4 집에 왔을 때, 나는 엄마가 요리하는 것을 보았다. (arrive, home)

→ ______________________________, I saw my mother cooking.

5 그 소식을 듣고 Bob은 울기 시작했다. (hear, the news)

→ ______________________________, Bob began to cry.

6 우리 할아버지는 연세가 아주 많으셔서 별로 건강하지 않으시다. (be, very old)

→ ______________________________, my grandfather is not very healthy.

B 우리말과 일치하도록 ( ) 안에 주어진 단어를 바르게 배열하시오.

1 테니스를 치다가 나는 발목을 삐었다. (I, playing, sprained, tennis)

→ ____ my ankle.

2 시간이 별로 없기 때문에 우리는 서둘러야 한다. (hurry, having, to, up, we, have, time, little)

→ ____.

3 그의 집 뒷길을 청소하다가 Paul은 동전 몇 개를 발견했다.
(the street, house, his, cleaning, behind)

→ ____, Paul found some coins.

4 시간이 없어서 그는 모든 문제를 풀 수 없었다. (couldn't, time, solve, running, he, out of)

→ ____ all the questions.

5 책을 읽으면서 나는 커피 한 잔을 마셨다. (I, reading, a, drank, book)

→ ____ a cup of coffee.

6 이 기차를 타면 너는 부산을 세 시간 안에 갈 수 있다. (get, Busan, train, taking, can, to, you, this)

→ ____ within three hours.

REVIEW TEST

Answer Key p.30

[1-5] 빈칸에 들어갈 알맞은 말을 고르시오.

1

I have no idea what to do with the ________ baby.

① cry ② cried
③ crying ④ to cry
⑤ to crying

2

The police found a suitcase ________ with money.

① fill ② fills
③ filled ④ filling
⑤ to fill

3

I was ________ about winning first prize.

① excite ② excites
③ exciting ④ excited
⑤ to excite

4

________ the sunrise, she made a wish.

① Watch ② Watches
③ Watching ④ Watched
⑤ Being watched

5

________ on the beach for too long, he got sunburned.

① Walk ② Walking
③ To walk ④ Walked
⑤ Being walked

6 다음 중 어법상 옳은 것은?

① The accident was very shocked.
② I was tiring with the work.
③ Eric was touching by the movie.
④ She sat talked on the phone.
⑤ The new drama series was really interesting.

7 빈칸에 들어갈 말이 순서대로 바르게 짝지어진 것은?

• The horror movie was very ________.
• I was ________ by the horror movie.

① bore – bore ② boring – boring
③ boring – bored ④ bored – boring
⑤ bored – bored

[8-9] 다음 중 밑줄 친 부분이 잘못된 것을 고르시오.

8

① The news was very surprising to her.
② The match isn't interesting to me.
③ The children sat drew a picture.
④ The barking dog is my neighbor's.
⑤ The new bed was very satisfying.

9 ① She bought a chair made of wood.
② The cat looking at me is cute.
③ Had a fever, I took some medicine.
④ Listening to music, I read some books.
⑤ I found something covered with white cloth.

빈출

[10-11] 밑줄 친 부분의 쓰임이 나머지 넷과 다른 것을 고르시오.

10 ① I talked to the girls taking photos.
② It was a really boring movie.
③ His job is delivering packages to customers.
④ The lady planting trees there is my aunt.
⑤ I heard her cooking something at night.

11 ① Being cute, she is popular at school.
② Being with you makes me happy.
③ Being tired, Olive took a rest.
④ Being in a bad mood, he didn't want to do anything.
⑤ Being poor at math, he always asked me questions.

서술형 빈출

[12-14] 밑줄 친 부분을 분사구문으로 바꿔 쓰시오.

12 When you leave the house, don't forget to lock the door.

→ ______________________, don't forget to lock the door.

13 As she thought of her family, she cried.

→ ______________________, she cried.

14 As he runs frequently, he keeps fit.

→ ______________________, he keeps fit.

[15-16] 밑줄 친 부분의 의미로 가장 적절한 것을 고르시오.

15 Having lunch together, they talked about moving to Seoul.

① Although they had lunch together
② Because they had lunch together
③ When they had lunch together
④ So they had lunch together
⑤ If they had lunch together

16 Being sick with a cold, I didn't go to school yesterday.

① As I was sick with a cold
② If I was sick with a cold
③ Before I was sick with a cold
④ Unless I was sick with a cold
⑤ Though I was sick with a cold

서술형

[17-18] ( ) 안의 말을 적절한 형태로 써서 문장을 완성하시오.

17 He has a cute hamster __________ Jerry. (call)

18 ______ today's newspaper, he became upset. (read)

서술형

[19-20] 우리말과 일치하도록 분사와 ( ) 안의 말을 이용하여 문장을 완성하시오.

19 시간이 없어서 나는 택시를 타야 했다.
(have, no time)

→ ______, I had to take a taxi.

20 나는 그의 영어 실력에 놀랐다. (amaze)

→ ______ at his English.

21 다음 중 보기의 밑줄 친 부분과 쓰임이 같은 것은?

보기	This is one of the biggest swimming pools in the world.

① The swimming girl is cute.
② There is no drinking water in the room.
③ I saw you riding a horse.
④ The boy skiing on the mountain is my cousin.
⑤ The people relaxing on the grass look happy.

서술형

[22-23] 우리말과 일치하도록 ( ) 안에 주어진 단어를 바르게 배열하시오.

22 그 남자를 보는 사람은 누구든지 우리에게 당장 알려주어야 한다.
(seeing, should, man, the, anyone)

→ ______ inform us immediately.

23 열심히 공부해서 그는 좋은 점수를 받았다.
(hard, studying, got, he)

→ ______ good grades.

서술형 고난도

[24-25] 어법상 틀린 부분을 찾아 바르게 고치시오.

24 Last summer, I went to Europe. Travel around, I met a lot of people. I was alone, but I was not boring. (2개)

25 I was so exciting to see a magic show yesterday. Watch the show, I was very amusing. It was so realistic that I couldn't look away. (3개)

UNIT 01

능동태와 수동태

A

( ) 안에서 알맞은 말을 고르시오.

1 James (solved, was solved) the math problem easily.

2 The musical (loves, is loved) by many people.

3 The car (is be washed, is being washed) by my brother now.

4 This movie (made, was made) in 2009.

5 The concert (will be holding, will be held) in the main hall.

6 Many students (respect, are respected) my English teacher.

7 This machine (was inventing, was invented) a long time ago.

8 Gyeongju (visits, is visited) by many tourists every year.

9 Pizza (is cooking, is being cooked) by my father.

10 Your order (will be cancel, will be canceled) within a few days.

B

밑줄 친 부분을 어법에 맞게 고치시오.

1 This ring will keep in my secret drawer.

2 She was injuring at the ski resort.

3 They will be divided the money equally.

4 The cookies are be baked in the oven now.

5 She was being taken a picture at that time.

6 Drones are use for many purposes.

7 The project is be doing by Brian now.

8 These days, a lot of people are loved that song.

9 The play will performed by some college students.

10 The wall was painted Samuel.

Answer Key p.31

C

다음을 수동태 문장으로 바꿔 쓰시오.

1 Oliver is writing an email.

→ ________________________________

2 My boss will change the meeting schedule.

→ ________________________________

3 My son painted the picture.

→ ________________________________

4 The little girl loves this doll.

→ ________________________________

5 The guests share the bathroom.

→ ________________________________

6 We will clean the office this weekend.

→ ________________________________

D

빈칸에 알맞은 말을 보기에서 골라 쓰시오. (단, 한 번씩만 쓸 것)

[1-4]

보기	will be finished	stole	is being repaired	was directed

1 The movie ______________ by Mr. Han.

2 Someone ______________ my purse yesterday.

3 The work ______________ tomorrow.

4 My car ______________ by him now.

[5-7]

보기	will be delivered	was designed	is being used

5 The house ______________ by my grandfather.

6 My laptop ______________ by my brother now.

7 The food ______________ soon.

WRITING PRACTICE

Answer Key p.31

A 우리말과 일치하도록 ( ) 안의 말을 이용하여 문장을 완성하시오.

1 이 시는 유명한 시인에 의해 쓰였다. (write)
→ This poem ______________________ a famous poet.

2 이 사진은 내 삼촌이 찍어주셨다. (take)
→ This picture ______________________ my uncle.

3 스테이크는 Luke에 의해 요리될 것이다. (will, cook)
→ The steak ______________________ Luke.

4 우리의 삶은 기술에 의해 바뀌고 있다. (change)
→ Our lives ______________________ technology.

5 이 영화는 많은 사람들에 의해 관람되었다. (see)
→ This film ______________________ many people.

6 자동차 사고가 지금 TV에서 보도되는 중이다. (report)
→ A car accident ______________________ on TV now.

B 우리말과 일치하도록 ( ) 안에 주어진 단어를 바르게 배열하시오.

1 많은 차들이 도로에 주차되어 있다. (the, parked, on, are, road)
→ A lot of cars ______________________.

2 이 모니터는 한국에서 만들어졌다. (was, Korea, this, monitor, in, made)
→ ______________________.

3 이 그림은 1990년에 그려졌다. (was, this, picture, painted)
→ ______________________ in 1990.

4 이 돈은 아픈 사람들을 돕는 데 쓰여질 것이다. (will, sick, people, be, used, help, to)
→ This money ______________________.

5 그 만화책은 나의 형에 의해 읽히는 중이다. (brother, is, read, my, by, being)
→ The comic book ______________________.

6 스페인어는 라틴 아메리카의 많은 나라에서 말해진다.
(is, many, Spanish, countries, spoken, in)
→ ______________________ in Latin America.

UNIT 02

수동태의 여러 가지 형태

Answer Key p.31

A

( ) 안에서 알맞은 말을 고르시오.

1 Claire (wasn't invited, didn't invited) to the wedding.
2 (Was, Did) the report written by you?
3 Your brother was heard (leave, leaving) the apartment.
4 This book was given (to, of) me by my friend.
5 The singer (called, was called) Little Prince by many people.
6 The jacket was bought (to, for) me by my father.
7 The puzzle can (is solved, be solved) by us.
8 He was made (doing, to do) the laundry by his wife.
9 She was heard (sing, singing) a sad song.
10 Some favors were asked (to, of) me by him.

B

밑줄 친 부분을 어법에 맞게 고치시오.

1 The black jeans were bought <u>to</u> me by my aunt.
2 Samantha was told <u>brush</u> her teeth.
3 He was made <u>clean</u> the restroom by his teacher.
4 <u>Did</u> this chocolate made by you?
5 All products must <u>tested</u> before they're sold.
6 A suspicious package was sent <u>for</u> her house by an unknown person.
7 This spaghetti <u>didn't cooked</u> by my mom.
8 The cat <u>named</u> Meow by my sister when it was little.
9 I was taught <u>to soccer</u> by a famous coach.
10 She was seen <u>enter</u> the room last night.

C

다음을 수동태 문장으로 바꿔 쓰시오.

1 Mr. Lee didn't write this novel.

→ ______________________________

2 You must keep milk in a cool place.

→ ______________________________

3 Did you push the button?

→ ______________________________

4 His parents allowed him to go camping.

→ ______________________________

5 When did they build this bridge?

→ ______________________________

D

다음을 주어진 말로 시작하는 수동태 문장으로 바꿔 쓰시오.

1 They gave him first prize.

→ He ______________________.

→ First prize ______________________.

2 They made me do the paperwork.

→ I ______________________.

3 I saw him run across the street.

→ He ______________________.

4 Her mom made her the long dress.

→ The long dress ______________________.

5 My family named the dog King.

→ The dog ______________________.

WRITING PRACTICE

Answer Key p.31

A 우리말과 일치하도록 ( ) 안의 말을 이용하여 문장을 완성하시오.

1 그 수학 문제는 누구에 의해서도 풀리지 않았다. (solve)

→ The math problem ____________________ by anyone.

2 이 소설은 Kim 씨에 의해 번역되었니? (novel, translate)

→ ____________________ by Mr. Kim?

3 이 스웨터는 찬물에 세탁되어야 한다. (must, wash)

→ This sweater ____________________ in cold water.

4 그 개가 마당에서 짖는 소리가 들렸다. (hear, bark)

→ The dog ____________________ in the yard.

5 그 예쁜 크리스마스 카드는 내 친구가 나에게 보낸 것이다. (send)

→ The pretty Christmas card ____________________ by my friend.

6 나는 아침 일찍 일어나도록 시켜졌다. (make, get up)

→ I ____________________ early in the morning.

B 우리말과 일치하도록 ( ) 안에 주어진 단어를 바르게 배열하시오.

1 그 이메일은 엉뚱한 사람에게 보내졌다. (wrong, person, sent, the, was, to)

→ The email ______________________________.

2 주방은 깨끗하게 유지되어야 한다. (be, clean, kept, should)

→ The kitchen ______________________________.

3 요리사가 그릴에 음식을 요리하고 있는 것이 보였다. (food, was, the chef, seen, cooking)

→ ______________________________ on the grill.

4 네가 더 열심히 노력한다면 너의 쓰기 실력이 향상될 수 있다.
(improved, your, can, be, writing skills)

→ ______________________________ if you work harder.

5 화재는 그 장치에 의해 야기되지 않았다. (fire, caused, not, the, was)

→ ______________________________ by the device.

6 그는 사무실에서 늦게까지 일하도록 강요받았다. (to, he, made, work, was, late)

→ ______________________________ at the office.

UNIT 03

주의해야 할 수동태

A

( ) 안에서 알맞은 말을 고르시오.

1 My bicycle was (run over, run over by) a fire truck.
2 Her brave story is known (to, at) lots of people in the world.
3 His room is filled (at, with) garbage.
4 His funny clothes (laughed, were laughed) at by his friends.
5 She (appeared, was appeared) in the street.
6 I (brought up, was brought up) by my grandparents.
7 He is satisfied (in, with) his new school.
8 My grandfather was looked up to (my family, by my family).
9 Are you interested (in, by) studying economics?
10 The books were covered (at, with) dust.

B

다음을 수동태 문장으로 바꿔 쓰시오.

1 Tina will take care of two boys.
→ ____________________

2 The results of the election surprised me.
→ ____________________

3 Her behavior disappointed me.
→ ____________________

4 My grandmother looked after the lost dog.
→ ____________________

5 The French cook looked down on my cooking.
→ ____________________

6 They will put off their visit for several days.
→ ____________________

Answer Key p.31

C 밑줄 친 부분을 어법에 맞게 고치시오.

1 The parade was putting off because of the typhoon.
2 David Beckham is known in most soccer fans.
3 I was surprised in their presentation.
4 My purse suddenly was disappeared.
5 Cheese made from milk.
6 Serena wasn't satisfied at her score.
7 The car accident was happened this morning.
8 My son will be looked after my sister tomorrow.
9 Our boss is looked up by all of us.
10 Be careful! The floor is covered of water.

D 빈칸에 알맞은 말을 보기에서 골라 쓰시오. (단, 한 번씩만 쓸 것)

[1-3]

보기	with	at	in

1 We were surprised ________ the score of the baseball game.
2 I am interested ________ action movies.
3 She is pleased ________ her success.

[4-6]

보기	with	of	to

4 This TV show is known ________ most Koreans.
5 This soup is made ________ vegetables.
6 My email box is filled ________ junk mail.

WRITING PRACTICE

Answer Key p.31

A 우리말과 일치하도록 ( ) 안의 말을 이용하여 문장을 완성하시오.

1 그 도로는 눈으로 덮여 있었다. (cover)
→ The road ______________________ snow.

2 James는 그 배우를 닮았다. (resemble, actor)
→ James ______________________.

3 이 아픈 사람들은 그 의사에 의해 돌보아진다. (take care of)
→ These sick people ______________________ the doctor.

4 많은 사람들이 그의 과학적 발견에 놀랐다. (surprise)
→ Many people ______________________ his scientific discovery.

5 태양이 구름 뒤에서 나타났다. (appear)
→ The sun ______________________ from behind the clouds.

6 이 웹 사이트는 잘못된 정보로 가득 차 있다. (fill)
→ This website ______________________ wrong information.

B 우리말과 일치하도록 ( ) 안에 주어진 단어를 바르게 배열하시오.

1 그 햄스터들은 그 어린 소년에 의해 보살핌을 받았다. (by, care, were, the hamsters, taken, of)
→ ______________________ the little boy.

2 그는 그 영화의 결말에 실망했다. (the, he, was, disappointed, ending, with)
→ ______________________ of the movie.

3 이 노래는 젊은 사람들에게는 알려져 있지 않다. (people, song, isn't, known, this, young, to)
→ ______________________.

4 나의 어머니는 하이킹에 관심이 있으시다. (in, mother, interested, my, hiking, is)
→ ______________________.

5 그는 그의 생일 파티에 만족했니? (he, with, birthday party, his, was, satisfied)
→ ______________________?

6 그 목걸이는 진주로 만들어졌다. (the, made, necklace, pearls, is, of)
→ ______________________.

REVIEW TEST

Answer Key p.32

[1-5] 빈칸에 들어갈 알맞은 말을 고르시오.

1 The sweater ________ by my mom.

① knit ② knits
③ to knit ④ knitted
⑤ was knitted

2 This computer must ________ quickly.

① fix ② is fixing
③ is fixed ④ be fixing
⑤ be fixed

3 I was made ________ home by Dad.

① stay ② stays
③ staying ④ to stay
⑤ stayed

4 The children were seen ________ computer games.

① playing ② played
③ be playing ④ be played
⑤ play

5 I was surprised ________ her income.

① to ② of ③ for
④ in ⑤ at

[6-7] 다음 중 어법상 틀린 것을 고르시오.

6
① The robot was named Kim.
② An action film will be shown on TV.
③ Your package is being delivered now.
④ The white laptop was had by Sam.
⑤ Pieces of paper were given to me.

7
① Were the flowers watered often?
② The film is loved by many people.
③ The shirt was bought to me by Zoe.
④ The desk was painted white by Dad.
⑤ The plan was delayed by them.

빈출

[8-9] 빈칸에 공통으로 들어갈 말을 고르시오.

8
- I was disappointed ________ the test result.
- I'm satisfied ________ my new car.

① of ② at ③ in
④ with ⑤ to

9
- This skirt was bought ________ me by my sister.
- The cookies were made ________ him by his mom.

① of ② at ③ by
④ for ⑤ to

[10-11] 다음 우리말을 영어로 바르게 옮긴 것을 고르시오.

10 그 질문은 그에 의해 답변될 수 있다.

① The question is answered by him.
② The question is being answered by him.
③ The question can be answered by him.
④ The question can answered by him.
⑤ The question can answer by him.

11 그 사진들이 Lisa에 의해 그에게 보내졌다.

① The pictures sent him by Lisa.
② The pictures were sent him by Lisa.
③ The pictures were sent to him by Lisa.
④ The pictures were sent for him by Lisa.
⑤ The pictures were sent of him by Lisa.

12 다음 중 어법상 옳은 것은?

① Did the cake was made by you?
② I didn't invited to her birthday party.
③ She was seen going out with Tom.
④ He was made wearing a seat belt by his mother.
⑤ Lunch was bought me by Tony.

서술형 빈출

[13-15] ( ) 안의 말을 이용하여 문장을 완성하시오.

13 The vacation will ____________ by my parents. (plan)

14 The dog was seen ____________ in the park. (run)

15 The children were made ____________ the room by Mr. Brown. (leave)

서술형

[16-19] 다음 문장을 수동태로 바꿀 때 빈칸에 알맞은 말을 쓰시오.

16 Amy taught them English.

→ They ________________________ by Amy.

17 Millions of fans love the singer.

→ The singer ________________________.

18 She looked after the children with love.

→ The children ________________.

19 Tom is upgrading my computer now.

→ My computer ________________ now.

서술형

[20-21] 우리말과 일치하도록 ( ) 안의 말을 이용하여 문장을 완성하시오.

20 그 비밀은 Benjamin이 나에게 이야기해줬다. (tell)

→ The secret ________________.

21 그 벽은 그의 그림으로 가득 차 있었다. (fill, paintings)

→ The wall ________________.

서술형

[22-23] 우리말과 일치하도록 ( ) 안에 주어진 단어를 바르게 배열하시오.

22 그 코치는 그 선수들로부터 존경을 받았다. (looked, by, to, players, up, the, was)

→ The coach ________________
________________.

23 나는 아빠에 의해 중국어를 배우게 되었다. (by, my, made, learn, was, to, Chinese, dad)

→ I ________________
________________.

서술형 고난도

[24-25] 어법상 틀린 부분을 찾아 바르게 고치시오.

24 My brother made a desk himself. He is interested by making things out of wood. (1개)

25 On Christmas Day, Ted was giving a gift by his parents. He was greatly pleased for it. (2개)

UNIT 01

부정대명사 I

( ) 안에서 알맞은 말을 고르시오.

1 (All, Every) the questions on the exam were difficult.

2 Ron and Harry are basketball players. (Both, Each) are good.

3 Do you have (any, every) problems with your chair?

4 (Each, Both) player has a chance to choose a card.

5 (Some, Every) girl in the school likes Jim.

6 I don't have a tablet. I want to have (it, one).

7 I'm hungry. I want to eat (some, any) food.

8 I don't like these white jeans. Show me some black (one, ones).

9 (All, Every) person wants to live happily.

10 I have a black cat. I like (it, one) very much.

B

빈칸에 알맞은 말을 보기에서 골라 쓰시오. (단, 한 번씩만 쓸 것)

[1-3]

보기	every	it	one

1 I would like to have a pet. Do you have ___________?

2 I can't find my library card. I need ___________ now.

3 ___________ student in the school is free to go home.

[4-6]

보기	both	all	any

4 ___________ my parents love me very much.

5 I don't have ___________ plans for this weekend.

6 ___________ the players have to follow the rules.

Answer Key p.32

C

다음 대화의 빈칸에 알맞은 말을 보기에서 골라 쓰시오.

보기	some	any	it	each	one

1 A: Would you like ________ coffee?
B: No, thanks.

2 A: Will you have a hot drink?
B: No, I want to have a cold ________.

3 A: Do you have ________ ideas about how to solve this problem?
B: Sorry, but I don't.

4 A: Do you have a child?
B: I have three sons. ________ has a different personality.

5 A: What are you doing?
B: I'm looking for my umbrella. I can't find ________.

D

우리말과 일치하도록 어법상 틀린 부분을 찾아 바르게 고치시오.

1 나는 두 명의 남동생이 있다. 둘 다 스포츠를 잘한다.
→ I have two brothers. Every are good at sports.

2 그녀는 나에게 빨간 티셔츠와 파란 것을 주었다.
→ She gave me a red T-shirt and a blue it.

3 나는 지금 동전을 조금도 가지고 있지 않다.
→ I don't have some coins now.

4 나는 모든 과목에서 A를 받고 싶다.
→ I want to get an A in every of my subjects.

5 우리는 각자 다른 꿈을 가지고 있다.
→ Every of us has a different dream.

6 나는 도서관에 책을 좀 빌리러 갔다.
→ I went to the library to borrow any books.

WRITING PRACTICE

Answer Key p.32

A 우리말과 일치하도록 ( ) 안의 말을 이용하여 문장을 완성하시오.

1 그의 모든 노래는 사랑에 관한 것이다. (song)

→ ______________________ are about love.

2 모든 운전자들은 교통법을 따라야 한다. (driver)

→ ______________________ has to follow the traffic laws.

3 나의 부모님은 두 분 다 영어 선생님이시다. (parent)

→ ______________________ are English teachers.

4 우리 각자는 다른 DNA 패턴을 가지고 있다. (us, have)

→ ______________________ a different DNA pattern.

5 모든 영화는 숨겨진 메시지가 있다. (every, have)

→ ______________________ a hidden message.

6 어제 나는 지갑을 잃어버렸다. 나는 새것을 사야 한다. (have to, buy, new)

→ Yesterday, I lost my wallet. ______________________.

B 우리말과 일치하도록 ( ) 안에 주어진 단어를 바르게 배열하시오.

1 모든 학생들은 제시간에 교실에 있어야 한다. (of, to, students, all, have, be, the)

→ ______________________________ in the classroom on time.

2 쿠키 좀 먹을래? (some, you, to, cookies, would, like, have)

→ ____?

3 나의 선생님은 우리에게 어떤 질문이 있는지 물으셨다. (questions, had, we, if, any, asked)

→ My teacher ______________________________.

4 내 여동생 둘 다 우리 엄마를 닮았다. (my mom, of, both, resemble, my sisters)

→ ____.

5 각각의 사람들은 자신만의 삶의 방식을 가지고 있다.
(person, each, own, his or her, lifestyle, has)

→ ____.

6 이번 여름 방학 때 계획이 좀 있니? (any, you, do, have, plans)

→ ______________________________ for this summer vacation?

UNIT 02

부정대명사 II

Answer Key p.32

A

( ) 안에서 알맞은 말을 고르시오.

1 The players helped (each others, one another) during the game.

2 I can do well next time. Give me (other, another) chance.

3 Sam and his friend are sharing a room with (another, each other).

4 I have two nephews. One lives in the US, and (the other, another) lives in Japan.

5 I went to three countries last year. One was Italy, (another, other) was France, and the other was Spain.

6 Can I drive a car in (others, another) country with my license?

7 Some people like baseball, and (others, the others) like basketball.

8 (One, Some) people agree with early education, but others don't.

9 There were ten rides in the amusement park. Some were scary, but (the others, the other) were not.

B

빈칸에 알맞은 말을 보기에서 골라 쓰시오. (단, 한 번씩만 쓸 것)

[1-3]

보기	each other	another	others

1 Ava and Jacob love ____________ very much.

2 Some go to work by bus and ____________ by subway.

3 This one is too expensive. Show me ____________ one.

[4-6]

보기	the others	one another	the other

4 We should be polite to ____________.

5 There are thirty students in my class; some students drink milk, but ____________ don't.

6 In this match, one team is going to win and ____________ is going to lose.

C 다음 대화의 빈칸에 알맞은 말을 보기에서 골라 쓰시오. (단, 한 번씩만 쓸 것)

보기	some one another others the other each other

1 A: Do you have children?

B: I have two sons. ___________ is four years old, and ___________ is two.

2 A: What menu item is popular at this restaurant?

B: ___________ customers like the pasta, and ___________ like the pizza.

3 A: How about this shirt?

B: I like its design, but I don't like the color. Can you show me ___________ color?

4 A: How did you meet ___________?

B: We worked at the same company.

D 빈칸에 알맞은 말을 보기에서 골라 쓰시오. (단, 한 번씩만 쓸 것)

[1-3]

보기	others like to get up late	he wants another pet
	the other is how to study	

1 He has a lot of cats and dogs, but ________________________________.

2 Some people like to get up early in the morning, but ________________.

3 I have two problems. One is what to study, and ______________________.

[4-6]

보기	the others didn't wear it	talked to each other
	often see one another	

4 He was the only boy wearing the uniform. _________________________.

5 The first time Jamie and Lucy met, they ___________________________ for a long time.

6 The three men are close friends and live in the same village. They ________ _________________________.

WRITING PRACTICE

Answer Key p.32

A 우리말과 일치하도록 빈칸에 알맞은 대명사를 쓰시오.

1 어떤 사람들은 사과를 좋아하고, 다른 어떤 사람들은 배를 좋아한다.
→ Some like apples, and ____________ like pears.

2 그들은 처음으로 만났다. 그들은 서로 악수를 했다.
→ They met for the first time. They shook hands with ____________.

3 나는 두 개의 펜을 샀다. 하나는 빨간색이고, 다른 하나는 파란색이다.
→ I bought two pens. ____________ is red, and ____________ is blue.

4 운동장에 20명의 아이들이 있다. 어떤 아이들은 하얀 모자를 쓰고 있고, 나머지 모든 아이들은 검은 모자를 쓰고 있다.
→ There are twenty children on the playground. ____________ are wearing white caps, and ____________ are wearing black ones.

5 이 셔츠는 아주 편하다. 나는 하나 더 사고 싶다.
→ This shirt is very comfortable. I want to buy ____________.

6 나는 세 명의 룸메이트가 있다. 한 명은 중국인이고, 다른 한 명은 스페인인이고, 나머지 한 명은 프랑스인이다.
→ I have three roommates. ____________ is Chinese; ____________ is Spanish; ____________ is French.

B 우리말과 일치하도록 ( ) 안에 주어진 단어를 바르게 배열하시오.

1 우리는 서로를 돌보아야 한다. (one, take care of, should, we, another)
→ ____.

2 Rachel과 Tim은 서로 바라보았다. (and, looked, Rachel, each, Tim, other, at)
→ ____.

3 나는 커피를 한 잔 더 마시고 싶다. (want, I, have, to, cup, another)
→ ____________________________________ of coffee.

4 어떤 사람들은 코트를 입었고, 다른 사람들은 입지 않았다.
(coats, didn't, wore, people, some, and, others)
→ ____.

5 나에게는 두 딸이 있다. 한 명은 디자이너이고, 다른 한 명은 의사이다.
(the, one, and, other, is, a doctor, a designer, is)
→ I have two daughters. ________________________________.

UNIT 03

재귀대명사

( ) 안에서 알맞은 말을 고르시오.

1 Last night, I wrote a letter to (me, myself).

2 The cat is cleaning (itself, themselves).

3 You can play this game (by, beside) yourself.

4 We should protect (themselves, ourselves).

5 He enjoyed (him, himself) on the last summer vacation.

6 Alice runs the blog (her, herself).

7 I bought (myself, itself) a gift on my birthday.

8 I love Lily (her, herself), not her looks.

9 I want to introduce (myself, yourself) to you.

10 Come on in, and make (you, yourself) at home.

밑줄 친 부분을 생략할 수 있으면 O표, 생략할 수 없으면 X표 하시오.

1 Jack is very proud of himself.

2 I made this soup myself.

3 Help yourself to this cake, please.

4 She herself was suffering from the disease.

5 The comedian was laughing at himself on the show.

6 Many people are looking for jobs themselves.

7 He calls himself a superstar.

8 He himself couldn't believe the result.

9 She was disappointed with herself.

10 An idea itself can be the start of a good work of art.

Answer Key p.32

C 다음 대화의 빈칸에 들어갈 알맞은 재귀대명사를 쓰시오.

1 A: Can you help me with my homework?
B: No. You must do it by ______________.

2 A: How was your vacation?
B: It was great. I enjoyed ______________ a lot.

3 A: Is he talking to ______________?
B: No, he is talking on the phone.

4 A: What is the main idea of your essay?
B: Actually, I ______________ don't understand my essay.

5 A: I'm nervous. Can I do it well?
B: Of course. Just believe in ______________.

D 빈칸에 알맞은 말을 보기에서 골라 적절한 형태로 바꿔 쓰시오. (단, 한 번씩만 쓸 것)

[1-3]

보기	by oneself　beside oneself　in itself

1 He was ______________________ with frustration after losing the game.

2 Gold is not useful ______________________.

3 My brother didn't help me. I had to clean up the house ______________________.

[4-6]

보기	seat oneself　help oneself to　excuse oneself

4 Logan, come here and ______________________ on the sofa.

5 She ______________________ and went home early.

6 Are you hungry? ______________________ these chips.

WRITING PRACTICE

Answer Key p.33

A 우리말과 일치하도록 재귀대명사와 ( ) 안의 말을 이용하여 문장을 완성하시오.

1 나는 저녁을 준비하다가 베었다. (cut)

→ ______________________ while I was preparing dinner.

2 그는 혼자서는 그 일을 끝낼 수 없다. (finish, job)

→ He can't ______________________.

3 애플파이를 마음껏 먹어라. (help, some apple pie)

→ ______________________.

4 내가 이 국수를 직접 만들었다. (make, these noodles)

→ ______________________.

5 그녀는 거울로 자신을 보고 있었다. (look at)

→ ______________________ in the mirror.

6 이것은 우리끼리의 얘기로만 간직하자. (keep, between)

→ Let's ______________________.

B 우리말과 일치하도록 ( ) 안에 주어진 단어를 바르게 배열하시오.

1 Sue가 직접 이 케익을 만들었다. (herself, cake, made, Sue, this)

→ ______________________.

2 그 소년은 집에 혼자 있었다. (stayed, himself, home, at, the boy, by)

→ ______________________.

3 그는 일어나서 옷을 입었다. (dressed, and, he, himself, got up)

→ ______________________.

4 다 먹으면 너는 자리를 떠나도 된다. (may, yourself, when, you, excuse)

→ ______________________ you are done eating.

5 나는 그 영화 자체는 좋아했지만, 그것의 광고들은 좋아하지 않았다. (movie, I, itself, liked, the)

→ ______________________, but not the advertisements for it.

6 그가 나를 찾지 못하자 "모습을 보여줘!"라고 소리쳤다. (yourself, he, shouted, show)

→ When he couldn't find me, ______________________!"

REVIEW TEST

Answer Key p.33

[1-5] 빈칸에 들어갈 알맞은 말을 고르시오.

1

_________ person has a unique fingerprint.

① Both ② Some
③ Each ④ All
⑤ Any

2

To win the basketball game, we all have to help _________.

① the other ② others
③ another ④ each others
⑤ one another

3

Do you have _________ plans for your birthday?

① all ② each
③ one ④ any
⑤ the other

4

I have two winter coats. One is black, and _________ is brown.

① another ② some
③ each ④ the other
⑤ the others

5

A: Do you need to buy a swimsuit? B: No, I already have _________.

① one ② it
③ any ④ all
⑤ another

[6-8] 다음 중 어법상 틀린 것을 고르시오.

6 ① Both of my sons are tall and healthy.
② I bought some fruit for lunch.
③ Every citizens have the right to vote.
④ My glasses are broken. I need new ones.
⑤ Do you have any ideas about how to lose weight?

7 ① I cooked the pizza myself.
② You should clean your room yourself.
③ I burned me while I boiled water.
④ I can't find any information about it.
⑤ Welcome. Make yourself at home.

8 ① He wanted to succeed for himself.
② Why did you watch the movie by you?
③ We share many things with each other.
④ All my friends are important to me.
⑤ I took two classes. One was English, and the other was science.

9 다음 중 밑줄 친 부분을 생략할 수 있는 것은?

① We enjoyed ourselves at the concert.
② She was talking to herself.
③ I drew these pictures myself.
④ Be careful not to hurt yourself.
⑤ He called himself a genius.

10 밑줄 친 부분의 쓰임이 나머지 넷과 다른 것은?

① This shirt is dirty. I need a new one.
② I don't have a pen. Do you have one?
③ We have two colors, but I like that one.
④ I lost my ruler. I have to buy one.
⑤ I need one more day to finish the job.

빈출

[11-12] 빈칸에 들어갈 말이 순서대로 바르게 짝지어진 것을 고르시오.

11

A: What do your three brothers do?
B: One is a lawyer, ________ is a doctor, and ________ is a scientist.

① the other – others
② another – the other
③ other – the other
④ another – the others
⑤ other – another

12

There are many people in the café. ________ drink coffee, and ________ drink tea.

① Some – others
② Some – the other
③ Another – the others
④ Every – all
⑤ Other – the others

13 다음 질문에 대한 대답으로 가장 적절한 것은?

A: Have you seen my pencil case?
B: Yes, ________________.

① you should buy one
② they're in your room
③ I saw one under the desk
④ I saw it on the table
⑤ there are some in the drawer

서술형

14 빈칸에 들어갈 알맞은 대명사를 쓰시오.

Many people in Canada speak two languages. One is English, and ________ is French.

서술형

15 밑줄 친 단어를 올바른 형태로 고쳐 쓰시오.

We must love us before we can love others.

서술형 빈출

[16-18] 빈칸에 공통으로 들어갈 알맞은 말을 쓰시오.

16

• I don't have ________ homework today.
• Does he have ________ brothers or sisters?

17

• ________ students were late for school.
• ________ read the book, but the others didn't.

18
- I like both of the dresses. I can't choose ________.
- A: Do you have an eraser?
  B: Yes, I have ________.

19 다음 우리말을 영어로 바르게 옮긴 것은?

빵을 마음껏 드세요.

① Please make you to some bread.
② Please make yourself to some bread.
③ Please help you to some bread.
④ Please help yourself at some bread.
⑤ Please help yourself to some bread.

서술형

[20-21] 우리말과 일치하도록 ( ) 안의 말을 이용하여 문장을 완성하시오.

20 나는 그 소식을 듣고 걱정에 제정신이 아니었다. (beside)

→ ________________ with worry after hearing the news.

21 너는 변명을 하려고 애쓰지 마라. (try to, excuse)

→ ________________.

서술형

[22-23] 우리말과 일치하도록 ( ) 안에 주어진 단어를 바르게 배열하시오.

22 그들은 크리스마스에 서로에게 카드를 보냈다. (they, to, one, sent, another, cards)

→ ________________ on Christmas Day.

23 나는 너의 모든 에세이들을 읽었다. (I, essays, read, your, of, all)

→ ________________.

서술형 고난도

[24-25] 어법상 틀린 부분을 찾아 바르게 고치시오.

24 Some people like dogs, and other like cats. I like both of them. (1개)

25 I have two brothers. They look similar to each another, but their personalities are very different. (1개)

UNIT 01

원급, 비교급, 최상급

A ( ) 안에서 알맞은 말을 고르시오.

1 Your bag is as (pretty, prettier) as mine.

2 Tim works (harder, hardest) than others.

3 This is the (cheaper, cheapest) model in the store.

4 This dress is (more beautiful, most beautiful) than that one.

5 The weather in Hawaii is as (good, better) as that in Florida.

6 This oven cooks food (many, much) faster than the old one.

7 I think love is the (more important, most important) thing in life.

8 He's running this company as (well, best) as his father did.

9 This parking lot is the (bigger, biggest) in the town.

10 The test was (very, a lot) more difficult than I expected.

B ( ) 안의 말을 이용하여 문장을 완성하시오.

1 His apartment building is much ______________ than mine. (tall)

2 Don is the ______________ of all the employees. (young)

3 James is the ______________ boy in my school. (popular)

4 The new elevator is ______________ than the old one. (fast)

5 Zoe didn't practice as ______________ as her rival. (hard)

6 An apple is ______________ than a lemon. (sweet)

7 I can skate as ______________ as Henry. (well)

8 February is the ______________ month of all. (short)

9 I am ______________ in painting than music. (interested)

10 Christine has the ______________ hair in her class. (long)

Answer Key p.33

C

밑줄 친 부분을 어법에 맞게 고치시오.

1 This is the spicy food in the restaurant.

2 This mountain isn't as higher as Mt. Halla.

3 I will save most money than I did last year.

4 Spring is the more dynamic season of the year.

5 This movie is most interesting than that one.

6 Finish this test as fastest as you can.

7 I like rice more to bread.

8 Your sunglasses are very prettier than mine.

9 This coffee is much bitter than that one.

10 He is as busier as his father.

D

주어진 문장과 의미가 통하도록 ( ) 안의 말을 이용하여 문장을 완성하시오.

1 The red box is 10 kg. The green box is 10 kg.
→ The red box is ______________________ the green one. (heavy)

2 The T-shirt is $20. The jacket is $30.
→ The jacket is ______________________ the T-shirt. (expensive)

3 Mary is 155 cm tall. Jen is 157 cm tall. Katie is 162 cm tall.
→ Katie is ______________________ the three. (tall)

4 Yuna can lift a 20 kg dumbbell. I can lift an 18 kg dumbbell.
→ Yuna is ______________________ me. (strong)

5 My sister has five bags. I have five bags too.
→ I have ______________________ my sister. (many bags)

6 Jamie is fourteen years old. Maria is fifteen years old. Harry is fifteen years old.
→ Jamie is ______________________ the three. (young)

WRITING PRACTICE

Answer Key p.33

A 우리말과 일치하도록 (   ) 안의 말을 이용하여 문장을 완성하시오.

1 나의 언니는 나보다 훨씬 똑똑하다. (much, smart)

→ My sister is ________________________________ me.

2 Mr. Lee는 한국에서 가장 부유한 남자이다. (rich, man)

→ ________________________________ in Korea.

3 이 노트북이 저것보다 더 저렴하다. (laptop, cheap)

→ ________________________________ that one.

4 Lauren의 키는 나만큼 크다. (tall)

→ ________________________________ me.

5 Lucy가 Jenny보다 더 건강하다. (healthy)

→ Lucy ________________________________.

6 그녀는 학교에서 가장 빠른 소녀이다. (fast, girl)

→ ________________________________ in the school.

B 우리말과 일치하도록 (   ) 안에 주어진 단어를 바르게 배열하시오.

1 내 자동차는 형의 것만큼 좋다. (is, good, my, car, as, as, brother's, my)

→ ________________________________.

2 Kevin은 나만큼 명석하다. (as, brilliant, is, Kevin, as, me)

→ ________________________________.

3 내 책상이 네 것보다 더 넓다. (is, yours, desk, than, my, wider)

→ ________________________________.

4 나에게는 내 집이 세상에서 가장 편한 곳이다. (the, house, my, is, place, comfortable, most)

→ ________________________________ in the world to me.

5 이 셔츠는 저 셔츠보다 훨씬 더 짧다. (than, that, shorter, even, one, is)

→ This shirt ________________________________.

6 이것이 그 영화에서 가장 유명한 부분이다. (the, movie, famous, of, part, most, the)

→ This is ________________________________.

UNIT 02

비교 구문을 이용한 표현

Answer Key p.33

A

( ) 안에서 알맞은 말을 고르시오.

1 My dog is (two, twice) as heavy as your dog.

2 The older he gets, the (more, most) he looks like his father.

3 She is one of the most successful (person, people) in the world.

4 The show is getting (interesting and interesting, more and more interesting).

5 Who is (shorter, shortest), you or your brother?

6 He was one of the (more handsome, most handsome) actors in the 1990s.

7 This book is (six, six times) thicker than that one.

8 Summer in Korea is getting hotter and (hotter, hottest).

9 Which are (smarter, smartest), dogs or cats?

10 The more I get to know him, (the little, the less) I like him.

B

( ) 안의 말을 이용하여 문장을 완성하시오.

1 The more she exercises, the ____________ she becomes. (healthy)

2 This smartphone is ____________ as expensive as that one. (two)

3 Liam is one of the ____________ names in the US. (popular)

4 The show is becoming ____________. (funny and funny)

5 Which car is ____________? This one or that one? (fast)

6 The deeper I sleep, the ____________ I feel. (good)

7 She is one of the ____________ women at the company. (kind)

8 The new TV is ____________ wider than the old one. (three)

9 Her hair is getting ____________. (short and short)

10 It is one of the greatest ____________ of all time. (movie)

C

밑줄 친 부분을 어법에 맞게 고치시오.

1 I have <u>four as many dolls as</u> my sister.

2 Which T-shirt is <u>most expensive</u>, this one or that one?

3 His cell phone is <u>twice as heavier as</u> mine.

4 The song has become <u>popularer and popularer</u>.

5 This device is ten times <u>lighter as</u> that one.

6 My cat becomes <u>more cute and cute</u> every day.

7 Van Gogh is one of the most <u>famous artist</u> in the world.

8 The more you rest, <u>the best</u> you will feel.

9 Who is <u>most popular</u>, Ron or Jim?

10 <u>The old</u> she gets, the more patient she becomes.

D

우리말과 일치하도록 빈칸에 알맞은 말을 보기에서 골라 적절한 형태로 바꿔 쓰시오.

보기	many slim long much tall popular

1 점점 더 많은 사람들이 내 블로그를 방문하고 있다.

→ ____________________ people are visiting my blog.

2 설악산과 지리산 중에서 어디가 더 높습니까?

→ Which is ____________________, Mt. Seorak or Mt. Jiri?

3 축구는 세계에서 가장 인기 있는 스포츠 중 하나이다.

→ Soccer is one of the ____________________ sports in the world.

4 더 오래 그녀와 함께할수록 더 많이 그녀를 좋아하게 된다.

→ _______________ I am with her, _______________ I like her.

5 그는 규칙적으로 운동을 한다. 그는 점점 더 날씬해지고 있다.

→ He exercises regularly. He is getting ____________________.

WRITING PRACTICE

Answer Key p.33

A 우리말과 일치하도록 ( ) 안의 말을 이용하여 문장을 완성하시오.

1 제주도는 세계에서 가장 아름다운 섬 중 하나이다. (beautiful, island)
→ Jeju Island is ________________ in the world.

2 그 가방은 점점 더 무거워졌다. (become, heavy)
→ The bag ________________.

3 네가 책을 더 많이 읽을수록 너는 더 똑똑해진다. (many books, smart)
→ ________________ you read, ________________ you become.

4 이 식당에서 파스타와 피자 중 어느 것이 더 맛있니? (delicious)
→ ________________ in this restaurant, the pasta or the pizza?

5 나의 부모님의 방은 나의 것보다 세 배만큼 더 크다. (large)
→ My parent's room is ________________ mine.

6 이 나뭇가지는 저것보다 네 배만큼 더 길다. (long)
→ This stick is ________________ that one.

B 우리말과 일치하도록 ( ) 안에 주어진 단어를 바르게 배열하시오.

1 Elon Musk는 세계에서 가장 부유한 사람 중 한 명이다. (richest, one, is, the, in, of, men)
→ Elon Musk ________________ the world.

2 날씨가 더 더워질수록 나는 아이스크림을 더 많이 먹는다.
(hotter, the, the, becomes, more, the, weather)
→ ________________ ice cream I eat.

3 공기가 점점 더 나빠지고 있다. (air, worse, is, and, getting, the, worse)
→ ________________.

4 Joel은 그의 여동생보다 두 배는 더 먹는다. (as, his, eats, twice, sister, much, as)
→ Joel ________________.

5 역사와 과학 중에 어느 과목이 더 쉽니? (history, which, or, subject, is, easier, science)
→ ________________?

6 독서는 요즘 가장 흔한 취미 중 하나이다. (one, hobbies, the, reading, of, is, common, most)
→ ________________ these days.

REVIEW TEST

1 다음 중 원급, 비교급, 최상급이 잘못 연결된 것은?

① sad – sadder – saddest
② quiet – quieter – quietest
③ healthy – healthyer – healthyest
④ carefully – more carefully – most carefully
⑤ delicious – more delicious – most delicious

[2-5] 빈칸에 들어갈 알맞은 말을 고르시오.

2

Yuram speaks English as ________ as Patrick does.

① well ② better
③ best ④ good
⑤ most

3

My grandfather is the ________ man in my town.

① old ② older
③ oldest ④ more old
⑤ most old

4

________ you study, the better you will do on the test.

① Many ② More
③ Most ④ The more
⑤ The most

5

This comic book is ________ more exciting than the last one.

① the ② very
③ as ④ much
⑤ many

[6-8] 다음 중 어법상 틀린 것을 고르시오.

6 ① Mt. Bukhan is the tallest mountain in Seoul.
② My room is twice as big as yours.
③ You're strongest than my father.
④ He is more handsome than his father.
⑤ He is one of the most popular sports stars in America.

7 ① He is the tallest boy in my class.
② Your car is much better than mine.
③ The warmer the weather becomes, the more often I go out.
④ The water is getting hotter and hotter.
⑤ This is one of the most beautiful building in Korea.

8 ① Your laptop is a lot faster than mine.
② More and more people are keeping pets.
③ She has twice as more earrings as I have.
④ The more you ask, the more you learn.
⑤ Which do you like better, soccer or baseball?

[9-10] 우리말과 일치하도록 할 때, 빈칸에 들어갈 말로 알맞은 것을 고르시오.

9

Shawn을 더 많이 알수록 나는 그를 더 믿게 된다.
→ The more I get to know Shawn, ________________.

① more I trust him
② most I trust him
③ the much I trust him
④ the more I trust him
⑤ the most I trust him

10

상황이 점점 더 나아졌다.
→ The situation got ________________.

① better and better
② better or better
③ good and good
④ best and best
⑤ good and better

11 빈칸에 들어갈 말로 알맞지 않은 것은?

The doll is ________ smaller than I thought.

① even ② far ③ much
④ a lot ⑤ very

서술형

12 표를 보고 ( ) 안의 말을 이용하여 문장을 완성하시오.

Item	Price
a yellow sweater	$30
a blue sweater	$30

→ A blue sweater is ________________ a yellow one. (expensive)

서술형 빈출

[13-15] 주어진 문장과 의미가 통하도록 ( ) 안의 말을 이용하여 문장을 완성하시오.

13

• Jacob is 165 cm tall.
• Liam is 172 cm tall.
• Tony is 168 cm tall.

→ Jacob is ________________ the three. (short, boy)

14

• Julie got a 90 on the English test.
• Harry got a 95 on the English test.

→ Julie got ________________ Harry on the English test. (a low score)

15

• My brother finished reading *Hamlet* in an hour.
• I finished reading *Hamlet* in three hours.

→ My brother finished reading *Hamlet* ________________ I did. (three, fast)

16 다음 중 어법상 옳은 것은?

① She became pretty and pretty.
② You're very kinder than Lisa.
③ Who is taller, Mitch or Kirk?
④ He plays the piano as better as his sister.
⑤ She is the more famous poet in Korea.

17 다음 중 밑줄 친 부분을 잘못 고친 것은?

① His voice is getting loud and loud.
→ louder and louder

② The many I have, the more I want.
→ more

③ I am as strongest as you.
→ strong

④ My mom can cook good than the chef.
→ best

⑤ She is one of the smaller girls in my class. → smallest

서술형

[18-20] 우리말과 일치하도록 ( ) 안의 말을 이용하여 문장을 완성하시오.

18 너는 치즈 케이크와 초콜릿 케이크 중 어느 것을 더 좋아하니? (which, much)

→ ______________________________,
cheesecake or chocolate cake?

19 낮이 점점 더 짧아지고 있다. (get, short)

→ The daytime is ____________________.

20 이 코끼리는 그 동물원에서 가장 큰 동물이다. (big, animal)

→ This elephant is ____________________
in the zoo.

서술형

[21-23] 우리말과 일치하도록 ( ) 안에 주어진 단어를 바르게 배열하시오.

21 이 다리가 저것보다 두 배 더 길다.
(this, as, twice, long, one, bridge, as, is, that)

→ ______________________________.

22 이번 수학 시험이 이전 것보다 훨씬 더 어려웠다.
(was, math, difficult, than, much, this, exam, more)

→ ______________________________
the previous one.

23 우리 학교는 한국에서 가장 오래된 학교 중 하나이다.
(schools, school, my, one, is, the, in, of, oldest)

→ ______________________________
Korea.

서술형 고난도

[24-25] 어법상 틀린 부분을 찾아 바르게 고치시오.

24 I didn't like her when I first met her. But the more I talked with her, more I understood her. (1개)

25 Which do you eat much often, meat or vegetables? Vegetables have more health benefits to meat. Try to eat vegetables as often as you can. (2개)

UNIT 01

시간, 이유, 결과의 접속사

Answer Key p.34

A

( ) 안에서 알맞은 말을 고르시오.

1 (Until, While) I come back, you should stay here.

2 The restaurant was so dirty (as, that) I didn't eat anything.

3 (That, While) I was taking a picture, somebody stole my bag.

4 (Before, Because) my computer didn't work, I couldn't finish my homework.

5 (After, Since) I don't have money, I can't buy that shirt.

6 She started to cry (when, until) she heard the sad story.

7 (As, That) he was on his way to the airport, he checked the flight schedule.

8 I sent the letter yesterday, (because, so) you'll receive it by this Friday.

9 We will have lunch after the movie (will be, is) over.

10 (So, Till) the train arrived, I was in the waiting room.

B

빈칸에 알맞은 말을 보기에서 골라 쓰시오. (단, 한 번씩만 쓸 것)

[1-4]

보기	since until when so

1 I was taking a shower ___________ the phone rang.

2 ___________ it's raining, I'll stay home this afternoon.

3 The movie was scary, ___________ I don't want to watch it again.

4 I will save money ___________ I have enough to buy a new computer.

[5-8]

보기	after while that as

5 You have to brush your teeth ___________ you eat something.

6 His voice was so loud ___________ everyone was able to hear it.

7 ___________ the actor lives near my house, I often see him.

8 I fell asleep ___________ I was watching the movie.

C 밑줄 친 부분을 어법에 맞게 고치시오.

1 When I called Chloe, she is writing a letter.
2 Elly was so angry with me as she didn't talk to me.
3 Until he will find the answer, he won't give up.
4 I was late this morning, because I had to hurry.
5 When I will go home, I will eat something.

D 빈칸에 공통으로 들어갈 말을 쓰시오.

1 • I was __________ scared that I couldn't sleep.
• Harry doesn't have any friends, __________ he feels lonely.

2 • __________ I entered the store, I saw the actress.
• __________ it was raining, the baseball game was canceled.

3 • __________ I was waiting for the bus, it started to rain.
• __________ he is good at writing, he is poor at speaking.

E 주어진 문장과 의미가 통하도록 빈칸에 알맞은 접속사를 보기에서 골라 쓰시오.

보기	so	while	after	because

1 Before I went to bed, I turned off the TV.
→ __________ I turned off the TV, I went to bed.

2 Since I didn't know his number, I couldn't call him.
→ __________ I didn't know his number, I couldn't call him.

3 As the crowd cheered, the singer took a bow.
→ __________ the crowd cheered, the singer took a bow.

4 As it was Sunday, the bank was closed.
→ It was Sunday, __________ the bank was closed.

WRITING PRACTICE

Answer Key p.34

A 우리말과 일치하도록 ( ) 안의 말을 이용하여 문장을 완성하시오.

1 그가 이메일을 하나 쓰는 동안, 그녀는 TV를 보았다. (write, email)

→ ______________________, she watched TV.

2 나는 이를 닦은 후에 잠자리에 들 것이다. (brush one's teeth)

→ I will go to bed ______________________.

3 너무 시끄러워서 나는 그의 목소리를 들을 수 없었다. (can, hear, voice)

→ It was too noisy, ______________________.

4 그 소설이 너무 재미있어서 Jen은 그것을 두 번이나 읽었다. (interesting, that)

→ The novel was ______________________ it twice.

5 네 숙제를 마칠 때까지 외출을 하지 마라. (finish, homework)

→ Don't go outside ______________________.

6 나는 오늘 오후에 테니스를 칠 것이기 때문에 테니스화를 가지고 왔다. (will, play)

→ I brought my tennis shoes ______________________ this afternoon.

B 우리말과 일치하도록 ( ) 안에 주어진 단어를 바르게 배열하시오.

1 몇몇 사람들은 그의 생각을 좋아하는 반면, 다른 사람들은 좋아하지 않는다.
(while, like, his, some people, idea)

→ ______________________, others don't.

2 나는 알람이 울리기 전에 잠이 깼다. (rang, the, up, alarm, before, woke)

→ I ______________________.

3 나는 너무 졸려서 계속 하품을 했다. (I, so, yawning, kept, that, sleepy)

→ I was ______________________.

4 봄이 올 때까지 나는 보스턴에서 머무를 것이다. (Boston, stay, comes, in, until, spring)

→ I'll ______________________.

5 나는 내 열쇠가 없었기 때문에 나의 남동생을 기다려야 했다.
(have, to, my key, had, as, didn't, I, I, wait for)

→ ______________________ my brother.

6 엄마는 나의 선생님을 만나신 후, 나에게 아무 말도 하지 않았다.
(didn't, my teacher, after, met, she, say, Mom)

→ ______________________ anything to me.

UNIT 02

조건, 양보의 접속사 / 명령문 + and, or ~

A ( ) 안에서 알맞은 말을 고르시오.

1 (Unless, Although) I took the medicine, I still have a headache.
2 Turn down the volume, (and, or) your ears will hurt.
3 (If, Unless) you don't give up, you'll be a good swimmer.
4 I won't take your picture (if, unless) you are ready.
5 Eat more vegetables, (and, or) you'll be healthy.
6 (If, Though) Jake is small, he is very strong.
7 Be on time, (and, or) you won't be allowed inside.
8 If you (didn't, don't) give my money back, I'll call the police.
9 (If, Unless) you get up early tomorrow, you will miss the first train.
10 Give me your address, (and, or) I'll send you the catalogue.

B 빈칸에 알맞은 말을 보기에서 골라 쓰시오. (단, 한 번씩만 쓸 것)

[1-3]

보기	if	although	and

1 Don't give up, __________ your dreams will come true.
2 __________ I'm not good at snowboarding, I enjoy it very much.
3 __________ it rains tomorrow, we won't wash our car.

[4-6]

보기	though	unless	or

4 Don't be late for class, __________ you'll miss some important things.
5 Good plans are useless __________ you follow them through.
6 __________ the heater was on, it was cold.

Answer Key p.34

C

주어진 문장과 의미가 통하도록 빈칸에 알맞은 접속사를 쓰시오.

1 Tell your mom the truth, and she will understand you.
→ __________ you tell your mom the truth, she will understand you.

2 If you take this pill, you'll feel much better.
→ Take this pill, __________ you'll feel much better.

3 He is my rival, but I respect him.
→ __________ he is my rival, I respect him.

4 Run fast, or you'll miss the school bus.
→ __________ you don't run fast, you'll miss the school bus.
→ __________ you run fast, you'll miss the school bus.

5 If you don't get enough sleep, you will be tired.
→ __________ you get enough sleep, you will be tired.
→ Get enough sleep, __________ you will be tired.

D

( ) 안의 접속사를 이용하여 주어진 두 문장을 한 문장으로 쓰시오.

1 I was tired last night. I went to the gym. (though)
→ ______________________________

2 Pull this string. The light will turn on. (and)
→ ______________________________

3 I come home early. I'll cook dinner for you. (if)
→ ______________________________

4 Stop laughing at him. He'll be very angry. (or)
→ ______________________________

5 You are busy. Let's go shopping. (unless)
→ ______________________________

WRITING PRACTICE

Answer Key p.34

A 우리말과 일치하도록 접속사와 ( ) 안의 말을 이용하여 문장을 완성하시오.

1 네가 나를 도와주지 않는다면, 나는 이 프로젝트를 마무리하지 못할 것이다. (help)
→ ______________________, I won't be able to finish this project.

2 비록 나는 배가 고팠지만, 그 케이크를 먹을 수는 없었다. 그것은 너무 달았다. (hungry)
→ ______________________, I couldn't eat that cake. It was too sweet.

3 여기서 기다려라, 그러면 누가 널 도와줄 것이다. (someone, help)
→ Wait here, ______________________.

4 더 이상 질문이 없다면, 당신은 가도 좋습니다. (have, more, question)
→ ______________________, you're free to go.

5 조심해라, 그러지 않으면 너는 다칠 것이다. (get hurt)
→ Watch out, ______________________.

6 나는 최선을 다했지만, 결과는 좋지 않았다. (do one's best)
→ ______________________, the result was not good.

B 우리말과 일치하도록 ( ) 안에 주어진 단어를 바르게 배열하시오.

1 내 집에서 당장 나가라, 그러지 않으면 경찰에 신고하겠다. (call, will, or, police, the, I)
→ Leave my house right now, ______________________.

2 네 선글라스를 써라, 그러면 그것이 너의 눈을 보호해 줄 것이다.
(sunglasses, put on, will, your, and, they)
→ ______________________ protect your eyes.

3 비록 비가 심하게 내렸지만, 그들은 축구를 했다. (played, it, heavily, rained, they, although)
→ ______________________ soccer.

4 네가 회원 카드가 없으면, 너는 그 방에 들어갈 수 없다.
(you, unless, enter, a, you, can't, membership card, have)
→ ______________________ the room.

5 네가 우산을 가지고 가지 않는다면, 너는 젖을 것이다.
(take, will, umbrella, you, get, you, if, your, don't)
→ ______________________ wet.

6 날씨가 나쁘면, 비행은 지연될 것이다. (weather, if, is, the, bad)
→ ______________________, the flight will be delayed.

REVIEW TEST

Answer Key p.34

[1-5] 빈칸에 들어갈 알맞은 말을 고르시오.

1 Someone called you ________ you were out.

① if ② so
③ unless ④ that
⑤ while

2 ________ Charlotte broke up with her boyfriend, she looked fine.

① If ② And
③ So ④ Unless
⑤ Though

3 I'll be on time ________ there is a traffic jam.

① if ② when
③ unless ④ since
⑤ while

4 The movie was so sad ________ I couldn't stop crying.

① since ② although
③ as ④ that
⑤ after

5 It was too dark, ________ I couldn't see anything.

① as ② so
③ or ④ because
⑤ since

[6-7] 두 문장의 의미가 비슷하도록 빈칸에 들어갈 알맞은 말을 고르시오.

6 After he finished his homework, he played soccer with his friends.
→ He finished his homework ________ he played soccer with his friends.

① if ② as ③ so
④ before ⑤ though

7 If you turn right, you'll see the bookstore.
→ Turn right, ________ you'll see the bookstore.

① and ② or ③ so
④ if ⑤ unless

8 다음 중 밑줄 친 부분이 자연스럽지 않은 것은?

① When he saw me, he ran away.
② Since I arrived late, I missed my bus.
③ Unless you don't buy a ticket, you cannot get in.
④ I stopped crying as my dad came in the room.
⑤ I went outside, although it was snowing.

빈출

9 밑줄 친 접속사의 의미가 나머지 넷과 다른 것은?

① As I lost my math textbook, I couldn't bring it.

② As I was sick, I couldn't go to his birthday party.

③ As today is a holiday, I won't go to work.

④ As I have never seen him, I don't know what he looks like.

⑤ As I opened the door, everyone yelled, "Surprise!"

[10-11] 다음 중 어법상 틀린 것을 고르시오.

10 ① When the train will arrive, I'll tell you.

② If I take a trip, I'll make detailed plans.

③ While I was away, he looked after my dog.

④ Tell me the truth, or you'll go to jail.

⑤ Though I like music, I don't play any musical instruments.

11 ① Be quiet, or you'll have to leave the room.

② If this computer doesn't work, use another one.

③ The cell phone is so expensive as I can't buy it.

④ Before I got on the bus, I took out my wallet.

⑤ Work hard, and you can become a great artist.

서술형 빈출

[12-15] 주어진 문장과 의미가 통하도록 빈칸에 알맞은 말을 쓰시오.

12 It was sunny, but it was cold outside.

→ __________ it was sunny, it was cold outside.

13 If I am not busy, I will help you move.

→ __________ I am busy, I will help you move.

14 Because I lost my brother's book, he is angry.

→ I lost my brother's book, __________ he is angry.

15 Unless you put on your coat, you'll be very cold.

→ Put on your coat, __________ you'll be very cold.

서술형

[16-17] 빈칸에 공통으로 들어갈 접속사를 쓰시오.

16
- __________ he was away, his sister took care of his cats.
- __________ I love Chinese food, my husband prefers Korean food.

17
- __________ I didn't know her name, I didn't introduce her.
- __________ I was getting on the train, I saw my best friend.

18 빈칸에 들어갈 접속사가 나머지 넷과 다른 것은?

① _____ you study hard, you'll fail the exam.
② _____ you take a taxi, you'll be on time.
③ You can stay here _____ you like.
④ _____ you see Jamie, give him this letter.
⑤ _____ it's warm tomorrow, I'll go hiking.

19 우리말과 일치하도록 할 때, 빈칸에 들어갈 말로 알맞은 것은?

> 비록 그는 어렸지만, 모든 것을 이해했다.
> → __________, he understood everything.

① As he was young
② Although he was young
③ Unless he was young
④ Because he wasn't young
⑤ When he wasn't young

서술형

[20-21] 우리말과 일치하도록 접속사와 ( ) 안의 말을 이용하여 문장을 완성하시오.

20 비록 그녀는 강했지만, 그녀는 그 경기에서 졌다. (strong)

→ _________ _________ _________ _________, she lost the game.

21 그가 돌아올 때까지 나는 여기 머무를 것이다. (come, back)

→ I will stay here _________ _________ _________ _________.

서술형

[22-23] 우리말과 일치하도록 ( ) 안에 주어진 단어를 바르게 배열하시오.

22 나는 스포츠에 관심이 있는 반면, 그녀는 음악과 예술에 관심이 있다.
(while, interested, in, I, am, sports)

→ ______________________________, she is interested in music and art.

23 물이 끓을 때 면을 냄비에 넣어라.
(put, boils, the, water, noodles, when, the)

→ ______________________________ into the pot.

서술형 고난도

[24-25] 어법상 틀린 부분을 찾아 바르게 고치시오.

24 Mom has always supported me. If I will win the gold medal at the Olympics, I will give it to her. (1개)

25 When I woke up in the morning, there were lots of presents under the Christmas tree. I was so surprised as I couldn't say a word. (1개)

UNIT 01

관계대명사

A ( ) 안에서 알맞은 말을 고르시오.

1 I met a man (who, which) had a nice sports car.
2 She wants to buy a bag (who, which) has a big pocket.
3 This is the book (whom, which) I ordered yesterday morning.
4 He isn't the boy (whom, whose) I gave the letter to.
5 This is the medicine (whom, which) you should take now.
6 I met a woman (whom, whose) daughter is a famous movie star.
7 She saw an old man (who, whose) was jogging in the park.
8 Give me the magazine (whom, which) is on the desk.
9 I saw a classroom (whose, which) had a broken window.
10 My family stayed at a hotel (which, whose) service was very good.

B 빈칸에 알맞은 말을 보기에서 골라 쓰시오.

보기	who	whose	which	whom

1 I have some friends ___________ want to be actresses.
2 The boy ___________ I like is standing over there.
3 He has the picture ___________ I took.
4 I know a man ___________ dream is very big.
5 Andrew has a girlfriend ___________ lives in the US.
6 This is a story ___________ I heard from my grandmother.
7 He is the man ___________ won the championship.
8 He is the doctor ___________ we saw on the news.
9 I'll buy a TV ___________ screen is very wide.
10 The restaurant ___________ I visited yesterday was very crowded.

Answer Key p.35

C

밑줄 친 부분을 어법에 맞게 고치시오. (단, that은 제외)

1 The man whom lives next door is my teacher.

2 This is the car whose I want to buy.

3 I'll eat the food whose I bought yesterday.

4 I know a girl who sister is a lawyer.

5 This is the wine whom she likes best.

6 She met a man whom is a famous violinist.

7 He is the actor which I like most these days.

8 This is the key whose I was looking for.

9 My boyfriend gave me a teddy bear which face is very cute.

10 I need someone which can help me.

D

다음 두 문장을 관계대명사를 이용하여 한 문장으로 쓰시오. (단, that은 제외)

1 The girl is my sister. + She is short.

→ ______________________________

2 I bought a scarf. + Its color is red.

→ ______________________________

3 I liked the song. + You sang it last night.

→ ______________________________

4 This is the watch. + It was made in Italy.

→ ______________________________

5 That's the man. + I saw him at the baseball stadium.

→ ______________________________

6 I know a girl. + Her birthday is the same as mine.

→ ______________________________

WRITING PRACTICE

Answer Key p.35

A 우리말과 일치하도록 관계대명사와 ( ) 안의 말을 이용하여 문장을 완성하시오. (단, that은 제외)

1 그는 스케이트보드를 잘 타는 소년이다. (ride a skateboard)

→ He is the boy ________________________ well.

2 강 중간에 있는 저 보트를 봐라. (look at, the boat)

→ ________________________ in the middle of the river.

3 Han 선생님은 모두가 존경하는 선생님이다. (everyone, admire)

→ Mr. Han is the teacher ________________________.

4 나는 색깔이 보라색인 꽃 한 송이를 갖고 싶다. (color, purple)

→ I want a flower ________________________.

5 이것이 내가 Jenny에게 준 책이다. (give)

→ This is the book ________________________ to Jenny.

6 나는 패션 디자이너가 되는 것이 꿈인 한 소년을 안다. (dream)

→ I know a boy ________________________ to become a fashion designer.

B 우리말과 일치하도록 ( ) 안에 주어진 단어를 바르게 배열하시오.

1 내가 지난주에 샀던 스마트폰이 작동하지 않는다. (the, last week, bought, which, I, smartphone)

→ ________________________________ isn't working.

2 나는 스테이크가 매우 맛있는 식당을 안다. (a, steak, very, is, delicious, whose, restaurant)

→ I know ________________________________.

3 이것은 그녀가 보살피고 있는 강아지이다. (dog, of, the, is, which, she, taking, care)

→ This is ________________________________.

4 그는 내가 선물을 주었던 남자이다. (gave, a, whom, the man, I, present, to)

→ He is ________________________________.

5 나는 엄마가 유명한 배우인 한 소녀를 만났다. (a girl, whose, actress, is, a, mom, famous)

→ I met ________________________________.

6 나는 아름다운 미소를 지닌 한 소년을 안다. (beautiful, who, boy, a, smile, a, has)

→ I know ________________________________.

UNIT 02

관계대명사 that, what / 관계대명사의 생략

Answer Key p.35

A

( ) 안에서 알맞은 말을 고르시오.

1 This is the tallest building (that, what) I've ever seen.
2 (That, What) I want to know is the main character's name.
3 The only thing (that, what) I care about is your opinion.
4 Tell me about the party (that, what) you want to go to.
5 I know the girl (whom, with whom) Harry came.
6 The cookies (that, what) you made were delicious.
7 Anyone (is bored, bored) with reading may do other things.
8 The girl to (that, whom) I sent an email hasn't answered yet.
9 I won't forget (that, what) you did for me.
10 The man (standing, is standing) over there is very tall.

B

다음 문장에서 생략할 수 있는 부분을 찾아 쓰시오. (생략할 수 있는 부분이 없으면 X표 하시오.)

1 The boy that is wearing a black cap is Tommy.
2 What you're looking for isn't in this room.
3 There's nothing that I can do now.
4 He is the professor who Mr. Brown was talking about.
5 My old friend who lives in Japan is going to visit me next week.
6 My uncle who is a travel agent told me an interesting story.
7 I tasted the soup which the cook made.
8 He has the biggest hands that I've ever seen.
9 The book which is written in English is not that difficult to read.
10 This is the apartment which I used to live in.

C 밑줄 친 부분을 어법에 맞게 고치시오. (단, 생략하기는 제외)

1 The things what I bought were not expensive.

2 I lost the wallet in that I had a lot of money.

3 Nobody believed that he told us.

4 Do you know the girl is talking to my teacher?

5 The man about that I was talking was very kind.

6 The museum about you were telling me was nice.

7 He was the most popular actor whom came from Australia.

8 I want to try that you recommended.

9 That was the longest movie whose I've ever seen.

10 I liked the speech what you gave yesterday.

D 다음 대화의 빈칸에 that과 what 중 알맞은 것을 쓰시오.

1 A: How was the concert last night?
B: It was the most amazing show __________ I've ever seen.

2 A: There was a man __________ was looking for you.
B: Who was he?

3 A: Are you saying that I have to do it alone?
B: No. That's not __________ I was telling you.

4 A: What do you need?
B: I need a big pot __________ I can grow some flowers in.

5 A: Do you think __________ you did was right?
B: Yes, I do.

6 A: Is this vest on sale as well?
B: No. I'm sorry, but that is one of our new fall products. However, I can show you a similar vest __________ is on sale.

WRITING PRACTICE

Answer Key p.35

A 우리말과 일치하도록 관계대명사와 ( ) 안의 말을 이용하여 문장을 완성하시오.

1 저 나무 옆에 서 있는 개는 늙어 보인다. (stand)
→ The dog ________________ next to that tree looks old.

2 이것은 내가 텔레비전을 보기 위해 앉는 소파이다. (the sofa, sit on)
→ This is ________________ to watch TV.

3 이 가방이 내가 찾고 있었던 것이다. (look for)
→ This bag is ________________.

4 내가 제안한 해결 방법은 효과가 없었다. (the solution, suggest)
→ ________________ didn't work.

5 테니스를 치고 있는 소년은 내 동생이다. (the boy, tennis)
→ ________________ is my brother.

6 네가 수영했던 수영장은 깨끗하지 않았다. (swim)
→ The pool in ________________ was not clean.

B 우리말과 일치하도록 ( ) 안에 주어진 단어를 바르게 배열하시오.

1 내가 어젯밤에 꾼 꿈은 아주 무서웠다. (night, last, I, scary, very, was, had)
→ The dream ________________.

2 신발을 파는 남자는 매우 친절했다. (selling, kind, was, shoes, very)
→ The man ________________.

3 네가 들고 있는 바로 그 책은 우리 아버지에 의해 쓰였다. (holding, very, book, you, that, the, are)
→ ________________ was written by my father.

4 그녀는 그 과제를 한 유일한 학생이었다. (only, the, student, homework, the, that, did)
→ She was ________________.

5 내가 매일 보는 쇼는 다음 달에 끝날 것이다. (end, watch, I, month, will, every day, next)
→ The show ________________.

6 이것은 내가 먹어본 가장 맛있는 케이크이다. (the, delicious, eaten, that, most, ever, I've, cake)
→ This is ________________.

UNIT 03

관계부사

A ( ) 안에서 알맞은 말을 고르시오.

1 This is the room (which, where) I found the key.
2 This is (how, the way how) I wrote the story.
3 I found a good website (why, where) I could chat with my friends.
4 I don't know the reason (why, who) he changed his mind.
5 This is the church (which, where) my parents got married.
6 Do you know the reason (when, why) she left the party so early?
7 I remember the day (when, where) you were late for school.
8 I didn't understand the reason (when, why) she painted the wall pink.
9 He didn't tell me (the way, the way how) he lost weight.
10 The day (how, when) you left was cloudy and gray.

B 빈칸에 알맞은 말을 보기에서 골라 쓰시오.

보기	when	where	why	how

1 December was the month __________ I first visited the city.
2 I wrote down the reasons __________ I quit the job.
3 Is that the house __________ his family lived?
4 She is trying to change __________ she dresses.
5 This is the swimming pool __________ he used to swim.
6 I remember the day __________ I came to school for the first time.
7 I know the store __________ you bought this candy.
8 I want to know __________ you were able to finish the work on time.
9 She doesn't know the reason __________ her sister is angry with her.
10 Fall is the season __________ we can eat a lot of fresh fruit.

Answer Key p.35

C

다음 두 문장을 관계부사를 이용하여 한 문장으로 쓰시오.

1 That is the way. + The woman succeeded in that way.
→ ______________________________

2 I remember the moment. + You walked into this room at that moment.
→ ______________________________

3 Tell me the reason. + I must take this class for that reason.
→ ______________________________

4 This is the park. + He exercises in the park every morning.
→ ______________________________

5 Tell me about the day. + You won first prize on the day.
→ ______________________________

6 This is the house. + I lived in this house when I was young.
→ ______________________________

D

두 문장의 의미가 같도록 빈칸에 알맞은 관계부사를 쓰시오.

1 Nine o'clock is the time at which my favorite drama starts.
→ Nine o'clock is the time __________ my favorite drama starts.

2 New York is the city in which he first met his wife.
→ New York is the city __________ he first met his wife.

3 I don't know the reason for which he called me last night.
→ I don't know the reason __________ he called me last night.

4 February is the month in which most students graduate from school.
→ February is the month __________ most students graduate from school.

5 I joined a club in which I can make many friends.
→ I joined a club __________ I can make many friends.

6 He told me the way in which he memorized fifty English words so quickly.
→ He told me __________ he memorized fifty English words so quickly.

WRITING PRACTICE

Answer Key p.36

A 우리말과 일치하도록 관계부사와 ( ) 안의 말을 이용하여 문장을 완성하시오.

1 여기가 그 사고가 일어났던 곳이다. (accident, happen)

→ This is the place ______________________.

2 나는 그가 그런 짓을 한 이유를 이해할 수 없다. (the reason, do)

→ I can't understand ______________________ such a thing.

3 그녀는 내가 일하는 도서관에서 공부를 한다. (work)

→ She studies at the library ______________________.

4 일요일은 내가 한가한 날이다. (the day, free)

→ Sunday is ______________________.

5 여기가 내가 태어난 그 병원이다. (hospital, be born)

→ This is ______________________.

6 나는 내가 별똥별을 봤던 밤을 잊을 수 없다. (the night, see)

→ I can't forget ______________________ a shooting star.

B 우리말과 일치하도록 ( ) 안에 주어진 단어를 바르게 배열하시오.

1 그는 그가 나를 방문한 이유를 내게 말했다. (the, visited, me, why, he, reason)

→ He told me ______________________.

2 네가 이 그림을 그린 방법을 내게 보여줘. (this, way, painted, you, the, picture)

→ Show me ______________________.

3 우리가 공부했던 교실은 매우 작았다. (where, the, we, studied, classroom)

→ ______________________ was very small.

4 그녀는 이 초콜릿을 만든 방법을 나에게 보여주었다. (made, how, this, she, chocolate)

→ She showed me ______________________.

5 나는 우리 부모님이 화나신 이유를 안다. (why, the, my parents, upset, are, reason)

→ I know ______________________.

6 우리가 만난 날에는 눈이 내렸다. (when, day, met, we, the)

→ It snowed on ______________________.

REVIEW TEST

Answer Key p.36

[1-5] 빈칸에 들어갈 알맞은 말을 고르시오.

1

This is the necklace __________ my mother gave me.

① who ② whom ③ whose
④ which ⑤ what

2

__________ he said that day touched many people.

① Who ② Whom ③ Whose
④ Which ⑤ What

3

Do you know the man to __________ Sarah is talking?

① that ② whom ③ whose
④ which ⑤ what

4

Owen is the boy __________ is very good at math.

① that ② whose ③ which
④ whom ⑤ what

5

I don't remember the store __________ I bought this dress.

① when ② where ③ why
④ how ⑤ which

[6-7] 다음 중 어법상 틀린 것을 고르시오.

6 ① The time when this happened is unknown.
② This is the salad that she made.
③ Stop singing the songs which I don't like.
④ I don't know the way how this device works.
⑤ Look at the food he is selling.

7 ① That is not what I'm trying to say.
② It is the most boring movie that I've ever seen.
③ This is the room where I often study in.
④ The day when I was late for the class was terrible.
⑤ Can you tell me the reason why you like poems?

8 다음 중 빈칸에 that을 쓸 수 없는 것은?

① He is the only person ________ I like.
② He has the same hat ________ I have.
③ It is the tallest tree ________ is in my town.
④ I can give you anything ________ you want.
⑤ I've seen the boy with ________ you came.

빈출

9 밑줄 친 부분의 쓰임이 나머지 넷과 다른 것은?

① I don't know who took my bag.
② I like singers who dance very well.
③ He is the man who runs this company.
④ I know the girl who caught the thief.
⑤ He is the guy who owns the French restaurant.

10 다음 중 밑줄 친 부분을 생략할 수 있는 것은? (2개)

① He is my friend who won first prize in the contest.
② The computer that I want to buy is too expensive.
③ The tower which is standing on the hill looks amazing.
④ The man for whom I am waiting hasn't come yet.
⑤ That is the boy whose father is a history teacher.

11 다음 중 어법상 옳은 것은?

① I love the people with that I work.
② Math is the subject I am interested in.
③ She has no friend with she can go to the movies.
④ She took the train where had many empty seats.
⑤ I broke the toy whose my little sister liked very much.

12 빈칸에 들어갈 말이 순서대로 바르게 짝지어진 것은?

- The thing ________ I am looking for is not here.
- ________ I need now is a break.

① what – What ② that – That
③ which – That ④ that – What
⑤ what – That

13 다음 우리말을 영어로 바르게 옮긴 것은?

네가 나에게 보내준 선물 고마워.

① Thank you for the gift you sent me.
② Thank you for the gift how you sent me.
③ Thank you for the gift that you sent me to.
④ Thank you for the gift whom you sent me.
⑤ Thank you for the gift what you sent me.

서술형 빈출

[14-15] 다음 두 문장을 관계대명사를 이용하여 한 문장으로 쓰시오.

14
- This is the house.
- Its stairs were broken.

→ ________________

15
- This is the game.
- I like it the most.

→ ________________

서술형

[16-17] 빈칸에 알맞은 관계부사를 쓰시오.

16 This laptop is small and light. This is the reason ___________ I like it.

17 Yesterday was the last day ___________ I worked for the company.

서술형

[18-19] 우리말과 일치하도록 ( ) 안의 말을 이용하여 문장을 완성하시오.

18 하와이는 우리가 신혼여행을 갔던 섬이다.
(the island, where, go)

→ Hawaii is ___________________ for our honeymoon.

19 나는 무대에서 기타를 치고 있는 저 남자를 좋아한다.
(play, guitar)

→ I like the man ___________________ on the stage.

서술형

[20-21] 다음 문장에서 생략할 수 있는 부분을 찾아 쓰시오.

20 This is the leather jacket that I bought last month.

21 Look at the bird which is flying high in the sky.

서술형

[22-23] 우리말과 일치하도록 ( ) 안에 주어진 단어를 바르게 배열하시오.

22 저곳이 우리 가족이 휴가 동안 머물렀던 호텔이다.
(stayed, at, hotel, family, the, my)

→ That is ___________________ during our vacation.

23 내 뒤에 앉아 있는 남자는 매우 잘생겼다.
(handsome, me, sitting, very, behind, is)

→ The man ___________________.

서술형 고난도

[24-25] 어법상 틀린 부분을 찾아 바르게 고치시오.

24 This is the village in that I grew up. I have very good memories of living there. (1개)

25 I will go to India next month. That I need now is some information about safety there. I want to know the way how I can travel safely. (2개)

UNIT 01

가정법 과거, 가정법 과거완료

( ) 안에서 알맞은 말을 고르시오.

1 If I (am, were) a doctor, I could help him.

2 If I were rich, I (will buy, would buy) the ring for you.

3 If she (studied, had studied) harder, she would have passed the test.

4 If I were healthy, I (can join, could join) the camping trip.

5 If it hadn't rained yesterday, I (can swim, could have swum) in the river.

6 If he (had called, has called) her last night, she wouldn't have answered.

7 If I had a security card, I (got, could get) into the building.

8 If I (would have, had) a car, I could go driving now.

9 If you (practiced, had practiced) harder, you could have done better.

10 If I (were, had been) young, I would try to be a singer.

B

밑줄 친 부분을 어법에 맞게 고치시오.

1 If I were you, I will believe him.

2 If you had helped me, I could finish my homework.

3 If I am not sick, I could play soccer.

4 If it had been sunny, she would gone to the swimming pool.

5 If I had more time, I will visit my grandparents.

6 If she had been there, she had been hurt.

7 If I were a teacher, I will make students exercise more.

8 If he had known the truth, he will have forgiven you.

9 If my car were bigger, we all can ride in it together.

10 If I were your father, I won't let you go there.

Answer Key p.36

C 다음 문장을 가정법으로 바꿀 때 빈칸에 알맞은 말을 쓰시오. (단, 주절의 조동사는 would를 쓸 것)

1 As he is busy, he isn't here with us.
→ If he ______________ busy, he ______________ here with us.

2 As he wasn't careful, he hurt his leg.
→ If he ______________ careful, he ______________ his leg.

3 As she didn't ask him, he didn't help her.
→ If she ______________ him, he ______________ her.

4 As you told a lie, he was angry.
→ If you ______________ a lie, he ______________ angry.

5 As she didn't take my advice, she failed.
→ If she ______________ my advice, she ______________.

6 As you didn't get up early enough, you missed the school bus.
→ If you ______________ early enough, you ______________ the school bus.

D 주어진 문장과 의미가 통하도록 빈칸에 알맞은 말을 쓰시오.

1 If Bob had a license, he could drive the car.
→ As Bob ______________ a license, he ______________ the car.

2 If I had had enough time, I would have studied all the subjects.
→ As I ______________ enough time, I ______________ all the subjects.

3 If they had won the game, they would have received the cash prize.
→ As they ______________ the game, they ______________ the cash prize.

4 If my eyesight were good, I wouldn't have to wear glasses.
→ As my eyesight ______________, I ______________ glasses.

5 If we had brought our own bag, we wouldn't have bought a plastic bag.
→ As we ______________ our own bag, we ______________ a plastic bag.

6 If she knew the truth, she would be angry at me.
→ As she ______________ the truth, she ______________ angry at me.

WRITING PRACTICE

Answer Key p.36

A 우리말과 일치하도록 ( ) 안의 말을 이용하여 문장을 완성하시오.

1 지금이 겨울이라면, 나는 스키를 타러 갈 텐데. (winter, now)

→ ______________________, I would go skiing.

2 내가 그의 전화번호를 잃어버리지 않았다면, 나는 그에게 전화할 수 있었을 텐데. (call)

→ If I hadn't lost his phone number, ______________________.

3 내가 만약 다시 학생이 된다면, 열심히 공부할 텐데. (hard)

→ If I were a student again, ______________________.

4 그녀가 더 조심했다면, 그 사고를 피할 수 있었을 텐데. (careful)

→ ______________________, she could have avoided the accident.

5 그가 약속이 없다면, 우리와 함께 할 수 있을 텐데. (have, join)

→ If he ____________ an appointment, he ____________ us.

6 내가 예약을 했었다면, 우리는 오랫동안 기다릴 필요가 없었을 텐데. (have to, wait)

→ If I had made a reservation, we ______________________ for a long time.

B 우리말과 일치하도록 ( ) 안에 주어진 단어를 바르게 배열하시오.

1 그녀가 집에 있다면, 택배를 받을 수 있을 텐데.
(home, receive, she, at, package, the, were, could)

→ If she ______________________.

2 그가 이기적이지 않다면, 많은 친구를 사귈 수 있을 텐데. (were, could, if, he, selfish, not, he, make)

→ ______________________ a lot of friends.

3 나의 할머니가 그 소식을 들으신다면, 행복해 하실 텐데.
(my grandmother, if, heard, be, she, the news, would)

→ ______________________ happy.

4 우리가 더 빨리 뛰었다면, 길을 건널 수 있었을 텐데.
(have, run, could, faster, we, crossed, had)

→ If we ______________________ the street.

5 내가 너라면, 그에게 편지를 쓸 텐데. (would, you, I, were, write, if, I)

→ ______________________ a letter to him.

6 그가 그 숙제를 끝냈다면, 그의 선생님이 화가 나지 않으셨을 텐데.
(finished, been, wouldn't, had, teacher, his, the homework, have)

→ If he ______________________ upset.

UNIT 02

I wish + 가정법, as if + 가정법

Answer Key p.36

A

( ) 안에서 알맞은 말을 고르시오.

1 I wish I (have, had) a lot of friends to talk to.

2 He talks as if he (were, had been) very angry, but he is just pretending.

3 It's hot today. I wish it (were, had been) cooler.

4 I wish you (be, were) kind to my friend Lisa. You're not kind to her.

5 Tommy talks as if the singer (be, were) his friend. In fact, he doesn't know him.

6 She acts as if she (are, were) a princess. In fact, she is not.

7 He looks as if he (cried, had cried) a while ago. In fact, he didn't.

8 Miranda talks as if she (is eating, had eaten) nothing. In fact, she ate more than all of us.

9 I wish I (ask, had asked) Mr. Yoon more questions. I still don't know much about him.

10 I wish I (bought, had bought) the magazine this morning. I don't have anything to read now.

B

( ) 안의 말을 이용하여 문장을 완성하시오.

1 I wish I ______________ younger than him right now. (be)

2 She talks as if she ______________ a hairdresser. In fact, she is not. (be)

3 She looks as if she ______________ a ghost. In fact, she didn't. (see)

4 He talks as if he ______________ in Africa. In fact, he never lived there. (live)

5 I don't play soccer well. I wish I ______________ soccer as well as Son Heungmin. (play)

6 He talks as if he ______________ the world. In fact, he didn't. (save)

7 The boy sometimes acts as if he ______________ a grown-up. (be)

8 I wish I ______________ class president, but I wasn't. (be elected)

9 Mr. Simpson talks as if he ______________ a doctor, but he was not. (be)

10 My brother talks as if he ______________ the dishes every day, but he never does. (do)

C 주어진 문장과 의미가 통하도록 빈칸에 알맞은 말을 쓰시오.

1 I am sorry that my apartment isn't bigger.

→ I wish ______________________________.

2 I am sorry that she found out the truth.

→ I wish ______________________________.

3 I am sorry that I didn't read more books when I was young.

→ I wish ______________________________.

4 In fact, my sister is not a teacher.

→ My sister talks as if ______________________________.

5 In fact, he was not a pilot.

→ He acts as if he ______________________________.

6 In fact, Emily never lived in that town.

→ Emily talks as if ______________________________.

D 주어진 문장과 의미가 통하도록 빈칸에 알맞은 말을 쓰시오.

1 I wish I knew how to play the flute.

→ I am sorry that ______________________________.

2 I wish I were as tall as you.

→ I am sorry that ______________________________.

3 I wish you had come to school yesterday.

→ I am sorry that ______________________________.

4 Jessica acts as if she knew him.

→ In fact, ______________________________.

5 He is answering as if he had understood everything.

→ In fact, ______________________________.

6 He talks as if he had gotten a hundred on the math exam.

→ In fact, ______________________________.

WRITING PRACTICE

Answer Key p.37

A 우리말과 일치하도록 ( ) 안의 말을 이용하여 문장을 완성하시오.

1 내가 그 영화의 주인공이라면 좋을 텐데. (the hero)

→ I wish ______________________ of the movie.

2 James는 마치 그가 거짓말을 하지 않았던 것처럼 말한다. (lie)

→ James talks ______________________.

3 나의 숙제를 더 일찍 끝냈더라면 좋을 텐데. (finish, homework)

→ I wish ______________________ earlier.

4 Sam은 마치 자신이 영화감독인 것처럼 행동하지만 그렇지 않다. (a movie director)

→ Sam acts ______________________, but he is not.

5 그녀가 어제 나를 방문했다면 좋을 텐데. (visit)

→ I wish ______________________ yesterday.

6 그녀는 마치 내가 그녀의 딸인 것처럼 나를 대한다. (be, daughter)

→ She treats me ______________________.

B 우리말과 일치하도록 ( ) 안에 주어진 단어를 바르게 배열하시오.

1 내가 영어를 잘한다면 좋을 텐데. (wish, I, speak, I, could, well, English)

→ ______________________.

2 그녀는 화가 난 것처럼 말한다. (if, she, annoyed, as, were, speaks, she)

→ ______________________.

3 내가 나의 선생님 말씀을 들었더라면 좋을 텐데. (listened, I, teacher, I, my, had, wish, to)

→ ______________________.

4 그는 마치 자기가 그 팀에서 최고의 선수인 것처럼 행동한다.
(the, he, if, acts, were, as, best, he, player)

→ ______________________ on the team.

5 내일이 월요일이 아니라면 좋을 텐데. (it, I, were, tomorrow, Monday, wish, not)

→ ______________________.

6 그는 오늘 아침에 운동했던 것처럼 말한다. (talks, exercised, he, as, he, if, had)

→ ______________________ this morning.

REVIEW TEST

[1-5] 빈칸에 들어갈 알맞은 말을 고르시오.

1 If I had time, I __________ you.

① help ② helped
③ helping ④ will help
⑤ would help

2 If I __________ harder, I could have received the scholarship.

① studied ② have studied
③ had studied ④ would study
⑤ would have studied

3 I wish my brother __________ here with us. But he is in Paris right now.

① be ② is
③ were ④ have been
⑤ had been

4 She was talking as if she __________ me yesterday. But she didn't.

① sees ② saw
③ seeing ④ has seen
⑤ had seen

5 If I __________ a scientist, I would make a big robot.

① be ② am
③ were ④ would be
⑤ would have been

[6-7] 다음 중 어법상 틀린 것을 고르시오.

6
① If I had time, I could go shopping.
② I wish I could swim well.
③ If I knew the way to the airport, I could pick you up.
④ I wish you came home yesterday.
⑤ She acts as if she owned this plane.

7
① If he had money, he could buy a bunch of roses.
② If I took his advice, I could have earned some money.
③ If I had passed the test, my mother would have been happy.
④ If I had heard the news, I would have told you.
⑤ If I were you, I would apologize first.

8 다음 중 어법상 옳은 것은?

① I wish she had finish her job on time.
② I wish he hasn't missed the train.
③ Bob cried as if he had heard sad news.
④ If she had a credit card, she'll buy the shoes.
⑤ If you tasted the soup, you would have liked it.

빈출

[9-11] 다음 우리말을 영어로 바르게 옮긴 것을 고르시오.

9

Zoe는 마치 가수인 것처럼 행동한다.

① Zoe acts as if she were a singer.
② Zoe acted as if she were a singer.
③ Zoe acts as if she had been a singer.
④ Zoe acted as if she had been a singer.
⑤ Zoe acts as if she will be a singer.

10

내가 답을 알았더라면, 너에게 알려주었을 텐데.

① If I know the answers, I will let you know.
② If I knew the answers, I would let you know.
③ If I knew the answers, I would have let you know.
④ If I had known the answers, I would let you know.
⑤ If I had known the answers, I would have let you know.

11

나에게 여동생이 있다면 좋을 텐데.

① I wish I have a sister.
② I wish I didn't have a sister.
③ I wish I had a sister.
④ I wish I had had a sister.
⑤ I want I hadn't had a sister.

빈출

[12-13] 다음 문장을 가정법으로 바르게 고친 것을 고르시오.

12

As I don't have an umbrella, I can't go home now.

① If I have an umbrella, I can't go home now.
② If I had an umbrella, I could go home now.
③ If I hadn't an umbrella, I couldn't go home now.
④ If I had had an umbrella, I could have gone home now.
⑤ If I hadn't had an umbrella, I couldn't have gone home now.

13

I'm sorry that I didn't see the movie.

① I wish I saw the movie.
② I wish I didn't see the movie.
③ I wish I had seen the movie.
④ I wish I hadn't seen the movie.
⑤ I wish I would have seen the movie.

14 빈칸에 공통으로 들어갈 말은?

• I wish I __________ with you now.
• You talk as if you __________ my professor.

① be ② was
③ were ④ have been
⑤ had been

서술형

[15-16] ( ) 안의 말을 이용하여 문장을 완성하시오.

15 If I ______________ time, I would watch the musical with you. (have)

16 I wish I ______________ how to play the piano when I was young. (learn)

서술형

[17-19] 다음 문장을 가정법으로 바꿀 때 빈칸에 알맞은 말을 쓰시오.

17 As I didn't read the question carefully, I couldn't solve it.

→ If I ______________ the question carefully, I ______________ it.

18 I am sorry that I laughed at her mistakes.

→ I wish I ______________ at her mistakes.

19 As it's not sunny, I won't go out.

→ If it ____________, I ____________ out.

서술형

[20-21] 우리말과 일치하도록 ( ) 안의 말을 이용하여 문장을 완성하시오.

20 내가 그 파일을 삭제하지 않았더라면 좋을 텐데. (erase, file)

→ I wish I ______________________.

21 그들은 뉴욕을 방문했던 것처럼 행동한다. (visit, New York)

→ They act ______________________

______________________.

서술형

[22-23] 우리말과 일치하도록 ( ) 안에 주어진 단어를 바르게 배열하시오.

22 네가 규칙을 따랐더라면, 너는 벌을 받지 않았을 텐데. (been, wouldn't, punished, had, followed, have, the rules, you)

→ If you ______________________

______________________.

23 그는 마치 자신이 나의 상사인 것처럼 나에게 말한다. (he, as, to, me, talks, if, he, my, boss, were)

→ ______________________

______________________.

서술형 고난도

[24-25] 어법상 틀린 부분을 찾아 바르게 고치시오.

24 My laptop is not working. I wish I can buy a new one. (1개)

25 When my brother got injured, I was far from home. If I had been home, I could take care of him. (1개)

UNIT 01 시제의 일치

Answer Key p.37

A

( ) 안에서 알맞은 말을 고르시오.

1 I heard that his wallet (is, had been) stolen.
2 Mom said that she (will, would) buy me jeans.
3 We learned at school that Mercury (is, was) the smallest planet.
4 He sent me a message saying that he (may, might) be late tomorrow.
5 He found that his pants (are, were) too small.
6 I didn't notice that she (has, had) been crying.
7 I heard that the Christmas holiday (is, will be) really important in the US.
8 I learned that the Republic of Korea (was, had been) established in 1948.
9 My father said that walls (have, had) ears.
10 We all know that two plus two (is, was) four.

B

밑줄 친 부분을 어법에 맞게 고치시오.

1 I heard that the early bird caught the worm.
2 The children learned that they had to stop at a red light at a crosswalk.
3 He learned that Seoul was the capital city of South Korea.
4 Jonathan read that exercise helped our brains work better.
5 My teacher explained that the Iraq War had broken out in 2003.
6 The boy learned that China was located in Asia.
7 I thought that my brother will pass the exam, and he did.
8 The book said that Columbus had discovered America.
9 The doctor said that oranges had a lot of vitamin C.
10 She was taught that Mars was farther from Earth than the moon.

C 문장의 주절을 과거시제로 바꿀 때, 빈칸에 알맞은 말을 쓰시오.

1 Tom says that he will arrive on time.
→ Tom said that he _______________ on time.

2 I know that he has finished his homework.
→ I knew that he _______________ his homework.

3 My teacher says that every cloud has a silver lining.
→ My teacher said that every cloud _______________ a silver lining.

4 The book says that Yi Sun-sin invented the Turtle Ship.
→ The book said that Yi Sun-sin _______________ the Turtle Ship.

5 We learn that the sun is much bigger than the earth.
→ We learned that the sun _______________ much bigger than the earth.

6 The children don't know that sweet potatoes grow underground.
→ The children didn't know that sweet potatoes _____________ underground.

7 He tells me that I can use his cell phone.
→ He told me that I _______________ his cell phone.

8 James doesn't know that the American Civil War broke out in 1861.
→ James didn't know that the American Civil War _____________ out in 1861.

9 She says that she has lost my bag.
→ She said that she _______________ my bag.

10 Dad says that all that glitters is not gold.
→ Dad said that all that glitters _______________ not gold.

11 I think that Luke will win first prize in the singing contest.
→ I thought that Luke _______________ first prize in the singing contest.

12 He knows that Einstein was born in Germany in 1879.
→ He knew that Einstein _______________ in Germany in 1879.

WRITING PRACTICE

Answer Key p.37

A 우리말과 일치하도록 ( ) 안의 말을 이용하여 문장을 완성하시오.

1 그는 지구가 둥글다는 것을 증명했다. (the earth, round)

→ He proved that ______________________.

2 그는 프로게이머가 되고 싶다고 말했다. (want, become)

→ He said that ______________________ a pro-gamer.

3 기상 캐스터는 내일 눈이 올 것이라고 말한다. (will, snow)

→ The weather forecaster says that ______________________ tomorrow.

4 그는 항상 인생은 짧다고 말했다. (life, short)

→ He always said that ______________________.

5 그녀는 제주도가 한국에서 가장 큰 섬이라는 것을 몰랐다. (big, island)

→ She didn't know that Jeju Island ______________________ in Korea.

6 나는 1차 세계대전이 1918년에 끝난 것을 몰랐다. (end)

→ I didn't know that the First World War ______________________ in 1918.

B 우리말과 일치하도록 ( ) 안에 주어진 단어를 바르게 배열하시오.

1 나는 그녀가 이미 떠났다는 것을 알았다. (that, she, left, knew, had, already)

→ I ____________________________________.

2 그는 UFO를 본 적이 있다고 말했다. (that, he, UFO, seen, a, had)

→ He said ____________________________________.

3 그는 그의 수업이 매일 9시에 시작한다고 말했다. (at, nine, class, he, starts, his, that, said)

→ ____________________________________ every day.

4 우리 선생님께서 체르노빌 참사가 1986년에 일어났다고 말씀하셨다.
(the Chernobyl disaster, that, my teacher, said, occurred)

→ ____________________________________ in 1986.

5 아버지는 항상 세월은 사람을 기다려 주지 않는다고 말씀하셨다.
(that, said, time and tide, no man, wait, for)

→ My father always ____________________________________.

6 나는 Kate에게 그녀가 한 시간 동안만 게임을 할 수 있다고 말했다.
(told, that, she, play, I, the game, could, Kate)

→ ____________________________________ for only one hour.

UNIT 02

화법

A

( ) 안에서 알맞은 말을 고르시오.

1 I (said, told) that I would buy a new dictionary.

2 He (said, told) me that he would change the menu at his restaurant.

3 She asked me (that, whether) I could bring her a glass of water.

4 The old man (asked, said) me how old I was.

5 My daughter asked me (if could she, if she could) go out with him.

6 James asked me (when would I, when I would) come home.

7 My teacher told us (if, that) she would give us a pop quiz.

8 The police officer asked him if (he had driven, had he driven) the car.

9 He asked me (if, that) Aria knew the secret.

10 Mom asked us (who had broken, had who broken) the vase.

B

다음을 간접화법으로 바꿀 때, 밑줄 친 부분을 어법에 맞게 고치시오.

1 She said to me, "I won't forget our promise."
→ She said me that she wouldn't forget our promise.

2 Mary said to me, "I need your help."
→ Mary told me that she needed your help.

3 He said to me, "Where did you buy your scarf?"
→ He asked me where had I bought my scarf.

4 She said to me, "Who sent you the package?"
→ She asked me who sent me the package.

5 Mike said to me, "Did you get my message?"
→ Mike asked me that I had gotten his message.

6 My father said to me, "I will buy you a new computer."
→ My father told me that I would buy you a new computer.

Answer Key p.37

C 다음을 간접화법으로 바꿀 때, 빈칸에 알맞은 말을 쓰시오.

1 She said to me, “When did you finish your homework?”
→ She asked me ________________________________.

2 He said to me, “I lost my wallet on the subway.”
→ He told me that ________________________________.

3 He said to me, “Will you join the club?”
→ He asked me ________________________________.

4 She said to me, “I ate a hamburger with my sister.”
→ She told me that ________________________________.

5 She said to me, “What do you want to be in the future?”
→ She asked me ________________________________.

6 My mother said to me, “Do you need to buy a new cell phone?”
→ My mother asked me ________________________________.

7 He said to me, “I worked for a design company.”
→ He told me that ________________________________.

D 다음을 직접화법으로 바꿀 때, 빈칸에 알맞은 말을 쓰시오.

1 I told my son that he had to study hard.
→ I said to my son, “________________________________.”

2 I asked him if he had liked the concert.
→ I said to him, “________________________________?”

3 He asked me when I would visit him.
→ He said to me, “________________________________?”

4 She asked me how I had known her email address.
→ She said to me, “________________________________?”

5 She told me that she would call me later.
→ She said to me, “________________________________.”

6 He asked her if she was working for the toy company.
→ He said to her, “________________________________?”

WRITING PRACTICE

Answer Key p.37

A 우리말과 일치하도록 ( ) 안의 말을 이용하여 문장을 완성하시오.

1 그녀는 나에게 새 컴퓨터를 사고 싶다고 말했다. (want)

→ She told me ________________________ a new computer.

2 나는 그녀에게 내가 그녀의 카메라를 빌려도 되는지 물어보았다. (can, borrow)

→ I asked her ________________________ her camera.

3 나는 나의 남동생에게 나와 대화할 시간이 있는지 물어보았다. (have, time)

→ I asked my brother ________________________ to talk with me.

4 나는 그에게 언제 설거지를 할 것인지 물어보았다. (will, do the dishes)

→ I asked him ________________________.

5 그녀는 나에게 자신이 나를 자랑스러워한다고 말했다. (be proud of)

→ She told me ________________________.

6 그는 나에게 Amy를 아는지 물어보았다. (ask, know)

→ He ________________________ Amy.

B 우리말과 일치하도록 ( ) 안에 주어진 단어를 바르게 배열하시오.

1 그는 나에게 어디에 사는지 물어보지 않았다. (ask, lived, where, me, I, didn't)

→ He ____.

2 엄마는 누가 그 선물을 나에게 주었는지 물어보셨다. (me, who, had, asked, me, given, Mom)

→ ____ the present.

3 나는 그에게 그가 말하는 것을 이해한다고 말했다. (understood, I, him, what, that, I, told)

→ ____ he said.

4 그는 나에게 내가 그의 컴퓨터를 사용했는지 물어보았다. (used, he, if, I, asked, me, had)

→ ____ his computer.

5 그녀는 나에게 자신은 나의 도움이 필요 없다고 말했다. (me, need, told, my, that, didn't, help, she)

→ She ____.

6 그는 나에게 배가 고픈지 물어보았다. (I, me, hungry, was, asked, if)

→ He ____.

REVIEW TEST

Answer Key p.38

[1-5] 빈칸에 들어갈 알맞은 말을 고르시오.

1

He thought that I ________ Italian.

① will study ② am studying
③ have studied ④ studied
⑤ study

2

I didn't understand why she ________ such a thing to him.

① had done ② will do
③ wants to do ④ is going to do
⑤ is doing

3

I didn't know that the moon ________ the tides.

① cause ② causes
③ will cause ④ was causing
⑤ had caused

4

She asked me ________ I had done my homework.

① that ② unless
③ if ④ what
⑤ though

5

He asked me where ________ him.

① did I meet ② I meet
③ had I met ④ I had met
⑤ had met I

[6-7] 다음 중 어법상 틀린 것을 고르시오.

6 ① He said he goes jogging every day.
② I thought his laptop wasn't working.
③ I understand why he won't come to the class.
④ I learned that water and oil didn't mix.
⑤ We knew that Dokdo Island belongs to Korea.

7 ① Mom asked me why I had been late.
② I thought the plan had been changed.
③ Dad asked me if I had a girlfriend.
④ He asked me that I had an ID card.
⑤ The research showed that sleep is important for one's health.

빈출

8 다음을 간접화법으로 바꿀 때, 빈칸에 들어갈 알맞은 말은?

Sam said to me, "Will you join us?"
→ Sam asked me ________________.

① that he would join us
② that I would join them
③ whether I would join them
④ if I will join us
⑤ if I would join us

빈출

[9-11] 대화를 읽고 빈칸에 들어갈 말이 순서대로 바르게 짝지어진 것을 고르시오.

9

John: Do you like action movies?
Sarah: Yes, I do.
→ John __________ Sarah __________ action movies.

① asked – that she liked
② told – if she liked
③ asked – if did she like
④ told – whether did she like
⑤ asked – whether she liked

10

Ted: Who is your favorite actor?
Ally: My favorite actor is Brad Pitt.
→ Ally __________ Ted __________ Brad Pitt.

① told – that her favorite actor was
② said – if her favorite actor was
③ told – that my favorite actor was
④ said – that her favorite actor was
⑤ told – whether her favorite actor was

11

Mom: Where did you get it?
Son: I can't tell you.
→ The mother __________ her son __________ it.

① asked – where did you get
② told – where did he get
③ asked – where had you get
④ told – where you gotten
⑤ asked – where he had gotten

12 빈칸에 들어갈 말로 알맞은 것은? (2개)

I thought that he __________ a poet.

① was ② has been
③ had been ④ were
⑤ will be

서술형

[13-14] ( ) 안의 말을 이용하여 문장을 완성하시오.

13 We learned that insects __________ six legs. (have)

14 Jonathan said that a little knowledge __________ a dangerous thing. (be)

서술형

[15-16] 다음을 간접화법으로 바꿀 때, 빈칸에 알맞은 말을 쓰시오.

15 My teacher said to us, "Did you bring your textbooks?"

→ My teacher asked us __________
__________.

16 I said to him, "How can I change my password?"

→ I asked him __________
__________.

17 다음 중 어법상 옳은 것은?

① I knew that English has twenty-six letters in its alphabet.
② I heard that her new album will be released soon.
③ I understood how the company has grown a lot.
④ He looked like he hasn't slept well last night.
⑤ I found that what he is saying is nonsense.

서술형

[18-19] 문장의 주절을 과거시제로 바꿀 때, 빈칸에 알맞은 말을 쓰시오.

18 I know that coffee has caffeine.

→ I knew that ____________________.

19 They believe that she will go to Paris.

→ They believed that ________________
____________________________________.

서술형

[20-21] 우리말과 일치하도록 ( ) 안의 말을 이용하여 문장을 완성하시오.

20 나는 펭귄은 날 수 없다는 것을 알았다. (can)

→ I knew that penguins ______________.

21 그녀는 내게 언제 내가 그 모자를 샀는지 물어보았다. (buy)

→ She asked me ____________________ the hat.

서술형

[22-23] 우리말과 일치하도록 ( ) 안에 주어진 단어를 바르게 배열하시오.

22 Susie는 매일 영어 단어 10개씩을 외운다고 말했다. (memorizes, that, said, Susie, she)

→ ____________________________________
ten English words every day.

23 나는 그녀에게 목이 마른지 물어보았다. (if, asked, she, thirsty, was, her, I)

→ ____________________________________.

서술형 고난도

[24-25] 어법상 틀린 부분을 찾아 바르게 고치시오.

24 William asked me why did I study Spanish. I told him that I wanted to travel in Spain. (1개)

25 It was very cold yesterday. Mom said that I have to dress warmly, but I didn't. And when I woke up this morning, I found that I had a cold. (1개)

MEMO

MEMO

MEMO

MEMO

MEMO

GRAMMAR

Inside

workbook

A 4-level grammar course
with abundant writing practice

Compact and concise English grammar
간결하고 정확한 문법 설명

Extensive practice in sentence writing
다양한 유형의 영어 문장 쓰기

Full preparation for middle school tests
내신 완벽 대비

+ Workbook with additional exercises
풍부한 양의 추가 문제

Answer Key

GRAMMAR Inside

LEVEL 2

A 4-level grammar course
with abundant writing practice

NE Neungyule

Answer Key

GRAMMAR Inside

LEVEL 2

CHAPTER

01 여러 가지 동사

UNIT 01 감각동사와 수여동사

CHECK UP p.12

1. ⓑ 2. ⓐ

PRACTICE p.13

STEP 1 1. new 2. interesting
3. him my secret 4. for 5. me
STEP 2 1. of 2. delicious 3. to 4. for
STEP 3 1. to me 2. to his parents 3. for me
STEP 4 1. felt cold 2. taste salty
3. her notebook to me 4. my diary to
5. me my teacher's name

UNIT 02 목적격 보어를 가지는 동사

CHECK UP p.14

1. ⓒ 2. ⓐ 3. ⓐ

PRACTICE p.15

STEP 1 1. travel 2. depressed 3. to wear
4. take 5. to water
STEP 2 1. shake[shaking] 2. to take 3. wait
4. warm 5. choose[to choose]
STEP 3 1. to clean 2. knock[knocking]
3. tell 4. to think
STEP 4 1. want you to choose
2. made us happy
3. felt something touch[touching]
4. let me have

GRAMMAR FOR WRITING pp.16-17

A 1. taste sour 2. named their baby Alice
3. You look young 4. allowed me to use
5. smells like curry 6. him wash the dishes
7. lent Bill my tent / lent my tent to Bill

B 1. This lake looks very deep 2. heard someone call her name 3. keeps food fresh 4. made a wedding dress for her 5. asked a favor of his neighbor 6. showed his scar to them

C 1. saw Mia talk[talking] to Henry
2. something fall[falling] from the sky
3. got me to join the book club 4. made me work until late last night 5. felt the wind blow[blowing] through her hair 6. let me ride my bike to school

D 1. children gifts / gifts to children
2. knock[knocking] on the door
3. the driver to stop the car

REVIEW TEST pp.18-21

1. ② 2. ① 3. ① 4. ③ 5. ② 6. ① 7. ② 8. ④ 9. ② 10. ② 11. ③ 12. ③ 13. steal[stealing] 14. use 15. to go 16. to me 17. of me 18. for his daughter 19. ② 20. tastes bitter 21. didn't[did not] let me enter 22. got me to keep a diary 23. ④ 24. The story sounded strange 25. I heard my sister play the violin 26. ①, ②, ⑤ 27. ③ 28. ③ 29. X, to 30. O 31. He helped us find the way 32. tiredly → tired 33. teach → to teach

1 감각동사(taste) + 형용사: ~한 맛이 나다
2 수여동사(lend) + 직접목적어 + to + 간접목적어
3 사역동사(make) + 목적어 + 동사원형
4 advise + 목적어 + to부정사(구)
5 지각동사(see) + 목적어 + 동사원형[현재분사]
6 ① 감각동사(feel) + 형용사 (smoothly → smooth)
7 ② find + 목적어 + 형용사 (excite → exciting)
8 ④는 for가 들어가야 한다.
9 감각동사(look, taste, smell, sound) + 형용사
10 ② get(~을 시키다) + 목적어 + to부정사(구)
11 ③ 사역동사(let) + 목적어 + 동사원형
12 사역동사(have) + 목적어 + 동사원형
13 지각동사(see) + 목적어 + 동사원형[현재분사]
14 사역동사(let) + 목적어 + 동사원형
15 allow + 목적어 + to부정사(구)
16 수여동사(give) + 직접목적어 + to + 간접목적어
17 수여동사(ask) + 직접목적어 + of + 간접목적어
18 수여동사(buy) + 직접목적어 + for + 간접목적어
19 ① usefully → useful ③ sadly → sad

④ arrive → to arrive ⑤ to bring → bring

20 감각동사(taste) + 형용사: ~한 맛이 나다

21 사역동사(let) + 목적어 + 동사원형

22 get(~을 시키다) + 목적어 + to부정사(구)

23 ④는 「수여동사 + 간접목적어 + 직접목적어」로 이루어진 4형식, 나머지는 「동사 + 목적어 + 목적격 보어」로 이루어진 5형식이다.

24 감각동사(sound) + 형용사: ~하게 들리다

25 지각동사(hear) + 목적어 + 동사원형[현재분사]

26 ③ looks like spicy → looks spicy
④ get some water of me → get me some water / get some water for me

27 b. play → to play
e. successfully → successful

28 • cleaning → to clean
• to bring → bring

29 수여동사(give) + 직접목적어 + to + 간접목적어

30 keep + 목적어 + 형용사(구)

31 help는 목적격 보어로 동사원형과 to부정사 둘 다 쓸 수 있다. 조건에서 6단어로 쓰라고 했으므로 동사원형으로 쓴다.

32 감각동사(look) + 형용사: ~하게 보이다

33 expect + 목적어 + to부정사(구)

CHAPTER 02 시제

UNIT 01 현재, 과거, 미래시제 / 진행형

CHECK UP p.24

1. ⓐ 2. ⓑ 3. ⓒ

PRACTICE p.25

STEP 1 **1.** takes **2.** entered **3.** was taking **4.** will send

STEP 2 **1.** ordered **2.** boils **3.** eating **4.** runs

STEP 3 **1.** knows **2.** took **3.** was singing **4.** am going to visit / will visit

STEP 4 **1.** is going to learn **2.** is washing dishes **3.** fixed my computer **4.** ride a bicycle

UNIT 02 현재완료

CHECK UP p.26

1. ⓒ 2. ⓒ 3. ⓑ 4. ⓒ

PRACTICE p.27

STEP 1 **1.** haven't seen **2.** sent **3.** has snowed **4.** has gone

STEP 2 **1.** Have you ever baked **2.** since **3.** learned **4.** have lived

STEP 3 **1.** has lost **2.** has come **3.** has gone

STEP 4 **1.** have forgotten **2.** has worked here for **3.** have already bought **4.** have been to **5.** Have you ever used

GRAMMAR FOR WRITING pp.28-29

A **1.** have just moved **2.** will[is going to] do volunteer work **3.** has worn those glasses for **4.** has met my parents **5.** is drying his hair **6.** turn red and yellow in fall **7.** graduated from elementary school

B **1.** What are you going to do **2.** My sister has broken my earphones **3.** Sue has liked to sing since **4.** I was watching a movie when **5.** My mother will be forty years old **6.** The restaurant opens at ten o'clock

C **1.** eats **2.** heard **3.** has been **4.** check **5.** has **6.** has taught **7.** was walking **8.** will help

D **1.** took a math quiz **2.** went to the dentist **3.** will[is going to] have dinner with Ryan **4.** will[is going to] practice the violin

REVIEW TEST pp.30-33

1. ① **2.** ② **3.** ③ **4.** ② **5.** ④ **6.** ③ **7.** ④ **8.** ⑤ **9.** ② **10.** ⑤ **11.** will[is going to] be **12.** has lived **13.** ⑤ **14.** ④ **15.** stayed **16.** is looking **17.** has gone **18.** has liked Mindy since **19.** Have you ever been **20.** has stolen my purse

21. met her boyfriend **22.** ③ **23.** I was writing an email to my friend **24.** I am going to join the movie club **25.** We have been friends for **26.** ③, ④ **27.** ② **28.** ② **29.** O **30.** X, heard [hear] **31.** X, won **32.** am believing → believe **33.** for → since, was taller → is taller

1 변함없는 진리는 항상 현재시제를 쓴다.

2 과거를 나타내는 부사구(last month)가 있으므로 과거시제가 와야 한다.

3 특정 시점(now)에 진행 중인 일을 나타내므로 현재진행형이 와야 한다.

4 소유를 나타내는 동사(have)는 진행형으로 쓰지 않는다.

5 과거부터 현재까지의 경험은 현재완료로 나타낸다.

6 ③ 변함없는 진리는 항상 현재시제를 쓴다. (was → is)

7 ④ 과거를 나타내는 부사구(last year)는 현재완료와 함께 쓸 수 없다. (has gone → went)

8 for + 기간: ~ 동안 / since + 시점: ~ 이래로

9 보기와 ②는 현재완료의 〈완료〉를 나타낸다. ①, ③은 〈경험〉, ④, ⑤는 〈계속〉을 나타낸다.

10 보기와 ⑤는 현재완료의 〈계속〉을 나타낸다. ①은 〈결과〉, ②는 〈경험〉, ③, ④는 〈완료〉를 나타낸다.

11 미래에 대한 예측을 나타낼 때 will이나 be going to를 쓴다.

12 과거의 어느 시점부터 현재까지 어떤 동작이나 일이 계속되고 있을 때 현재완료를 쓴다.

13 ① will[is going to] ride ② is running ③ was ④ lost

14 첫 번째 빈칸은 과거를 나타내는 부사구(last Saturday)가 있으므로 과거시제가 와야 한다. 두 번째 빈칸은 since가 있으므로 현재완료가 와야 한다.

15 과거를 나타내는 부사구(last summer)가 있으므로 과거시제가 와야 한다.

16 특정 시점(now)에 진행 중인 일을 나타내므로 현재진행형이 와야 한다.

17 과거 행동으로 인한 결과가 현재까지 영향을 미치고 있을 때 현재완료를 쓴다.

18 과거의 어느 시점부터 현재까지 어떤 동작이나 일이 계속되고 있을 때 현재완료를 쓴다.

19 과거부터 현재까지의 경험은 현재완료로 나타낸다.

20 과거 행동으로 인한 결과가 현재까지 영향을 미치고 있을 때 현재완료를 쓴다.

21 과거를 나타내는 부사구(last year)가 있으므로 과거시제가 와야 한다.

22 A의 말을 듣고 즉흥적으로 결심한 일을 나타내므로 will을 쓴다.

23 과거진행형(be동사의 과거형 + v-ing)이 와야 한다.

24 be going to + 동사원형

25 과거 어느 시점에서부터 현재까지 계속되고 있는 상태를 나타내므로 현재완료를 쓴다.

26 ① am knowing → know ② will play → has played ⑤ is → was

27 I am liking the boy band BTS.
→ I like the boy band BTS.
Do you ever been to Jeonju?
→ Have you ever been to Jeonju?

28 • is having → has • needed → need
• have lived → lived

29 이미 정해진 미래의 계획을 나타낼 때 be going to를 쓴다.

30 감각을 나타내는 동사(hear)는 진행형으로 쓰지 않는다.

31 과거를 나타내는 부사구(last year)가 있으므로 과거시제가 와야 한다.

32 인지를 나타내는 동사(believe)는 진행형으로 쓰지 않는다.

33 for + 기간: ~ 동안 / since + 시점: ~ 이래로
현재를 나타내는 부사(now)가 있으므로 현재의 사실이나 상태를 나타내는 현재시제를 써야 한다.

CHAPTER 03 조동사

UNIT 01 can, may, will

CHECK UP p.36

1. ⓐ **2.** ⓒ

PRACTICE p.37

STEP 1	**1.** can't **2.** play **3.** Would **4.** will
STEP 2	**1.** can **2.** May[Can] **3.** could
STEP 3	**1.** rain **2.** be able to **3.** to drive **4.** save
STEP 4	**1.** may[can] have **2.** won't be late **3.** may be **4.** will finish **5.** is able to run

UNIT 02 must, should

CHECK UP p.38

1. ⓐ **2.** ⓒ **3.** ⓐ **4.** ⓑ

PRACTICE p.39

STEP 1	**1.** turn **2.** must **3.** don't have to

	4. cannot **5.** must not
STEP 2	**1.** follow **2.** not change **3.** had to come **4.** don't have to worry
STEP 3	**1.** should **2.** can't **3.** must
STEP 4	**1.** should not sleep **2.** must be **3.** must not smoke **4.** will have to take

UNIT 03 would like to, had better, used to

CHECK UP p.40

1. ⓒ **2.** ⓑ **3.** ⓒ **4.** ⓐ

PRACTICE p.41

STEP 1	**1.** to have **2.** had better **3.** used to **4.** had better not
STEP 2	**1.** had better **2.** would like to **3.** would
STEP 3	**1.** had better not **2.** would like to **3.** used to
STEP 4	**1.** used to have **2.** would like to see **3.** had better look for **4.** used to be a hospital **5.** Would you like to go

GRAMMAR FOR WRITING pp.42-43

A **1.** can't[isn't able to] speak **2.** may snow **3.** would like to invite **4.** would[used to] visit **5.** must be angry **6.** had better not study **7.** had to go

B **1.** will be able to meet him **2.** didn't use to eat dessert **3.** Can you turn on the heater **4.** You don't have to take his advice **5.** You should not lie to me **6.** He may not meet you

C **1.** will start **2.** had better not drink **3.** used to play **4.** would like to have **5.** can't be

D **1.** must not smoke **2.** have to speak quietly **3.** may eat or drink

REVIEW TEST pp.44-47

1. ④ **2.** ④ **3.** ② **4.** ③ **5.** ② **6.** ① **7.** ④ **8.** ③ **9.** ④ **10.** ② **11.** ① **12.** ⓐ may ⓑ must **13.** ④ **14.** had **15.** to **16.** ④ **17.** ④ **18.** used to be **19.** may not want **20.** ③ **21.** may use **22.** can't[cannot] play **23.** He doesn't have to go to work **24.** I would like to buy a new smartphone **25.** Would you lend me this book **26.** ①, ③ **27.** ④ **28.** ③ **29.** X, not talk **30.** X, be **31.** O **32.** uses to → used to, would like live → would like to live **33.** helped → help, had to → have to

1 have to + 동사원형: ~해야 한다(의무)

2 used to + 동사원형: ~하곤 했다(과거의 습관)

3 should + 동사원형: ~해야 한다

4 보기와 ③은 '~해도 된다(허가)'의 의미이고, ①, ②, ④, ⑤는 '~일지도 모른다(불확실한 추측)'의 의미이다.

5 ② 미래의 가능은 will be able to를 쓴다. (will can → will be able to)

6 ① had better + 동사원형: ~하는 것이 낫다(충고, 경고) (has better → had better)

7 don't have to: ~할 필요가 없다(= don't need to, need not)

8 must + 동사원형: ~해야 한다(= have to)

9 ④ must + 동사원형: ~임에 틀림없다(강한 추측) (has to → must)

10 ② would like to + 동사원형: ~하고 싶다 (have → to have)

11 Can[Could, Will, Would] you ~?: ~해 주시겠습니까?

12 ⓐ may + 동사원형: ~해도 된다(허가)
ⓑ must + 동사원형: ~해야 한다(의무)

13 must + 동사원형: ~임에 틀림없다(강한 추측) / may + 동사원형: ~일지도 모른다(불확실한 추측)

14 had better + 동사원형: ~하는 것이 낫다(충고, 경고) / had to + 동사원형: ~해야 했다(과거 의무)

15 would like to + 동사원형: ~하고 싶다 / used to + 동사원형: ~이었다(과거의 상태)

16 ①, ②, ③, ⑤는 '~할 수 없다'의 의미이고, ④는 '~일 리가 없다'의 의미이다.

17 ①, ②, ③, ⑤는 '~해야 한다(의무)'의 의미이고, ④는 '~임에 틀림없다(강한 추측)'의 의미이다.

18 used to + 동사원형: ~이었다(과거의 상태)

19 may not + 동사원형: ~않을지도 모른다(불확실한 추측)

20 had better not + 동사원형: ~하지 않는 것이 낫다(충고, 경고)

21 can: ~해도 좋다(= may)

22 be not able to + 동사원형: ~할 수 없다(= can't)

23 don't have to + 동사원형: ~할 필요가 없다

24 would like to + 동사원형: ~하고 싶다

25 Would you + 동사원형: ~해 주시겠습니까?

26 ② will can → will be able to ④ to meet → meet
⑤ would → used to

27 a. wearing → wear d. being → be

28 • able to not → not able to
• go → to go

29 should의 부정문은 should not으로 쓴다.

30 used to + 동사원형: ~이었다(과거의 상태)

31 had better + 동사원형: ~하는 것이 낫다(충고, 경고)

32 used to + 동사원형: ~하곤 했다(과거의 습관) / would like to + 동사원형: ~하고 싶다

33 should + 동사원형: ~해야 한다 / have to + 동사원형: ~해야 한다

CHAPTER 04 to부정사

UNIT 01 명사적 용법의 to부정사

CHECK UP p.50

1. ⓐ **2.** ⓒ **3.** ⓒ

PRACTICE p.51

STEP 1 **1.** It, to watch American dramas **2.** It, to travel around the world **3.** It, to run 100 m in seven seconds

STEP 2 **1.** what to say **2.** where to stay **3.** who(m) to see

STEP 3 **1.** to teach students **2.** to draw pictures **3.** to memorize thirty English words a day **4.** to buy a watch

STEP 4 **1.** wanted to have **2.** how to use **3.** It, to eat

UNIT 02 형용사적 용법의 to부정사

CHECK UP p.52

1. ⓒ **2.** ⓒ **3.** ⓑ

PRACTICE p.53

STEP 1 **1.** to eat **2.** to finish **3.** to love

STEP 2 **1.** with **2.** to **3.** in

STEP 3 **1.** is to visit **2.** are to return **3.** was to see **4.** are to stay

STEP 4 **1.** am to be home **2.** nothing cold to drink **3.** many traffic rules to follow

UNIT 03 부사적 용법의 to부정사

CHECK UP p.54

1. ⓒ **2.** ⓑ **3.** ⓒ

PRACTICE p.55

STEP 1 **1.** to understand **2.** to know **3.** to learn **4.** to work

STEP 2 **1.** not to be late for class **2.** to be a famous poet **3.** to see you in New York **4.** to take a walk

STEP 3 **1.** 나는 건강해지기 위해서 다이어트를 할 것이다. **2.** 그 노인은 100세까지 살았다. **3.** 나는 새 겨울 외투를 사기 위해 상점에 갔다. **4.** 같은 실수를 하다니 그녀는 어리석은 것이 틀림없다. **5.** 그가 노래하는 것을 듣는다면 너는 그를 가수로 생각할 것이다.

STEP 4 **1.** to hear about her death **2.** is easy to learn **3.** to be a great writer **4.** to look for my cat

UNIT 04 to부정사의 의미상의 주어, too ~ to-v, enough to-v

CHECK UP p.56

1. ⓑ **2.** ⓒ **3.** ⓑ **4.** ⓒ

PRACTICE p.57

STEP 1 **1.** of you **2.** small enough **3.** too sour **4.** for her

STEP 2 **1.** for **2.** of **3.** for **4.** of

STEP 3 **1.** rich enough to buy the island **2.** too small for me to put all my books **3.** so easy that she can read

4. so big that he can't pass through this hole

STEP 4 **1.** too lazy to finish **2.** silly of you to tell **3.** exciting for me to cook **4.** old enough to understand

GRAMMAR FOR WRITING pp.58-59

A **1.** wants to be a singer **2.** wore sunglasses to[in order to, so as to] protect **3.** It, to meet new people **4.** is easy to use **5.** grew up to be a supermodel **6.** to believe Jake's words **7.** too busy to have lunch / so busy that she couldn't have lunch

B **1.** old enough to make a decision **2.** Give me something hot to drink **3.** I don't know when to call him **4.** are looking for a bench to sit on **5.** It is very hard for her to eat less **6.** I am to arrive at the station

C **1.** to learn English **2.** enough to buy **3.** to collect pictures **4.** to fail the exam **5.** not to remember **6.** cold to drink

D **1.** surprised to meet **2.** how to get to **3.** too short to ride

REVIEW TEST pp.60-63

1. ④ **2.** ⑤ **3.** ③ **4.** ③ **5.** ⑤ **6.** ④ **7.** ② **8.** ③ **9.** ①, ③ **10.** ③ **11.** ④ **12.** to hear **13.** to visit / I should visit **14.** too complicated for him to do **15.** large enough to hold **16.** what to do **17.** ④ **18.** ② **19.** ⑤ **20.** only to miss the train **21.** To hear him play the piano **22.** ③ **23.** big enough to fit all of these clothes **24.** any paper to write on **25.** ② **26.** ①, ③, ⑤ **27.** ② **28.** ③ **29.** O **30.** X, of you **31.** The song is difficult to sing **32.** finishing → finish **33.** buying → to buy, write → to write

1 It은 가주어, to learn 이하가 진주어이다.

2 talk는 자동사이므로 목적어를 취하려면 전치사(to)가 필요하다.

3 too ~ to-v: 너무 ~하여 …할 수 없다

4 결과를 나타내는 부사적 용법의 to부정사

5 사람의 성향이나 성질을 나타내는 형용사(rude) 뒤에서 to부정사의 의미상의 주어는 「of + 목적격」으로 나타낸다.

6 ①, ②, ③, ⑤는 형용사적 용법의 to부정사, ④는 목적을 나타내는 부사적 용법의 to부정사이다.

7 ② live는 자동사이므로 목적어를 취하려면 전치사(in)가 필요하다. (to live → to live in)

8 ③ -thing 등으로 끝나는 대명사 뒤에 수식하는 형용사가 있을 때, to부정사는 형용사 뒤에서 수식한다. (to wear nice → nice to wear)

9 사람의 성향이나 성질을 나타내는 형용사(kind, polite) 뒤에서 to부정사의 의미상의 주어는 「of + 목적격」으로 나타낸다.

10 보어로 쓰인 명사적 용법의 to부정사

11 ① too difficult ② to hear ③ of you ⑤ to tell

12 감정의 원인을 나타내는 부사적 용법의 to부정사

13 when to-v: 언제 ~할지(= when + 주어 + should + 동사원형)

14 too + 형용사 + to-v: 너무 ~하여 …할 수 없다

15 형용사 + enough to-v: ~할 만큼 충분히 …하다

16 what to-v: 무엇을 ~할지

17 ① reading → to read ② to found → to find ③ to visiting → to visit ⑤ live → to live

18 보기와 ②는 목적을 나타내는 부사적 용법의 to부정사이고, ①, ④, ⑤는 명사적 용법, ③은 형용사적 용법의 to부정사이다.

19 ①, ②, ③, ④는 for가 오고, ⑤는 of가 와야 한다.

20 결과를 나타내는 부사적 용법의 to부정사

21 조건을 나타내는 부사적 용법의 to부정사

22 ③ too + 형용사 + to-v: 너무 ~하여 …할 수 없다(= so + 형용사 + that + 주어 + can't + 동사원형) (can → can't)

23 형용사 + enough to-v: ~할 만큼 충분히 …하다

24 형용사적 용법의 to부정사

25 의미상의 주어 「for + 목적격」은 to부정사 앞에 쓴다. (It is important for teenagers to make friends.)

26 ② losing → to lose
④ of children → for children

27 b. so weak → too weak d. for you → of you

28 • enough hard → hard enough
• for you → of you

29 보어로 쓰인 명사적 용법의 to부정사

30 사람의 성향이나 성질을 나타내는 형용사(kind) 뒤에서 to부정사의 의미상의 주어는 「of + 목적격」으로 나타낸다.

31 형용사를 수식하는 부사적 용법의 to부정사

32 주어를 설명하는 「be to-v」 용법(의무)

33 형용사적 용법의 to부정사 / 명사적 용법의 to부정사(목적어)

CHAPTER
05 동명사

UNIT 01 동명사의 쓰임

CHECK UP p.66

1. ⓑ 2. ⓑ 3. ⓒ

PRACTICE p.67

STEP 1 1. drawing 2. trying 3. Meeting 4. watching
STEP 2 1. eating 2. riding 3. designing[to design] 4. Taking[To take]
STEP 3 1. going camping with his family 2. Eating too much fast food 3. not keeping her promise
STEP 4 1. is busy cooking 2. good at speaking 3. smiling at me 4. feel like watching

UNIT 02 동명사와 to부정사

CHECK UP p.68

1. ⓑ 2. ⓒ 3. ⓒ

PRACTICE p.69

STEP 1 1. to get 2. waiting 3. to buy 4. to send
STEP 2 1. to exercise 2. reading 3. playing 4. lying
STEP 3 1. to study 2. dancing 3. to have
STEP 4 1. Avoid eating 2. likes watching 3. decided to learn 4. tried using 5. forgot borrowing money

GRAMMAR FOR WRITING pp.70-71

A 1. decided to sell their house 2. forgot to take 3. hates getting[to get] up 4. remember meeting him 5. couldn't[could not] help looking at 6. making a mistake 7. Laughing[To laugh] a lot is good

B 1. has finished fixing the car 2. try using a different password 3. doesn't mind donating lots of money 4. Staying up every night is 5. brush my teeth before going to bed 6. His new album is worth buying

C 1. teaching Japanese 2. Being honest 3. to send 4. buying the milk 5. eating fast food 6. is busy solving

D 1. completing the marathon 2. busy preparing dinner 3. to go to the concert

REVIEW TEST pp.72-75

1. ④ 2. ⑤ 3. ④ 4. ④ 5. ④ 6. ② 7. ⑤ 8. ② 9. ⑤ 10. to fail → failing 11. bringing → to bring 12. ② 13. ② 14. using 15. to set 16. to change 17. shopping 18. ⑤ 19. Finding a good job is not easy 20. about not going camping 21. He loves taking a walk with his dogs 22. is busy doing his math homework 23. He practices speaking 24. forgets to take her cell phone 25. meeting 26. ③, ⑤ 27. ⑤ 28. ④ 29. X, to travel 30. O 31. X, going to 32. to learn → learning 33. to buy → buying

1 quit은 동명사만 목적어로 취하는 동사이다.
2 decide는 to부정사만 목적어로 취하는 동사이다.
3 remember v-ing: (과거에) ~했던 것을 기억하다
4 cannot help v-ing: ~하지 않을 수 없다
5 ④ 전치사의 목적어로는 동명사가 와야 한다. (cook → cooking)
6 ② forget to-v: (앞으로) ~할 것을 잊다 (calling → to call)
7 mind는 동명사만 목적어로 취하는 동사이다.
8 promise는 to부정사만 목적어로 취하는 동사이다.
9 try to-v: ~하려고 노력하다[애쓰다]
10 전치사의 목적어로는 동명사가 와야 한다.
11 remember to-v: (앞으로) ~할 것을 기억하다
12 ① to missing → missing[to miss]
③ play → playing ④ sell → selling[to sell]
⑤ Read → Reading[To read]
13 ① seeing → to see ③ giving → to give
④ to practice → practicing
⑤ to watch → watching

14 try v-ing: 시험 삼아 ~하다[해 보다]
15 forget to-v: (앞으로) ~할 것을 잊다
16 agree는 to부정사만 목적어로 취하는 동사이다.
17 go v-ing: ~하러 가다
18 ① to buy ② thinking ③ to join ④ attending
19 동명사가 문장의 주어 역할을 한다.
20 동명사의 부정은 동명사 앞에 not을 붙인다.
21 동명사가 목적어 역할을 한다.
22 be busy v-ing: ~하느라 바쁘다
23 practice는 동명사만 목적어로 취하는 동사이다.
24 forget to-v: (앞으로) ~할 것을 잊다
25 remember v-ing: (과거에) ~했던 것을 기억하다
26 ③ Tell → Telling[To tell] ⑤ meeting → to meet
27 a. go → going d. to prepare → preparing
28 • to read → reading
29 wish는 to부정사만 목적어로 취하는 동사이다.
30 on v-ing: ~하자마자
31 feel like v-ing: ~하고 싶다
32 enjoy는 동명사만 목적어로 취하는 동사이다.
33 be worth v-ing: ~할 가치가 있다

CHAPTER 06 분사

UNIT 01 현재분사와 과거분사

CHECK UP p.78

1. ⓑ 2. ⓒ 3. ⓑ

PRACTICE p.79

STEP 1 1. shocked 2. sitting 3. left 4. smiling 5. checked

STEP 2 1. that crying girl 2. watching 3. looked surprised 4. picture painted

STEP 3 1. lost 2. sleeping 3. made 4. talking 5. wearing

STEP 4 1. the boring movie 2. an email written 3. looked excited 4. found my dog sleeping

UNIT 02 분사구문

CHECK UP p.80

1. ⓐ 2. ⓒ 3. ⓑ

PRACTICE p.81

STEP 1 1. Reading 2. talking 3. Being 4. Listening

STEP 2 1. Cleaning my room, I found some money. 2. Coming after 8:00 p.m., you can get a discount. 3. Being ill, she won't go to work today.

STEP 3 1. Because[As, Since] he stood[was standing] so long in the rain 2. If you go straight 3. Although he had an exam the next day

STEP 4 1. Finishing our homework 2. Listening to music 3. Turning right

GRAMMAR FOR WRITING pp.82-83

A 1. was really boring 2. broken glass 3. interesting stories 4. He looked worried 5. everything written 6. standing in front of the door 7. kept her car parked

B 1. Seeing me, the baby began
2. The police saw the thief hiding
3. Hating meat, he didn't order
4. Leaving now, you will catch
5. Do you know a man named Greg Smith
6. Walking down the street, I met

C 1. a. tiring b. tired
2. a. boring b. bored
3. a. shocking b. shocked
4. a. excited b. exciting

D 1. a picture taken
2. Talking on the phone
3. building the sandcastle
4. wearing sunglasses

REVIEW TEST pp.84-87

1. ④ 2. ④ 3. ③ 4. ② 5. ① 6. ③ 7. ② 8. ③ 9. ④ 10. ① 11. Being sick 12. Exercising regularly 13. ④ 14. ② 15. ④ 16. Sitting 17. shocking 18. locked 19. ④ 20. the car damaged 21. was disappointing 22. Those girls building 23. Studying in Korea 24. I heard him playing the guitar 25. Smiling brightly, he waved 26. ②, ③, ⑤ 27. ④ 28. ④ 29. O 30. X, speaking 31. X, drawn 32. building → built 33. ridden → riding, injuring → injured

1 '떠오르는'의 의미로 현재분사가 와야 한다.
2 '초대된'의 의미로 과거분사가 와야 한다.
3 '이야기를 하면서'의 의미로 현재분사가 와야 한다.
4 시간이나 때를 나타내는 분사구문(= As I walked ...)
5 ② Hear → Hearing ③ interesting → interested ④ writing → written ⑤ bored → boring
6 감정을 느끼게 할 때는 현재분사, 감정을 느낄 때는 과거분사를 쓴다.
7 이유를 나타내는 분사구문
8 조건을 나타내는 분사구문
9 ④ 감정을 느낄 때는 과거분사를 쓴다. (boring → bored)
10 ① '불리는'의 의미로 과거분사가 와야 한다. (calling → called)
11 부사절의 주어가 주절의 주어와 같을 때, 부사절의 접속사와 주어를 생략하고 동사를 「v-ing」 형태로 바꾼다.
12 부사절의 주어가 주절의 주어와 같을 때, 부사절의 접속사와 주어를 생략하고 동사를 「v-ing」 형태로 바꾼다.
13 ①, ②, ③, ⑤는 현재분사, ④는 동명사이다.
14 ①, ③, ④, ⑤는 현재분사, ②는 동명사이다.
15 ①, ②, ③, ⑤는 분사, ④는 동명사이다.
16 이유를 나타내는 분사구문(= As I sat ...)
17 감정을 느끼게 할 때는 현재분사를 쓴다.
18 '잠긴'의 의미로 과거분사가 와야 한다.
19 ④ used car: 중고차 (use → used)
20 '손상된'의 의미로 과거분사가 와야 한다.
21 '실망하게 하는'의 의미로 현재분사가 와야 한다.
22 '만들고 있는'의 의미로 현재분사가 와야 한다.
23 시간이나 때를 나타내는 분사구문
24 목적격 보어 역할을 하는 현재분사구
25 동시동작을 나타내는 분사구문(= As he smiled brightly, ...)
26 ① writing → written ④ breaking → broken
27 a. interesting → interested c. Taken → Taking
28 • stood → standing
29 감정을 느낄 때는 과거분사를 쓴다.
30 '말하는'의 의미로 현재분사가 와야 한다.
31 '그려진'의 의미로 과거분사가 와야 한다.
32 '지어진'의 의미로 과거분사가 와야 한다.
33 '타고 있던'의 의미로 현재분사가 와야 한다.
'부상당한'의 의미로 과거분사가 와야 한다.

CHAPTER 07 수동태

UNIT 01 능동태와 수동태

CHECK UP p.90

1. ⓒ 2. ⓑ 3. ⓑ

PRACTICE p.91

STEP 1 1. made 2. is used 3. is being made 4. will be released

STEP 2 1. This website is visited by many people. 2. The bird was watched by the scientists. 3. Kate will be chosen as the best actress (by them). 4. The chocolate cookies are being baked by John now.

STEP 3 1. was solved 2. is being held 3. will be painted 4. is shared

STEP 4 1. was drawn by 2. will be built 3. is being recorded 4. is elected by

UNIT 02 수동태의 여러 가지 형태

CHECK UP p.92

1. ⓑ 2. ⓑ 3. ⓒ

PRACTICE p.93

STEP 1 1. Was 2. to 3. playing 4. must be followed

STEP 2 1. was not invited 2. must be kept 3. to wash 4. for me

STEP 3 1. was made to wake up early by my mom 2. are taught English by Mr. Smith 3. was advised to eat more

	vegetables by my doctor **4.** can be removed easily (by you)
STEP 4	**1.** Were these pictures taken **2.** was made for me **3.** was heard talking **4.** was called Princess by

UNIT 03 주의해야 할 수동태

CHECK UP p.94

1. ⓒ **2.** ⓑ

PRACTICE p.95

STEP 1	**1.** was taken care of **2.** disappeared **3.** is covered with **4.** resembles
STEP 2	**1.** was put off by my boss **2.** is looked up to by Sophia **3.** are satisfied with life
STEP 3	**1.** in **2.** of **3.** with **4.** to
STEP 4	**1.** was laughed at by **2.** was surprised at **3.** was filled with **4.** were run over by

GRAMMAR FOR WRITING pp.96-97

A **1.** was written by **2.** is being built **3.** will be put off **4.** was made to guide **5.** was bought for me **6.** was sent to me **7.** disappeared

B **1.** should be kept secret **2.** Was the computer broken by you **3.** was seen standing at the bus stop **4.** was not baked by me **5.** He is called an angel by his friends **6.** Mowgli was brought up by wolves

C **1.** am satisfied with **2.** is being repaired **3.** can be made by anyone **4.** was told to get **5.** should be covered with

D **1.** are pleased with **2.** is disappointed with[at] **3.** is surprised at **4.** is taken care of by

REVIEW TEST pp.98-101

1. ⑤ **2.** ① **3.** ⑤ **4.** ④ **5.** ④ **6.** ⑤ **7.** ④ **8.** ② **9.** ④ **10.** ⑤ **11.** was read **12.** to keep **13.** be held **14.** ⑤ **15.** ② **16.** was filmed by my favorite director **17.** was made a superstar by that sitcom **18.** is looked up to by many workers **19.** ③ **20.** is liked by **21.** was told to us **22.** was laughed at by **23.** will be caught by the police **24.** Important issues are being talked about **25.** My little brother was heard crying **26.** ②, ③ **27.** ② **28.** ④ **29.** Was the child rescued by the hero **30.** O **31.** X, brought up by her uncle **32.** by → with **33.** been → being, many → by many

1 드레스가 디자인된 것이므로 수동태가 되어야 한다.

2 4형식 문장의 수동태에서 직접목적어를 주어로 수동태를 만들 때 동사 send는 간접목적어 앞에 전치사 to를 쓴다.

3 수동태의 미래시제: will be + v-ed

4 사역동사의 수동태에서 make 다음에 목적격 보어로 쓰인 동사원형은 to부정사로 바뀐다.

5 be surprised at: ~에 놀라다

6 ① was disappeared → disappeared
② 소유를 나타내는 타동사(have)는 수동태로 쓰이지 않는다.
③ built → was built
④ 상태를 나타내는 타동사(resemble)는 수동태로 쓰이지 않는다.

7 ④ 수동태의 미래시제: will be + v-ed (will being finished → will be finished)

8 ② 지각동사 다음에 목적격 보어로 쓰인 동사원형은 수동태 문장에서 현재분사나 to부정사로 바뀐다. (read → reading[to read])

9 4형식 문장의 수동태에서 직접목적어를 주어로 수동태를 만들 때 동사 make는 간접목적어 앞에 전치사 for를 쓴다.

10 동사구의 수동태에서 동사구는 수동태로 바꿀 때 하나의 동사로 취급한다.

11 잡지는 읽히는 것이므로 수동태가 되어야 하며 과거를 나타내는 표현(in the past)이 있으므로 과거시제 수동태를 쓴다.

12 사역동사의 수동태에서 make 다음에 목적격 보어로 쓰인 동사원형은 to부정사로 바뀐다.

13 수동태의 미래시제: will be + v-ed

14 be satisfied with: ~에 만족하다
be filled with: ~로 가득 차다

15 4형식 문장의 수동태에서 직접목적어를 주어로 수동태를 만들 때 동사 give는 간접목적어 앞에 전치사 to를 쓴다.
be known to: ~에게 알려지다

16 수동태의 과거시제: be동사의 과거형 + v-ed

17 5형식 문장에서 목적어가 수동태의 주어가 되고, 목적격 보어가 명사인 경우 그대로 쓴다.

18 동사구의 수동태에서 동사구는 수동태로 바꿀 때 하나의 동사로 취급한다.
19 be disappointed with[at]: ~에 실망하다
20 수동태: be + v-ed
21 4형식 문장의 수동태에서 직접목적어를 주어로 수동태를 만들 때 동사 tell은 간접목적어 앞에 전치사 to를 쓴다.
22 동사구의 수동태에서 동사구는 수동태로 바꿀 때 하나의 동사로 취급한다.
23 조동사의 수동태: 조동사 + be + v-ed
24 수동태의 진행형: be동사 + being + v-ed
25 지각동사의 수동태에서 지각동사 다음에 목적격 보어로 쓰인 동사원형은 현재분사나 to부정사로 바뀐다.
26 ① wrote → written ④ practice → to practice
⑤ for me → to me
27 c. by → of[from] e. for → with
28 • was happened → happened
29 수동태의 의문문: be동사 + 주어 + v-ed?
30 수동태: be + v-ed
31 동사구의 수동태에서 동사구는 수동태로 바꿀 때 하나의 동사로 취급한다.
32 be filled with: ~로 가득 차다
33 수동태의 진행형: be동사 + being + v-ed
수동태에서는 행위자 앞에 by를 붙인다.

CHAPTER 08 대명사

UNIT 01 부정대명사 I

CHECK UP p.104

1. ⓐ **2.** ⓑ

PRACTICE p.105

STEP 1	**1.** one **2.** any **3.** all **4.** Each **5.** ones
STEP 2	**1.** some **2.** any **3.** some **4.** any
STEP 3	**1.** one **2.** Both **3.** every **4.** All **5.** it
STEP 4	**1.** get one **2.** some fresh strawberries **3.** Both of us like **4.** Each was

UNIT 02 부정대명사 II

CHECK UP p.106

1. ⓐ **2.** ⓑ **3.** ⓒ **4.** ⓒ

PRACTICE p.107

STEP 1	**1.** another **2.** each other **3.** One, the other **4.** Some, others
STEP 2	**1.** others **2.** each other / one another **3.** another[another one] **4.** the other
STEP 3	**1.** the others **2.** one another **3.** others **4.** another, the other
STEP 4	**1.** each other / one another **2.** another **3.** Some, others **4.** One, the other

UNIT 03 재귀대명사

CHECK UP p.108

1. ⓒ **2.** ⓒ **3.** ⓐ

PRACTICE p.109

STEP 1	**1.** myself **2.** himself **3.** themselves **4.** by myself
STEP 2	**1.** X **2.** O **3.** O **4.** X
STEP 3	**1.** beside **2.** by **3.** between
STEP 4	**1.** in itself **2.** do your homework yourself **3.** help yourself to **4.** excused himself

GRAMMAR FOR WRITING pp.110-111

A **1.** Both of us attend / We both attend **2.** Each person has **3.** need some coins **4.** hurt himself **5.** another one **6.** One is a desktop, the other

B **1.** I like English itself **2.** Every person wants to live **3.** made a snack for themselves **4.** All her money was stolen **5.** have known each other for ten years **6.** Some foreigners like kimchi, but others don't

C 1. one 2. it 3. any 4. ourselves 5. both 6. the other

D 1. burned herself 2. each other / one another 3. another is, the other is

REVIEW TEST

pp.112-115

1. ① 2. ② 3. ⑤ 4. ⑤ 5. ① 6. ⑤ 7. ① 8. ⑤ 9. ④ 10. by herself 11. yourself 12. Some, the others 13. ones 14. ⑤ 15. ② 16. another 17. some 18. ④ 19. cut yourself 20. Every student 21. both practice 22. ② 23. All of us were very tired 24. we enjoyed ourselves very much 25. help yourself to the dessert 26. ①, ③, ④ 27. ② 28. ③ 29. O 30. X, others 31. O 32. another → the other 33. are → is, make you at home → make yourself at home

1 앞에서 언급된 것과 동일한 것을 가리킬 때 it을 쓴다.
2 앞에 언급된 것과 같은 종류의 불특정한 사람이나 사물을 가리킬 때 one을 쓴다.
3 each는 '각각(의)'의 의미로 단수 취급한다.
4 one another는 '서로'의 의미로 보통 셋 이상일 때 쓴다.
5 '약간(의)'의 뜻으로 의문문에는 주로 any를 쓴다.
6 ⑤ 뒤의 명사가 복수이므로 all을 쓴다. (Every → All)
7 ① '자신'의 의미이므로 재귀대명사를 쓴다. (introduce me → introduce myself)
8 ⑤ one ~ the other ...: (둘 중의) 하나는 ~, 나머지 하나는 ... (other → the other)
9 another: 또 다른(= one more)
10 by oneself: 홀로, 혼자서(= alone)
11 burn oneself: 데다, 화상을 입다
12 some ~ the others ...: 어떤 것[사람]들은 ~, 나머지 모든 것[사람]들은 ...
13 앞에 언급된 것과 같은 종류의 불특정한 사물을 가리키고 복수형이 와야 하므로 ones를 쓴다.
14 긍정문이나 권유문에서는 '약간(의)'의 의미로 주로 some을 쓴다.
15 every는 단수 취급 / 「all of + 명사」는 뒤에 오는 명사의 수에 일치
16 another: 또 하나 다른 것 / one ~, another ..., the other ...: (셋 중의) 하나는 ~, 다른 하나는 ..., 나머지 하나는 ...
17 권유문에서는 주로 some을 쓴다. / some ~ others ...: 어떤 것[사람]들은 ~, 다른 어떤 것[사람]들은 ...
18 some ~ others ...: 어떤 것[사람]들은 ~, 다른 어떤 것[사람]들은 ...
19 cut oneself: 베이다
20 every: 모든(단수 취급)
21 both: 둘 다(복수 취급)
22 ②는 강조용법(생략 가능)이고 ①, ③, ④, ⑤는 재귀용법이다.
23 all: 모두, 모든 것
24 enjoy oneself: 즐거운 시간을 보내다
25 help oneself to: ~을 마음껏 먹다
26 ② some → any ⑤ any → some
27 c. each another → each other / one another
d. have → has
28 · Each of us have → Each of us has
· Both of my parents was → Both of my parents were
29 앞에 언급된 것과 같은 종류의 불특정한 사람이나 사물을 가리킬 때 one을 쓴다.
30 some ~ others ...: 어떤 것[사람]들은 ~, 다른 어떤 것[사람]들은 ...
31 by oneself: 홀로, 혼자서(= alone)
32 one ~ the other ...: (둘 중의) 하나는 ~, 다른 하나는 ...
33 every: 모든(단수 취급)
make oneself at home: 편히 쉬다[지내다]

CHAPTER 09 비교

UNIT 01 원급, 비교급, 최상급

CHECK UP

p.118

1. ⓐ 2. ⓑ 3. ⓒ

PRACTICE

p.119

STEP 1 1. longest 2. far 3. high 4. more exciting
STEP 2 1. more 2. largest 3. cold 4. earlier
STEP 3 1. cheaper than 2. the tallest 3. as fast as
STEP 4 1. much stronger than 2. as well as 3. more difficult than 4. the most famous actress

UNIT 02 비교 구문을 이용한 표현

CHECK UP p.120

1. ⓒ **2.** ⓒ **3.** ⓑ **4.** ⓐ **5.** ⓒ

PRACTICE p.121

STEP 1 **1.** ten times **2.** inventions **3.** the angrier **4.** more

STEP 2 **1.** bigger and bigger **2.** more difficult **3.** four times **4.** the busiest cities

STEP 3 **1.** longer and longer **2.** The more slowly, the more **3.** the most beautiful

STEP 4 **1.** quieter and quieter **2.** The earlier, the sooner **3.** Who is richer **4.** three times bigger than

GRAMMAR FOR WRITING pp.122-123

A **1.** as cheap as **2.** getting warmer and warmer **3.** the tallest building in **4.** much more money than **5.** one of the happiest days **6.** Which is closer **7.** The longer, the more tired

B **1.** is one of the greatest writers **2.** Who is younger, Paul or Alice **3.** three times bigger than my hometown **4.** became more and more famous **5.** twice as much money as me **6.** The higher I climbed, the colder it became

C **1.** hotter than **2.** as cool as **3.** the hottest **4.** far longer than **5.** the oldest **6.** four times as heavy as / four times heavier than

D **1.** the slowest **2.** four times as fast as **3.** faster than **4.** three times faster than

REVIEW TEST pp.124-127

1. ④ **2.** ③ **3.** ① **4.** ③ **5.** ② **6.** ④ **7.** ② **8.** ④ **9.** ④ **10.** three times as much as / three times more than **11.** as hot **12.** the highest **13.** younger than **14.** ⑤ **15.** ① **16.** cheaper than **17.** The nicer, the better **18.** ② **19.** The higher, the colder **20.** five times as expensive as / five times more expensive than **21.** Which do you like more **22.** ⑤ **23.** is twice as thick as the notebook **24.** His English is getting better and better **25.** Carter is one of the most famous magicians in the world **26.** ③, ⑤ **27.** ② **28.** ② **29.** X, larger and larger **30.** O **31.** X, most crowded cities **32.** as → than **33.** cheapest → the cheapest, fast → faster

1 ④ strong - stronger - strongest
2 비교급 + than: ~보다 더 …한
3 as + 원급 + as: ~만큼 …한
4 the + 비교급 ~, the + 비교급 ...: ~하면 할수록 더 …하다
5 Who ~ 비교급, A or B?: A와 B 중에서 누가 더 ~한가?
6 ④ 비교급 + and + 비교급: 점점 더 ~한 (bright and bright → brighter and brighter)
7 ② 배수사 + as + 원급 + as ~: ~의 몇 배로 …한 (four → four times)
8 (A) one of the + 최상급 + 복수명사: 가장 ~한 것들 중 하나
(B) Who ~ 비교급, A or B?: A와 B 중에서 누가 더 ~한가?
9 ④ Which ~ 비교급, A or B?: A와 B 중에서 어느 것이 더 ~한가?
① of ② heavier ③ rich ⑤ most famous
10 배수사 + as + 원급 + as ~(= 배수사 + 비교급 + than): ~의 몇 배로 …한
11 as + 원급 + as: ~만큼 …한
12 the + 최상급: 가장 ~한
13 비교급 + than: ~보다 더 …한
14 비교급을 강조할 때는 비교급 앞에 much, a lot, even, far 등을 쓴다.
15 ② heavy and heavier → heavier and heavier
③ very → much[a lot, even, far]
④ more people → the more people
⑤ boy → boys
16 비교급 + than: ~보다 더 …한
17 the + 비교급 ~, the + 비교급 ...: ~하면 할수록 더 …하다
18 ② 미나는 하니보다 몸무게가 더 나간다. (lighter → heavier)
19 the + 비교급 ~, the + 비교급 ...: ~하면 할수록 더 …하다
20 배수사 + as + 원급 + as ~(= 배수사 + 비교급 + than): ~의 몇 배로 …한
21 Which ~ 비교급, A or B?: A와 B 중에서 어느 것이 더 ~한가?
22 ⑤ as + 원급 + as: ~만큼 …한 (better → well)
23 배수사 + as + 원급 + as ~: ~의 몇 배로 …한
24 비교급 + and + 비교급: 점점 더 ~한
25 one of the + 최상급 + 복수명사: 가장 ~한 것들 중 하나
26 ① harder → hard

② nearest → the nearest
④ best → better

27 b. taller → tall
e. farthest → farther, hardest → harder

28 · hottest → hot
· more popular → most popular
· artist → artists

29 비교급 + and + 비교급: 점점 더 ~한

30 Which ~ 비교급, A or B?: A와 B 중에서 어느 것이 더 ~한가?

31 one of the + 최상급 + 복수명사: 가장 ~한 것들 중 하나

32 비교급 + than: ~보다 더 …한

33 the + 최상급: 가장 ~한 / 비교급 + than: ~보다 더 …한

CHAPTER 10 접속사

UNIT 01 시간, 이유, 결과의 접속사

CHECK UP p.130

1. ⓑ **2.** ⓐ **3.** ⓒ

PRACTICE p.131

STEP 1 **1.** As **2.** While **3.** so **4.** that **5.** starts

STEP 2 **1.** before **2.** so **3.** Since **4.** while **5.** that

STEP 3 **1.** that **2.** tell **3.** cleaned[was cleaning]

STEP 4 **1.** after I had dinner **2.** until[till] you are ready **3.** Since[Because, As] he worked **4.** When[As] you leave **5.** so cold that

UNIT 02 조건, 양보의 접속사 / 명령문 + and, or ~

CHECK UP p.132

1. ⓐ **2.** ⓒ **3.** ⓐ

PRACTICE p.133

STEP 1 **1.** Though **2.** If **3.** Unless **4.** and

STEP 2 **1.** miss **2.** leave **3.** Follow **4.** study

STEP 3 **1.** Unless **2.** Though[Although] **3.** and **4.** or

STEP 4 **1.** If you see Jenny **2.** Unless you are quiet **3.** Though[Although] I was tired **4.** or you will be

GRAMMAR FOR WRITING pp.134-135

A **1.** before you called **2.** If you change your plans **3.** so I gave a present **4.** so vivid that I could remember **5.** until[till] your class is over **6.** While I was traveling / While I traveled **7.** and I will forgive you

B **1.** Although I took the medicine
2. As I entered the room, everyone
3. Since it was Sunday, the shop was
4. After he finishes lunch, he will wash
5. Unless you bring the receipt, you can't
6. Put on your coat, or you will

C **1.** stayed at home all day **2.** moved to Paris **3.** see this photo **4.** taste better **5.** say sorry to him **6.** was cooking in the kitchen

D **1.** before we watched the movie **2.** that we cried a lot **3.** When we got out of the movie theater **4.** until it stopped raining

REVIEW TEST pp.136-139

1. ④ **2.** ② **3.** ② **4.** ③ **5.** ① **6.** ③ **7.** ③ **8.** ④ **9.** ② **10.** ⑤ **11.** before **12.** and **13.** While **14.** ⑤ **15.** until it stops **16.** If he is not busy / Unless he is busy **17.** ② **18.** ④ **19.** As **20.** while[While] **21.** until[till] my dream comes true **22.** or you'll make a mistake **23.** have dinner together after Jimmy comes back **24.** Since her son was sick, she was worried **25.** so scared that he screamed **26.** ①, ④, ⑤ **27.** ③ **28.** ③ **29.** O **30.** X, comes back **31.** X, so **32.** very → so **33.** If → Unless 또는 move → don't move

1 while: ~하는 동안

2 though: ~에도 불구하고, 비록 ~지만
3 so: 그래서
4 so ~ that ...: 매우[너무] ~해서 …하다
5 명령문, and ~: ~해라, 그러면 …할 것이다
6 ③ after: ~한 후에 / before: ~하기 전에 (after → before)
7 ③ 조건을 나타내는 부사절에서는 현재시제가 미래시제를 대신한다. (will tell → tells)
8 명령문, or ~: ~해라, 그러지 않으면 …할 것이다
if: ~한다면, ~라면
unless: 만약 ~하지 않으면(= if ~ not)
9 ①, ③, ④, ⑤는 '~이기 때문에'의 의미이고, ②는 '~할 때'의 의미이다.
10 ①, ②, ③, ④는 If가 들어가야 하고, ⑤는 Unless가 들어가야 한다.
11 after: ~한 후에 / before: ~하기 전에
12 명령문, and ~: ~해라, 그러면 …할 것이다
13 while: ~인 반면에
14 ⑤ though: ~에도 불구하고, 비록 ~지만
15 시간의 부사절에서는 현재시제가 미래시제를 대신한다.
16 unless: 만약 ~하지 않으면(= if ~ not)
17 ⓐ because ⓑ when ⓒ though ⓓ that
18 ④ 조건을 나타내는 부사절에서 현재시제가 미래시제를 대신한다.
① move ② that ③ and ⑤ Though[Although]
19 as: ~이기 때문에, ~할 때
20 while: ~하는 동안, ~인 반면에
21 until[till]: ~(할 때)까지
22 명령문, or ~: ~해라, 그러지 않으면 …할 것이다
23 after: ~한 후에
24 since: ~이기 때문에
25 so ~ that ...: 매우[너무] ~해서 …하다
26 ② won't → doesn't ③ Unless → If 또는 don't get up → get up
27 c. and → or d. too → so
28 · As → Though[Although]
· Though → Because[As, Since]
29 so ~ that ...: 매우[너무] ~해서 …하다
30 시간의 부사절에서는 현재시제가 미래시제를 대신한다.
31 so: 그래서
32 so ~ that ...: 매우[너무] ~해서 …하다
33 unless: 만약 ~하지 않으면(= if not)

CHAPTER 11 관계사

UNIT 01 관계대명사

CHECK UP p.142

1. ⓐ **2.** ⓒ **3.** ⓒ

PRACTICE p.143

STEP 1 **1.** whose **2.** who **3.** which **4.** whom

STEP 2 **1.** whose **2.** which **3.** who **4.** whom

STEP 3 **1.** Yesterday, I met a girl who is from Mexico. **2.** I want to buy a smartphone whose screen is large. **3.** Mr. Lee is a teacher who(m) a lot of students respect. **4.** The dress which the actress is wearing is very beautiful.

STEP 4 **1.** which is[was] **2.** whose fur is **3.** who lives **4.** who(m) Lily likes

UNIT 02 관계대명사 that, what / 관계대명사의 생략

CHECK UP p.144

1. ⓑ **2.** ⓑ **3.** ⓒ **4.** ⓑ

PRACTICE p.145

STEP 1 **1.** that **2.** playing **3.** what **4.** that **5.** which

STEP 2 **1.** that was **2.** X **3.** X **4.** that **5.** X

STEP 3 **1.** that **2.** What **3.** that **4.** what

STEP 4 **1.** the language spoken in Brazil
2. The subjects I like
3. What she wants for Christmas
4. was the first person that arrived

UNIT 03 관계부사

CHECK UP p.146

1. ⓐ 2. ⓑ 3. ⓑ 4. ⓒ

PRACTICE p.147

STEP 1 1. where 2. how 3. why 4. when
STEP 2 1. where 2. why 3. when 4. how
STEP 3 1. This is the elementary school where I used to go. 2. That is how Harry solved the problem. 3. Liz told me the reason why she left the party early. 4. April 1 is the day when people play jokes.
STEP 4 1. the time when the musical starts
2. the reason why he studied French
3. the shop where you bought your skirt

GRAMMAR FOR WRITING pp.148-149

A 1. old friend who[that] knows
2. whose father is a famous composer
3. the very house (that) I'm looking for
4. (that[which]) he saw yesterday
5. the reason why[for which] he moved
6. how[the way] I made the potato pizza
7. The girl (that[who(m)]) I fell in love with

B 1. You can drink anything that is
2. throw away the shoes I don't wear anymore
3. the day when the second semester begins
4. This is the gym where I exercise
5. The person drinking coffee over there
6. what I like about her

C 1. which has a lot of vitamin C
2. that I didn't agree with
3. that my friend recommended
4. whose job is to design clothes
5. where we can eat Greek food
6. why I was depressed yesterday
7. how I got my job
8. when the car accident happened

D 1. whose tire is flat
2. what she said to me
3. who is walking the dog

REVIEW TEST pp.150-153

1. ① **2.** ④ **3.** ③ **4.** ⑤ **5.** ② **6.** ⑤ **7.** ④ **8.** ③ **9.** ③ **10.** ② **11.** ③ **12.** ③ **13.** ① **14.** I want to meet the author who[that] wrote the *Dark Tower* series. **15.** Today is the day when[on which] my final exams are over. **16.** how **17.** that **18.** when **19.** whose rules are simple **20.** where I want to go **21.** that was **22.** that **23.** the first person that heard the news **24.** gave me what I needed **25.** that I bought my smartphone in **26.** ②, ④, ⑤ **27.** ⑤ **28.** ③ **29.** X, how[the way] **30.** X, where[at which] **31.** X, why[for which] **32.** whose → who(m)[that] 또는 생략 **33.** whom → who[that]

1 사람이 선행사일 때는 주격 관계대명사로 who를 쓴다.
2 동물이 선행사일 때는 주격 관계대명사로 which를 쓴다.
3 소유격 관계대명사 whose를 쓴다.
4 선행사를 포함한 관계대명사 what을 쓴다.
5 장소를 나타내는 선행사 다음에는 관계부사 where를 쓴다.
6 ⑤ 소유격 관계대명사 whose를 써야 한다. (which → whose)
7 ④ 선행사 the way와 관계부사 how는 함께 쓰지 않는다. (the way how → how[the way])
8 ③ which 전치사가 관계대명사 앞에 올 경우 관계대명사 that을 쓸 수 없다.
9 ①, ②, ④, ⑤는 관계대명사이고, ③은 의문사이다.
10 목적격 관계대명사는 생략 가능하다.
11 ① which → where[in which]
② in where → where[in which]
④ for that → why[for which]
⑤ what → that[which]
12 첫 번째 빈칸에는 앞에 전치사가 있으므로 관계대명사 which가, 두 번째 빈칸에는 관계부사 where가 적절하다.
13 목적격 관계대명사가 와야 하고, 선행사가 the last의 수식을 받으므로 관계대명사 that을 쓴다.
14 사람이 선행사일 때는 주격 관계대명사로 who[that]를 쓴다.
15 시간을 나타내는 선행사 다음에는 관계부사 when을 쓴다.
16 방법을 나타내는 관계부사 how를 쓴다.
17 선행사가 사람과 동물인 경우 관계대명사 that을 쓴다.
18 시간을 나타내는 선행사 다음에는 관계부사 when을 쓴다.
19 소유격 관계대명사 whose를 쓴다.
20 장소를 나타내는 선행사 다음에는 관계부사 where를 쓴다.
21 뒤에 분사구가 올 때 「주격 관계대명사 + be동사」는 생략 가능하다.
22 목적격 관계대명사는 생략 가능하다.
23 서수가 선행사인 경우에는 주로 관계대명사 that을 쓴다.
24 선행사를 포함한 관계대명사 what을 쓴다.
25 목적격 관계대명사 that을 쓰고, that 앞에는 전치사가 올 수

없으므로 전치사는 관계대명사절 끝에 쓴다.

26 ① whom → who[that] ③ which → what

27 a. which → who[that] b. what → which[that]

28 • what → which[that] • which → who[that]

29 선행사 the way와 관계부사 how는 함께 쓰지 않는다.

30 장소를 나타내는 선행사 다음에는 관계부사 where를 쓴다.

31 이유를 나타내는 선행사 다음에는 관계부사 why를 쓴다.

32 사람이 선행사일 때는 목적격 관계대명사로 who(m) 또는 that을 쓰거나 생략한다.

33 사람이 선행사일 때는 주격 관계대명사로 who[that]를 쓴다.

CHAPTER 12 가정법

UNIT 01 가정법 과거, 가정법 과거완료

CHECK UP p.156

1. ⓑ **2.** ⓑ **3.** ⓒ **4.** ⓑ

PRACTICE p.157

STEP 1	**1.** were **2.** could have seen **3.** wouldn't be **4.** had gotten
STEP 2	**1.** would not buy **2.** could have gone **3.** spoke **4.** had heard
STEP 3	**1.** weren't[were not], could go **2.** had known, could have called **3.** knew, could invite **4.** hadn't[had not] stolen, wouldn't[would not] have gone
STEP 4	**1.** were, could watch **2.** had enough money, would travel **3.** had not been full, would have eaten

UNIT 02 I wish + 가정법, as if + 가정법

CHECK UP p.158

1. ⓑ **2.** ⓒ **3.** ⓑ **4.** ⓒ

PRACTICE p.159

STEP 1	**1.** liked **2.** hadn't spent **3.** were **4.** had seen
STEP 2	**1.** had gone **2.** didn't[did not] have **3.** were
STEP 3	**1.** hadn't[had not] had a fight with my brother **2.** were in the same class **3.** cleaned her room every day **4.** hadn't[had not] heard the news
STEP 4	**1.** I wish I were good at singing **2.** I wish I had brought an umbrella **3.** he speaks Chinese as if he were

GRAMMAR FOR WRITING pp.160-161

A **1.** were, wouldn't[would not] give up **2.** I wish I could sleep **3.** had arrived, could have met **4.** I had brought my sunglasses **5.** it were a human **6.** had hurried up, could have taken **7.** had taken, wouldn't[would not] have failed

B **1.** I wish I were a grown-up **2.** I would have gone on a picnic **3.** we would have more fun **4.** wish I had not told my secret **5.** behaves as if she were a five-year-old kid **6.** He talked as if he had been to Spain

C **1.** could play **2.** had, could give **3.** had bought **4.** weren't, couldn't go **5.** had happened **6.** had missed, would have been **7.** could drive

D **1.** would[could, might] buy this dress **2.** I had more time **3.** I hadn't[had not] lost my gloves

REVIEW TEST pp.162-165

1. ④ **2.** ⑤ **3.** ② **4.** ④ **5.** ② **6.** ① **7.** ⑤ **8.** ⑤ **9.** ③ **10.** ⑤ **11.** ⑤ **12.** had **13.** were **14.** had called **15.** stopped, would be **16.** had apologized, would have forgiven **17.** hadn't[had not] happened **18.** ② **19.** had, could drive **20.** hadn't[had not] lied **21.** winter vacation were longer **22.** ④ **23.** as if the math test had been easy **24.** I had not bought the expensive coat

25. If she weren't busy, she could go **26.** ①, ③, ④, ⑤ **27.** ③ **28.** ③ **29.** X, knew **30.** X, would call **31.** O **32.** went → had gone **33.** as if I am → as if I were, have worried → worry

1 가정법 과거: If + 주어 + 동사의 과거형, 주어 + would[could, might] + 동사원형
2 가정법 과거완료: If + 주어 + had v-ed, 주어 + would[could, might] + have v-ed
3 I wish + 가정법 과거: I wish + 주어 + 동사의 과거형
4 I wish + 가정법 과거완료: I wish + 주어 + had v-ed
5 as if + 가정법 과거: as if + 주어 + 동사의 과거형
6 ① I wish + 가정법 과거: I wish + 주어 + 동사의 과거형 (has → had)
7 ⑤ 가정법 과거완료: If + 주어 + had v-ed, 주어 + would[could, might] + have v-ed (saw → had seen)
8 가정법 과거완료: If + 주어 + had v-ed, 주어 + would[could, might] + have v-ed
9 가정법 과거: If + 주어 + 동사의 과거형, 주어 + would[could, might] + 동사원형
10 가정법 과거완료: If + 주어 + had v-ed, 주어 + would[could, might] + have v-ed
11 I wish + 가정법 과거완료: I wish + 주어 + had v-ed
12 I wish + 가정법 과거: I wish + 주어 + 동사의 과거형
13 가정법 과거에서 if절의 be동사는 주어의 인칭에 관계없이 were를 쓴다.
14 as if + 가정법 과거완료: as if + 주어 + had v-ed
15 가정법 과거: If + 주어 + 동사의 과거형, 주어 + would[could, might] + 동사원형
16 가정법 과거완료: If + 주어 + had v-ed, 주어 + would[could, might] + have v-ed
17 I wish + 가정법 과거완료: I wish + 주어 + had v-ed
18 ① can → could
③ have worked → had worked
④ have not missed → had not missed
⑤ will have told → would have told
19 가정법 과거: If + 주어 + 동사의 과거형, 주어 + would[could, might] + 동사원형
20 가정법 과거완료: If + 주어 + had v-ed, 주어 + would[could, might] + have v-ed
21 I wish + 가정법 과거: I wish + 주어 + 동사의 과거형
가정법 과거에서 be동사는 주어의 인칭에 관계없이 were를 쓴다.
22 가정법 과거에서 be동사는 주어의 인칭에 관계없이 were를 쓴다.
23 as if + 가정법 과거완료: as if + 주어 + had v-ed
24 I wish + 가정법 과거완료: I wish + 주어 + had v-ed
25 가정법 과거: If + 주어 + 동사의 과거형, 주어 + would[could, might] + 동사원형
26 ② haven't been → hadn't been / weren't
27 c. have bought → buy
d. can introduce → could introduce
28 • drive → had driven
• practiced → had practiced
29 as if + 가정법 과거: as if + 주어 + 동사의 과거형
30 가정법 과거: If + 주어 + 동사의 과거형, 주어 + would[could, might] + 동사원형
31 가정법 과거완료: If + 주어 + had v-ed, 주어 + would[could, might] + have v-ed
32 I wish + 가정법 과거완료: I wish + 주어 + had v-ed
33 as if + 가정법 과거: as if + 주어 + 동사의 과거형
가정법 과거: If + 주어 + 동사의 과거형, 주어 + would[could, might] + 동사원형

CHAPTER 13 일치와 화법

UNIT 01 시제의 일치

CHECK UP p.168

1. ⓐ **2.** ⓑ

PRACTICE p.169

STEP 1	**1.** had been **2.** grow **3.** wins **4.** was
STEP 2	**1.** moves **2.** is **3.** was
STEP 3	**1.** would win **2.** had lost **3.** started **4.** makes
STEP 4	**1.** you did your best **2.** was built **3.** snakes sleep

UNIT 02 화법

CHECK UP p.170

1. ⓒ

PRACTICE p.171

STEP 1 **1.** told **2.** if **3.** she had bought **4.** who had kicked

STEP 2 **1.** said (that) it would snow on Christmas Day **2.** asked me if[whether] I liked musicals **3.** told Tom (that) I had something to tell him **4.** asked me where I was going **5.** said (that) he had gotten an F in history **6.** asked me who had sent the fax **7.** asked me if[whether] I wanted to change the schedule **8.** asked Lisa how she had made the potato pizza

STEP 3 **1.** told, he wanted **2.** asked, if[whether] she could borrow my **3.** asked, why I liked

GRAMMAR FOR WRITING pp.172-173

A **1.** asked me if[whether] I liked **2.** (that) water boils **3.** (that) the Korean War started **4.** she wants to travel **5.** (that) Japan is **6.** (that) my sister wore **7.** asked me why I wanted to become

B **1.** told me that he had already seen
2. asked me if I could speak English
3. said that two heads are better
4. asked me who lived in that big house
5. heard that Picasso was born in Spain
6. told me that she had met my teacher

C **1.** (that) he would go to America to study
2. what he wanted to study in America
3. (that) he planned to study marketing
4. if[whether] she had heard the noise
5. what had happened
6. (that) there had been a car accident

D **1.** if[whether] he could play the drums
2. humans first landed on the moon in 1969
3. (that) she had ridden a bike along the river

REVIEW TEST pp.174-177

1. ② **2.** ② **3.** ③ **4.** ② **5.** ④ **6.** ④ **7.** ① **8.** ② **9.** ② **10.** ④ **11.** ⑤ **12.** ④ **13.** the earth moves around **14.** told me (that) I looked young **15.** asked me what I would do **16.** is **17.** started **18.** freezes **19.** told me (that) he had had a fight with his girlfriend **20.** asked me what had made me think so **21.** Amy asked me if[whether] I wanted some coffee **22.** said that he always goes to school **23.** asked me how I had solved the problem **24.** asked me if I had finished my homework **25.** (that) she would go to the baseball stadium **26.** ①, ⑤ **27.** ③ **28.** ③ **29.** X, is **30.** X, I liked **31.** O **32.** will → would **33.** have → had, told → asked

1 주절의 시제가 과거인 경우 종속절에는 과거 또는 과거완료가 와야 한다.

2 과학적 사실, 일반적 진리는 주절의 시제와 상관없이 항상 현재시제를 쓴다.

3 역사적 사실은 주절의 시제와 상관없이 항상 과거시제를 쓴다.

4 의문사가 없는 의문문의 화법 전환에서 접속사는 if[whether]를 쓴다.

5 주절의 시제가 과거인 경우 종속절에는 과거 또는 과거완료가 와야 한다.

6 ④ 과학적 사실, 일반적 진리는 주절의 시제와 상관없이 항상 현재시제를 쓴다. (was → is)

7 ① 의문사가 없는 의문문의 화법 전환에서 if 다음의 어순을 「주어 + 동사」로 바꾼다. (did I like → I liked)

8 의문사 다음의 어순을 「주어 + 동사」로 바꾸고, 인용 부호 안의 인칭대명사는 전달자에 맞춰서 바꾸고, 동사도 시제에 맞춰 바꾼다.

9 목적어가 없는 경우 전달동사는 say를 쓴다. 인칭대명사를 전달자에 맞춰 바꾸고, 동사도 시제에 맞춰 바꾼다.

10 의문문의 경우 전달동사는 ask이다. 의문사가 없으므로 접속사 if[whether]를 쓰고, 어순을 「주어 + 동사」로 바꾸고 인칭대명사를 전달자에 맞춰 바꾸고, 동사도 시제에 맞춰 바꾼다.

11 의문문의 경우 전달동사는 ask이다. 어순을 「의문사 + 주어 + 동사」로 바꾸고, 인칭대명사를 전달자에 맞춰 바꾸고, 동사도 시제에 맞춰 바꾼다.

12 주절이 과거인 경우 종속절의 시제는 과거 또는 과거완료가 되어야 한다.

13 과학적 사실, 일반적 진리는 주절의 시제와 상관없이 항상 현재시제를 쓴다.

14 목적어가 있는 경우 전달동사는 tell을 쓰고, 주절의 시제에 맞춰 종속절의 시제를 과거로 쓴다.

15 전달동사는 ask를 쓰고, 의문사 다음의 어순을 「주어 + 동사」로 바꾼다. 인용 부호 안의 인칭대명사는 전달자에 맞춰서 바꾸고, 동사도 시제에 맞춰 바꾼다.

16 속담은 주절의 시제와 상관없이 항상 현재시제를 쓴다.

17 역사적 사실은 주절의 시제와 상관없이 항상 과거시제를 쓴다.

18 과학적 사실, 일반적 진리는 주절의 시제와 상관없이 항상 현재시제를 쓴다.

19 목적어가 있는 경우 전달동사는 tell을 쓴다. 인칭대명사를 전달자에 맞춰 바꾸고, 동사도 시제에 맞춰 바꾼다.

20 의문문의 경우 전달동사는 ask를 쓰고, 의문사가 주어인 경우에는 「의문사 + 동사」의 어순을 그대로 쓴다. 인칭대명사를 전달자에 맞춰 바꾸고, 동사도 시제에 맞춰 바꾼다.

21 의문문의 경우 전달동사는 ask이다. 의문사가 없는 의문문일 때 접속사 if[whether]를 쓰고, 어순을 「주어 + 동사」로 쓰고 동사도 시제에 맞춰 쓴다.

22 평서문의 간접화법: say + (that +) 주어 + 동사

23 의문사가 있는 의문문의 간접화법: ask + (목적어 +) 의문사 + 주어 + 동사

24 의문사가 없는 의문문의 간접화법: ask + (목적어 +) if[whether] + 주어 + 동사

25 평서문의 간접화법: tell + 목적어 + (that +) 주어 + 동사

26 ② had he → he had ③ was → is
④ had become → became

27 b. that → if[whether] d. had I → I had

28 • had I done → I had done • had died → died

29 과학적 사실, 일반적 진리는 주절의 시제와 상관없이 항상 현재 시제를 쓴다.

30 의문사가 있는 의문문의 간접화법: ask + (목적어 +) 의문사 + 주어 + 동사

31 의문사가 주어인 경우에는 「의문사 + 동사」의 어순을 그대로 쓴다.

32 주절의 시제가 과거인 경우 종속절의 시제는 과거 또는 과거완료가 되어야 한다.

33 주절의 시제가 과거인 경우 종속절의 시제는 과거 또는 과거완료가 되어야 한다. / 의문사가 없는 의문문의 간접화법: ask + (목적어 +) if[whether] + 주어 + 동사

workbook
Answer Key

GRAMMAR Inside

LEVEL 2

GRAMMAR BASICS

01 문장의 성분 p.2

A **1.** Cats, eat **2.** You, should go **3.** The picture, was painted **4.** His grandparents, took care of **5.** My love for my family, will last **6.** Exercising every day, keeps **7.** You and I, have to finish **8.** My younger sister, laughed at **9.** That he didn't receive my letter, must be **10.** What she borrowed from me, was

B **1.** 수식어 **2.** 동사 **3.** 수식어 **4.** 주어 **5.** 보어 **6.** 목적어 **7.** 보어 **8.** 목적어 **9.** 보어 **10.** 동사

02 품사 p.3

A **1.** about **2.** always **3.** salt **4.** listen **5.** pretty **6.** language **7.** oh **8.** the **9.** with **10.** now

B **1.** 대명사 **2.** 전치사 **3.** 감탄사 **4.** 동사 **5.** 접속사 **6.** 형용사 **7.** 명사 **8.** 부사 **9.** 부사 **10.** 접속사

03 구와 절 p.4

A **1.** 구 **2.** 구 **3.** 절 **4.** 구 **5.** 구 **6.** 절 **7.** 절 **8.** 구 **9.** 절 **10.** 절

B **1.** i **2.** j **3.** c **4.** f **5.** a **6.** e **7.** h **8.** g **9.** b **10.** d

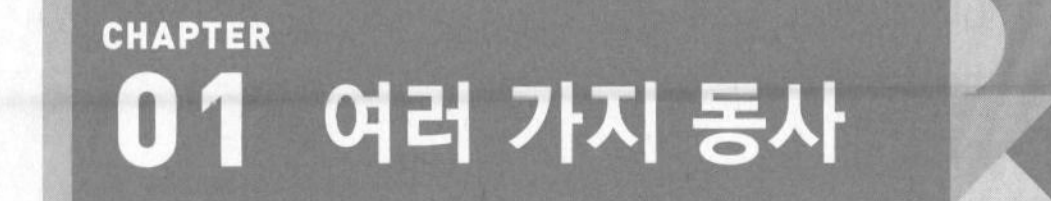

CHAPTER 01 여러 가지 동사

UNIT 01 감각동사와 수여동사 pp.5-6

A **1.** young **2.** sweet **3.** my son a bike **4.** fresh **5.** to me **6.** a doll **7.** for **8.** good **9.** her **10.** to

B **1.** to my brother **2.** for my younger sister **3.** to his daughter **4.** to us **5.** of you **6.** to her **7.** for her mother

C **1.** to you **2.** great **3.** bad **4.** some money **5.** soft **6.** to me **7.** terrible **8.** beautiful **9.** to us **10.** me

D **1.** like **2.** for **3.** to **4.** to **5.** of **6.** for **7.** for **8.** to **9.** to **10.** to

WRITING PRACTICE p.7

A **1.** looks heavy **2.** lent a beautiful necklace to **3.** tastes fantastic **4.** bought me a long dress / bought a long dress for me **5.** smell sweet **6.** gave her his locker key / gave his locker key to her

B **1.** bought her a trendy T-shirt **2.** looked really sleepy **3.** asked them various questions **4.** This potato pizza smells delicious **5.** sent the wrong product to her customer **6.** wrote lots of letters to me

UNIT 02 목적격 보어를 가지는 동사 pp.8-9

A **1.** study **2.** taking **3.** to come **4.** useful **5.** smile **6.** to listen **7.** sing **8.** go **9.** a hero **10.** to enter

B **1.** burn[burning] **2.** Harry **3.** to study **4.** take **5.** fight[fighting] **6.** to go **7.** fresh **8.** to help **9.** move[to move] **10.** to take

C **1.** tell **2.** to come **3.** to get up **4.** to turn down **5.** repair **6.** take[taking] **7.** find[to find] **8.** jump[jumping] **9.** to do **10.** take

D **1.** so happy **2.** playing the violin at the concert **3.** the father of pop music **4.** to come to my birthday party **5.** swim in the pool **6.** to stay out late

WRITING PRACTICE p.10

A **1.** wanted me to tell **2.** saw your dog run[running] **3.** advised me to say sorry **4.** got me to do **5.** found the show boring **6.** calls me a little princess

B **1.** keeps her room clean **2.** had me bring his camera **3.** saw his car stop in front of **4.** asked me to be quiet **5.** made him our president **6.** made me eat more vegetables

REVIEW TEST pp.11-13

1. ① **2.** ③ **3.** ④ **4.** ② **5.** ③ **6.** ② **7.** ⑤ **8.** ④ **9.** ② **10.** ④ **11.** ③ **12.** ③ **13.** play[playing] **14.** make **15.** ① **16.** for her **17.** of me **18.** to him **19.** gives energy to plants **20.** sounds different **21.** I had him make a call **22.** He asked me to return his book **23.** I want you to make dinner **24.** exercise → to exercise, healthily → healthy **25.** pictures for you → pictures to you, picking → to pick

CHAPTER 02 시제

UNIT 01 현재, 과거, 미래시제 / 진행형 pp.14-15

A **1.** is going to see **2.** visited **3.** goes **4.** is talking **5.** was watching **6.** make **7.** bought **8.** has **9.** am looking **10.** was

B **1.** wear **2.** wrote **3.** knows **4.** is taking **5.** were **6.** teaches **7.** will[am going to] learn **8.** is **9.** planned **10.** are eating

C **1.** was **2.** will[am going to] go **3.** started **4.** is **5.** traveled **6.** is watching **7.** feels **8.** won't[am not going to] watch **9.** knows **10.** was playing

D **1.** will[am going to] cook **2.** gets **3.** am writing **4.** passed **5.** was riding

WRITING PRACTICE p.16

A **1.** visited his office **2.** is looking for her purse **3.** Frogs hibernate **4.** sent three emails **5.** will[is going to] repair his car **6.** The library opens

B **1.** I play tennis with my father **2.** moved to Seoul three years ago **3.** are going to take the train **4.** is making dinner at home **5.** The basketball game will start **6.** was playing with my friend

UNIT 02 현재완료 pp.17-18

A **1.** used **2.** has studied **3.** have been **4.** hasn't read **5.** for **6.** lost **7.** has gone **8.** has read **9.** saw **10.** since

B **1.** has been **2.** has never had **3.** went **4.** has gone **5.** cleaned **6.** have met

C **1.** have known **2.** has lost **3.** has gone **4.** have left **5.** has eaten **6.** has been

D **1.** 나는 아직 수학 숙제를 끝내지 못했다. **2.** Stella는 멕시코에 5년째 살고 있다. **3.** 너는 독일 음식을 먹어 본 적이 있니? **4.** 나는 이미 옷을 빨았다. **5.** Harry는 우리 집을 여러 번 방문했다. **6.** Earl과 나는 다섯 살 때부터 친한 친구이다. **7.** 내 상사는 출장차 서울에 가고 없다. **8.** 누군가 호텔에 여행 가방을 두고 갔다. **9.** Jenny는 방금 그녀의 엄마의 생일 선물을 샀다. **10.** 나는 중국에 가 본 적이 없다.

WRITING PRACTICE p.19

A **1.** have been to **2.** has already read **3.** have never seen **4.** has snowed **5.** have gone to **6.** has worked here since

B **1.** She has just arrived **2.** I have watched the movie **3.** found her necklace yesterday **4.** He has used this computer for **5.** The doctor has not arrived **6.** She has lost her English textbook

REVIEW TEST pp.20-22

1. ② **2.** ② **3.** ④ **4.** ④ **5.** ③ **6.** ③ **7.** ④ **8.** ③ **9.** ② **10.** ④ **11.** ⑤ **12.** ⑤ **13.** ③ **14.** ① **15.** have been **16.** is brushing **17.** met **18.** has broken **19.** has worked **20.** drink **21.** was talking **22.** He fixed the machine **23.** She is going to be sixteen years old **24.** was → is **25.** invites → invited, was liking → liked

CHAPTER
03 조동사

UNIT 01 can, may, will pp.23-24

A **1.** play **2.** spend **3.** wasn't able to **4.** be **5.** may **6.** be **7.** take **8.** was **9.** Will **10.** be able to

B **1.** be **2.** May[Can] **3.** Will[Would, Can, Could] **4.** leave **5.** to apply **6.** can[may] **7.** live **8.** couldn't[was not able to] **9.** be able to **10.** to jump

C **1.** May[Can] **2.** may **3.** couldn't **4.** Will[Would, Could] **5.** may[can] **6.** can

D **1.** 네가 원한다면 내 크래커를 먹어도 된다. **2.** 나는 네 생일에 너를 위해 노래를 부를 것이다. **3.** 그들은 그 기계를 고칠 수 있다. **4.** 너는 오늘 저녁에 네 친구들과 영화를 보러 가도 된다. **5.** 우리는 우주를 여행할 수 있을 것이다. **6.** 그의 이야기는 사실이 아닐지도 모른다. **7.** 너희 부모님은 그 소식에 놀랄지도 모른다. **8.** 그는 내게 아무 말도 하지 않을 것이다. **9.** 당신의 이메일 주소를 제게 말해 주시겠어요? **10.** 나는 중국어를 읽을 수 있지만, 말은 전혀 못한다.

WRITING PRACTICE p.25

A **1.** may know **2.** may[can] borrow **3.** will be able to lend **4.** could[was able to] run **5.** couldn't[wasn't able to] finish **6.** Will[Would, Can, Could] you take care of

B **1.** may tell a lie about **2.** Can you stop by the post office **3.** may come into my house **4.** is able to dive from **5.** Will you carry this baggage for me **6.** won't be able to finish the report

UNIT 02 must, should pp.26-27

A **1.** stop **2.** must not **3.** should **4.** can't **5.** do **6.** save **7.** take **8.** should **9.** had to **10.** don't have to

B **1.** have to pay **2.** need not **3.** doesn't have to **4.** should not **5.** Did **6.** to run **7.** return **8.** speak **9.** had to **10.** can't [cannot] / may not

C **1.** should **2.** cannot **3.** must not **4.** need not **5.** must

D **1.** 너는 친구들을 비웃어서는 안 된다. **2.** 저 개는 매우 영리한 게 틀림없다. **3.** 너는 그 파일을 복사할 필요가 없다. 나는 이미 복사본을 갖고 있다. **4.** 문을 여는 또 다른 방법이 틀림없이 있을 것이다. **5.** 우리는 소풍이 끝나면 우리의 쓰레기를 주워야 한다. **6.** 나는 그녀를 만나기 위해 하루를 기다려야 했다. **7.** 너는 결승전을 준비해야 한다. **8.** 너는 치과에 가야만 할 것이다. **9.** 그는 밤을 새야 했다. **10.** Tony는 그의 방에 있을 리가 없다. 나는 그가 집에 들어오는 것을 보지 못했다.

WRITING PRACTICE p.28

A **1.** should practice **2.** has to hand in **3.** must be difficult **4.** This camera can't [cannot] be **5.** She doesn't have to leave **6.** had to spend

B **1.** They don't need to wear masks **2.** You should solve these questions **3.** You must be quiet in this room **4.** I had to wear a uniform **5.** We don't need to follow **6.** I should finish the report

UNIT 03 would like to, had better, used to pp.29-30

A **1.** have **2.** study **3.** would like to **4.** used to **5.** used to **6.** didn't use to **7.** had better not **8.** Would **9.** used to **10.** had better

B **1.** would like to **2.** used to **3.** had better **4.** used to **5.** had better **6.** used to **7.** would like to **8.** had better **9.** would like to **10.** used to

C **1.** would like to **2.** had better **3.** used to **4.** had better **5.** used to

D **1.** 너는 저녁으로 뭘 먹고 싶니? **2.** 그녀는 Tom에게 그녀의 돈을 빌려주지 않는 것이 낫겠다. **3.** 너는 지하철을

타는 게 낫겠다. **4.** Dave는 예전에는 부유한 남자였다. **5.** 예전에는 이곳에 오래된 집이 있었다. **6.** 아무도 그와 일하고 싶어 하지 않는다. **7.** 나는 이번 주말에 컴퓨터 게임을 하고 싶다. **8.** 우리 엄마는 예전에 농구 선수였다. **9.** Dan은 그가 건강했을 때 혼자 여행하곤 했다. **10.** 너는 우선 과학 숙제를 하는 것이 낫겠다.

WRITING PRACTICE p.31

A **1.** used to go **2.** would like to look **3.** would like to buy **4.** used to live **5.** had better not take part in **6.** had better get

B **1.** Peter would take a walk **2.** Greg didn't use to be kind **3.** You had better be on time **4.** Did you use to think **5.** had better not swim **6.** What would you like to do

REVIEW TEST pp.32-34

1. ④ **2.** ③ **3.** ⑤ **4.** ⑤ **5.** ③ **6.** ④ **7.** ② **8.** ② **9.** ① **10.** ⑤ **11.** ④ **12.** ④ **13.** ③ **14.** may[can] **15.** used to **16.** had better **17.** ⑤ **18.** She should relax before going **19.** You have to be careful **20.** doesn't have[need] to **21.** would like to **22.** to **23.** must **24.** don't had better → had better not **25.** like → like to, able → be able 또는 will → are

CHAPTER 04 to부정사

UNIT 01 명사적 용법의 to부정사 pp.35-36

A **1.** It **2.** to stay **3.** to become **4.** to take **5.** to go **6.** to carry **7.** to wear **8.** not to see **9.** to go **10.** to move

B **1.** It, to keep two cats in this small house **2.** It, to finish the homework before dinner **3.** It, to go to Europe this summer **4.** It, to make her follow my order **5.** It, to listen to his advice **6.** It, to exercise regularly

C **1.** how to solve the problem **2.** who(m) to ask about my application **3.** where to go next **4.** what to prepare for dinner **5.** how to arrange the furniture **6.** when to start recording

D **1.** to buy **2.** to clean / cleaning **3.** not to accept **4.** where to buy / where I should buy **5.** when to tell / when we should tell **6.** to invite / inviting **7.** what not to do / what they should not do **8.** to finish **9.** to go **10.** how to read / how I should read

WRITING PRACTICE p.37

A **1.** It, to visit new places **2.** what to say **3.** to edit the magazine **4.** It, to score 100 **5.** decided to leave **6.** need to fix the computer

B **1.** 200 dollars to rent this tent **2.** decide where to go for summer vacation **3.** It was wise to buy the tickets **4.** wanted to go back and get **5.** to learn how to cook steak **6.** what to prepare for the trip

UNIT 02 형용사적 용법의 to부정사 pp.38-39

A **1.** to do **2.** warm to drink **3.** to sell **4.** to deal **5.** to be **6.** is to study **7.** sweet to eat **8.** to talk to **9.** to finish **10.** to write in

B **1.** to study **2.** to answer **3.** to call **4.** to ask **5.** to lead **6.** to explain

C **1.** in **2.** to **3.** on **4.** with **5.** with **6.** to **7.** on **8.** in

D **1.** is to arrive **2.** was to be **3.** is to meet **4.** are to be married **5.** are to clean **6.** are to enjoy

WRITING PRACTICE p.40

A **1.** important to say **2.** to paint with **3.** is to pay **4.** was to start **5.** any friends to talk to **6.** was never to see

B **1.** is looking for a roommate to live with **2.** don't have anything to worry about **3.** was not to return to his hometown **4.** needs something pretty to wear

5. send me something to read
6. the best season to visit the island

UNIT 03 부사적 용법의 to부정사 pp.41-42

A 1. to see 2. To get 3. to be 4. to solve 5. to walk 6. to see 7. To see 8. to buy 9. to be 10. to go

B 1. to start his new job 2. To hear his accent 3. to be a hundred years old 4. to carry in my pocket 5. to have such a wonderful family 6. To make your vacation fun

C 1. to help 2. To get 3. to arrive 4. only to fail 5. to keep

D 1. Dean은 노래 대회에서 우승하여 행복했다. 2. 그 소식을 들으면 그녀는 실망할 것이다. 3. 나는 그 이야기를 들어서 슬펐다. 4. 그는 자라서 세계 최고의 미용사 중 한 명이 되었다. 5. 미국에서 공부하기 위해서 나는 영어를 더 열심히 공부해야 한다. 6. 그 교회는 여기서 가기에 꽤 나 어렵다. 7. 우리는 챔피언전에서 우승하기 위해 더 연습해야 한다. 8. Logan은 일하러 갔지만 휴일인 것을 알게 되었다. 9. 저 큰 컨테이너들은 옮기기 쉽지 않다. 10. 네 아빠를 깨우지 않도록 조심해라.

WRITING PRACTICE p.43

A 1. to[in order to, so as to] log in 2. angry to find out 3. grew up to be 4. was careless to drop 5. difficult to write 6. To hear him

B 1. only to find it closed 2. To see her dance, you would think 3. is very hard to pass 4. shocked to hear the news 5. are pleased to see you again 6. to get into a good university

UNIT 04 to부정사의 의미상의 주어, too ~ to-v, enough to-v pp.44-45

A 1. for me 2. too large 3. so tired 4. for me 5. of Jane 6. to reach 7. smart enough 8. to understand 9. of him 10. to do

B 1. for 2. of 3. of 4. for 5. of 6. for 7. of 8. for 9. of 10. for

C 1. enough to touch 2. too big for me to drive 3. strong enough to lift 4. fast enough to win 5. cheap enough for young students to buy 6. too small to contain

D 1. 그 티셔츠는 내가 입기에 너무 작다. 2. 그 소녀는 그 수수께끼를 풀 만큼 충분히 똑똑했다. 3. 내 아들은 그 드라마를 보기에 너무 어리다. 4. 그 커피는 내가 마시기에 충분히 달았다. 5. 그 영화는 내가 이해하기 너무 어려웠다. 6. 그는 그 답을 찾아낼 만큼 충분히 영리했다.
7. 내 여동생은 개를 키우기에는 너무 조심성이 없다.
8. Mark는 유명한 배우가 될 만큼 충분히 재능이 있다.
9. 이 책은 내가 그만 읽기에는 너무 재미있다.
10. 그 텔레비전은 내가 살 수 있을 만큼 충분히 저렴하다.

WRITING PRACTICE p.46

A 1. to do your best 2. of you to leave 3. is too young to take the subway 4. light enough to carry 5. too embarrassed to answer 6. foolish of you to behave

B 1. he was too small to join a basketball team 2. is sharp enough to cut the paper 3. was too heavy for me to carry 4. is so hot that I can't sleep 5. It was wise of her not to touch 6. It is easy for Koreans to learn Japanese

REVIEW TEST pp.47-49

1. ④ 2. ⑤ 3. ④ 4. ① 5. ③ 6. ④ 7. ② 8. ② 9. ⑤ 10. ③ 11. ③ 12. to accept 13. where to get off / where I should get off 14. too spicy for me to eat 15. strong enough to support 16. what to do 17. ⑤ 18. ③ 19. ③ 20. to find himself 21. is difficult to guess 22. smart enough to pass the test 23. something nice to give to my friend 24. saying → to say 25. travel → to travel / traveling, what do → what to do / what I should do

CHAPTER
05 동명사

UNIT 01 동명사의 쓰임 pp.50-51

A **1.** Waiting **2.** building **3.** Taking **4.** doing **5.** repairing **6.** finishing **7.** going **8.** watching **9.** not smoking **10.** crying

B **1.** taking **2.** dancing[to dance] **3.** holding **4.** watching[to watch] **5.** telling **6.** listening **7.** studying **8.** Living[To live] **9.** making **10.** skiing

C **1.** meeting a lot of people during the trip **2.** Understanding my parents **3.** collecting comic books **4.** Pointing at someone **5.** is busy making her new album

D **1.** 매일 일기를 쓰는 것은 쉽지 않다. **2.** 내가 가장 좋아하는 활동은 내 아이들과 하이킹하는 것이다. **3.** Lyle은 그의 친구들과 낚시하러 갔다. **4.** Tony는 어제 저녁 식사를 준비하느라 바빴다. **5.** Jina는 오늘 밤 외출하고 싶지 않다. **6.** Peter는 그녀의 제안에 웃지 않을 수 없었다. **7.** 내가 이 병을 여는 것을 도와줄래? **8.** 그 셔츠들은 멋져 보이니까 살 가치가 있다. **9.** 여행에서 돌아오자마자 그는 당장 다시 여행을 가고 싶어 했다.

WRITING PRACTICE p.52

A **1.** writing[to write] a travel blog **2.** is not interested in making **3.** talked about changing **4.** was good at playing basketball **5.** couldn't[could not] help telling the truth **6.** is worth reading

B **1.** She was proud of winning **2.** was busy writing a report **3.** is biting his nails **4.** Maggie didn't finish eating dinner **5.** Respecting different cultures is important **6.** He was afraid of speaking

UNIT 02 동명사와 to부정사 pp.53-54

A **1.** to go **2.** doing **3.** buying **4.** to feel **5.** to go **6.** to lock **7.** to buy **8.** to clean **9.** knocking **10.** traveling

B **1.** to buy **2.** moving **3.** to leave **4.** to turn **5.** writing **6.** shooting **7.** being **8.** taking **9.** to call **10.** to see

C **1.** living **2.** to bring **3.** running **4.** to open **5.** meeting **6.** to win **7.** to go **8.** fighting **9.** to tell **10.** studying

D **1.** 그 아기는 나를 보자마자 울기 시작했다. **2.** 차 열쇠 가져오는 거 잊지 마. **3.** Diane은 건강을 위해 담배 피우는 것을 그만뒀다. **4.** 그는 일에 집중하려고 애썼지만, 그럴 수 없었다. **5.** Nick은 그 청바지를 한번 입어보았다. **6.** 우리 엄마는 커피 마시는 것을 아주 좋아하신다. **7.** 그녀는 수프에 소금을 넣은 것을 잊어버려서 소금을 약간 더 추가했다. **8.** William은 Zoe에게 돈을 빌려줬던 것을 기억했다. **9.** 그녀는 휴대 전화를 받으려고 멈춰 섰다. **10.** 외출할 때 난로를 끄는 것을 기억해라.

WRITING PRACTICE p.55

A **1.** avoided eating **2.** wanted to see his daughter **3.** enjoys taking pictures **4.** promised to give us **5.** stopped working **6.** remember meeting him

B **1.** She forgot to call her mother **2.** Would you mind bringing me **3.** Mandy stopped to smell the roses **4.** should keep practicing until the competition **5.** She likes spending time with Tom **6.** Remember to make a reservation

REVIEW TEST pp.56-58

1. ④ **2.** ④ **3.** ③ **4.** ② **5.** ③ **6.** ⑤ **7.** ④ **8.** ⑤ **9.** ④ **10.** do → doing **11.** bringing → to bring **12.** making → to make **13.** ① **14.** ② **15.** to take **16.** eating **17.** seeing **18.** ④ **19.** Using your phone in the dark **20.** She has a bad habit of sleeping **21.** Ted likes to meet new people **22.** practiced speaking **23.** stopped listening to music **24.** to think → thinking **25.** to be → being, to throw → throwing

CHAPTER
06 분사

UNIT 01 현재분사와 과거분사 pp.59-60

A **1.** talking **2.** written **3.** bored **4.** satisfied **5.** sleeping **6.** known **7.** reading **8.** exciting **9.** amazing **10.** named

B **1.** shocking **2.** interested **3.** waiting **4.** excited **5.** surprised **6.** broken **7.** spoken **8.** playing **9.** looking **10.** boring

C **1.** wearing **2.** made **3.** satisfying **4.** built **5.** interested **6.** tired **7.** cut **8.** dancing **9.** exciting **10.** playing

D **1.** painted by Picasso **2.** wearing a long coat **3.** carrying a yellow backpack **4.** imported from India **5.** practicing basketball in the rain

WRITING PRACTICE p.61

A **1.** covered with paper **2.** singing on the stage **3.** fix the broken door **4.** sounded amazing **5.** three bottles filled with **6.** had a tree planted

B **1.** The man sat talking on the phone **2.** That skirt worn by Susie **3.** The boy waiting for me over there **4.** a very interesting person to talk to **5.** the picture taken by the paparazzi **6.** Who was the man having dinner with you

UNIT 02 분사구문 pp.62-63

A **1.** Handing **2.** sitting **3.** Hugging **4.** Seeing **5.** Wanting **6.** Being **7.** Turning **8.** Lying **9.** Wearing **10.** Smiling

B **1.** Looking out the window **2.** Taking the bus **3.** Feeling tired **4.** Lifting heavy boxes **5.** Wanting to learn how to play tennis **6.** Putting down his book

C **1.** Though he was upset with her
2. As[While] I sat[was sitting] on the beach
3. If you turn right at City Tower
4. When she got off the bus / While she was getting off the bus **5.** Because[As, Since] I had no money **6.** After I had dinner

D **1.** 내 차례를 기다리면서 나는 잡지를 읽었다. **2.** 그 결과들에 압도되어 그녀는 한마디도 할 수 없었다. **3.** 그를 나의 집에 데려가서 나는 그에게 구경을 시켜주었다. **4.** 일이 끝나고 나면 피곤해서 나는 아무것도 하고 싶지 않다. **5.** 한국인이어서 그는 항상 김치와 밥을 먹는 것을 좋아한다. **6.** 공항에 도착했을 때 나는 어머니께 전화했다. **7.** 교통 혼잡을 뚫고 운전하면서 그는 늦게 도착하는 것에 대해 걱정하였다. **8.** 라디오를 들으면서 James는 숙제를 했다. **9.** 잠자리에 들기 전에 나는 항상 알람을 맞춘다. **10.** 왼쪽으로 돌면 너는 집 한 채를 보게 될 것이다.

WRITING PRACTICE p.64

A **1.** Taking the subway **2.** Crossing the old bridge **3.** Feeling depressed **4.** Arriving home **5.** Hearing the news **6.** Being very old

B **1.** Playing tennis, I sprained
2. Having little time, we have to hurry up
3. Cleaning the street behind his house
4. Running out of time, he couldn't solve
5. Reading a book, I drank
6. Taking this train, you can get to Busan

REVIEW TEST pp.65-67

1. ③ **2.** ③ **3.** ④ **4.** ③ **5.** ② **6.** ⑤ **7.** ③ **8.** ③ **9.** ③ **10.** ③ **11.** ② **12.** Leaving the house **13.** Thinking of her family **14.** Running frequently **15.** ③ **16.** ① **17.** called **18.** Reading **19.** Having no time **20.** I was amazed **21.** ② **22.** Anyone seeing the man should **23.** Studying hard, he got **24.** Travel → Traveling, boring → bored **25.** exciting → excited, Watch → Watching, amusing → amused

CHAPTER
07 수동태

UNIT 01 능동태와 수동태 pp.68-69

A **1.** solved **2.** is loved **3.** is being washed **4.** was made **5.** will be held **6.** respect **7.** was invented **8.** is visited **9.** is being cooked **10.** will be canceled

B **1.** be kept **2.** was injured **3.** will divide **4.** are being baked **5.** was taking **6.** are used **7.** is being done **8.** love **9.** will be performed **10.** by Samuel

C **1.** An email is being written by Oliver. **2.** The meeting schedule will be changed by my boss. **3.** The picture was painted by my son. **4.** This doll is loved by the little girl. **5.** The bathroom is shared by the guests. **6.** The office will be cleaned this weekend (by us).

D **1.** was directed **2.** stole **3.** will be finished **4.** is being repaired **5.** was designed **6.** is being used **7.** will be delivered

WRITING PRACTICE p.70

A **1.** was written by **2.** was taken by **3.** will be cooked by **4.** are being changed by **5.** was seen by **6.** is being reported

B **1.** are parked on the road **2.** This monitor was made in Korea **3.** This picture was painted **4.** will be used to help sick people **5.** is being read by my brother **6.** Spanish is spoken in many countries

UNIT 02 수동태의 여러 가지 형태 pp.71-72

A **1.** wasn't invited **2.** Was **3.** leaving **4.** to **5.** was called **6.** for **7.** be solved **8.** to do **9.** singing **10.** of

B **1.** for **2.** to brush **3.** to clean **4.** Was **5.** be tested **6.** to **7.** wasn't[was not] cooked **8.** was named **9.** soccer **10.** entering[to enter]

C **1.** This novel wasn't[was not] written by Mr. Lee. **2.** Milk must be kept in a cool place (by you). **3.** Was the button pushed by you? **4.** He was allowed to go camping by his parents. **5.** When was this bridge built (by them)?

D **1.** was given first prize (by them), was given to him (by them) **2.** was made to do the paperwork (by them) **3.** was seen running[to run] across the street (by me) **4.** was made for her by her mom **5.** was named King by my family

WRITING PRACTICE p.73

A **1.** wasn't[was not] solved **2.** Was this novel translated **3.** must be washed **4.** was heard barking[to bark] **5.** was sent to me **6.** was made to get up

B **1.** was sent to the wrong person **2.** should be kept clean **3.** The chef was seen cooking food **4.** Your writing skills can be improved **5.** The fire was not caused **6.** He was made to work late

UNIT 03 주의해야 할 수동태 pp.74-75

A **1.** run over by **2.** to **3.** with **4.** were laughed **5.** appeared **6.** was brought up **7.** with **8.** by my family **9.** in **10.** with

B **1.** Two boys will be taken care of by Tina. **2.** I was surprised at the results of the election. **3.** I was disappointed with[at] her behavior. **4.** The lost dog was looked after by my grandmother. **5.** My cooking was looked down on by the French cook. **6.** Their visit will be put off for several days (by them).

C **1.** was put off **2.** to **3.** at **4.** disappeared **5.** is made **6.** with **7.** happened **8.** by my sister **9.** looked up to **10.** with

D **1.** at **2.** in **3.** with **4.** to **5.** of **6.** with

WRITING PRACTICE p.76

A **1.** was covered with **2.** resembles the actor **3.** are taken care of by **4.** were surprised at **5.** appeared **6.** is filled with

B 1. The hamsters were taken care of by 2. He was disappointed with the ending 3. This song isn't known to young people 4. My mother is interested in hiking 5. Was he satisfied with his birthday party 6. The necklace is made of pearls

REVIEW TEST pp.77-79

1. ⑤ 2. ⑤ 3. ④ 4. ① 5. ⑤ 6. ④ 7. ③ 8. ④ 9. ④ 10. ③ 11. ③ 12. ③ 13. be planned 14. running[to run] 15. to leave 16. were taught English 17. is loved by millions of fans 18. were looked after with love by her / were looked after by her with love 19. is being upgraded by Tom 20. was told to me by Benjamin 21. was filled with his paintings 22. was looked up to by the players 23. was made to learn Chinese by my dad 24. by → in 25. giving → given, for → with

CHAPTER 08 대명사

UNIT 01 부정대명사 I pp.80-81

A 1. All 2. Both 3. any 4. Each 5. Every 6. one 7. some 8. ones 9. Every 10. it

B 1. one 2. it 3. Every 4. Both 5. any 6. All

C 1. some 2. one 3. any 4. Each 5. it

D 1. Every → Both 2. it → one 3. some → any 4. every → all 5. Every → Each 6. any → some

WRITING PRACTICE p.82

A 1. All (of) his songs 2. Every driver 3. Both (of) my parents 4. Each of us has 5. Every movie has 6. I have to buy a new one

B 1. All of the students have to be 2. Would you like to have some cookies 3. asked if we had any questions 4. Both of my sisters resemble my mom 5. Each person has his or her own lifestyle 6. Do you have any plans

UNIT 02 부정대명사 II pp.83-84

A 1. one another 2. another 3. each other 4. the other 5. another 6. another 7. others 8. Some 9. the others

B 1. each other 2. others 3. another 4. one another 5. the others 6. the other

C 1. One, the other 2. Some, others 3. another 4. each other

D 1. he wants another pet 2. others like to get up late 3. the other is how to study 4. The others didn't wear it 5. talked to each other 6. often see one another

WRITING PRACTICE p.85

A 1. others 2. each other / one another 3. One, the other 4. Some, the others 5. another 6. One, another, the other

B 1. We should take care of one another 2. Rachel and Tim looked at each other 3. I want to have another cup 4. Some people wore coats, and others didn't 5. One is a designer, and the other is a doctor

UNIT 03 재귀대명사 pp.86-87

A 1. myself 2. itself 3. by 4. ourselves 5. himself 6. herself 7. myself 8. herself 9. myself 10. yourself

B 1. X 2. O 3. X 4. O 5. X 6. O 7. X 8. O 9. X 10. O

C 1. yourself 2. myself 3. himself 4. myself 5. yourself

D 1. beside himself 2. in itself 3. by myself 4. seat yourself 5. excused herself 6. Help yourself to

WRITING PRACTICE p.88

A **1.** I cut myself **2.** finish the job by himself **3.** Help yourself to some apple pie **4.** I made these noodles myself / I myself made these noodles **5.** She was looking at herself **6.** keep this between ourselves

B **1.** Sue made this cake herself / Sue herself made this cake **2.** The boy stayed at home by himself **3.** He got up and dressed himself **4.** You may excuse yourself when **5.** I liked the movie itself **6.** he shouted, "Show yourself

REVIEW TEST pp.89-91

1. ③ **2.** ⑤ **3.** ④ **4.** ④ **5.** ① **6.** ③ **7.** ③ **8.** ② **9.** ③ **10.** ⑤ **11.** ② **12.** ① **13.** ④ **14.** the other **15.** ourselves **16.** any **17.** Some **18.** one **19.** ⑤ **20.** I was beside myself **21.** Don't try to excuse yourself **22.** They sent cards to one another **23.** I read all of your essays **24.** other → others **25.** each another → each other / one another

CHAPTER 09 비교

UNIT 01 원급, 비교급, 최상급 pp.92-93

A **1.** pretty **2.** harder **3.** cheapest **4.** more beautiful **5.** good **6.** much **7.** most important **8.** well **9.** biggest **10.** a lot

B **1.** taller **2.** youngest **3.** most popular **4.** faster **5.** hard **6.** sweeter **7.** well **8.** shortest **9.** more interested **10.** longest

C **1.** spiciest **2.** high **3.** more **4.** most dynamic **5.** more interesting **6.** fast **7.** than **8.** much[a lot, even, far] **9.** more bitter / bitterer **10.** busy

D **1.** as heavy as **2.** more expensive than **3.** the tallest (girl) of **4.** stronger than **5.** as many bags as **6.** the youngest (person) of

WRITING PRACTICE p.94

A **1.** much smarter than **2.** Mr. Lee is the richest man **3.** This laptop is cheaper than **4.** Lauren is as tall as **5.** is healthier than Jenny **6.** She is the fastest girl

B **1.** My car is as good as my brother's **2.** Kevin is as brilliant as me **3.** My desk is wider than yours **4.** My house is the most comfortable place **5.** is even shorter than that one **6.** the most famous part of the movie

UNIT 02 비교 구문을 이용한 표현 pp.95-96

A **1.** twice **2.** more **3.** people **4.** more and more interesting **5.** shorter **6.** most handsome **7.** six times **8.** hotter **9.** smarter **10.** the less

B **1.** healthier **2.** twice[two times] **3.** most popular **4.** funnier and funnier **5.** faster **6.** better **7.** kindest **8.** three times **9.** shorter and shorter **10.** movies

C **1.** four times as many dolls as **2.** more expensive **3.** twice as heavy as **4.** more and more popular **5.** lighter than / as light as **6.** cuter and cuter **7.** famous artists **8.** the better **9.** more popular **10.** The older

D **1.** More and more **2.** taller **3.** most popular **4.** The longer, the more **5.** slimmer and slimmer

WRITING PRACTICE p.97

A **1.** one of the most beautiful islands **2.** became heavier and heavier **3.** The more books, the smarter **4.** Which is more delicious **5.** three times as large as / three times larger than **6.** four times as long as / four times longer than

B **1.** is one of the richest men in **2.** The hotter the weather becomes, the more **3.** The air is getting worse and worse **4.** eats twice as much as his sister **5.** Which subject is easier, history or science **6.** Reading is one of the most common hobbies

REVIEW TEST pp.98-100

1. ③ **2.** ① **3.** ③ **4.** ④ **5.** ④ **6.** ③ **7.** ⑤ **8.** ③ **9.** ④ **10.** ① **11.** ⑤ **12.** as expensive as **13.** the shortest boy of **14.** a lower score than **15.** three times as fast as / three times faster than **16.** ③ **17.** ④ **18.** Which do you like more **19.** getting shorter and shorter **20.** the biggest animal **21.** This bridge is twice as long as that one **22.** This math exam was much more difficult than **23.** My school is one of the oldest schools in **24.** more I understood → the more I understood **25.** much → more, to meat → than meat

CHAPTER 10 접속사

UNIT 01 시간, 이유, 결과의 접속사 pp.101-102

A **1.** Until **2.** that **3.** While **4.** Because **5.** Since **6.** when **7.** As **8.** so **9.** is **10.** Till

B **1.** when **2.** Since **3.** so **4.** until **5.** after **6.** that **7.** As **8.** while

C **1.** was **2.** that **3.** finds **4.** so **5.** go

D **1.** so **2.** As **3.** While

E **1.** After **2.** Because **3.** While **4.** so

WRITING PRACTICE p.103

A **1.** While he wrote[was writing] an email **2.** after I brush my teeth **3.** so I couldn't hear his voice **4.** so interesting that Jen read **5.** until[till] you finish your homework **6.** because[as, since] I will play tennis

B **1.** While some people like his idea **2.** woke up before the alarm rang **3.** so sleepy that I kept yawning **4.** stay in Boston until spring comes **5.** As I didn't have my key, I had to wait for **6.** After Mom met my teacher, she didn't say

UNIT 02 조건, 양보의 접속사 / 명령문 + and, or ~ pp.104-105

A **1.** Although **2.** or **3.** If **4.** unless **5.** and **6.** Though **7.** or **8.** don't **9.** Unless **10.** and

B **1.** and **2.** Although **3.** If **4.** or **5.** unless **6.** Though

C **1.** If **2.** and **3.** Although[Though] **4.** If, Unless **5.** Unless, or

D **1.** Though I was tired last night, I went to the gym. / I went to the gym though I was tired last night. **2.** Pull this string, and the light will turn on. **3.** If I come home early, I'll cook dinner for you. / I'll cook dinner for you if I come home early. **4.** Stop laughing at him, or he'll be very angry. **5.** Unless you are busy, let's go shopping. / Let's go shopping unless you are busy.

WRITING PRACTICE p.106

A **1.** If you don't help me / Unless you help me **2.** Though[Although] I was hungry **3.** and someone will help you **4.** If you don't have more questions / Unless you have more questions **5.** or you'll get hurt **6.** Though[Although] I did my best

B **1.** or I will call the police **2.** Put on your sunglasses, and they will **3.** Although it rained heavily, they played **4.** Unless you have a membership card, you can't enter **5.** If you don't take your umbrella, you will get **6.** If the weather is bad

REVIEW TEST pp.107-109

1. ⑤ **2.** ⑤ **3.** ③ **4.** ④ **5.** ② **6.** ④ **7.** ① **8.** ③ **9.** ⑤ **10.** ① **11.** ③ **12.** Though[Although] **13.** Unless **14.** so **15.** or **16.** While **17.** As **18.** ① **19.** ② **20.** Although[Though] she was strong **21.** until[till] he comes back **22.** While I am interested in sports **23.** When the water boils, put the noodles **24.** will win → win **25.** as → that

CHAPTER
11 관계사

UNIT 01 관계대명사 pp.110-111

A **1.** who **2.** which **3.** which **4.** whom **5.** which **6.** whose **7.** who **8.** which **9.** which **10.** whose

B **1.** who **2.** who(m) **3.** which **4.** whose **5.** who **6.** which **7.** who **8.** who(m) **9.** whose **10.** which

C **1.** who **2.** which **3.** which **4.** whose **5.** which **6.** who **7.** who(m) **8.** which **9.** whose **10.** who

D **1.** The girl who is short is my sister.
2. I bought a scarf whose color is red.
3. I liked the song which you sang last night.
4. This is the watch which was made in Italy.
5. That's the man who(m) I saw at the baseball stadium. **6.** I know a girl whose birthday is the same as mine.

WRITING PRACTICE p.112

A **1.** who rides a skateboard **2.** Look at the boat which is **3.** who(m) everyone admires **4.** whose color is purple **5.** which I gave **6.** whose dream is

B **1.** The smartphone which I bought last week
2. a restaurant whose steak is very delicious
3. the dog which she is taking care of
4. the man to whom I gave a present / the man whom I gave a present to
5. a girl whose mom is a famous actress
6. a boy who has a beautiful smile

UNIT 02 관계대명사 that, what / 관계대명사의 생략 pp.113-114

A **1.** that **2.** What **3.** that **4.** that **5.** with whom **6.** that **7.** bored **8.** whom **9.** what **10.** standing

B **1.** that is **2.** X **3.** that **4.** who **5.** X **6.** X **7.** which **8.** that **9.** which is **10.** which

C **1.** that[which] **2.** in which
3. what / the thing(s) that[which]
4. talking / that[who] is talking **5.** whom
6. about which **7.** that[who] **8.** what / the thing(s) that[which] **9.** that[which]
10. that[which]

D **1.** that **2.** that **3.** what **4.** that **5.** what **6.** that

WRITING PRACTICE p.115

A **1.** that[which] is standing **2.** the sofa that[which] I sit on **3.** what[the thing that[which]] I was looking for **4.** The solution that[which] I suggested **5.** The boy who[that] is playing tennis **6.** which you swam

B **1.** I had last night was very scary **2.** selling shoes was very kind **3.** The very book that you are holding **4.** the only student that did the homework **5.** I watch every day will end next month **6.** the most delicious cake that I've ever eaten

UNIT 03 관계부사 pp.116-117

A **1.** where **2.** how **3.** where **4.** why **5.** where **6.** why **7.** when **8.** why **9.** the way **10.** when

B **1.** when **2.** why **3.** where **4.** how **5.** where **6.** when **7.** where **8.** how **9.** why **10.** when

C **1.** That is how the woman succeeded. **2.** I remember the moment when you walked into this room. **3.** Tell me the reason why I must take this class. **4.** This is the park where he exercises every morning. **5.** Tell me about the day when you won first prize. **6.** This is the house where I lived when I was young.

D **1.** when **2.** where **3.** why **4.** when **5.** where **6.** how

WRITING PRACTICE p.118

A **1.** where the accident happened **2.** the reason why he did **3.** where I work **4.** the day when I'm free **5.** the hospital where I was born **6.** the night when I saw

B **1.** the reason why he visited me **2.** the way you painted this picture **3.** The classroom where we studied **4.** how she made this chocolate **5.** the reason why my parents are upset **6.** the day when we met

REVIEW TEST pp.119-121

1. ④ **2.** ⑤ **3.** ② **4.** ① **5.** ② **6.** ④ **7.** ③ **8.** ⑤ **9.** ① **10.** ②, ③ **11.** ② **12.** ④ **13.** ① **14.** This is the house whose stairs were broken. **15.** This is the game which[that] I like the most. **16.** why **17.** when **18.** the island where we went **19.** (who[that] is) playing the guitar **20.** that **21.** which is **22.** the hotel my family stayed at **23.** sitting behind me is very handsome **24.** in that → where[in which] **25.** That → What / The thing that[which], the way how → how[the way]

CHAPTER 12 가정법

UNIT 01 가정법 과거, 가정법 과거완료 pp.122-123

A **1.** were **2.** would buy **3.** had studied **4.** could join **5.** could have swum **6.** had called **7.** could get **8.** had **9.** had practiced **10.** were

B **1.** would **2.** could have finished **3.** were **4.** would have gone **5.** would visit **6.** would have been **7.** would make **8.** would have **9.** could ride **10.** wouldn't[would not] let

C **1.** weren't[were not], would be **2.** had been, wouldn't[would not] have hurt **3.** had asked, would have helped **4.** hadn't[had not] told, wouldn't[would not] have been **5.** had taken, wouldn't[would not] have failed **6.** had gotten up, wouldn't[would not] have missed

D **1.** doesn't[does not] have, can't[cannot] drive **2.** didn't[did not] have, didn't[did not] study **3.** didn't[did not] win, didn't[did not] receive **4.** isn't[is not] good, have to wear **5.** didn't[did not] bring, bought **6.** doesn't [does not] know, isn't[is not]

WRITING PRACTICE p.124

A **1.** If it were winter now **2.** I could have called him **3.** I would study hard **4.** If she had been more careful **5.** didn't[did not] have, could join **6.** wouldn't[would not] have had to wait

B **1.** were at home, she could receive the package **2.** If he were not selfish, he could make **3.** If my grandmother heard the news, she would be **4.** had run faster, we could have crossed **5.** If I were you, I would write **6.** had finished the homework, his teacher wouldn't have been

UNIT 02 I wish + 가정법, as if + 가정법 pp.125-126

A **1.** had **2.** were **3.** were **4.** were **5.** were **6.** were **7.** had cried **8.** had eaten **9.** had asked **10.** had bought

B **1.** were **2.** were **3.** had seen **4.** had lived **5.** played[could play] **6.** had saved **7.** were **8.** had been elected **9.** had been **10.** did

C **1.** my apartment were bigger **2.** she hadn't [had not] found out the truth **3.** I had read more books when I was young **4.** she were a teacher **5.** had been a pilot **6.** she had lived in that town

D **1.** I don't[do not] know how to play the flute **2.** I'm[I am] not as tall as you

3. you didn't[did not] come to school yesterday
4. Jessica doesn't[does not] know him
5. he didn't[did not] understand everything
6. he didn't[did not] get a hundred on the math exam

WRITING PRACTICE p.127

A 1. I were the hero 2. as if he hadn't[had not] lied 3. I had finished my homework 4. as if he were a movie director 5. she had visited me 6. as if I were her daughter

B 1. I wish I could speak English well 2. She speaks as if she were annoyed 3. I wish I had listened to my teacher 4. He acts as if he were the best player 5. I wish it were not Monday tomorrow 6. He talks as if he had exercised

REVIEW TEST pp.128-130

1. ⑤ 2. ③ 3. ③ 4. ⑤ 5. ③ 6. ④ 7. ② 8. ③ 9. ① 10. ⑤ 11. ③ 12. ② 13. ③ 14. ③ 15. had 16. had learned 17. had read, could have solved 18. hadn't[had not] laughed 19. were sunny, would go 20. hadn't[had not] erased the file 21. as if they had visited New York 22. had followed the rules, you wouldn't have been punished 23. He talks to me as if he were my boss 24. can → could 25. could take → could have taken

CHAPTER 13 일치와 화법

UNIT 01 시제의 일치 pp.131-132

A 1. had been 2. would 3. is 4. might 5. were 6. had 7. is 8. was 9. have 10. is

B 1. catches 2. have to 3. is 4. helps 5. broke 6. is 7. would pass 8. discovered 9. have 10. is

C 1. would arrive 2. had finished 3. has 4. invented 5. is 6. grow 7. could use 8. broke 9. had lost 10. is 11. would win 12. was born

WRITING PRACTICE p.133

A 1. the earth is round 2. he wanted to become 3. it will snow 4. life is short 5. is the biggest island 6. ended

B 1. knew that she had already left 2. that he had seen a UFO 3. He said that his class starts at nine 4. My teacher said that the Chernobyl disaster occurred 5. said that time and tide wait for no man 6. I told Kate that she could play the game

UNIT 02 화법 pp.134-135

A 1. said 2. told 3. whether 4. asked 5. if she could 6. when I would 7. that 8. he had driven 9. if 10. who had broken

B 1. told 2. my help 3. where I had bought 4. who had sent me 5. if[whether] I had gotten 6. (that) he would buy me

C 1. when I had finished my homework
2. he had lost his wallet on the subway
3. if[whether] I would join the club
4. she had eaten a hamburger with her sister
5. what I wanted to be in the future
6. if[whether] I needed to buy a new cell phone
7. he had worked for a design company

D 1. You have to study hard 2. Did you like the concert 3. When will you visit me 4. How did you know my email address 5. I will call you later 6. Are you working for the toy company

WRITING PRACTICE p.136

A 1. (that) she wanted to buy 2. if[whether] I could borrow 3. if[whether] he had time 4. when he would do the dishes 5. (that) she was proud of me 6. asked me if[whether] I knew

B **1.** didn't ask me where I lived **2.** Mom asked me who had given me **3.** I told him that I understood what **4.** He asked me if I had used **5.** told me that she didn't need my help **6.** asked me if I was hungry

REVIEW TEST pp.137-139

1. ④ **2.** ① **3.** ② **4.** ③ **5.** ④ **6.** ④ **7.** ④ **8.** ③ **9.** ⑤ **10.** ① **11.** ⑤ **12.** ①, ③ **13.** have **14.** is **15.** if[whether] we had brought our textbooks **16.** how I could change my password **17.** ① **18.** coffee has caffeine **19.** she would go to Paris **20.** can't[cannot] fly **21.** when I had bought **22.** Susie said that she memorizes **23.** I asked her if she was thirsty **24.** did I study → I studied **25.** have to → had to